THE CORPORATION, ETHICS, AND THE ENVIRONMENT

THE CORPORATION, ETHICS, AND THE ENVIRONMENT

EDITED BY

W. Michael Hoffman,
Robert Frederick, and
Edward S. Petry, Jr.

Foreword by Gregory H. Adamian

From the Eighth National Conference on Business Ethics
Sponsored by the Center for Business Ethics at Bentley College

QUORUM BOOKS
WESTPORT, CONNECTICUT • LONDON

Library of Congress Cataloging-in-Publication Data

National Conference on Business Ethics (8th : 1990 : Bentley College)
   The corporation, ethics, and the environment / edited by W.
 Michael Hoffman, Robert Frederick, and Edward S. Petry, Jr.
   p. cm.
   "From the Eighth National Conference on Business Ethics sponsored
 by the Center for Business Ethics at Bentley College."
   Includes bibliographical references.
   ISBN 0-89930-603-9 (lib. bdg. : alk. paper)
   1. United States—Industries—Environmental aspects—Congresses.
 2. Business ethics—United States—Congresses.   3. Industry—Social
 aspects—United States—Congresses.   I. Hoffman, W. Michael.
 II. Frederick, Robert.   III. Petry, Edward S.   IV. Bentley College.
 Center for Business Ethics.   V. Title.
 HC110.E5N32   1990a
 363.7'08'0973—dc20   90-8402

British Library Cataloguing in Publication Data is available.

Library of Congress Catalog Card Number: 90-8402
ISBN: 0-89930-603-9

First published in 1990

Quorum Books, 88 Post Road West, Westport, CT 06881
An imprint of Greenwood Publishing Group, Inc.

Printed in the United States of America

363.708
N277
1990

∞™

The paper used in this book complies with the
Permanent Paper Standard issued by the National
Information Standards Organization (Z39.48-1984).

10 9 8 7 6 5 4 3 2

Contents

Figures and Tables

Tables

Foreword

GREGORY H. ADAMIAN

Every two years for the last fifteen years, Bentley College, through its Center for Business Ethics, has been privileged to organize and host this important, intellectually challenging, and timely series of conferences. I especially emphasize their timeliness. Anyone familiar with the subjects covered by past conferences can only be impressed by their topicality. "The Ethics of Mergers and Acquisitions," "Ethics and the Multinational Enterprise," and "Ethics and the Management of Computer Technology" are the subjects of a few recent conferences that could have been taken from the newspaper headlines of those particular years.

This year's topic, "Business, Ethics, and the Environment," is no exception. For the last five years or so, an ever-swelling chorus of voices has expressed profound concern over the way humanity is mistreating the earth. Concern for our environment was first expressed on a mass scale in the 1960s, not coincidentally around the same time of the first widespread movements for nuclear disarmament. I say not coincidentally because each of these phenomena—massive pollution of the planet and the creation of greater numbers of more sophisticated nuclear weapons—threatens us with the total destruction of life on earth.

Some small progress has been made in recent years toward the lessening of the threat of nuclear war. The ascendance to power in the Soviet Union of somewhat more enlightened, pragmatic leadership and our own government's prudent, realistic response to that leadership have held out hope for more progress in the future. Perhaps this small diminishment in the nuclear threat underlies the new vigor with which men and women all over the world are confronting the fouling of our environment. We see in the cooperation that has recently been demonstrated between East and West a model of the kind of international cooperation necessary to win substantial victories in the battle to clean up the planet.

This cooperation is especially crucial in relation to Third World countries and emerging industrial countries. Pollution is sometimes mistakenly thought to be found only in the First World. However, in the Second and Third worlds the environmental battle, long overlooked, is gaining the attention it deserves. Gas emissions from fossil fuels burned in the Third World are expected to grow from 20 percent of all such emissions today to 60 percent by 2050. In the next century 95 percent of world population growth will occur in the Third World, putting additional stress on already endangered ecological systems.

We hear much about the destruction of rain forests in nations like Brazil. The development attendant on such devastation spurs economic growth in the short term but at the cost of ecological chaos in the longer term. The environment of the industrialized nations, denizens of less-developed countries point out, has already been ravaged, affording most citizens the highest standard of living in the world. Our moral admonitions carry little weight in the face of this seeming hypocrisy. Such adversarial relations are profoundly counterproductive.

We are beginning to see some examples of more forward-looking cooperation in the international arena. The banks that have made enormous loans to Third World countries now speak of "sustainable growth." They recognize that loans made to poorer countries cannot be repaid if the environment that supports the economy is plundered in the process. The banks are now doing what they can to encourage ecological responsibility and economic growth.

What about in our own country? Unfortunately an adversarial tone too often prevails here as well. A recently published survey revealed that almost 75 percent of Americans believe that business has a "definite" responsibility to reduce air and water pollution; but the same survey disclosed that only 29 percent of those same respondents avoided using dangerous aerosol products as a matter of course; only 20 percent regularly recycled newspapers; only 9 percent regularly used public transportation or car pools rather than driving alone; and only 3 percent volunteered for local community clean-up efforts. It is on this individual level that improvements must begin. Albert Gore, one of the Senate's most environmentally conscious members, put it this way: "We must now create a new pattern of thinking in which we once again see ourselves as part of the ecological system in which we live."

Animosity has traditionally existed between environmental advocates and those whom they perceive as the enemy—business. While it is true that many segments of the business community have been slow to respond to ecological imperatives, it is also true that some naturalists have been equally slow to recognize the positive contributions of the business community. Participation in these proceedings is one indication of the corporate world's increasing sensitivity to environmental issues. Greater cooperation between the two groups is essential. The enormous and adverse economic implications presented by a dying environment dictate that antagonism be replaced by cooperation. Economic growth and a sensible environmental policy need not be mutually exclusive goals; they are, in fact, dependent. After all, the ultimate interests of environmentalists and corporate leaders are the same, just as the ultimate interests of Third World governments and First World bankers are alike, as well as those of political leaders in the East and West.

The task is formidable and important. As one observer said, "The more we get out of the world, the less we leave, and in the long run we shall have to pay our debts at a time that may be very inconvenient for our own survival." This conference can perhaps in some way help us to "create the new pattern of thinking" that Senator Gore described. We can then begin to reduce the debt, or at least slow its accumulation, and perhaps put off that ominous day of reckoning.

Acknowledgments

The Eighth National Conference on Business Ethics and other activities of the Center for Business Ethics were made possible in part by grants from the following: Arvin Industries; Robert W. Brown, M.D.; Champion International Corporation; the Council for Philosophical Studies (sponsored by the National Endowment for the Humanities); the General Mills Foundation; General Motors Corporation; the Goodyear Tire and Rubber Company; Midland-Ross, Inc.; the Motorola Foundation; Norton Company; Primerica Corporation; Raytheon Company; the Raytheon Charitable Foundation; Rexnord, Inc.; Richardson-Merrill, Inc.; the Rockefeller Foundation; Semline, Inc.; Stop and Shop Manufacturing Companies; F. W. Woolworth Company; and Exxon Education Foundation. On behalf of the center, we wish to thank these contributors and all of the participants of the Eighth National Conference for sharing with us their support and ideas. We also wish to thank Anne Glynn, Sally Lydon, and Peter Rubicam for all their help with the conference and this book.

Introduction

ROBERT FREDERICK

On October 26 and 27, 1989, the Center for Business Ethics at Bentley College held its Eighth National Conference on Business Ethics. The topic of the conference was "Business, Ethics, and the Environment." Prominent members of business, government, academic, and public interest groups made presentations. Many of those presentations are collected in this book, and others are in a companion volume.

The conference marked a departure from a number of other discussions on business and the environment since the major focus of the conference was not the monetary cost-benefit of environmental protection. Instead most of the papers were intended specifically to address the ethical obligations businesses may have for protecting the environment. If there are such obligations, then businesses are morally required to consider them when business activity has an adverse effect on the environment. But are businesses obligated to protect the environment, and if so, why are they? To answer these questions, I hope the framework I outline will help orient, in a sometimes complex conceptual landscape, readers unfamiliar with the contours of the debate.

An ancient and compelling ethical principle, one that almost everyone accepts, is the brief rule: Do no harm. One reason this rule, usually called the "harm principle," is so compelling is the conviction we share that causing harm violates a moral right. As it stands, however, the injunction to do no harm is much too brief to be of any real help. It needs to be expanded and clarified if we are to use it as a moral guide in complex situations. One way to do it is,

(1) If a certain type of human activity or endeavor causes unwarranted harm to a person or some other entity, then that activity violates the moral right of that person or entity not to be harmed.

Note that this version of the harm principle does not state that all the harm a person may suffer violates the right not to be harmed but only that all unwarranted harm does. In order to apply the principle, then, something more needs to be said about the notion of unwarranted harm.

Unwarranted harm is a difficult concept to analyze since there are different kinds of harm and many different circumstances under which someone might allege that harm is unwarranted and hence violates rights. As a rough cut, however, I suggest that the harm an activity causes is unwarranted if the following two conditions are met: (1) the harm is not offset or ameliorated to any significant extent by some corresponding benefit the activity generates, and (2) the harm can be prevented without causing other significant harm that outweighs the benefit of prevention.

The requirement for showing that harm is unwarranted is very strong. It probably would not be easy to show that both conditions are met. The requirement could be made weaker by saying that harm is unwarranted if at least one of them is met; however, I will use the stronger version in this introduction.

There is no generally accepted formula I am aware of that determines when a harm is significantly offset or ameliorated by a benefit. Moreover, in my view, harms and benefits may be incommensurable in many cases. There may be no objective standard of measurement, monetary or otherwise, that we can use to quantify harms and benefits and see if the former is to any degree offset or ameliorated by the latter. Nevertheless, I believe that judgments about the relative weight of harms and benefits are unavoidable. Surgery is harmful, but in most (not all) cases, we judge that the benefit of improved health offsets the harm of the pain caused by surgery, even though there is no standard against which pain and improved health can be measured. Economic activity is another example. Industrial accidents happen, factories shut down, the stock market takes a plunge, pollutants are released into the atmosphere; in all these cases people suffer harm. But here also we judge that in the main the benefits of economic activity offset the harm it causes although, once again, there may be no objective way to measure one against the other.

Sometimes, of course, we judge that harms are not offset by benefits. Sometimes surgery causes more harm than good, and the same is true of economic activity. For example, the economic benefits of slavery and child labor did not offset the harm they caused. Much of the debate about business and the environment is about harms versus benefits. It is a serious mistake to think that harms and benefits can be quantified and compared, but it is equally a mistake to think that we can make no judgments at all about their relative weight.

The final point concerns condition 2. Preventing a harmful activity, even when the harm is not offset by the benefits it produces, may cause other serious harm that outweighs the advantage gained by stopping the activity. For example, the illegal trade in addictive drugs causes harm that is not significantly offset by any benefit, but some argue that preventing this trade would cause other harm that would be too costly to bear. Consequently the trade should not be prevented but legalized. A more controversial example is clear-cutting tropical rain forests. The long-term ecological harm this causes may outweigh any immediate economic benefit, but stopping the activity would deprive many people of their only means of livelihood and further impoverish certain Third World countries.

If this account of unwarranted harm is provisionally acceptable, then the next step in the expansion and clarification of the harm principle is:

(2) If a human activity or endeavor violates the moral right of a person or other entity not to be harmed, then that harm ought to be prevented by stopping the activity or, if it cannot be entirely stopped without causing other significant harm, modifying it so as to minimize the harm it causes.

Step 2 is based on the thesis that moral rights imply moral duties. For instance, if Jones has the right not to be harmed, then I have a duty not to harm Jones. Thus, if some activity of mine violates Jones's right not to be harmed, I have a duty to stop or at least modify the activity. Furthermore, if I am unwilling to stop or modify the activity, then step 2 implies that other persons are morally required to see to it that I do not continue harming Jones.

Both steps apply to any human activity that causes unwarranted harm. In a business context they apply as follows: Suppose business activity X has adverse effects on the environment that cause harm to certain persons or entities. Further suppose such harm is unwarranted since it is not significantly offset or ameliorated by the benefits that economic activity brings to those persons or entities and it can be prevented without causing other significant harm that outweighs the benefit of prevention. Then, there are moral grounds for either preventing activity X or modifying it to ensure that the environmental damage it causes is minimized, since to allow it to continue violates the right of certain persons or entities not to be harmed.

To take a specific example, suppose business activity X is disposing of toxic industrial wastes in a way that eventually pollutes area groundwater. If it could be shown that the pollution causes unwarranted harm to the local residents, it would follow that there are moral grounds for altering the method of disposal.

Someone who rejected the conclusion of this argument would have to show either that the proposed ethical principle is inapplicable, that no harm is caused, or that it cannot be claimed that the harm caused is unwarranted since it does not satisfy the suggested characterization of unwarranted harm. On the other hand, even if the conclusion is accepted, the controversy is not ended. The argument can continue over how and to what extent the damage should be prevented or minimized and who should ensure that it is prevented or minimized.

It seems unlikely to me that any of the contributors to this book would reject the ethical principle as long as those harmed are existing human beings. But the same is not true if, as several contributors argue, the harm is done to future generations of human beings, animals, or the environment itself. For instance, suppose there will be no significant greenhouse effects from burning fossil fuels for another hundred years. Someone might argue that although no human beings alive now will suffer harm from greenhouse effects, future generations will be harmed. Thus, assuming such harm is unwarranted, burning fossil fuel should be severely curtailed.

Similar arguments can be given on behalf of animals. If animals have the right not to be harmed, then if they are caused unwarranted harm, their rights are violated. Some contributors to this book deny that animals have rights. It is, one contributor claims, "hopelessly sentimental" to believe that they do. If this is correct, then although we may want to avoid harming animals, there are no moral reasons not to do so since the harm principle does not apply to them.

But the same might be said about future generations. How can something that does not exist have a moral right that implies a duty on our part to preserve the environment? And if neither animals nor future generations have rights, why shouldn't we exploit the environment as we see fit as long as we do not cause unwarranted harm to existing persons?

In order to answer this question fully, we would have to examine in detail arguments for the rights of animals and future generations, but there may be a way to answer without undertaking this lengthy task. Some of the contributors suggest that the broad-based public support for environmental protection cannot be explained by the methods of rational risk assessment. Instead it is a deeply held public value, an attitude or sense of obligation toward other persons and the natural world. If this is correct, then one reason businesses should protect the environment is prudential: when things the public values are damaged or destroyed by what is generally believed to be a willful disregard for the public interest, legislative and regulatory restrictions are usually not far behind. And when these are ineffective, direct public action against the offender is an option sometimes taken. Thus, protecting the environment, even in circumstances where there is no question of the violation of rights, also protects the self-interest of business.

The difficulty with this approach, however, is that it does not necessarily give any particular business a good reason for eliminating or minimizing an environmental problem it causes. A businessperson could quite consistently agree that protecting the environment is a public value that deserves support and at the same time argue that as long as no person is caused unwarranted harm, there is no overriding reason to spend stockholder money to solve the problem. Protecting the environment may be beneficial, but in the absence of decisive moral considerations, it must take its place in line with all the other good things to do, had we but enough time and money.

I will leave the public value approach aside for a moment and return to the main argument. The second way to show that no moral right has been violated by an action that damages the environment is to show that no harm was caused to any person, or to animals and future generations, if they have rights. There can be two areas of disagreement here. The first concerns what counts as harm, and the second is whether the harm actually occurred or will occur. There are many different kinds of harm, but an uncontroversial example is immediate and undeniable physical harm directly caused by, for instance, toxins discharged into rivers used as a source of drinking water. If the harm is not immediate but supposedly will occur in the future, perhaps years in the future, and if the causal connection between environmental damage or pollutants and physical harm is less than clear, the case that a certain type of business activity causes physical harm by environmental damage is much more difficult to establish. For example, it is sometimes alleged that in twenty or thirty years, certain pollutants will cause an increase in the rate of various cancers or other disorders. But an examination of the evidence that backs up these claims often reveals questionable assumptions and research that is at best in its initial stages.

Furthermore, the problem is not only the empirical one of gathering enough evidence to establish that harm will occur. It is also conceptual. If we can point to no specific person who is harmed now, no rights are violated now, so why should a business be obligated to change its current procedures to prevent harm that may occur at some unspecified date in the future to some unspecified person or persons?

These are complex issues. The empirical problem of showing that harm will occur at some future date has two distinct parts: deciding on some standard of evidence that, it is generally agreed, is sufficient to justify present steps to prevent future harm and showing in particular cases that the standard is or is not met.

Disagreement about the standard of evidence seems to lie at the center of many contemporary debates about the environment. Some corporations demand a very stringent standard. In legal terms, they want the evidence to show beyond a reasonable doubt that environmental damage will cause harm. Others require a less strict standard—only that the preponderance or weight of evidence shows that harm will occur. For example, Du Pont apparently used the less strict standard when it decided to stop making chlorofluorocarbons (CFCs).

I believe the less strict standard should apply. The reason is that the moral requirement not to cause harm overrides whatever qualms there may be about the strength of the evidence. A preponderance of evidence, though it may not be as strong or unequivocal as we might wish, is reason enough to act to prevent harm that may occur in the future. I concede, however, that much more needs to be said about this.

Assuming the proposed standard of evidence is adopted, there remains the problem of determining whether the standard is met in specific instances. For instance, is there a preponderance of evidence that CFCs cause depletion of the ozone layer or that greenhouse gases will cause the icecaps to melt? Individual businesspersons might reasonably object that evaluating the evidence is beyond their competence and that without any determination about the quality of the evidence it would be foolhardy for them to act.

The objection is well taken, but I deny that businesspersons are thereby absolved of all responsibility. Businesses have the responsibility to find out whether the evidence justifies action, if not through their own efforts then by banding together to support independent and objective evaluations of the evidence. For example, suppose the chemical industry agreed to submit the CFC problem to an independent scientific organization for evaluation, to support additional research if needed, and to abide by that organization's decision about the evidence. In my view this would be an ethically responsible course of action. It would also be an action that would require immense changes in business attitudes and government policy. It may seem idealistic to advocate such a course of action, but the alternative is more lengthy debate about the evidence, and continued delay may prove disastrous. Some way to decide about the quality of the evidence must be adopted—if not the one proposed, then some other one. We cannot wait until the issue is moot.

There remains the conceptual problem: in brief, if no one is harmed now, then no rights are violated now, so why should businesses change their procedures? In order to answer this question, consider one of those fanciful examples so dear to the heart of philosophers. Suppose an evil scientist constructs a superintelligent robot. He enters the name and address of every living American into the robot's memory and then instructs the robot to select one of those persons at random and in about twenty years or so go to that person's home and cause him or her serious physical harm. If we learned about the scientist's nefarious plan, would we be morally justified in preventing him from carrying it out, by force if necessary? Surely we would. And we would dismiss as frivolous any claim on his part that since no one has been harmed, no rights have been violated. It is justification enough for us to act that if we were to allow the scientist to continue, rights would be violated. If this is correct, then it implies that if an action in the present were to cause harm in the future and thus would violate a right in the future, we are morally justified in requiring action to prevent or minimize that harm. This is an important extension of the ethical principle I gave earlier, which does not obviously have this implication. It allows us to say to an individual manager that he or she is morally obligated now to prevent harm that may occur long after the manager has gone to another job. It may even justify present action to protect the rights of future generations.

The final stage of the argument is to show that the harm caused is unwarranted. If both conditions in the characterization of unwarranted harm are not met, then the conclusion does not follow. For example, suppose businesses are convinced that greenhouse gases will cause some warming of the earth's atmosphere and that as a consequence ocean levels will rise several feet and harm some coastal residents. They still could argue that the benefits of the economic activities that generate greenhouse gases offset the harm done to coastal residents. Alternatively they could argue that stopping those activities would cause other significant harm, such as loss of jobs, that outweighs any benefit gained. If either point could be shown, the harm caused does not qualify as unwarranted in the sense I have characterized it.

The greenhouse case is complex since it asks us to make judgments about the relative weight of present benefits (economic activity) against future harms (rising sea levels) and existing harms (loss of jobs) against future benefits (maintaining sea levels). It is not clear to me how rationally to make such judgments, but it is clear that a procedure for making them is needed. Many kinds of business activity cause some degree of harm and can be stopped only at the cost of causing other harm. If we consider causing any harm at all morally unacceptable, then we will find ourselves in a moral dilemma from which there is no escape. Thus we need have some way of determining whether harm is unwarranted and hence morally prohibited.

Finally, if it is shown that a certain economic activity causes environmental damage that in turn causes unwarranted harm, who should take the lead in stopping the activity or minimizing the harm it causes: business, government, or some other organization? Since an adequate discussion of this problem would require many pages, I will not pursue it further except to mention two points. First, if businesses are to take the lead in environmental action, they must do so in a manner that does not place individual businesses at a competitive disadvantage. Otherwise the potential is created for other kinds of unwarranted harm. Second, placing major responsibility on government for environmental protection does not relieve businesses of their moral obligations. If necessary, businesses may have to lobby the government to impose regulation that prevents or minimizes unwarranted harm caused by economic activity. This is directly contrary to prevailing business attitudes, but it may be one way businesses can discharge their moral obligations.

I have only touched on many of the issues discussed in this book. In conclusion I return briefly to the point that environmental protection is a public value. I centered my discussion around the rights of individuals and argued that the public value of environmental protection does not always provide individual businesspersons with reasons to change their business policies. But it would be a mistake to dismiss this value too lightly. The decisions we make now about the environment are decisions about the kind of world we want to live in and the kind of world we want to leave to our heirs. Each decision shapes that world, sometimes in ways that can be changed, sometimes irrevocably. Many decisions about the environment are of the latter kind. No doubt some of them do violate rights not to be harmed. These should be dealt with by appropriate means. But others of equal or greater magnitude do not clearly violate any rights. Perhaps they cannot even be evaluated within the conceptual framework of rights. This seems to me a genuine possibility. It does not mean that we cannot evaluate them at all from a moral viewpoint, but it may mean that we need to consider whether we have moral obligations to ourselves, to future generations, to animals, and to the environment that go beyond the rights these things may or may not have. The place to begin this investigation is with the values we hold—the things we hope our actions will preserve or protect. It is here, if anywhere, that we can truly begin to deal with the environmental dilemmas we face.

I

BUSINESS, ETHICS, AND THE ENVIRONMENT: AN OVERVIEW

1

Terre Gaste

PETER A. FRENCH

It is characteristic of the stories of the Celtic tradition that pivotal events occur near springs, fords, forest clearings, or special trees. These sacred sites were defended by a king or knight who could be challenged in order to test his ability to protect the special place. The spot is guarded not just because it is sacred but because the prosperity of the people, or so they believed, depends on the strength and the resolve of the defender to protect the sacred springs and forests. If the defender—Frazier called him "The King of the Wood"—loses virility, if the place is no longer safe, according to Celtic mythology, the land is magically transformed into Terre Gaste, the Wasteland of which T. S. Eliot wrote.[1] The Celtic legends forged a link between environmental protection and long-term communal prosperity. The link lies in the responsibility shouldered by the defender to guard the sacred spot and that of the people to ensure that the appropriate defender was on the spot.

Celtic mythology is invigorating, sometimes brutal, and certainly pagan. Still the Celts' doctrine of the sacred spots and the threat of magical barrenness speaks across millennia and worldviews. The Celts were nature worshippers; hence they had deep religious reasons to guard the environment. More important for us, they understood the need to locate responsibility for environmental protection with those who can have a positive effect on that goal. Although the people did bear the responsibility of ensuring that the defender remained capable of his task, grooming and sending challengers to test the vigor of the defender, the defender held the ultimate responsibility for preventing the onset of the Wasteland.[2] Failure resulted in beheading.

One of the major problems we have in conceptualizing responsibility for environmental protection is that of identifying roles in the first place. The care of the environment is often left to everyone—egalitarian but also ineffective. If we want to prevent the Wasteland from becoming the human habitat of the future, we need a moral and metaphysical theory that lays the responsibility where it can do some genuine good and where it makes moral sense to assign it. The idea that we should place long-term environmental protection on the shoulders of each of us is the kind of nonsense produced by the atomistic individualism that is characteristic of modern political-moral theory and that it renders individuals, at the very least, frustrated and leaves the important job undone, often barely started.

In spring 1989, a week or so after the *Exxon Valdez* piled into a reef and befouled the waters and shores of Prince William Sound with 11 million gallons of oil, a Wall Street analyst of some reputation was interviewed on national television (CNN). The gist of his position was that disasters of this sort are bound to occur in the industry and should be understood as a cost the society must absorb for its oil-based economy. He went on to argue that neither Exxon nor individuals either on the tanker or in the company ought to be held responsible for the incident. In effect, he claimed, no person, natural or corporate, ought to be held to account or liable for damages. It seemed to him that Exxon was making a magnanimous gesture in voluntarily cleaning up the damaged region. The startled reaction of the other discussants left a few awkward moments of silent airtime before someone attempted a rejoiner.

When I first heard this view expressed, like so many others, I was shocked. Here was just another free enterpriser (all he needed was an eye patch and a parrot) defending big business as it desecrates the earth. Responding to his position, however, is not as simple as it sounds. To do so one must be prepared to dynamite some of the most cherished and firmly placed cornerstones of the political liberalism that has dominated Western academic discussion of moral responsibility for centuries. I am prepared to trade that sort of desecration to bring the other under control.

There are enormous problems with motivating responsibility ascriptions with respect to the environment. One reason, no doubt, is that traditional theories of ownership, such as Locke's, exclude waste. Hence, it is rather hard to get people to accept ownership of things they throw away, flush away, or spill. Although the ownership of waste would make a useful study, that is not my interest. I want to argue that establishing a ground for holding us, an aggregate of individual natural persons, responsible for environmental protection is virtually impossible from within the liberal individualist tradition. In other words, no sensible responsibility relationship to which we as individuals are a party can exist from which individual responsibility for environmental protection can be derived.

Environmental protection, for moral purposes, cannot be based on any relationship that might be imagined between us, collectively or individually, and other species. Consider what I have elsewhere called the "input conditions of responsibility-ascription."[3] The formula for responsibility recently sketched by Edmund Pincoffs[4] exposes them: A imputes C to B on account of D, in the light of E, and in the absence of F. C is an event, condition, or state of affairs, usually an unpleasant one(s). If the event is the oil spill on Prince William Sound, the question is whether A [you or me] can impute it to Exxon (B^1) or the tanker captain (B^2) or both, and so on. D is an activity (or activities) or action (or actions) performed by B, and E is the set of role requirements that establish B's relationship to A and to the event. F is the defense, excuses, or justifications B could offer. Pincoffs's formula is for responsibility ascription, and so C is the focus, an untoward event. But if the concern is responsibility assignment, then we need to look primarily at the relationship between A and B—what I will call the responsibility relationship—and at E—the role requirements. In short, my interest is not in nailing the party liable for the oil spill; it is in establishing the assignment of responsibility for environmental protection. In terms of the Celtic traditions, it is not in pinpointing and then beheading the particular lax defender but in determining who ought to be the defenders and what their duties should be. In effect we need to uncover the requirements for being a responsible party in long-term environmental matters. Who or what can play the part of B?

Insofar as we are talking of moral matters, B must be a person. It makes no moral sense to hold, for example, sea otters or whales responsible for whatever they might do to mess up the ecosystem. If we are to be strict, we should probably say that only those persons who stand in a responsibility relationship can ascribe responsibility to each other. That, however, is a long way from actual practice. I do not stand in any responsibility relationship with Jim Bakker, but I ascribe blame to him for his misdeeds. A (in Pincoffs's formula) need not be linked to B in a relationship that generates responsibilities on B in order for A to ascribe responsibility to B for some C, failure to meet them. But for that ascription to make sense, it must be the case that B does have a responsibility to do something that would have prevented C, and for B to have such a responsibility, there must be a party $\langle P \rangle$ with whom B has a relationship that defines roles and duties. The problem for environmental protection is to discover the parties B and P. No one is responsible to the sea otters for their protection. Is anyone responsible to anyone else for the protection of the sea otters? Of course, laws are in place protecting elements of the environment, so violators theoretically owe the state an obligation on which they have defaulted. But is it a moral obligation? Is the state a person and hence a suitable party to the relationship? The preponderance of thinkers in the Western liberal tradition would be reluctant to say it is.

Typical of the discussion of environmental responsibility is the view that protection of the environment, species, and so on is owed to future generations. Of course, we should protect it for ourselves as well, but in either case these are difficult claims to understand or cash out. Protect it for what? for our possible enjoyment? for someone else's possible enjoyment? How many of us are ever going to visit the shores of Prince William Sound? It is not on my vacation wish list. It surely is not likely to be enjoyed by the millions on millions of people living on the Indian subcontinent or in Africa. There are bothersome discriminatory tendencies to protectionism based on possible future enjoyment of existing people. At least future generations are safer candidates since we do not know what their interests will be or how they may need to use the environment. Many people talk as if we ought to leave it to them in good repair. But why?

It seems to me that environmental protection as a long-term project depends on persons existing now being in a responsibility relationship with the generations of persons who will (or may) exist in the remote future. Yet it is very difficult to see how any relationship deep enough to support responsibility assignment can exist between any persons existing today and distant generations. I reject as grossly sentimental the view that we have a responsibility to protect the environment because it contains living things that have rights. Again, a responsibility to whom? and with respect to what role requirements? Although I admit to certain negative feelings about some birds, I have nothing against flora and fauna, all creatures great and small. I would rather they continued living than not, and I support organizations that work to protect them. But it is a matter of charity, not obligation, especially in such cases as the sea otters.

Returning then to the possibility that a moral responsibility relationship with respect to the environment exists between people now existing and future generations, we should note that traditional liberal individualist theories utterly fail to provide the basis for such a relationship. Consider the important thinkers of that tradition: Thomas Hobbes and John Locke. As Brian Barry[5] notes, any attempt to create the relationship must account for the asymmetry in power to harm between those persons now in existence and future generations. As the environmentalists remind us, we can certainly make those in the future worse off, but they will never be able to reciprocate. They can tarnish our reputations, but that is hardly comparable to the messes in which we can force them to live. We, individually and in the aggregate, can materially hurt or help them. They can neither hurt nor help us.

For Hobbes, as Barry notes, "morality offers convenient articles of peace."[6] But insofar as Hobbes's view depends on the relative equality in ability to harm each other of the parties to the social contract, Hobbesian responsibility relations cannot be established between us and future generations. Moral obligations for him depend on mutual risks of harm. We have no Hobbesian reasons to respect whatever interests in the environment future generations may have.

Lockean entitlement protection hardly fares better in motivating a responsibility relationship across generations. That is no surprise, for Locke's property theory is in no small measure responsible for our carelessness with the environment. For Locke, and more recently Robert Nozick,

Provided an individual has come by a good justly, he may justly dispose of it any way he likes. . . . Since we have a right to dispose of our property as we wish, subsequent generations could not charge us with injustice if we were to consume whatever we could in our lifetimes and direct that what was left should be destroyed at our deaths.[7]

Or we can destroy it as we go along and owe nothing to those in the future.

I have no recipe for the proper use and care of the environment. That is not my interest here. Instead I want to locate the stewardship obligations in a responsibility relationship that makes sense, and not in mystical extensions of the traditional views. I believe that our concept of responsibility assignment embodies Michael Walzer's position that obligations to others depend on actual relationships with them.[8] "Actual relations" does not mean equality in the ability to cause each other harm. I, for example, have such a relationship with my children and my students. But how can any of us have an actual relationship with generations of people who will not be born until we are long dead? The answer is that there are persons who exist now who can have actual relations with the generations of the future: corporations or corporate-like entities.[9]

The major reason that atomistic individualism has such problems with future generation relations, and this is evident in both liberal politics and libertarian economics, is that it treats corporations merely as things—legal fictions, shorthands for aggregations of natural persons. They have no moral standing. As such they cannot enter into obligation-generating relationships; only their members can.

The actions of corporations can be understood as redescriptions of the actions of humans, and corporate internal decision structures provide the licenses for such redescription.[10] Corporations can do a number of things that are not sensibly reduced to the actions of those associated with them: join cartels, manufacture automobiles, enter bankruptcy, set the price of goods and services, and so forth. In a number of places I have elaborated on the ways corporations act and how they manifest corporate intentionality. Corporate-like entities make decisions, have rights and duties in law, carry on nonlegal relationships with other corporations and with human persons: the whole spectrum of activities and relationships we associate with persons. They are historical entities with births, lives, and deaths. They flourish and decline, succeed and fail. Roger Scruton has pointed out that they can "even be leading characters in a drama (as in Wagner's *Die Meistersinger*)."[11]

The next step in the analysis will not appeal to many of those who are at least willing to allow corporations entry into the moral community. I want to argue that not only are corporations persons in a full-fledged moral sense but that corporations are essential elements of the moral world. Robert Solomon hints at this when he writes that "business is a social practice not an activity of isolated individuals."[12] It can take place only in "a culture with an established set of procedures and expectations" that are not open to tinkering by individual human beings.[13] The maintenance of the business culture is, according to Solomon, a prerequisite for the prosperity of a nation and, he sometimes says and sometimes implies, of the happiness, in the Aristotelian sense, of the individual members of the society. The corporate culture's existence and character are clearly central to Solomon's conception of the good life. It is also not, he assures us, the product of an invisible hand operating to our benefit unbeknown to or unintended by any of us.

Jean-Jacques Rousseau, G. W. F. Hegel, and F. H. Bradley provide a rather different perspective on the place of corporate-like entities than is offered by the individualists of liberal political theory. It is with them that I want to associate. Each, albeit in his own way, suggests that in nature humans are only potential persons. To achieve full moral personhood, humans must associate with and within corporate institutions. The dependency relationship between individuals and corporate entities, on these theories, runs in just the opposite direction from that found in the traditional individualist's theory. Corporations are not things cobbled together for certain purposes but mere means. They put flesh on the bones of the abstract independent actors of Kantian or Rawlsian theory. According to the individualist, corporate institutions gain whatever legitimacy they may have from a "subservience to the state—the supreme institution in which the sum of human contracts is inscribed. . . . The state tends to be seen as the only permissible corporate person."[14] The epitome of this view was intoned by the leaders of the French Revolution who wrote: "A state that is truly free ought not to suffer within its bosom any corporation."[15] Totalitarianism was not far behind. For the Hegelian there is an internal relation between corporate personalities and natural persons.[16] By that I mean that the corporate entities provide something to humans in the absence of which we would be something less than human. Call it culture, historical identity, *bildung*. The Hegelian view is that our relations with others and within corporate-like entities are essential to any adequate understanding of our identities and to the notion of rational agency. Bradley tells us that

what we call an individual man is what he is because of and by virtue of community. . . . If we suppose the world of relations in which he was born and bred, never to have been, then we suppose the very essence of him not to be; if we take that away, we have taken him away.[17]

To act rationally is not to choose on the basis of abstract utility maximization. It is to act to foster one's interests, and those interests are intimately and inextricably interwoven within the corporations and corporate-like personalities with which one is associated.

In the absence of such a view of corporations there is no basis for long-term obligations in society. Suppose that corporate-like entities were what the atomistic individualists say they are: aggregations, mere fictions of law and commerce. In such a world, we may assume, individuals can contract to assign responsibilities, and they can also enter into noncontractual relations with each other based on affection and companionship in which responsibility assignments will play some role. But none of these responsibilities will endure much beyond the death of one or both of the parties. Love is wonderful, but its obligations hardly can be said to last after the lovers have died. It is no wonder that we feel impotent as individuals with respect to the protection of the environment. It is not just that there is little any one of us can do to make a difference when we live; it is that we cannot ensure that what we do will survive us. We will never enter into the actual personal responsibility relationship with future generations that is necessary to ground an obligation in us not to do them harm by despoiling their environment. As Roger Scruton has noted, "The care for future generations must be entrusted to persons who will exist when they exist: and if there are no such persons surrounding me, how can I have that care except as a helpless anxiety?"[18]

But surrounding me, intermingling with my very identity, are exactly the sort of persons who will exist (or are likely to exist) when future generations are the existing generations. The responsibility relationships to future generations can be sensibly articulated through corporate-like entities. The maintenance of the environment in order to protect those generations from the Wasteland is a reasonable responsibility of corporations. Indeed they are the best bearers of it, and through each of our identity dependency relations with those corporations, we share the obligation. Not to meet it individually would be to act less than rationally, for it would be to act in ways discordant with one's own essential elements. In effect, an ecological imperative is to be unpacked from our essential dependence on the personalities of corporate-like entities.

Atomistic individualists cheat themselves out of participation in meaningful long-range responsibility relationships. Their purposes in living must be drastically limited and no doubt account for their typical cynicism about almost everything over the long haul. It is no wonder that they put what hope they have in invisible hands. The springs, forests, and waterways of our planet cannot long withstand the treatment they have received from both corporate and natural persons. Environmental protection is essential to the prosperity of those who will live in the future, but only corporate entities can be sensibly assigned responsibility for that protection, and individual humans participate in the task as they achieve their individual identities in their corporate associations. There seems to me to be a close analogy between our role in environmental protection and that which the ordinary Celt played with respect to the defender of the sacred spot.

NOTES

I especially want to thank Roger Scruton for his extremely helpful insights into this problem and for pushing me to expand my corporate personhood theory in these directions.

1. J. G. Frazier, *The Golden Bough* (London, 1949), p. 2.

2. See John Darrah, *The Real Camelot* (London, 1981) esp. pt. 1.

3. Peter A. French, "Responsibility and the Moral Role of Corporate Entities," in *Business and the Humanities*, ed. T. Donaldson (forthcoming).

4. Edmund Pincoffs, "The Practices of Responsibility-Ascription," in *Proceedings and Addresses of the American Philosophical Association* 61, no. 5 (June 1988): 827.

5. Brian Barry, "Justice between Generations," in *Law, Morality, and Society*, ed. P. M. S. Hacker and J. Raz (Oxford, 1977) pp. 268–84.

6. Ibid., p. 270.

7. Ibid., pp. 272–73.

8. Michael Walzer, *Obligations* (Cambridge, 1970), chap. 1.

9. I use the terms *corporations* and *corporate-like entities* to refer to any organizations that function through corporate decision structures. Hence, churches, government, and so-called nonprofit organizations would qualify.

10. Peter A. French, *Collective and Corporate Responsibility* (New York, 1984), chaps. 3, 4, 12.

11. Roger Scruton, "Corporate Persons," in *Proceedings of the Aristotelian Society*, Supplemental Volume (forthcoming).

12. Robert Solomon, "Business and the Humanities: An Aristotelian Approach to Business Ethics" in *Business and the Humanities*.

13. Ibid.

14. Scruton, "Corporate Persons."

15. Quoted in F. W. Maitland, "Moral Personality and Legal Personality," in *Collected Papers*, vol. 3, ed. H. A. L. Fisher (Cambridge, 1911).

16. See G. W. F. Hegel, *The Phenomenology of Spirit* (1807) and *The Philosophy of Right* (1821), esp. Additions, para. 75.

17. F. H. Bradley, *Ethical Studies* (1876; Oxford University Press, 1962), p. 166.

18. Scruton, "Corporate Persons."

2

Animism Redivivus: Are New Visions of Nature a Threat to Homo Sapiens?

WALTER W. BENJAMIN

INTRODUCTION

Rational and prudential planning regarding the long-term interests of nature and future humans is being undercut by environmental fanaticism and zero-risk absolutism. For a nontraditional, adolescent culture, such attitudes are not new. We have a penchant for asking more than our institutions can deliver, whether we gear up for wars against cancer and poverty, health perfectionism, or a life free of pain. As a society we are prone to faddism, irresistibly jumping from one cause to another, unwilling to accept the premise that our finitude makes problematic crucial human problems.

Voices are shrill; "doomsters" among us seem to enjoy creating what *Science Magazine* has labeled the "scare of the week": alar in apples, aflatoxins in corn, bovine growth hormone in milk, and cyanide in grapes.[1] A public interest group led by actress-turned-toxicologist Meryl Streep can force public schools in major cities to withdraw apple products. Two grapes containing 3 millionths of 1 gram of cyanide almost destroyed an industry in Chile. Our public officials, forced to live in the werewolf world of "health risks," too often make no reasonable counterargument and entertain no effort to demonstrate that benefits far outweigh risks.

Are we becoming too careful for our own good? Despite scares, I contend we have never been safer. The primary environmental causes of premature death and disease are still the same they were decades ago: smoking, diets rich in fat and lean in fiber, lack of exercise, and alcohol abuse.

The etiology of our predicament can be revealed in reviewing philosophies of nature.

TRADITIONAL VIEWS OF NATURE

The Western perspective on nature is a composite of two philosophical streams: Judaic-Christian and Greek–natural law. From the Old Testament we have two seemingly contradictory motifs: "The earth is the Lord's and the fullness thereof" (Psalm 24:1) and "The heavens are the Lord's Heavens, but the earth he has given to mankind" (Psalm 115:16).

To whom does the earth really belong? What are the consequences of holding title?[2] "Then God said: 'Let us make man in our image, after our likeness. And let them have dominion over the fish of the sea, and over the birds of the air, and over cattle and over all the earth and over every creeping thing that creeps upon the earth'. And God blessed them, and said, 'multiply, fill the earth and SUBDUE it; and have DOMINION over every living thing that moves upon the earth' " (Genesis 1:26). Some environmental commentators, such as Lynn White, see this as the locus classicus of the dichotomy between nature and homo sapiens.[3] For centuries, he charges, these texts have been a scriptural blank check for continued human imperialism and despoliation of nature.

But most biblical theologians believe our discontinuity with and over nature cannot be based on a few proof-texts. Moreover, Adam and Eve were subsequently "to till" (*shamar* = "to watch" or "to preserve") the Garden of Eden, which can also be rendered "to serve" or "to be a slave to."[4] In addition, the Hebrew words "to take dominion" suggest nothing more than the basic needs of settlement and agriculture. The theme is "stewardship," not "ownership" of nature. Yet having been given a position of power over creation, humans sever or abuse this relationship with God by means of sin, such as idolatry and hubris. Disharmony and brokenness within human nature lead to rebellion, war, and exploitation without.[5]

For twenty centuries the church has been the nurturing mother to many ecologically sensitive movements. St. Francis of Assisi, the prototypical saint, saw nature as the veil of the divine and gave homilies to animals, birds, and fish.[6] He incarnated the nature mysticism as it existed in the thirteenth century. Indeed, the ideal Christian way of living for over a thousand years, the monastic movement, spawned communities of men and women who lived in empathetic union with nature in sustainable, self-contained communities.

The medieval church, moreover, was suspicious that commerce would feed the fires of greed and avarice, one of the seven deadly sins. The agricultural vocations were prized because real wealth was generated only by the soil and flocks. Even Martin Luther wondered, "How could a guilder beget a guilder?" Thus, usury was forbidden.

But technology was not eschewed. During the Middle Ages, English Cistercians were honored as the foremost breeders of sheep. And the father of genetics, an Augustinian monk, Gregor Mendel, did his experiments on cross-fertilizing sweet peas. Clearly those who would place the cause of our ecological crisis on the Judaic-Christian tradition regarding nature have not made their case.

Nonetheless, for the past few centuries there has been a struggle within the Christian churches between two ethical paradigms—the ethics of nature—the sacro-symbiotic model—and the ethics of history—the power-plasticity model.[7] The former ties human activity to the paradigm of the circle. To be ethical demands that one be in harmony and balance with seasonal, menstrual, and cosmic cycles. Nature reveals a design, a pattern of law, a preexistent harmony, to which humans must a priori conform. To break with sacred and archetypal patterns is to act "unnaturally" or to go "against nature." This ethic repudiates abortion, sterilization, fertilization outside the womb, and suicide. Death is but a rhythm of nature, to be gracefully accepted. This is a conservative, agrarian, and holistic ethic that tends to see hubris in much of recent technology.

The ethics of history, the power-plasticity model, interprets biblical "dominion" as God releasing homo sapiens from the tyranny of the cycle. Nature is alien and independent of humans and possesses little inherent value. The circle is broken to become a line of time that can be changed to achieve individual and collective goals. Humans can bend "his-tory" or "her-story" and shape their future, family, and environment to the ends they hold dear. One does not have to endure drought, flood, genetic disease, and untimely pregnancy fatalistically. The demonic, antihuman forces resident in nature need to be tamed, if not destroyed. Death is something to be overcome, outwitted. Obviously the power-plasticity model has sunk deeply into our moral imagination; we are corporately homo technologicus. Individualistic, progressive, and youthful cultures, unlike traditional ones like Bohemia and Austria, tend to treat people, as well as nature, in functional terms. Moreover, Protestantism has a greater affinity for the ethics of history; Roman Catholicism, the ethics of nature.

Greek philosophy and Stoic natural law are the origin of the Western "scale of being" paradigm that has been dominant in shaping our view of nature. It viewed nature as layered. From inert matter at the base of the pyramid of life, we proceed upward through raw matter, mineral, vegetable, lower to higher animals, homo sapiens, to noncorporeal angelic life, to God. Each species had its own niche depending on its being or essence, that is, the quality of its physical, rational, and spiritual life. The Stoic principle that "the lower good must serve the higher" saw its embodiment in soil that served to produce grass, which in turn was eaten by cows, whose milk, hide, and meat nourished humans. Although we are biologically linked to the animal kingdom, an infinite gap separated us because of our possession of *nous* (mind) or the image of God. Homo sapiens closed the teleological circle by glorifying God. It was both a sacred and experiential paradigm imposed on a world that was assumed to be quite tidy. Obviously the cosmic hierarchic template meant that nature and God decreed that the ecclesiastical and political order, from supplicant to pope, from serf to king, should be hierarchic as well.

Today, from an ecological point of view, the natural world is much more integrated and systematically unified than the Greek position postulated. The biotic mantle of the earth is one because its living components are coevolved and mutually interdependent. The Christian and Greek views of nature are condemned by many as being "homocentric," allowing a "cowboy ethic" and an "ecological holocaust."[8] Where hierarchies exploit, models of holism unite—hence, the plea for a new ecological ethic.

ORIGINS OF THE NEW ENVIRONMENTALISM

I could not but feel with a sympathy full of regret all the pain that I saw around me, not only that of men, but that of the whole creation. From this community of suffering I have never tried to withdraw myself. (Albert Schweitzer)

The historic roots of the new environmental absolutism are to be found in a rebirth of Animism, the earliest of all cosmic and religious sentiments, which held that all of nature was alive due to the spirits (*anima* = soul) that inhabited all objects and living things in nature. All reality (trees, mountains, stones, rivers) was imbued with consciousness and possessed a kind of invisible electricity, or *mana,* that only medicine men or shamans could release or constrain. Such spirits brought either health or disease, fertility or impotency. Most often, however, they held humanity in thralldom; humans were under, not over, nature. The potentially demonic power had to be propitiated by sacrifices, incantations, and prayer.

While we turn animals into objects and use them to serve the complicated ends of our destiny, animists include them in their community and treat them subjectively and personally, but they pay a high price in terms of fear. They are paralyzed by the violent and tragic in nature. A central Eskimo shaman named Aua, queried about Eskimo beliefs, answered, "We do not believe. We fear."[9]

Jeremy Rifkin tends to think like an animist. For him nature is sacro-symbiotic. An economist by training, he assumes the worst regarding genetic engineering, believing that effects would be "subtle, cumulative, irreversible, and catastrophic."[10] We are handcuffed by the determinism of nature because of evolutionary natural selection. We need to endure our fate. We should change neither phenotype nor genotype to eliminate diabetes, hemophilia, muscular dystrophy, Huntington's chorea, or dozens of other genetic diseases. Nor should we develop nitrogen fixation on corn or use bacteria to make vegetables frost resistant. He prefers litigation in place of scientific dialogue and impedes much potentially beneficial technology in the courts rather than discuss reasonable trade-offs. Rifkin pleads that the process of secularization should be stopped, that "the resacralization of nature stands before us as the great mission of the coming age."[11] Ironically he overlooks the fact that the very technology that created our predicament will be necessary to lead us out of it.

Pantheism, the cosmology of many nineteenth-century literary romantics such as William Wordsworth, Elizabeth Barrett Browning, and Alfred, Lord Tennyson, also worshipped Nature (always capitalized). Pantheists see the world as God's body. Revelation was not found in church, Scripture, or dogma but by resting on the bosom of Nature. Pantheists looked with horror on the environmental effects of the Industrial Revolution as canals, mines, railroads, and factories began to make England the workshop of the world. While industry, invention, and technology raised millions out of endemic poverty, the romantics saw only a zero-sum paradigm: Britannia's "green and pleasant land" and verdant shires were being destroyed by the "Satanic Mills." Nature was their shrine, within which they discovered the numinous, the mysterious tremendum, and the ecstatic.

Today the Sierra Club and Greenpeace continue the ethos of pantheism. Preservation rather than conservation, a "lock-up" mentality rather than multiple use, aesthetics rather than economics, is their focus. The being, not utility, of nature is valued. Eagles, whales, dolphins, and harp seals are inviolate. An annual theophany is a week of backpacking in the wilderness where, if one is lucky, one will not hear sound from or sight another human. Since the average income of a club member is $76,800, they willingly pay the additional cost of lumber, oil, and minerals that their political agenda saddles on a less fortunate blue-collar brother. It is the wealthy and the educated who will be the primary beneficiaries of the maintenance and expansion of pristine environments. The rural poor will be denied the fruits of development, and the urban poor will continue to choke on pollution that cannot be exported (an example is the Sierra Club affirmed "nondegradation" decision that required the Environmental Protection Agency to preserve pristine air in underdeveloped areas).[12]

In West Germany, home of the world's largest drug and chemical industry, the biotechnology industry has not licensed a new plant in over a year because of a phobia over gene splicing. In a replay of the Andromeda strain myth of twenty-five years ago, a politician stated, "What killer life forms, what environmental dangers, what biological epidemics can we now expect if gene technology is carried on?"[13] A strange trinity of the green party, the communists, and some Lutheran parishes has exacerbated fears by circulating stories of mutant microbes and gene-spliced "sheep as big as grizzlies." Yet the plan of BASF, the chemical giant, was to make an experimental cancer medicine by using the process of altering the genes of a human intestinal bacteria so that the bugs' innards would secrete the medicine. The process has been going on for a decade in the making of many drugs without accident. "They accept all the advantages of technology," researcher Peter Meyer commented. "They get food cheaper than they ever have. They have unlimited energy. They just aren't prepared to accept any risk."[14] They turn to political coercion because they cannot win the scientific debate.

"Ultimately, you can't do work that isn't approved by your neighbors," says Rolf-Dieter Acker, BASF's head of biotechnology research. It will continue to fight the pantheist greens and their loyalists but plans to locate its main gene research laboratory in a more hospitable setting, Boston.[15]

Nathan Hare, a black philosopher, is critical of the "suburban ecology" of whites for its idolatry of redwood trees and pristine water for water-skiing, fishing, swimming, or "just to look at." It neglects a more important black ecology: the socioeconomic oppression in the ghetto. Pantheists can easily find God in a sunset but never in the haunting eyes of a black child of the ghetto. A 760-page record of the Conservation Foundation in Virginia in 1965 had only a half-page devoted to black concerns. The bourgeois "colonizer milks dry the resources and labor of the colonized to develop and improve his own habitat while leaving that of the colonized starkly 'underdeveloped.' "[16]

We should be wary of a pantheistic renaturalization—the purely ecological reconstruction of our culture. We should be able to mitigate the pride and spirit of domination that came out of the Enlightenment without refashioning the shackles of humanity to the despotisms of nature.

SOME INHERENT DANGERS IN THE NEW ENVIRONMENTALISM

Specism

As we shift from a homocentric to a more holistic vision of the cosmos, we must not overlook the real dangers inherent in those who propose radical remedies. For a number of philosophers—Patrick Corbett, Peter Singer, Michael Peters, Andrew Linzey, Richard Ryder, Ruth Harrison—liberation must extend beyond blacks, homosexuals, and women to nonhumans: "We require expansion of the great principles of liberty, equality and fraternity over the lives of animals. Let animal slavery join human slavery in the graveyard of the past."[17] The late U.S. Supreme Court Justice William O. Douglas once wrote, in a dissenting opinion, that the day should come when "all of the forms of life will stand before the court—the pileated woodpecker as well as the coyote and bear, the lemmings as well as the trout in the streams."[18] Animal liberationists, in making their case for extending "rights" to animals, argue that dolphins and chimpanzees often manifest greater rationality than babies, the senile, and those afflicted with Altzheimer's.

As a principle this is beautiful; operationally it throws us into what ethicists call a moral sponge. The jargon of specism is confused, tangled, and frequently bizarre. Like religious fundamentalists who anthropomorphize the divine, it anthropomorphizes the natural world. Animal rightists speak in poetry but want to be accredited as scientists. It is another extension of the "more-sensitive-than-thou" movements of our time. In spite of ideology, few antispecist philosophers know where to draw the line between dragonflies, mice, robins, snail darters, monkeys, and humans. Serving the demands of equity is difficult enough in treating subjects that are alike. How do we measure and evaluate those that are unlike?

Rights to a "Livable Environment"

William Blackstone affirms that "each person has a right qua human being" to a pristine environment because it is the essential entitlement necessary to fulfill human capacity.[19] As a pole star by which to steer, this principle is fine. But just as perfect health is impossible if fate has given us a bad genetic deck of cards, so too neither the state nor nature can deliver an ideal environment—nor can insurance companies. The "acts of God" provision—drought, earthquakes, floods, hurricanes—protects them from litigation due to the vagaries of nature. After the eruption of Mount St. Helens, tens of thousands of square miles in the northwestern part of the United States were unfit for habitation for months. Northern Minnesota in the winter is a serendipitous experience for me, but for most others it is the nation's icebox.

What constitutes "livable"? Moreover, when a right for a pure environment clashes with other rights—for example, a well-paying job, which might be available only in a city with smog—which right must give way?

The Denigration of Homo Sapiens

Animal liberationists realize that if humanity can be lowered to the level of animals or animals raised to the level of humans, expanding rights to cover animals would be easier. While Charles Darwin, Sigmund Freud, B. F. Skinner, and sociobiologists have revealed our genetic, psychic, or physiological linkage to animals, most animal advocates link emotional and thought capacities to animals. "Whether we choose the rabbit or the child or the insect," comments Andrew Linzey, the foremost theologian in the animal rights arena, "are all essentially *subjective matters* [my emphasis] with nothing but human preference to determine our choice."[20] Or again, "How can we know that God values elephants *more* than he does flies, or rabbits *more than* potatoes?"[21] J. D. Salinger's retort in *Catcher in the Rye* regarding this near deification of animals is fitting: "Sentimentality is loving something more than God does."

Thus a whole category of animals—cats, rats, mice, chimps, cows, deer—has rationality, emotions, pain, and aesthetic capacity attributed to them. For classical philosophy this new Copernican Revolution is disturbing because it undercuts human dignity in five categories:

1. Conceptual Thought: Humans have a brain; they can create language, symbols, dream, and imagine. "When a chimp can tell me anything worth listening to," commented an undergraduate philosophy major, "I'll listen!"

2. Capacity for Technology: Pure science has no utilitarian function and all technology is not bad. In explaining the rite of circumcision, the Talmud states, "Man must finish what God has started." There is synergy between nature and humans.

3. Range of Emotions: Animals do not have guilt. Instead they have fear-guilt, like my dog when he digs holes in the yard. I experience fear-guilt when driving 70 miles an

hour and hear a siren behind me. (When the patrolman passes me and pulls over the porsche ahead of me, then I experience "guilt.")

4. Cultural Lamarckism: We are not genetically fixed. We must learn how to start a fire. And unlike animals whose genetic code programs them, we create, transform, and transmit our culture.

5. Freedom from Instinctual Fixation: The nature versus nurture debate is endless, but we do have freedom within limits to shape a more humane world.

A responsible ecology movement has little to gain by denigrating the glory of homo sapiens. We should be proud anthropocentrists. It is not egocentric to affirm that nature serves homo sapiens. Totalitarianism, whether ecological or political, begins with the disparagement of human uniqueness. Beauty is not in the sunset or flower but in the human aesthetic perceiver. The significance of the Age of Reason, the Renaissance, and the Enlightenment is often missed by radical environmentalists and animal advocates.

The psychiatrist Willard Gaylin sees a measure of self-hate, a residue from campus life of the sixties, in an inordinate love of plants and animals.[22] Ecological terrorists who drive spikes into trees in the Northwest that severely injure lumbermen may have pathological personal biographies. Activists who destroy scientific laboratories and prevent animal research from uncovering the etiology of AIDS and dozens of other diseases are telling us more about themselves than the technology they oppose.

THE RIGHTS OF FUTURE HUMANS

Classical moral tradition gives us little help regarding our obligations to future humans. Yet we sense a vague generalized duty to them, as when we leave wood and a clean campsite for unknown future campers. The problem is that the further we project into the future, the greater are the unknowability and unpredictability. We do not know much about all the children who will be born during the next eight months, though their genetic makeup is entirely fixed.[23] Yet we can form some generalized rules.

First, we need to strike a judicious balance between qualitative and quantitative factors. Our duty is to respect the ecological carrying capacity as understood at the time. The Club of Rome's five criteria—population, pollution, industrialization, nonrenewable resources, poverty—need to be monitored. Yet life in Holland with its 625 people per square mile is not automatically more "nasty, brutish, and short" than the United States with its 85. Clearly in some Third World countries such as Bangladesh, this is the case. Human life, both now and in the future, requires more than mere existence but the capacity to "live well."

Second, affirm negative rights even if positive rights are problematical. Just as negative eugenics (eliminating deleterious genes and diseases) is ethically to be preferred to positive eugenics (breeding in desirable characteristics), so too it is easier to gain consensus on what not to bequeath to future humans. Negative rights are similar to the Hippocratic Code—*primum non nocere* ("Above all, do no harm"). Farmers cannot dictate what their children and grandchildren should grow on the farm that they inherit but should leave them as much topsoil as possible so they have the freedom to make that decision. We have negative duties to protect the environmental commons and pass unpoisoned land, air, and water to future generations.

Third, affirm the benefits and limits of future technology. Clearly the Club of Rome was overly pessimistic regarding its "if present trends continue" scenario.[24] A judicious balance must be struck between human inventiveness and human culpability. Few of us would continue to choose to smoke on the grounds that by the time we fall victim to disease, a cure will have been found for cancer. It would be selfish of our generation to continue to poison common goods in the naive assumption that future humans will develop a technology to clean up the mess we have bequeathed to them. It is best to err on the side of safety. Each generation should assess itself the costs of its own pollution.

Fourth, near-future persons have greater claims than distant-future persons: "Men have no right to put the well-being of the present generation wholly out of the question," wrote Edmund Burke. "Perhaps the only moral trust with any certainty in our hands is the care of our own time."[25] It is a truism that altruism dissipates with time and distance. We would not honor a mother who starved her own children for the interests of the destitute in Bangladesh or for the hungry in the twenty-first century. I contribute to college funds for my grandchildren but not to those who may carry my genes in the twenty-second century. I am ignorant about their number, condition, and need. It would be unjust, therefore, to leave today's poor in poverty because of the mysterious claims of the distant poor. Near-future persons are generations whose size and fate we more directly control. We must allow them to inherit basic resources as good as ours without undue cost.

Fifth, a social contract links our present and future generations. John Locke, to whom the founding fathers looked for a formulation of the moral and political principles, said that among our duties to others was a prepolitical "state of nature."[26] Today we are in a "state of nature" toward distant persons. I have a duty to pick up broken glass from my sidewalk even though I do not know how many people may be endangered. We are social beings, not Robinson Crusoes. We make payment on the sacrifices our posterity bequeathed to us by giving equally good or better to our descendents.

SOME SUGGESTIONS

First, we need to clarify our moral discourse. "Rights language" cannot be applied to flora and fauna because, while they may be "subjects of a life," we do not impute to them moral duties. A "bad" man we deem a criminal who has misused his freedom in rejecting the legal-ethical norms of the community. A "bad" dog may have merely followed a genetic imprint. Thus, the scale of being still has ecological utility, for it apportions duties to levels of life given their being. I propose that we restrict "rights language" to homo sapiens, "welfare language" to animals, and "sustainability language" to the rest of nature's goods. All life is wondrous, but not all life should be classed as either sacred or inviolate.

Second, we must unmask zealotry. We must label the radical proanimalists for what they are—antihumanists. A so-called animal liberation front in April 1989 caused $100,000 damage in "freeing" 1,000 animals at the University of Arizona. Thirty were mice carrying the disease cryptosporidium, which can be fatal to immunosuppressed individuals and malnourished children. There is no known treatment.[27] Vigilante vandalism is a sad commentary on the Luddite mentality and scientific ignorance of tens of thousands of Americans captured by zealotry. As one who has a relative suffering from a genetic disease for which relief is possible through future animal research, I feel a sense of outrage that biomedical researchers are maligned by Hollywood celebrities who "major in minors." The notion that young men and women undergo the arduous pilgrimage in route to Ph.D.s and M.D.s just for a chance to torture innocent furry creatures in the laboratory is itself an act of intellectual torture.

The "nature good, man-made bad" ideology of many ecological zealots rarely informs us of the hazards of nature's own pesticides. The Food and Drug Administration estimates that the average American consumes about 45 micrograms of possibly carcinogenic man-made pesticide residues a day. Yet there are 500 micrograms of natural carcinogens in a cup of coffee (hydrogen peroxide and methylglyoxal), 185 micrograms of natural carcinogenic formaldehyde in a cola, and 760 micrograms of carcinogenic estragole in a leaf of basil.[28] According to biologist Bruce Ames, plants have learned through evolution that chemical warfare is a great way to fight off fungi, insects, and animal predators—even human predators.

Third, we must eschew environmental apocalypticism. In spite of the fact that prophets of doom have had a dismal record from Malthus to the present, we continue to be prone to the Chicken Little syndrome. (Two Texas A&M professors, Charles Maurice and Charles W. Smithson, in their work, *The Doomsday Myth*, have traced the crisis mentality back to seventeenth-century England where a shortage of wood was expected to cripple the British Navy and raise the cost of heating homes beyond the means of most families. Instead a century-long rise in the price of wood hastened the development of coal as a superior fuel.) Unlike religious soothsayers, however, environmental gloom-and-doomers are supposed to have data on their side. Yet most are imperfect seers, and their predictions in the 1960s—jets ruining the atmosphere, an impending ice age, Lake Erie forever dead—have not been validated. It is wise to pamper the earth now, but apocalyptic predictions of doom should remain the province of religious cults.

There is enough nihilism in our present mental climate without doomsday scenarios' increasing the gospel of despair. Doomsdayers accept all problems and reject all solutions. They leave little room for hope, imagination, creativity, or expanded awareness. It is as if one inherited a beautiful garden and then devoted one's full attention to pulling the weeds and casting out the bugs, only to be left with a plot of stunted and wilted vegetables. We should not allow ourselves to be trapped in a gigantic zero-sum game. We need to expand our concept of nature beyond the earth. In time we may be able to remove toxic wastes and waste-producing activities from the terrestrial biosphere while gaining access to the continuous and virtually limitless flow of solar energy streaming past the earth. We need, in sum, to listen to softer voices.

Fourth, let us speak the language of trade-offs. Pristine environments existed from the Stone Age until the dawn of the Industrial Revolution. Yet longevity was short and life anything but idyllic. A modicum of environmental degradation is the necessary price we pay for the benefits of a technological culture. We cannot use oil, chemicals, iron ore, nuclear, wind, or solar power without trade-offs. The more we spend on cleanliness as a moral ideal, the less we have left to spend on real health threats. We need waste dumps just as we need prisons and halfway houses. Forests of virgin pine and dolphins can be protected, but then the poor may be unable to afford homes and tuna. "Factory farms" can be abolished and chickens liberated to scratch for food in the open air, but then chicken may cost as much as sirloin in the supermarket. We can shame women into wearing cloth coats and all become vegetarians, but then trappers, farmers, and cattle ranchers will join the welfare rolls. We can grow vegetables and fruits without the benefit of scientific horticulture, but our grocery bills will escalate, and we have to endure more bugs, smut, and worms.

Finally, we should prefer public to private monitoring. The past few years have seen the creation of dozens of private ecological groups. Environmental buccaneers and their attorneys bring scores of actions against corporations and almost never against public agencies, often for nothing more substantive than noncompliance with voluminous paperwork regulations.[29] Critics charge that an "environmental enforcement cartel," motivated by "bounty-hunting," brings little public benefit as lawyers seek to maximize private reward. In September 1989 an organization called the National Toxics Campaign coerced several small grocery chains into selling "pesticide-free" fresh produce by threatening a boycott. The Environmental Protection Agency, Food and Drug Administration, and Agricultural Department attempted to stem the panic and criticized the group for "seeking to create a major crisis of confidence" in the nation's food supply.[30]

We should watch for hidden political agendas of the "disaster lobby." Since we know that nations make more prudent decisions when there is a hopeful ethos, we should point to real environmental gains. New York air today is far cleaner than was the air over Sam Johnson's wood-and-coal burning London. On balance the automobile has probably ameliorated human health by getting rid of tons of urban horse manure. Case upon case could be cited similarly.

Ecological issues are complex. They are not solved by means of conspiracy theories where ecological saviors do battle with bad people and evil corporations. Nor is it helpful to torture moral discourse and resacralize all living beings. Good ecological ethics is arrived at through an arduous process involving prudence, tolerance, empathy, the weighing of evidence and outcomes, and active listening. We can only hope that such virtues will increase in the future.

NOTES

1. *St. Paul Pioneer Dispatch,* May 21, 1989.

2. Eugene Hargrove, ed., *Religion and Environmental Crisis* (London: University of Georgia Press, 1986), p. 38.

3. Lynn White, Jr., "The Historical Roots of Our Ecological Crisis," *Science* 155 (1967):1203–7.

4. Susan Power Bratton, "Christian Ecotheology and the Old Testament," in Hargrove, *Religion and Environmental Crisis,* p. 64.

5. Ibid., p. 65.

6. See Roger D. Sorrell, *St. Francis of Assisi and Nature: Tradition and Innovation in Western Christian Attitudes toward the Environment* (Oxford: Oxford University Press, 1988).

7. Richard A. McCormick, "Theology and Bioethics," *Hastings Center Report* (March-April 1989): 8.

8. S. K. Shader-Frechette, "Spaceship Ethics," in *Environmental Ethics* (Pacific Grove: Boxwood Press, 1981), p. 46.

9. Barry Lopez, "The Mind of the Hunter," *Harper's Magazine* (March 1987): 30.

10. *Discover* (June 1986): 61.

11. Jeremy Rifkin, *Algeny* (New York: Viking Press, 1983), p. 252.

12. Richard B. Stewart, "Paradoxes of Liberty, Integrity and Fraternity: The Collective Nature of Environmental Quality and Judicial Review of Administrative Action," in *Environmental Ethics,* pp. 143–44.

13. *Wall Street Journal,* September 1, 1989.

14. Ibid.

15. Ibid.

16. Nathan Hare, "Black Ecology," in *Environmental Ethics,* pp. 229–33.

17. Peter Singer, "Animal Liberation," in *Environmental Ethics,* p. 103.

18. Steven Zak, "Ethics and Animals," *Atlantic Monthly* (March 1989): 73.

19. William Blackstone, "Ecology and Rights," in *Environmental Ethics,* p. 133.

20. Andres Linzey, *Christianity and the Rights of Animals* (New York: Crossroad Publishing, 1987), p. 78.

21. Ibid., p. 77.

22. Willard Gaylin, "In Praise of the Man-made Animal," Nobel Conference Address, Gustavus Adolphus College, October 13, 1982.

23. Annette Baier, "For the Sake of Future Generations," in *Earthbound* (New York: Random House, 1984), p. 219.

24. Donella H. Meadows, *The Limits to Growth* (New York: Universe Books, 1972), pp. 190–200.

25. *Forbes Magazine,* February 20, 1989.

26. Baier, "For the Sake of Future Generations," p. 217.
27. *St. Paul Dispatch,* April 4, 1989.
28. *Wall Street Journal,* September 22, 1989.
29. Ibid., September 18, 1989.
30. *St. Paul Dispatch,* September 12, 1989.

Can a Corporation Have an Environmental Conscience?

KENNETH E. GOODPASTER

We are rediscovering our concern for the environmental impact of institutional action. After a decade and a half of relative silence, the environmental theme is once again on the national agenda, as it was in the early seventies. During this silence, the business community has in many ways and for many reasons become more comfortable with a moral vocabulary that should improve the dialogue. More than ever before corporations are open to the suggestion that they need a conscience as much as they need a strategy. For these reasons, my answer to the title question of this chapter—can a corporation have an environmental conscience?—is yes. But there is more to the story, for the conditions that must be satisfied if there is to be an environmental conscience are significant, extending the boundaries of business ethics.

First, corporations must be clear about the concept of conscience in general, distinguishing it clearly from its counterfeits: public relations, government relations, competitive strategy, a marketing orientation, legal compliance, and issues management. Corporate conscience may have secondary effects that connect with each of these arenas, but it is not to be confused with any one of them or it loses its meaning. In other places, I have referred to this as distinguishing Type 3 thinking (the ethics of conviction) from Type 2 thinking (the ethics of external constraint) and Type 1 thinking (the ethics of self-interested competition).[1]

Second, management must take steps to orient, institutionalize, and sustain the corporate conscience or value system in ways that are as realistic as those that guide strategy formulation and implementation. Rhetoric and value statements are not enough. Rewards, incentives, controls, audits, and clear leadership action are critical to this task. Management must be "given permission" to think and act environmentally, a condition that affects organizations more deeply than statements or credos. As important, leadership must give itself permission to think and act in ways that have hitherto been considered somewhat beyond the standard limits of stockholder, and even stakeholder, concern. And where specific environmental needs outstrip the power, and therefore the responsibility, of the individual corporation (since ought implies can), conscience demands more—reaching out to and eventually with other corporations in an industry, a geographical area, or a technological network in an effort to be part of a solution, rather than part of a problem.

CONSCIENCE: THE BASIC IDEA

In the last years of the nineteenth century, Harvard philosopher Josiah Royce offered an account of conscience that remains relevant today. Conscience, Royce wrote, frees us from the illusion that our neighbors are "less real" than ourselves and guides us to act accordingly:

The realization of one's neighbor, in the full sense of the word realization, is indeed the resolution to treat him as if he were real, that is, to treat him unselfishly. But this resolution expresses and belongs to the moment of insight. Passion may cloud the insight in the very next moment. It always does cloud the insight after no very long time. It is as impossible for us to avoid the illusion of selfishness in our daily lives, as to escape seeing through the illusion at the moment of insight.

Royce reminded us that conscience works against a kind of entropy in human nature—backsliding toward the pursuit of self-centered purposes. We may slide back occasionally or even regularly, but we understand this process for what it is: failing to maintain our perspective as neighbors in a shared environment.

The thrust of this view is not toward eliminating self-interest or private purpose; these are often productive and constructive forces. It is toward adjusting the basic attitude that guides an individual in adopting and pursuing purposes. The development of conscience can be seen as a kind of Copernican Revolution in the realm of practical decision making. The decision maker no longer sees himself or herself as at the center of the social or even the biological universe. Other persons—and the environment—are not simply resources to be used but invite and deserve consideration independently. Conscience emerges, by nature, nurture, or (more likely) both, as a practical surrender of self-centered thinking.[2]

In the remainder of this chapter, I shall discuss a framework for integrating managerial decision making with an environmental conscience as understood above. For ease of reference and recall, I will name the framework PASCAL, after the French philosopher-mathematician Blaise Pascal (1623–1662) who remarked in reference to ethics that "the heart has reasons the reason knows not of."

SEGMENTING DECISIONS USING
THE PASCAL FRAMEWORK

Since conscience avoids excessively self-centered, goal-driven behavior, it can and arguably should affect every phase of the decision-making process. I will elaborate on these phases using the PASCAL acronym: perception, analysis, synthesis, choice, action and learning.[3]

Perception

The first step in the process of integrating business decisions and environmental conscience is perception. All decision making begins with the decision maker's perception of his or her environment. Perception is not a passive and neutral process as we are sometimes tempted to think. Observers have long recognized that perception has an active aspect to it and that an agent gathers, structures, and packages information in accordance with certain interests and purposes. Drug addicts, for example, often refuse to look at the effects of their habits on themselves and those around them. To look, presumably, might lead to action that would be painful or difficult. Perception is here distorted by the fear of withdrawal or the pursuit of euphoria.

Everyone's perception is active and selective. It is impossible for us to know all the facts, past, present, and future, that bear on a decision before us. And even if it were possible, we could not realistically keep all the relevant ones before our mind at once. Thus the ethical aspect of perception has to do with how an actor scans the environment and selects what is of concern to conscience.

A conscientious decision maker will gather and take seriously not only information that has to do with the accomplishment of self-interested goals but also information about the effects of contemplated behavior on the social and biological environment. In the words of law professor Christopher Stone, the perception of the conscientious decision maker is "stamped with moral categories."

A company that carefully researched markets and revenue projections for selling its pesticides in Third World countries while ignoring information about safety standards, health effects, and environmental impact would exhibit a lack of moral perception. Conscience influences perception by distinguishing ethically important information from background information of other kinds. For many years, what we now refer to as thermal pollution was not perceived by most companies as a significant by-product. Only in the wake of discussions of the greenhouse effect and global warming is this perception being activated. The environmentally sensitive corporation scans for the whole truth about its products and operations. If its aerosol propellants may be affecting the ozone layer, it conducts careful and objective research. It does not hide conclusions from that research that might be problematic as, for example, Manville Corporation was alleged to have done with research on health effects of asbestos.

Perception also includes an assessment of what the corporation can and cannot do. Some environmental problems (like global warming) are too large in scale for resolution by one company or even one industry. In such cases, the appropriate response may be coalition rather than inaction. The Valdez Principles in the context of the environment, like the Sullivan Principles in the context of South Africa, offer one concrete way for this coalition to happen.

In summary, moral perception calls not only for attention to what can and should be done but also to who is best able to do it. Here are some of the questions a perceptive company (through its management) should ask:

1. What are the most salient facts in this situation, both strategically and environmentally?
2. Who are the principal decision makers who must respond to the issue in question? Who really decides?
3. What are the principal choices (options) facing these decision makers?
4. What are the short- and long-term implications of each option?

Analysis

The second step in conscientious decision making is a thoughtful analysis of the pros and cons of each perceived option. Analysis builds on perception and takes it further. An environmentally responsible decision maker identifies the key stakeholders but also looks at the holistic effects of each option. In the pesticide example, key stakeholders include the company itself, the competition, the U.S. government, the host government in the Third World country, the local distributors, the farmworkers, and perhaps indirectly U.S. consumers as well, if there are secondary effects of the use of this pesticide on the U.S. market (such as residues on imports).

A holistic environmental outlook will also take into account problems associated with using more and more chemical pesticides to accomplish less and less (the treadmill effect) and the general ecosystemic effects of pesticide use in contrast, say, with biological pest controls that use natural pest enemies (sometimes referred to as integrated pest management).

Simply making a list of direct and indirect (or primary and secondary) stakeholders for each option or choice available is a useful exercise in any decision-making process. It enriches the decision maker's perception of the full implications of each course of action. It is what is often referred to as stakeholder analysis. This step should include, but not be limited to, what some call a cost-benefit analysis of the implications of the proposed action for each of the primary and secondary stakeholders identified earlier. There are other approaches to the ethical pros and cons of an action besides calculating its measurable benefits and costs, including a careful evaluation of the human rights involved and a consideration of the decision maker's independent duties to the affected parties (honesty, promise keeping, avoidance of coercion). Some might be tempted to construe benefits and costs as equivalent to pros and cons, but this can end up confusing rather than clarifying a decision. Not all moral reasoning (pro-con argument) is of the benefit-cost variety.

One of the limitations of stakeholder analysis as a concept is that it tends to focus the decision maker on discrete classes of affected parties without much attention to the incremental and systemic effects of actions. These effects are often the most relevant ones when the environment is our concern. We can, of course, choose to list the environment or even future generations among the stakeholders in our analysis, but in doing so we must be aware that we are straining the concept somewhat. Perhaps a better strategy is to treat particular stakeholders and the environment as two fundamental classes of effects to be analyzed in a responsible decision, like figure and ground.

Once one has identified the stakeholders and environmental effects, a matrix can be constructed with the columns representing the costs, benefits, rights, and duties that either support or discourage the option in question. Pros for the company may be clear, in the form of high margins and high market share on a patented product that may be banned for use in the U.S. Pros for the host country and farmers may also be significant, in the form of improved crop yields and reduced hunger. Cons may include not only poisonings and direct health effects on farmworkers but indirect effects on U.S. consumers and host country ecosystems.

Analysis is not simply an exercise in altruism. Most people would put themselves (their company, the objectives of their job) at or near the top of their list of stakeholders. This natural tendency is hardly a failure of conscience. The failure would be to include only oneself or one's company. Ethics includes rational self-interest and self-respect in addition to respect for others. Analysis does not in and of itself resolve a problem or make a decision. It is, after all, only analysis (taking apart), not synthesis (putting together), choice, or action. But neither is it a purely detached, intellectual exercise. The very process of identifying affected parties and environmental effects involves the use of the imagination in a way that can lead to a natural empathetic or caring response to those parties in the synthesis, choice, and action phases of decision making. This is a contingent connection, however, not a necessary one.

It is possible that once we have taken the analytical step, our perception of the situation, the options available to us, or the key decision makers may change. If so, we can loop back through the perception step again. The risks associated with a given pesticide to the farmworker, for example, might lead us to modify the marketing option under consideration to include special labeling provisions. Here are some of the questions implicit in the analysis step:

1. Who are the direct (and indirect) stakeholders associated with each option? (Consider not only individuals, groups, companies, industries, countries, and other groups but the environment itself.)

2. For each direct and indirect stakeholder and each option, what are the benefits conferred, rights upheld, or duties fulfilled by the decision maker toward that stakeholder?

3. For each direct and indirect stakeholder and each option, what are the costs incurred, rights abridged, or duties set aside by the decision maker toward that stakeholder?

4. Have any additional options or direct (indirect) stakeholders surfaced in the course of this analysis that need to be factored in? the environment itself?

Synthesis

The third step or segment of the process is often the most difficult. Here the analytical matrix constructed in the previous two segments must be transformed into a preference of one option over the other available options, leading to a choice or decision.

The decision maker normally seeks a resolution of two potential tensions at this point: (1) between self-interest and concern for others (what we can call the partiality problem) and (2) among different ways of expressing concern for others (what we can call the impartiality problem). Philosopher Thomas Nagel refers to the second as the combinatorial problem. Of course, the most attractive solution to the combinatorial problem would be a simple (or complex) mathematical function. Historically Jeremy Bentham and (to a lesser extent) John Stuart Mill offered a utilitarian "calculus" in which only nonmoral benefits and costs were allowed into the analysis phase of a decision (to avoid circular reasoning) and maximization for the greatest number of the "benefit-cost ratio" was the key in the synthesis stage.

While straightforward, however, this approach to synthesis has some drawbacks. One is that it assumes more quantifiability of human goods and bads than we are often able to achieve. Another is that it allows (in principle) serious costs to minorities in the name of modest gains to the majority. Fairness is not clearly a virtue of this kind of synthesis.

There are other formulas for synthesizing the stakeholder analysis, such as maximizing the well-being of the least advantaged member of the stakeholder group. Such a formula is referred to as contractarian. But most formulas have problems and are vulnerable to counterexamples and exceptions. The contractarian formula is sometimes criticized for leading to an extreme and unacceptable form of liberalism that gives insufficient attention to the values of the community and the environment as a whole. This is not to say that any kind of synthesis will do. Some ways are clearly more convincing than others. Pure egoism, for example, is an implausible way since it ignores both the partiality problem and the impartiality problem altogether.

In their book on the moral education of children, psychologists Michael Schulman and Eva Mekler draw upon a widely held view of the foundations of morality when they observe that

moral behavior has two components: Its intention must be good, in the sense that its goal is the well-being of one or more people; and it must be fair or just, in the sense that it considers the rights of others without prejudice or favoritism. Helping my friend gain an unwarranted advantage over others may be kind to him but it is not fair, and thus not an instance of moral behavior. Treating everybody equally cruelly may be fair, but it is not kind and, therefore, it is not moral.[4]

Most philosophers agree that an ethical framework must include a principle of justice (fairness) and a principle promoting the common good (kindness). The precise formulations of such principles are the subjects of lengthy treatises, and I shall not go into detail here. It is sufficient to point out that respect for the dignity of the individual and for the welfare of the group are the key operating principles in most frameworks.

Whether a distinct, basic principle of respect for the biological environment should be included as part of any adequate synthesis is a question that has received some attention in recent years but deserves more. It is tempting to think that environmental issues can ultimately be reduced to issues of benevolence and justice toward human beings, at least long term, but some have questioned this view, and we would do well to listen to the reasons.

In the pesticide example, the risks to the health of the workers and environment in the Third World country, as well as the secondary risks to consumers in our own country, may outweigh the gains of both my company (profit) and the host country (improved food production). Much depends on the technique used to quantify these risks and outcomes. On the other hand, even if the quantification came out with a clearly preferred option (in terms of benefit-cost), the decision maker may invoke other moral principles, such as fairness to the least advantaged, and arrive at a different ethical conclusion.

The main point is that there must be some reflective and self-aware process of prioritizing the pros and cons in the analysis into a central tendency, an orientation toward action. And it behooves us to try to be explicit about the criteria that we are employing when we eventually attempt this synthesis. Consistency about these criteria in applications to other cases may be a major test of their adequacy.

The history of ethics suggests that the process of synthesis, of coming to a thoughtful appraisal of the ethical weights of the pros and cons for each option, is neither mechanical nor arbitrary. Often dialogue with others about a case will lead to synthesis and convergence in ways that solitary reflection does not. On the other hand, consensus is neither a necessary nor a sufficient condition for final truth in ethics or in any other domain of inquiry.

Synthesis involves sincerely identifying or empathizing with each stakeholder group—what Royce would have called "realizing my neighbor." It may also involve a kind of holistic ecological respect that goes beyond empathy with any particular stakeholder group. The main point is that it is not enough to acknowledge distantly and intellectually that a certain stakeholder or the environment as a whole will be affected in such and such a way, any more than such cursory consideration would be enough if the tables were reversed.

As with analysis, attempts at synthesis can lead to new perceptions and new insights about stakeholders and the environment, sending the decision maker through previous steps before continuing. Here are some of the questions that need to be answered in an attempt to take the synthesis step:

1. What are the main strategic and functional imperatives associated with each of the options (e.g., policy issues, marketing or production concerns, finance or control problems, personnel issues)? How do these criteria combine toward self-interest and the achievement of management goals, competitiveness, and legality?

2. How are the following criteria factored into our consideration of the options at hand: maximizing benefit-cost for all affected stakeholders, maximizing the well-being of the least advantaged stakeholders, and other basic duties, including a fundamental respect for the integrity of the environment?

3. Is there a clear preponderance of pros or cons associated with one of the options? If so, a synthesis is easier, and the choice is clearer.

4. If there is not convergence, are there creative ways to align conscience with business objectives in this case, perhaps by finding new options (revisit perception and analysis?)?

It is perhaps worth reminding ourselves, however, that an attempt at synthesis (or some kind of principled resolution of potentially conflicting arguments for different options) may not succeed and that choice must take place nevertheless. In other words, synthesis is not the same as choice; it precedes it. It is like the dialogue preceding the "cutting off" that the word *decision* has at its root.

Choice

The fourth step or segment in the process is making a choice. It might be thought that this step was either the whole process, or at least the termination of the process, but it is neither. It is not the whole process because there is more to decision making than choosing. Decision making has a beginning (perception), a middle (analysis, synthesis, choice), and a further course (action and learning). Choice is conditioned by what goes before it and can be modified in future cases by what comes after.

Choice is a consequence of the need for closure, the need to terminate efforts at synthesis. Decision makers do not have the luxury of unlimited time for perception, analysis, and synthesis, even if more time would often improve the quality of their decision. Choices must be made, even when the best option is not apparent or when two or more options compete strongly for primacy in the decision maker's consciousness.

When senior management at Du Pont had to make a decision regarding the continued production of its Freon products in the face of considerable evidence about their negative effects on the ozone layer, competitive disadvantage was clearly a factor along with concern about the environment. In the end, no simple synthesis was possible, but a choice was made. The product would be discontinued regardless of competitor behavior.[5] Similarly, when Ashland Oil Company considered its options in January 1988 after one of its storage tanks burst and spilled a million gallons of diesel fuel into the Monongahela River outside Pittsburgh, there was conflict between self-interest and candor about the spill. John Hall, the chief executive officer, made a choice, against the advice of key lawyers, to be open and take responsibility for the spill and cleanup. Just over a year later, we saw Exxon leadership make a different choice in the case of the *Valdez* oil spill.[6]

When the time for decision is at hand, the decision maker must finally rely on the balancing effects of perception, analysis, and synthesis. Judgment is always and in the end a matter of balance, and balance is something we seek through the discipline of looking at the whole truth, considering stakeholders and the environment, and striving for a principled or consistent response—a response of the whole person or organization. Here are some questions involved in the choice step:

1. Is this the time for choice, or is there some value in delay? When is a decision necessary?

2. Is the decision maker in a mentally and emotionally balanced state for making a choice, relatively free from the potentially distorting effects of anxiety or pressure?

3. If the time is now, which option best fits managerial, stakeholder, and environmental requirements?

4. What is the decision?

Action

The fifth stage or segment of conscientious decision making is implementation or action. In this context, action means more than just initiating a course of events and walking away. It includes a plan by which one or several initiatives are timed, sequenced, and monitored with a view to realizing the decision arrived at in the preceding segment.

Perception has led to analysis, analysis to synthesis, and synthesis to choice. Now the decision maker must pay close attention to the effective and ethical means available for achieving the ends chosen. We all know which road is paved with good intentions. Responsible decision making includes attention to detail and consistency in the implementation of a decision. Carelessness, cowardice, or inconsistency can subvert well-made decisions in important ways. And someone who, out of the best of motives, tries to coerce another person into doing "the right thing" as part of a well-reasoned plan may be both ineffective and wrong. Parents of teenagers understand well the challenges that decision making presents on this front.

It is morally self-defeating to implement a decision to avoid harming some stakeholders (e.g., shareholders or consumers) through an action plan that in the process does just as much harm to other stakeholders (e.g., suppliers or employees or the environment). Here are some useful questions to improve the action step:

1. Having arrived at an option that is ethically acceptable and coordinated with the decision maker's objectives, what is the implementation plan?

2. What changes, if any, in organizational structure, systems, personnel, incentives, and so forth will be required? What is the time frame for each part of the plan?

3. Are the contemplated means and methods themselves ethically acceptable, or is the decision maker slipping into an "end justifying means" frame of mind?

Learning

We do not always think of conscientious decision making as a learning process, but it surely is. It is a process of guessing outcomes on more or less reliable data, weighing hard-to-commensurate values, internalizing roles and positions, identifying with strangers, deciding what to do, and finally observing and living with the results of our actions.

As a decision maker experiences the outcome of a moral choice, not just the external outcome but the internal one as well, the entire decision-making process can be affected. Self-esteem may increase or decrease, leading to modifications (or not) in the perceptual net, the analytic tools, the approach to synthesis, choice, and action planning. Such a learning process is clearly, if slowly, unfolding with the implementation of affirmative action programs in the United States. Racial and gender discrimination are perceived and analyzed differently by most of us today than they were twenty years ago.

The same kind of learning seems to be taking place in the environmental arena. We are more prepared today than in times past to take seriously the effects of corporate behavior on environmental pollution, resource conservation, and the preservation of species, for example, than ever before. We learn. It is no contradiction to say that we have an ethical responsibility to keep tabs on our responsibly made ethical decisions, to reverse them if and when the situation warrants. Another learning step that we have taken in recent years is from what might be called industry principles to impact principles. In the past when the action of a given company was contributing to a problem even though the company was (alone) not to blame, we would look to local laws or industry norms for some kind of resolution, as with automobile safety standards. Sometimes, however, as we learned in South Africa, the problem is not industry specific. It has to do with the joint impact of many or all industries on a social problem (racial injustice). Such problems call for sets of principles that cut across industries and focus on a problem area directly. The Sullivan Principles served this purpose for many years in the South African context. The newly issued Valdez Principles can serve this purpose in relation to the environment.[7]

It is possible to block the learning process, of course, by not paying attention to the outcomes of our decisions. The penchant for "not wanting to know" or "plausible deniability" (as Americans discovered during the Iran-contra hearings) can in fact undermine the ethical judgment of a decision maker by preventing the completion of the feedback loop from action to perception. Such blockage can be tragic if it frustrates growth. Also tragic can be the attitude that all ethical learning takes place at one's mother's knee and so does not continue into adult life. Such an attitude not only flies in the face of facts and experience but predisposes us against the kind of reflective follow-through that can help us to make positive changes in our ethical outlook over time.

Some useful questions at the learning stage in the process are:

1. Have adequate provisions been made to monitor the action plan as it unfolds?
2. Will feedback be prompt and reliable, permitting reassessment and reevaluation if necessary?
3. Does this decision (its values and its impact) have implications for other similar decisions within the organization or outside it? What are its lessons?

Figure 3.1
The PASCAL Framework for Decision Making I

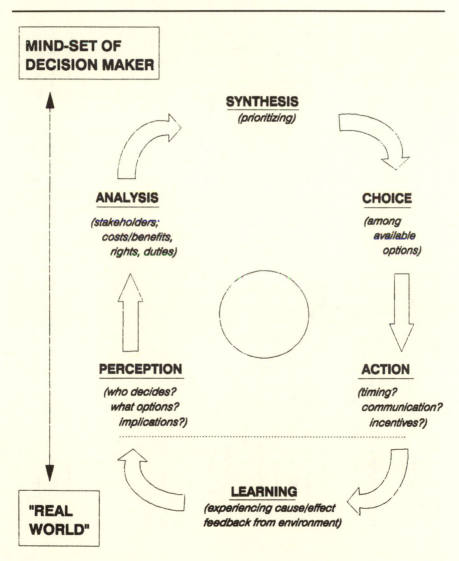

Figure 3.2
The PASCAL Framework for Decision Making II

PERCEPTION or fact gathering about the options available and their short- and long-term implications:

1. What are the most salient facts in this situation, both strategically and environmentally?

2. Who are the principal decision makers who must respond to the issue in questions? Who really decides?

3. What are the principal choices (options) facing these decision makers?

4. What are the short- and long-term implications of each option?

ANALYSIS of implications with specific attention to affected parties and to decision makers' goals, objectives, values, and responsibilities:

1. Who are the direct (and indirect) stakeholders associated with each option? (Consider not only individuals, groups, companies, industries, and other groups, countries, but the environment itself.)

2. For each direct and indirect stakeholder and each option, what are the costs incurred, rights abridged, or duties set aside by the decision maker toward that stakeholder?

3. Is there a clear preponderance of pros or cons associated with one of the options? If so, a synthesis is easier, and the choice is clearer.

4. If there is not convergence, are there creative ways to align conscience with business objectives in this case, perhaps by finding new options (revisit perception and analysis)?

CHOICE among the available options based on the stakeholder synthesis:

1. Is this the time for choice, or is there some value in delay? When is a decision necessary?

2. Is the decision maker in a mentally and emotionally balanced state for making a choice, relatively free from the potentially distorting effects of anxiety or pressure?

3. If the time is now, which option best fits managerial, stakeholder, and environmental requirements?

4. What is the decision?

3. For each direct and indirect stakeholder and each option, what are the costs incurred, rights abridged, or duties set aside by the decision maker toward that stakeholder?

4. Have any additional options or direct (indirect) stakeholders surfaced in the course of this analysis that need to be factored in? the environment itself?

SYNTHESIS of stakeholder analysis according to priorities that obtain in the mind-set of the decision maker:

1. What are the main strategic and functional imperatives associated with each of the options (e.g., policy issues, marketing or production concerns, finance or control problems, personnel issues)? How do these criteria combine toward self-interest and the achievement of management goals, competitiveness, and legality?

2. How are the following criteria factored into our consideration of the options at hand: maximizing benefit-cost for all affected stakeholders, maximizing the well-being of the least advantaged stakeholders, and other basic duties, including a fundamental respect for the integrity of the environment?

ACTION or implementation of the decision through charges to specific individuals or groups, resource allocation, incentives, controls, feedback:

1. Having arrived at an option that is ethically acceptable and coordinated with the decision maker's objectives, what is the implementation plan?

2. What changes, if any, in organizational structure, systems, personnel, incentives, etc., and so forth will be required? What is the time frame for each part of the plan?

3. Are the contemplated means and methods themselves ethically acceptable, or is the decision maker slipping into an "end justifying means" frame of mind?

LEARNING from the outcome of the decision, leading to reinforcement of modification (for future decisions) of the way the previous steps were taken:

1. Have adequate provisions been made to monitor the action plan as it unfolds?

2. Will feedback be prompt and reliable, permitting reassessment and reevaluation of necessary?

3. Does this decision (its values and its impact) have implications for other similar decisions within the organization or outside it? What are its lessons?

SUMMARY AND CONCLUSION

I have summarized the PASCAL framework in figure 3.1 and have collected in figure 3.2 the questions associated with each step in the process. These questions, in conjunction with the wheel diagram, are intended to help us organize and display our thinking about the ethical aspects of a given business decision. Thus, we have in PASCAL a kind of anatomy of conscientious corporate decision making. A list of questions does not, of course, constitute a panacea or a simple way out of difficult choices. There is no such simple way for adults. Mature moral judgment is as precious a commodity as it is rare, but it is an attribute increasingly demanded of the professional manager and a sine qua non of business leadership.

The shift from corporate self-interest as an operating philosophy to respect for law and markets is an important one. Moving from there to a genuine concern for fairness and the common good marks another ethical quantum jump. The frontier of an environmental conscience for the corporation seems to go still further in many ways, inviting a global consciousness every bit as challenging as that demanded by international competition. Biological sustainability is ultimately a prerequisite for corporate policy.

NOTES

1. See my Ruffin Lecture, "Ethical Imperatives and Corporate Leadership," University of Virginia (April 1988), forthcoming in *Business Ethics: The State of the Art* (Oxford: Oxford University Press, 1989).

2. I have explained and defended this view in "On Being Morally Considerable," *Journal of Philosophy* (June 1978).

3. The framework is depicted in figure 3.1. Each of the six segments or moments on the wheel indicates a component process in the framework that is influenced by the conscience of the decision maker at the hub or center. The dotted line represents the contact between the turning of thought and the hard surface of reality. We can imagine the rotation of the wheel from mental and emotional processes in the decision maker to cause-effect processes in the "real world" outside. Learning takes place when a decision maker observes the results of action and reprocesses those results with an eye toward improvement. In ethics, as in other aspects of practical life, good judgment comes from an active, yet reflective, process.

4. Michael Schulman and Eva Mekler, *Bringing Up a Moral Child* (Reading, Mass.: Addison-Wesley, 1985).

5. See *Du Pont Freon Products Division* (A) and (B), HBS Case Services 8-389-111 and 112.

6. See *Ashland Oil, Inc.: Trouble at Floreffe (A) (B) (C) (D)*, HBS Case Services N9-390-017, 018 019, 020; and *Exxon Corporation: Trouble at Valdez*, HBS Case Services N9-390-024.

7. For a summary of the Valdez Principles, see the *New York Times*, September 10, 1989, p. 6F.

4

Hazardous Wastes: Ethical Dilemmas of Ends and Means, Heroes and Villains

PAUL STEIDLMEIER

It was not uncommon, even as late as the 1950s, to see pictures of cities dotted with factories whose smokestacks spewed forth clouds emblematic of progress. In the past decade Americans have come to realize that economic progress is a two-edged sword. Paralleling the country's dazzling ascent to the threshhold of a trillion-dollar economy is its descent into the morass of environmental pollution.

Paradoxically environmental pollution has historically been considered a necessary by-product of economic "progress." Americans got a crash course in the ephemeral nature of such progress beginning in the late seventies with highly publicized eco-catastrophes. First there was Love Canal, a community in Niagara, New York, that had to be evacuated following a twenty-five-year period of groundwater pollution by hazardous waste. Next the "Valley of the Drums" took center stage, when leaking storage barrels turned part of Kentucky into one of most hazardous places in the nation. And then in the eastern Missouri community of Times Beach, oil-contaminated dioxin invaded the soil and water. The edifice of progress was shaken as the economic foundations of modern life were perceived to be sitting on an ominous ecological fault line.

THE EXTENT OF THE PROBLEM

In the developed countries a consensus has slowly emerged in the past decades that continued abuse of the environment spells planetary disaster. Thomas Marx (1986) charts the life cycle of the environmental protection issue. Phase 1 saw the rise of social expectations coincident with the publication of *Silent Spring* by Rachel Carson in 1962. Second was a transformation of these expectations into a political issue, particularly with the political platform of Senator Eugene McCarthy in 1968. The third phase ushered in legislation in the form of the Environmental Protection Agency (EPA) in 1971. This launched the so-called environmental decade, which led to the fourth phase of social control of the environment by means of emissions standards, pollution fines, product recalls, and environmental permits.

Significant policies are beginning to be forged in areas of toxic wastes and the atmosphere's ozone layer. There is, nevertheless, considerable resistance to ecological business practices in the area of acid rain. In many developing countries the situation is far more ominous. Good ecology seems to be a luxury. Ecological concerns appear to be the enemy of economic development. Ecological deterioration in many countries is fueled by empty stomachs. Each of these problems presents a special set of technological, economic, political, and moral issues.

In an attempt to visualize the magnitude of the problem the EPA put it this way (EPA, 1987, p. 1):

There are 240,000,000 people in the United States. Try to imagine a ton of hazardous waste piled next to each one of them, with another ton added each and every year.

Hazardous waste is produced in this country at the rate of 700,000 tons per day. That's 250 million tons per year—enough to fill the Superdome in New Orleans 1500 times over.

Everyone agrees that there is environmental pollution, yet there is surprisingly little agreement as to its extent. A good overview of the measurement issue is provided by Christopher Harris, William Want, and Morris Ward (1987, pp. 12–48) in their book, *Hazardous Waste: Confronting the Challenge.* The first attempt to develop an estimate of the amount of hazardous waste was made by the Batelle Memorial Institute in 1974 in a report commissioned by the EPA. That report estimated that American industry produced 8.9 million metric tons (mmt) of hazardous waste a year. Few people believed that report, and in 1979 the EPA commissioned Arthur D. Little and Co. to do another study.

The ensuing report estimated hazardous wastes of 33.8 mmt. At the same time in another study, conducted by Putnam, Hayes and Bartlett Inc., the estimate was placed at 41 mmt. All of these reports left observers frustrated. As a result the EPA commissioned yet another study in 1982. Westat Inc. studied generators covered by the Resource Conservation and Recovery Act (RCRA) and arrived at an estimate of 150 mmt. In 1984 Westat revised that figure to 264 mmt. Even then hazardous wastes coming from sources not regulated by RCRA were not included.

Data remain fragmentary. Nonetheless, even the 264 mmt estimate for 1984 is alarming. The distribution of such wastes across the country is by no means uniform. Nine states generate wastes in excess of 10 mmt, while fifteen produce less than 1 million. In ranking industries, chemicals account for 47.9 percent, followed by primary metals at 18 percent and petroleum and coal products at 11.8 percent. Nonmetallic inorganic liquids and sludge account for 42 percent. Twenty-one other pollutants are ranked, and their pollution contribution ranges from 8 percent to less than 1 percent.

Most alarming is the way in which waste products have been managed. Water disposal accounts for 47 percent: 25 percent injected into wells and 22 percent through the sewage system. Surface impoundment accounts for 19 percent; then follow hazardous waste landfill with 13 percent and sanitary landfill with 10 percent. Together these four methods account for 70 percent of waste management.

The costs to industry are highest for the wood preserving industry, whose chemical and allied products industries, major pollutants, spend the most for cleanup in aggregate terms, but this amounts to only 1.8 percent of sales and 3.2 percent of value added.

Methods of waste management have proved to be disastrous. Industry not only has polluted water and land areas; its disposal methods have created an additional problem of cleaning up dumps. The Comprehensive Environmental Response, Compensation and Liability Act of 1980 (CERCLA), the Superfund program, was intended to clean up the mess, and other aspects of legislation were to prevent new dumps from being created. This act was reauthorized with amendents in 1986 (EPA, 1986c). In 1980 the EPA estimated that there were some 8,000 priority sites that needed to be cleaned up. By 1986 the number had risen to 25,194 (EPA, 1986a, p. 6).

The state of environmental pollution continues to be alarming. The EPA has made some progress in cleaning up some dumps and water pollution, but its progress has been slow. Clearly much remains to be done. Even more alarming is the fact that prevention of future pollution has not been ensured. Industries continue to spew forth pollutants in ever increasing numbers.

ETHICAL PROTAGONISTS: A FRAMEWORK

Ecological interests have grown to become a matter of major concern only within the past thirty years. From the beginning the debate has taken an ethical tone. There is a tangle of different positions regarding ecology and the environment. For purposes of discussion I have summarized them under three general typologies: preecological economism, legal-market ecology strategies, and public policy (interventionist) ecology strategies. Although these typologies represent oversimplifications of the positions of representative groups, they are nonetheless adequate to reveal some important differences in ethical analysis on the part of various protagonists.

It is important to examine why different people reach far different conclusions from analysis of the "facts." In this case the legitimacy of moral argument is framed by four factors (table 4.1): assumptions regarding empirical facts, institutional and personal loyalties and predispositions, overall worldview, and methods of reasoning (Potter, 1970, chap. 1).

All three protagonists appear to be talking about the same descriptive phenomenon: environmental pollution caused by hazardous wastes. But that is only partially true. Observers hold different positions about the seriousness of the

Table 4.1
Determinants of Moral Argument

Determinants	Preecological Economism	Liberal/Market Ecologists	Public Policy Ecologists
Empirical assessment	minimal	moderate; dispute real culprits	maximum dispute real culprits
Loyalties	local interests; faith in technology and business efficiency	ideal market; anti-intervention by government; legal tort approach	interests of those hurt by pollution interventionist against business
Methods of reasoning	technocratic; economic rationality	legal and economic rationality	political rationality statutory law
Worldview	economic utilitarian progress	classic liberal individualism	communitarian, expressed in public choice models

problem because they rely on different sampling and forecasting techniques while assuming often radically different technology sets both now and in the future. The moral problem of the environment is not merely a present problem. In fact, in most discussions it is the nature of the supposed future catastrophe as well as our obligations to future generations that primarily frames the discourse. This is not to underestimate present problems. Rather it is to draw attention to the fact that moral discourse in this area is to a great extent based on estimates of future probabilities as well as on determining present facts and responsibilities. Empirical uncertainty regarding "what it is we are talking about" necessarily introduces a dynamic element into moral analysis. Empirical reference points must be continually revised. With this caveat, it is nonetheless possible to compare the broad outlines of moral positions. In doing this three other determinants come into play.

Attention must be paid to different modes of reasoning, for they lead to different truths and serve as the foundation for what a person is willing to consider reasonable. Moral reasoning proves to be especially complex, for it is based not only on empirical fact but on an ontological worldview whose components may not all be either clear or distinct. Worldview embraces not only clear and distinct ideas but myth and symbols, narratives and history; it expresses a sense of overall human destiny and purpose. In essence, worldview provides the prism through which one views the empirical data. To complicate the matter even more, both worldview and representation of the facts are notoriously open to bias on both individual and social levels. The ethical debate about the environment, therefore, is simultaneously one of sorting out biases and reasonably interpreting the empirical facts in terms of a worldview. Ethical reasoning, as opposed to strict empiricism, for example, is inherently multilevel and encompasses levels of meaning that are not always susceptible to rationalization in clear and distinct concepts.

With this backdrop I specifically analyze hazardous wastes in terms of two considerations: acts of pollution and agents of pollution. This approach is summarized in table 4.2. It embodies a twofold thrust. First, are acts of pollution, considered as general types of action, morally right or wrong? Second, in a specific case, are the people who do the polluting morally culpable? Are they good or bad?

PREECOLOGICAL ECONOMISM

In analyzing the action of pollution, those holding the preecological position I term economism contend that there is an inherent conflict between economic growth and competitiveness, on the one hand, and environmental concerns, on the other. Proponents of this position are not antiecology. Rather they rank it as a secondary concern and a long-term one at that.

To understand this position it is important to examine the prism through which proponents view the facts of the matter. Historically this group tends to under-

Table 4.2
A Moral Diagnostic Moral Category

	Preecological Economists	Legal/Market Ecologists	Public Policy Ecologists
Descriptive Phenomenon	pollution	pollution	pollution
Analysis of the action			
Social Purpose (end)	economic progress as the engine of all social progress	harmony of individual interests	growth is subordinate to ecology
Values	utility of nature	individual liberty in relation to nature and others	nature as a sacred common good; rights of nature
Means	technical feasibility on a sound cost-benefit basis	management of commons through market and legal/compensatory means	regulation through public policy and institutions

Consequences	principle of double effect; trade-offs	accountability of individuals/associations to third parties	obligations of present generation to future; priority of public good
Analysis of the agent			
Individual Intention	economic progress is intended; pollution is accidental	rational self-interest balanced with others	individual interest subject to common interest
Degree of freedom	economic necessity constrains moral freedom	contractual freedom	public coercion may be necessary
Conscience	economic values over ecology	individual/group rights plus contractual duties to others	ecology cannot be a trade-off to economic interests

estimate both the extent and the seriousness of the problem. That is, their esti-mated costs of environmental pollution pale before the array of benefits allegedly ushered in by economic progress. More important, they believe that a thriving economy and a flourishing technological infrastructure provide the formula that will eventually lead to the sound economic handling of the problem. Some important predispositions frame the discourse. First, there is an act of faith in technology that economically reasonable solutions will eventually be found. There are also prominent loyalties to specific communities—the company, work-ers, local towns, and other economic stakeholders in the affected companies and industries—whose economic livelihood depends on a company or an industry staying profitable and competitive. The method of reasoning is based on a worldview of economic progress and is decidedly technocratic and economic in nature. This concatenation of analytical factors yields a set of moral priorities that justifies the term *economism*.

Turning to legitimating values, the preecological economists take a utilitarian approach to nature. In this case, nature is primarily to serve economic progress (defined in terms of gross output). Further, when it comes to the appropriate means for preserving the environment, preecological economism suggests that actions be governed by questions of cost or profit and technological feasibility.

In analyzing the consequences of pollution, this group employs the ethical principle of double effect, where pollution is an externality or unintended by-product of economic progress. The benefits of the latter outweigh the effects of the former and therefore can be morally justified as the lesser of two evils.

Regarding analysis of polluting agents, economism finds that those causing pollution do not intend to do so. They intend economic progress even though the exhaust of that engine may burn our eyes temporarily. There are economic constraints on freedom. Preecological economists claim that the intense pressure to meet more fundamental needs creates a volatile social instability that cannot be ignored. In effect, the constraints on our livelihood are coercive and force hard choices between the lesser of two evils rather than between a clear good or bad.

Economism has shown itself to be resilient to what it perceives as a negative operating environment fomented by those favoring big government. The strategy is to exploit loopholes and to seek nonregulated environments. For example, there has been a startling new movement to dispose of wastes by sending them to the Third World (Shabecoff, 1988a). The primary targets are debt-ridden poor countries. The EPA reports 400 to 500 applications a year to export U.S. wastes. While it may cost waste generators $250 to $350 per ton to dispose of wastes domestically, some developing countries will accept wastes for as little as $40 per ton. Such choices are justified in terms of economic rationality. Both North American and Western European concerns are known to engage in such prac-tices. Furthermore, groups such as Greenpeace allege that the open seas are increasingly becoming a dumping ground for such wastes. At present there are no truly effective international controls.

The preecological mind-set is more widespread than might be expected. It is clearly strongest among people whose economic interests are immediately adversely affected by tough ecological policy. In many parts of the developing world, ecological concern appears to be a luxury. It does not rank with the basic needs of food, shelter, clothing, habitat, and health. Ecological hazards, on the other hand, have little immediate impact on those burying toxic wastes. The problem is exacerbated by those countries strapped for foreign exchange. But even in the developed world local communities, unions, and businesses often oppose ecological policies on the grounds of immediate economic interests.

THE MARKET–COMMON LAW APPROACH

The legal-market ecologists tend to deplore the devastation of the environment; however, they frame the question within an individualist (atomistic) view of society. They contend that individuals and/or free associations of people who cause harm to others by polluting the environment should be held liable for damages to third parties.

The worldview of legal-market ecologists embodies a quasi-libertarian and contractual approach to ecology. The relation of people to nature is to be governed by the free choice of individuals, conditioned by the fact that all enjoy due liberty. This group examines whether the self-interest of one party also respects the legitimate self-interest of others. To ensure that it does, they favor market incentives and legal redress of abuses.

Legal-market ecologists find the consequences of the dumping of hazardous wastes unacceptable, but they also find public policy interventions unnecessarily coercive as well as wasteful and inefficient. The medicine is worse than the disease. These ecologists oppose any big government coercion while insisting on the honoring of contracts between free agents.

Government has a role to facilitate the functioning of legal and market mechanisms. It should not, however, be the principal actor on the scene. Groups of this persuasion, such as the Heritage Foundation and the CATO Institute, have been highly vocal critics of Superfund because in principle they view the government's role as both ethically coercive and inefficient (Bovard, 1987). Furthermore, they believe that the Superfund program does more harm than good and has also deterred private enterprise from voluntarily cleaning up; that is, it inhibits the emergence of ecological market forces.

In moral critique these groups concentrate on five issues: the ranking system, finance mechanisms, the approach to liability, inefficiency, and the selection of improper means to the end (Bovard, 1987; Heritage Foundation, 1980, 1985a, 1985b).

EPA's hazardous ranking system (HRS), the foundation of Superfund, is attacked as arbitrary and often misleading. One study found that a site's HRS score is almost entirely determined by the amount of information readily available about a site and how many people live near a site rather than by any rigorous measure of risk. The Congressional Office of Technology Assessment is cited as saying that the score for hazard potential is based on only the most hazardous substance in the site rather than a composite of all constituents. However, all substances are used to quantify the magnitude of the hazard, so, for example, if there were a thousand barrels of industrial waste at a site and one of them contained PCBs, the site's rating would assume pervasive PCBs (polychlorinated biphenyl). Clearly National Priority List (NPL) standards are not very rigorous. Morally, the problem is misrepresentation of fact.

Another problem with the Superfund is its financing procedures, which these critics assert impose an unjust burden on certain citizens. The Superfund program is financed primarily through a special tax levied on the oil and petrochemical industries that raises about $300 million each year. In addition, approximately 10 percent of the total Superfund collections ($44 million annually) comes from general treasury revenues. This is flawed because the bulk of the funds comes from a relatively narrow sector of American industry, which is not responsible for creating most of the nation's hazardous wastes. On this point the CATO Institute differs from the Congressional Budget Office regarding the facts. The latter states that the oil and petrochemical industries produce about 60 percent of total industrial toxic waste. CATO denies this and therefore asserts that taxing the oil and chemical industries is unfair and also creates little incentive to reduce waste production among firms in other industries that actually generate the bulk of hazardous waste. These tax provisions also carry with them negative economic and social consequences, for they threaten to hamstring the U.S. petrochemical industry. The moral problem is one of unjust distribution of benefits and costs.

Perhaps the most damaging attack on the Superfund concerns its liability mechanisms. According to its detractors, the EPA has intentionally disregarded equity and fairness in its prosecution of alleged Superfund offenders. The EPA has allegedly consistently interpreted the Superfund legislation to maximize its own arbitrary authority and minimize private companies' chances of avoiding conviction. To allocate responsibility for the cost of the entire cleanup of a dumpsite, all EPA needs to prove is that a company contributed a single barrel of waste to the problem. EPA's official policy manual is cited as stating that to achieve the agency's goal of obtaining 100 percent of the cost of cleanup, it will be necessary in many cases to require a settlement contribution greater than the percentage weight contributed by each private responsible party (PRP) to the site. Critics charge that EPA seeks out corporations with substantial financial resources and tries to force them to pay the full cost of a cleanup. The joint-and-several-liability burden extends not only to cleanup costs but also to any future cleanup or damage costs connected with the wastes transported from the original hazardous waste site, as well as to any personal damage suits from plaintiffs claiming to be harmed by the waste site. Many corporate critics of Superfund see joint-and-several liability as the biggest single impediment to private voluntary cleanups. EPA perceives voluntary cleanup efforts as a confession of guilt and an invitation to hold a company responsible for all cleanup costs at a site, regardless of the company's proportional share of the waste.

Another major Superfund failing is that it has done little to protect the environment. It a utilitarian sense, it has wasted scarce resources and contributed little. After six years and over a billion dollars spent, critics charge, only ten sites have been cleaned up, and several of those still leak. Three-quarters of the federal Superfund budget has allegedly been spent on litigation and endless studies. The program mainly serves to feed an inefficient bureaucracy.

Finally, Superfund represents the wrong means to the end. It is argued that a better approach to funding the inevitable industry contribution to Superfund, especially as it relates to hazardous waste sites, would be to build in economic incentives. For example, by placing a tax on wastes at the point of disposal, a charge with a sliding scale based on the potential hazard of the waste, the government would encourage industry to seek more economically feasible alternatives, such as recycling or incineration. Although the government has a role in cleaning up hazardous waste sites, there is no need for it to invoke its police powers and effectively claim eminent domain over the thousands of factories around the country. By greatly expanding government control, EPA minimizes private corporations' freedom to deal effectively with their own problems. If the main threat to private companies was the law of torts (common law), they would be confronted with a much more effective threat to their livelihood. It is improper to rely on the government when private solutions are available. Relying on common law instead of statutory regulation would leave control to the marketplace. This would allow for private parties to have more leeway, as opposed to the excessive regulation by the government.

These groups clearly link their noninterventionist market approach with the legal framework. In doing so they make several assumptions. It is argued that the marketplace is best equipped to handle the environment. The profit incentive combined with the severe penalties involved in a possible adverse common law suit are enough to resolve these problems.

A possible solution is found in property rights. For example, currently there is little or no recognition of property rights in groundwater, where the greatest danger from hazardous waste is found. Thus, no private entity or individual has an incentive to monitor the condition of groundwater and protect it against pollution. Trusting the protection of groundwater to accountable private sources would be far more effective than trusting it to various groups of bureaucrats, each insisting that he or she is not responsible. Groundwater rights could be established in the same way that property rights for oil were established. Once groundwater is no longer seen as a free good, there will be an entirely different attitude toward those who contaminate it. Every property owner is in effect a police person overseeing his or her own rights. Creating property rights in groundwater would vastly increase the number of people with a strong incentive to protect our environment.

This position, which would rely on market forces and the law, possesses a coherent logic. It is open to question, however, with respect to its operational assumptions. Common law provides a logical framework for handling environmental problems. Congress has debated a variety of toxic victims compensation systems since 1977 but has not yet enacted any legislation. When the Superfund law was passed in 1980, several proposed personal injury compensation provisions were deleted and replaced by a section directing that a study be undertaken to evaluate the adequacy of existing common law and statutory remedies in redressing chemical-caused health effects. Up to this point, however, it has not proved to be adequate in practice (Harris, Want, and Ward, 1987, pp. 51–56), for the following reasons:

1. Rulings by various courts have proved to be inconsistent among themselves.
2. The legal system has historically emphasized compensation over prevention and future protection of the public.
3. Bringing suit is very costly, which deters potential plaintiffs.
4. Lawsuits are invariably brought after the fact. They are therefore not preventive except insofar as a ruling may be assumed to establish legal precedent and in this way function as a deterrent.
5. The technological complexity of environmental problems leaves few courts equipped to handle them. This leads judges to transfer problems to government agencies, which supposedly have expertise.

The belief in a market approach is logically based and not to be facilely discounted. The fact that the federal government has allocated billions of dollars to clean up toxic substances has stimulated technological innovation and spurred many new companies to enter this new market. Environmental Treatment and Technologies Corporation is an example of such a company. The company specializes in on-site abatement of hazardous waste. James L. Kirk, chairman and chief executive officer, has said that he "doesn't know an industry that is going to grow as fast as this one." Environmental Treatment is currently doing $136 million a year in business and has responded to hundreds of emergencies. The main challenge facing it is to maintain rapid growth as its industry evolves and competition heats up. Another leading company is Waste Management Inc., which in 1988 earned $464 million on sales of $3.5 billion. It will spend up to $60 million to construct a state-of-the-art landfill. One major uncertainty is the degree to which the public will accept a particular means of handling hazardous waste, a special problem in the case of incineration. For example, Waste Management has also operated a subsidiary, Ocean Combustion Service, which incinerated wastes some 100 miles off the coast of Europe. The Europeans have set a ban on this practice (beginning in 1994). Waste Management has agreed, partly because it sees the Common Market as a primary target for expansion. The point of these examples is to show that a new industry is emerging to handle toxic wastes. The likelihood is that it will grow significantly.

THE PUBLIC POLICY APPROACH

The market-legal approach is logically coherent; however, its operational assumptions have not yet been borne out. Because of the problems associated with common law solutions to environmental pollution and to the fact that markets have not stemmed the problem, public policy ecologists feel that a federal statutory law is needed to protect U.S. citizens from the dangers posed by hazardous waste abandoned at sites throughout the nation.

Public policy ecologists see the environment as a common heritage and insist that economic concerns be subordinated to maintaining the integrity of the environment. In many ways those in this camp insist that good ecology and sound economics are not in conflict (the argument turning on the definition of "good" and "sound"). The public policy position sees nature as a common possession that is not only useful but sacred and therefore cannot be left to a utilitarian economic calculus or libertarian caprice. They suggest a higher norm than either economic utilitarianism or individual liberty, which I term a public good approach.

The result is that this group is interventionist, favoring strict regulation, public policy, and government institutions. This group finds that public policy is the only way to get everyone to act. To neglect it is to ignore those who suffer as well as our obligation to future generations.

Public policy protagonists tend to see polluters as driven by greed and narrow self-interest such that they must be forcibly restrained. At the same time they see market forces as placing coercive limits on freedom such that one pollutes in order to survive. They see public policy as improving the market and actually increasing the freedom to act responsibly. Finally, with respect to conscience this group emphasizes the collective bonds uniting all of humanity and the necessity for public action to preserve the public good.

The social ethical program this groups favors is evident from recent history. Congressional action during the 1970s (an era that came to be called the environmental decade) included several statutes intended to narrow the range of acceptable disposal options. In 1970 the Clean Air Act was passed to improve air quality throughout much of the country. In 1972 the amendments to the Federal Water Pollution Control Act (known as the Clean Water Act) were passed to improve surface water quality throughout the country. Having addressed major air pollution and water pollution challenges in 1970 and 1972, Congress in 1976 turned its attention to the solid waste dilemma. In that year, it passed the Resource Conservation and Recovery Act (RCRA). The RCRA established comprehensive authority for federal regulation of hazardous waste. As knowledge about the health and environmental impacts of waste disposal increased, Congress revised the RCRA in 1984 with the passage of the Hazardous and Solid Waste Amendments (HSWA).

The Comprehensive Environmental Response, Compensation and Liability Act of 1980 (CERCLA) was passed by Congress and became the first major response to the problem on a national level. Funded from 1980 to 1985 by a $1.6 billion Hazardous Waste Trust Fund, this act gave the federal government broad authority to respond to emergencies involving uncontrolled releases of hazardous substances and to develop long-term solutions for the nation's most serious hazardous waste problems. It was renewed in 1986.

Despite the flurry of this legislation, many in this camp remain profoundly dissatisfied. Barry Commoner, the director for the Center for the Biology of Natural Systems at Queens College of the City University of New York, has stated that the EPA practices bad science and bad policy and is failing to protect the environment (1988). In 1988 he gave a speech to the EPA that focused on production technology and the scientific basis of the regulatory process. Dr. Commoner believes that environmental pollution is a nearly incurable disease, but it can be prevented. Environmental degradation is built into the modern instruments of production. Most of our environmental problems are the inevitable result of the sweeping changes in the technology of production that transformed the U.S. economic system after World War II. Only in the few instances in which the technology of production has been changed has the environment been substantially improved. Production technology, however, remains mostly unchanged.

Attempts are therefore made to trap the pollutant in an appended control device. This improves the environment at best only modestly, and in some cases not at all. If a pollutant is attacked at the point of origin, it can be eliminated; once it is produced, it is too late. Unfortunately the legislative base of the U.S. environmental program was created without reference to the origin of the crisis it was supposed to solve. Our environmental laws do not discuss the origin of environmental pollutants—why we are afflicted with pollutants that the laws were designed to control. Because environmental legislation ignored the origin of the assault on environmental quality, it has dealt only with its subsequent effects. And having defined the disease (environmental pollution) as a collection of symptoms, the legislation mandates only mitigating measures. The notion of preventing pollution—the only measures that really work—appears but fitfully in the environmental laws and has never been given any administrative force.

Dr. Commoner believes that the great majority of the assaults on the environment are preventable. His approach would mean sweeping changes in the major systems of production—agriculture, industry, power production, and transportation. This represents social (as contrasted with private) governance of the means of production. He contends that such measures would also lead to greater economic efficiency and argues that a good deal of the U.S. economic decline derives from the fact that the new, highly polluting post–World War II production technologies were based on large-scale, centralized, capital- and energy-intensive facilities. Thus, the country's overall economic efficiency is now heavily encumbered by low capital productivity and low energy productivity, so the technological changes that reduce environmental impact can also improve economic productivity. For example, by reducing fuel consumption, decentralized electric power systems improve not only air pollution but the economic efficiency of power production as well.

Today's largely unsuccessful regulatory effort is based on a defective but now well-established process. First, EPA estimates the degree of harm represented by different levels of numerous environmental pollutants. Next, some "acceptable" level of harm is chosen, and emission and/or ambient concentration standards that can presumably achieve that risk level are established. Polluters are expected to respond by introducing control measures that will bring emissions or ambient concentrations to the required levels. If the regulation survives the inevitable challenges from industry, the polluters will invest in the appropriate control systems. If all goes well, and it frequently does not, at least some areas of the country and some production facilities are then in compliance with the regulation. The net result is that the "acceptable" pollution level is frozen in place. The industries, having heavily invested in the equipment designed just to reach the required level, are unlikely to invest in further improvements. The public, having been told that the accompanying hazard is "acceptable," is likely to be equally satisfied.

Clearly this process is the inverse of a preventative public health approach. It strives not for the continuous improvement of environmental health but for the social acceptance of some, hopefully low, risk to health. Thus, some level of pollution and some risk to health is the "unavoidable" price that must be paid for the material benefits of modern technology. The preventative approach, however, aims at progressively reducing the risk to health. The present regulatory approach, by setting a standard of "acceptable" exposure to the pollutant, erects an administrative barrier that blocks further improvement in environmental quality.

How is it decided when to stop and where to set standards? Since the pollutants' ultimate effect can often be assessed by the number of lives lost, the risk-benefit analysis requires that a value be placed on a human life, so in practice the risk-benefit equation masquerades as a science. It thus deprives society of the duty to control moral questions (how many people should be allowed to die?). Therefore one result of failing to adopt the preventative approach to environmental quality is that the regulatory agencies have been driven into positions that seriously diminish the force of social morality. The response to this retrogressive policy is that polluters can justify their action and the public its apathy. This erodes the integrity of regulation and diminishes the public faith in the meaning of environmental legislation.

A related area of concern is the impact of the current process in the area of science. Although the scientific participants may be convinced that their decisions are even-handed and objective, the consequences are not. Each such decision means that some people will save a good deal of money and others will spend more, that some people will be more concerned about their childrens' health and others less. For a few people, the decision creates a political problem and, for a few others, a welcome political opportunity. These are the facts of regulatory life. In this situation there is an understandable tendency to find purely scientific grounds, which appear to be free of economic or other judgments, for unequivocal standards of exposure—a firm line below which there is a simple message: "healthy." The no-effect level is such a standard and a threshold level below which it can be said, on presumably objective and scientific grounds, that all is well. On the other hand, if there is a linear relationship between dosage and effect, determining the allowable standard moves from the seemingly solid realm of science to the more arguable domain of judgment of policy. Since every level of exposure, no matter how small, will result in a comparable degree of medical risk, the choice of an "acceptable" standard must somehow balance the expected harm against some other value—the supposed worth of a human life or the cost of controlling or cleaning up the pollutant. However, if the risk assessment is changed—for example, by increasing the dosage expected to generate a particular risk level—the standard can be altered without changing the social judgment, thus avoiding the contentious area of discourse.

There is an inherent contradiction between science and policy. In this context, the relevant attributes of science are its demand for rigorous, validated methods independent of the expected results and its objectivity or the independence of the data and analysis used to reach the results from the interests of those affected by them. In contrast, policy is defined as "prudence or wisdom in the management of affairs" and "management or procedure based primarily on material interest." None of us is ready to prescribe what should be done to remedy the environmental failure. This will require the courage to challenge the taboo against even questioning the current dominance of private interests over the public interest. It calls for good science and wise politics.

CONTINUING DILEMMAS AND NEW FACTORS IN THE EQUATION

The past decades have seen a transformation of the ecological question. The most notable change is that of social values and conscience. There is a new moral perception of the problem. In the developed world people are no longer willing to accept environmental pollution as a necessary trade-off with livelihood. This is not the case, at least to the same degree, in the developing world. The main controversies today are not whether but how and the structure of incentives as well as of liability. The analysis of both of these issues has been profoundly affected by the dynamic and rapidly changing nature of pivotal variables. Principal developments include the following:

1. Improved empirical methods that allow for a better modeling of the environment and more accurate data.
2. Emerging technologies to reduce the production of hazardous wastes, as well as effectively treat whatever wastes are generated.
3. The development of new industries and markets to handle wastes.

4. A clarification of the legal foundations of the environment, particularly mechanisms of liability.

5. Improvements in public policy processes.

Clearly as any of these areas change, moral analysis must be accordingly revised, for these variables transform the moral characteristics of environmental actions and also affect the responsibility of moral agents.

Congress, EPA, private enterprise, and the public are challenged to seek reliable long-term solutions to the problem of managing hazardous wastes. Sound policy is multifaceted. It must address the economic effects of policy, improve the functioning of markets and the law, and increase the efficiency of public agencies. There are some recent indications that society's "ecological efficiency" is growing. Indeed ends and means are in much sharper focus today than thirty years ago, and polluters can less easily escape culpability.

REFERENCES

Bovard, James. 1987. "The Real Superfund Scandal." *Policy Analysis,* Cato Insitute, August 14.

Bussey, John. 1987. "Softer Approach: Dow Chemical Tries to Shed Tough Image and Court the Public." *Wall Street Journal,* November 27.

Commoner, Barry. 1986. "Failure of the Environmental Effort." Center for the Biology of Natural Systems, Queens College, CUNY, January 12.

Environmental Protection Agency. 1986a. *Superfund: A Six-Year Perspective.* Washington, D.C., October.

Environmental Protection Agency. 1986b. *RCRA Orientation Manual.* Washington, D. C., January.

Environmental Protection Agency. 1986c. *Major Provisions of Superfund Amendments and Reauthorization Act of 1986.* Washington, D. C., October 17.

Environmental Protection Agency. 1987. *Superfund: Looking Forward, Looking Back.* Washington, D. C., April.

Hahn, Robert W. 1988. "An Evaluation of Options for Reducing Hazardous Waste." *Harvard Environmental Law Review* 21, 1:201–30.

Harris, Christopher, William Want, and Morris Ward. 1987. *Hazardous Waste: Confronting the Challenge.* Westport, Conn.: Quorum Books.

Harthill, Michalann. 1984. *Hazardous Waste Management: In Whose Backyard?* Boulder, Colo.: Westview Press and American Association for the Advancement of Science.

Heritage Foundation. 1985a. "Superfund Extension: How Much Is Enough?" *Backgrounder.* Washington, D. C., April 3.

Heritage Foundation. 1980. "'Superfund' Legislation." *Issue Bulletin,* September 17.

Heritage Foundation. 1984. "The Super Problems with Superfund Extension." Executive Memorandum, Washington, D. C., September 16.

Heritage Foundation, 1985b. "The Many Hazards of a Mega-Superfund." *Backgrounder.* "Washington, D. C., June 10.

Ketchum, Bostwick H. 1985. *Nearshore Waste Disposal*. New York: Wiley.

McElfish, James M., Jr. 1987. "State Hazardous Waste Crimes." *Environmental Law Reporter* 17, (December): 10465–77.

Marx, Thomas J. 1986. "Integrating Public Affairs and Strategic Planning." *California Management Review* 29, 1 (Fall): 141–48.

Mazmanian, Daniel, and David Morrell. 1988. "The Elusive Pursuit of Toxics Management." *Public Interest* (Winter): 81–98.

Morgenthaler, Eric. 1987. "Ecology Effort: A Florida Utility Wins Naturalists' Praise for Guarding Wildlife." *Wall Street Journal*, July 5, pp. 1, 19.

New York Times. 1987. "Superfund Cleanups Termed Lax." November 24, p. C11.

Piasecki, Bruce. 1984. *Beyond Dumping: New Strategies for Controlling Toxic Contamination*. Westport, Conn.: Quorum Books.

Piasecki, Bruce, and Gary A. Davis. 1987. *America's Future in Toxic Waste Management: Lessons from Europe*. Westport, Conn.: Quorum Books.

Potter, Ralph. 1970. *War and Moral Discourse*. Richmond, Va.: John Knox Press.

San Francisco Chronicle. 1988. "EPA to Query on Cancer Risk Acceptability." July 22, p. A32.

Shabecoff, Philip. 1988a. "Irate and Afraid, Poor Nations Fight Efforts to Use Them as Toxic Dumps." *New York Times*, July 5, p. C4.

Shabecoff, Philip. 1988b. "Congress Report Faults U.S. Drive on Waste Cleanup." *New York Times*, June 18, pp. 1, 8.

Schneider, Keith. 1987. "Radioactive Waste Is Turned into Fertilizer in Oklahoma." *New York Times*, November 16, pp. A1, B5.

Schneider, Keith. 1988. "California Town Elegantly Solves a Basic Problem." *New York Times*, January 24, p. 20.

Schwab, Jim. 1988. "Hazardous Waste: What Goes Around Comes Around—Federal Legislation Prompted State Involvment in Hazardous Waste Management." *Planning* 54 (February): 18–20.

Sheppard, Nathaniel, Jr. 1987. "Toxic Waste a Growing U.S. Export." *San Francisco Chronicle*, July 17, p. A4.

Wartzman, Rick. 1988. "A Low Profile CEO's High-Profile Mess." *Wall Street Journal*, January 12, p. 42.

5

Straws in the Wind: The Nature of Corporate Commitment to Environmental Issues

D. KIRK DAVIDSON

What kind of commitment is the U.S. business community making to improving the environmental problems so much in the news? Is it superficial and oriented toward public relations, or does it reflect a real understanding of the critical nature and potential scope of the problems? Is public pressure forcing businesses to deal with environmental concerns, is the business community only reluctantly complying with regulations it has opposed and delayed, or is it taking a leadership role in searching out solutions? Are U.S. businesses concentrating only on trying to control the most obvious environmental brushfires, or do they recognize longer-range, systemic problems that need to be addressed?

A preliminary survey and review of the straws in the wind indicates no easy generalizations on these questions. While some individual companies are making strong commitments in this area and while there may be a consensus on the need to address certain environmental problems, these are still isolated examples. There is as yet no general agreement within the business community as to what the environmental problems are, how serious they are, how they should be addressed, or who should address them.

In 1972 there appeared a small, technical, but surprisingly readable book, *Limits to Growth*, which focused attention on some serious global environmental problems. The authors first created a computer model of the entire world's economic and environmental processes. Then, charting the course of five indexes—population growth, declining physical resources, industrial growth, diminishing food supplies, and increasing pollution—they went on to show that because of the slow but inexorable power of compound growth in these five factors, there would be severe environmental and economic breakdowns as early as the middle of the next century if the world economies continued in their existing patterns.

Coming as it did near the zenith of this country's newly discovered interest in environmental matters, *Limits to Growth* won praise from environmental groups and others who understood the link between economic growth and ecological disruptions.[1] But the book also raised criticism and doubts. Mathematicians and other scientists disputed the author's modeling methodology. More important for our purpose, the underlying concepts of the book dared to question the wisdom and efficacy of one of the most fundamental principles of business: growth itself. Is not growth at the very heart of every business manager's strategy? As a recent television documentary proclaimed, "No corporation believes in limits to growth; staying the same size is commercial blasphemy."[2]

Julian Simon and the late Herman Kahn, two business-oriented researchers and writers, argued that it was useless and just plain wrong to talk about limited resources. If and when the supply of any resource began to shrink, its price would rise, just as Adam Smith had predicted more than two hundred years ago. This would lead to declining use of the resource, the recovery of formerly uneconomic sources, wider exploration for new sources, and the search for suitable substitutes.[3] Simon has even disputed the widespread concern regarding population growth by claiming that population is in fact the ultimate resource; greater numbers of people are the source of the world's wealth and are therefore the solution rather than the problem.[4]

Limits to Growth gained very little circulation within the business community itself. One might have thought that major corporations would be concerned about the state of the world's economy and environment fifty or sixty years ahead. As has been noted so frequently, however, the planning horizon for most corporations, at least in the United States, is far shorter than that. Also company chiefs much preferred the good news and rosy scenarios that Kahn predicted, and so he was a frequent and popular speaker on the corporate lecture circuit.

The problems raised by *Limits to Growth* refused to fade, however. They surfaced again in the *Global 2000 Report,* issued in 1980 at the end of the Carter administration, and a year before that they had appeared in a different context in the so-called Brandt commission report.[5]

Most recently these interrelated economic and ecological issues have been the subject of a report published in 1987 by the World Commission on Environment and Development, chaired by Gro Harlem Brundtland, prime minister of Norway.[6] Growth per se is no longer ruled out; instead the report looks for "sustainable development." Still, there are a number of direct links between this recent publication and its 1972 predecessor. The Brundtland commission specifically recognizes the links between population pressures and issues on the one hand and poverty, development, and the environment on the other. It speaks dramatically of the conflict between short-range gains and long-term losses:

Many present efforts . . . to meet human needs and to realize human ambitions are simply unsustainable. . . . They draw too heavily, too quickly, on already overdrawn environmental resource accounts. They may show profits on the balance sheets of our generation, but our children will inherit the losses. We borrow environmental capital from future generations with no intention or prospect of repaying. They damn us for our spendthrift ways, but they can never collect on our debt to them.[7]

Circulation of the commission's report, *Our Common Future*, began in 1988, a time of increasing concern for environmental issues: the severe drought in the United States, more scientific evidence supporting theories on global warming and ozone depletion, *Time* magazine's Planet-of-the-Year award to the environmentally battered earth,[8] a new president and administration claiming the environment as one of their prime concerns, and early in 1989 the Exxon oil spill in Valdez, Alaska. Yet in spite of the fact that the report is addressed to private enterprises as well as to governments, it has received little recognition in corporate America.

Why not? Are these issues not a genuine concern of business? Do not environmental problems, along with the interrelated development problems, threaten the vitality and viability of business firms and institutions in the fast-approaching twenty-first century? How can business reconcile the saving graces and the dark sides of growth?

MIXED MESSAGES FROM BUSINESS

Where and how can one take the pulse of the business community to get answers to such questions? One might start with a look at umbrella groups such as the Business Roundtable and the Conference Board. When asked about the business community's response to or involvement in environmental matters, a spokesperson for the Business Roundtable responded that that group did not take positions on such issues. Its one recent exception was the publication of an economic analysis in March 1988 strongly criticizing the Clean Air Act under consideration by the U.S. Senate at that time. The report claimed that the bill would jeopardize at least 300,000–600,000 jobs, and David M. Roderick, chairman of the Business Roundtable's Environmental Task Force and also chairman of USX Corporation, stated, "This bill would be the most expensive environmental legislation ever adopted and the least cost effective."[9] Regardless of the merits of this specific piece of legislation the Roundtable's report in both substance and tone was hardly sympathetic to the environmentalist point of view.

On the other hand, and as an example of the contradictory evidence one finds, Roderick is personally responsible for two significant environmentally oriented accomplishments. He has led USX out of what a company spokesperson called "the Dark Ages" of environmental thinking into the light of not only cleaning up the company's facilities at a cost of $250 billion per year but also adopting a longer-range rather than a damage control strategy. Roderick was also instrumental in founding the International Environmental Bureau, which studies and reports on the interaction of business and the environment from a global perspective.

Another major business umbrella organization, the Conference Board, in its monthly publication, *Across the Board,* has called attention regularly to environmental issues.[10]

The oil and chemical industries provide a reasonable starting point to look at individual companies. Both industries produce and sell products that can cause environmental damage, and both employ production processes that can create serious pollution and/or toxic waste problems. It is interesting to look at what the firms in these two industries say about themselves in their annual reports. Here again there is contradictory evidence. Of the four major chemical producers surveyed, three highlighted environmental issues and achievements, while the fourth made almost no mention of the subject.

Du Pont, in the traditional letter to its shareholders, reported that the company was committed to end its production of chlorofluorocarbons (CFCs) by the end of the century, if not earlier.[11] Later the report elaborated on this commitment and also stated that Du Pont had spent some $600 million in operating costs during the year on pollution control.

Dow's letter from chairman Frank Popoff noted the company's "concern for the environment" and that Dow would "receive the World Environment Center's Gold Medal for international corporate environmental achievement." Later in the report the company described its Waste Reduction Always Pays program. Monsanto's chief executive officer, Richard Mahoney, wrote to his shareholders of the company's "commitment to the . . . protection of the environment," and two full pages of the report were devoted to details. By contrast, in the Rohm and Haas 1988 Annual Report, there is no mention of environmental issues except for a vague reference under "Corporate Affairs" to a concern that the company handle its products and wastes responsibility.

Of the oil companies' annual reports surveyed, Chevron stood well above the others in emphasizing its environmental commitment:

We're not just reacting. . . . We need to look ahead and help identify solutions to environmental problems. We're reemphasizing our philosophy that environmental concerns must be an integral part of every manager's business plans. We want to improve the level of public dialogue and to work with environmental groups, the community and various levels of government.[12]

Clearly, this does not signal agreement with environmental groups on every issue; the following paragraph of chairman Kenneth Derr's letter called for opening the Arctic National Wildlife Refuge for oil exploration.

Shell's letter to its shareholders made only brief mention of protection of the environment. Unocal, Phillips, Mobil, Arco, and Exxon did not find the subject important enough to include in the introductory letter, although Unocal and Phillips did make passing references to the subject elsewhere in their reports.

Exxon's annual report is particularly interesting in the light of the controversy over the way the company has managed or mismanaged the Valdez oil spill.

Exxon's four major business groups are highlighted: oil exploration and production, oil refining and marketing, chemicals, and coal. Each of these four businesses stirs up plenty of environmental worries, yet nowhere in the report does Exxon even mention the subject of environmental problems or issues.

The obligatory letter to shareholders in an annual report is not the only indication of the priority a company gives to an issue. Chevron's emphasis is borne out, however, by the millions of dollars it spends on institutional advertising promoting its species conservation and other environmental efforts. It is also borne out in a thoughtful speech to the California Manufacturers Association (CMA) by former chairman George M. Keller calling for a new philosophy connecting industry and the environment, a recognition that regulation has been necessary, an end to mutual distrust and a lowering of the "emotional thermostat," and a willingness for industry to accept its responsibilities and go beyond mere compliance, as well as take a share of the credit for the progress that has been made.[13]

It is interesting to take a second look at Arco. That company under Thornton Bradshaw and Robert Anderson gained a reputation for a strong sense of responsibility toward all social issues, including the environment, and so it is all the more significant that chairman Lodwrick Cook and president Robert Wycoff's letter to the shareholders in Arco's 1988 annual report did not raise the subject. Furthermore, in a recent speech to the CMA, Cook adopted a somewhat more adversarial tone than was characteristic of Bradshaw or Anderson:

The environmental leaders should have to tell us how many U.S. jobs, how much of our standard of living, they are asking us to sacrifice. . . .
The hard fact is that the U.S. could restrict itself environmentally to the point we're not able to function competitively in world society, let alone maintain our leadership position.

Does this signal a new point of view for Arco? Not necessarily. Arco's manager of corporate environmental protection, June Lindstedt-Siva, has written a position paper, "Environmental Issues of the 1990s," in which she states:

[Arco] can no longer afford the traditional industry approach of just objecting to legislation after it is proposed, we should play a more active role as policies and legislation are being developed. . . . Some of [our] recommendations will lead to increased costs and changes in the status quo. This approach would require considerably more resources than we currently devote to these areas, but, if successful, the benefits of assuming leadership would far exceed the costs over the long-term.[14]

MORE STRAWS IN THE WIND

Other bits of evidence can be reported from discussions with these chemical and oil firms. The Brundtland commission report, *Our Common Future,* describes the all-too-familiar problems of development and of the environment:

- more hungry people in the world
- more illiteracy
- more people without safe water
- millions of acres of productive land become worthless each year
- acid precipitation kills lakes and forests
- gradual global warming from the burning of fossil fuels
- depletion of the planet's protective ozone shield
- toxic wastes poisoning the food chain and water supplies

These problems also cast a shadow on the environment in which the U.S. business community will be operating in the coming decades, yet none of the chemical firms and only three of the nine oil companies surveyed had ever heard of the commission or its report.[15]

William Ruckelshaus, the United States's only member of the Brundtland commission, agrees that the report has had little circulation to date within the business community because the media to a large extent have ignored it. His hope is that this will change. He notes that whereas the dire message of *Limits to Growth* has been received with skepticism and resistance by the business community, he anticipates eventually a more positive reaction to *Our Common Future* because of its emphasis on the possibility of "sustainable development."[16]

My survey of oil and chemical firms confirmed the short-run nature of U.S. business planning so often decried. Long-range planning was defined most often by the respondents as from three to five years into the future. A few said, with little conviction, their firms nominally looked ten years ahead. Several firms noted that this had changed significantly since the 1970s, initiated by more of an interest (perhaps a fad) in "futuristic" planning. Fueled by such thinking from both social scientists and natural scientists, the business community tried its hand at long-range planning.[17] By the end of the 1980s, however, after severe recessions, mounting foreign competition, continuing pressures to increase productivity, and other problems, such long-range planning was viewed by the respondents as valueless and frivolous.

Also to emerge from the survey was an interesting paradox. During the 1970s, with the onrush of social legislation and regulation and in the bloom of interest and debate over corporate social responsibility, some firms enthusiastically embraced an environmentalist point of view. Now, however, after years of neglect by the Reagan administration, environmental concerns are less likely to be priority items on corporations' agendas in spite of the mounting scientific evidence regarding acid rain, the greenhouse effect, groundwater pollution, and so on. Just as the fears and speculations of the 1970s are gaining scientific credibility, interest and involvement on the part of the business community seem to be waning. The Brundtland commission report suggested that this paradox is true for more than just the business community:

The present decade has been marked by a retreat from social concerns. Scientists bring to our attention urgent but complex problems bearing on our very survival. . . . We respond by demanding more details, and by assigning the problems to institutions ill equipped to cope with them.[18]

This waning concern is reflected in the business press. For example, the *Wall Street Journal* did not even review or mention the Brundtland commission report, as vital as its findings may be for business, although it did manage to find space over the years for reviews of books on medieval prostitution and the life of John Lennon. In fact the only reference to Gro Harlem Brundtland during the time of the publication of the report was a light-hearted story about the number of women in the Norwegian government and "doing dishes" after a cabinet meeting. Furthermore, in describing environmental concerns, the *Journal* is more likely to poke fun at the disagreements among scientists over future predictions than to provide any sort of balanced report on the issues.[19]

Some observers can find a silver lining, however. William Halal at the George Washington University writes that

American society as a whole is undergoing a remarkable change. . . . Where once the youthful interest in unconstrained growth, material consumption, and hard technology was unquestioned, now the country is moving toward a more pragmatic, mature ethic that accepts the reality of limits.[20]

Halal defines and recommends "smart growth" as a compromise and answer to environmental problems.

Certainly there are any number of firms, for whatever combination of motives—compliance, concern for the environment, public relations, and sometimes even outright profit—that have developed programs of recycling, pollution control, and resource conservation. The conversion of USX to a believer in environmentalism is a shining example.

CONTENTION IN LOS ANGELES

What happens when companies bump up against the unyielding realities of specific environmental problems? For five years or more the Southern California Air Quality Management District has been wrestling with putting together a specific plan to meet Environmental Protection Agency air quality standards by the end of the century. Any plan must deal with both stationary and moving sources of pollution, and both raise problems for the oil industry. In the last year or two the district has pushed hard toward a plan that would substitute methanol for gasoline by the early 1990s and eventually eliminate the use of petroleum-based fuels altogether. The oil firms, primarily through the Western States Petroleum Association (WSPA), have been a major player and have consistently advocated a plan that, they have argued, would achieve better results at a lower cost.

The two sides found no compromise. In December 1988, as the district pushed for a vote of its board, WSPA and its allies urged yet another delay in the hopes of swinging public opinion to their side and did in fact find a loophole by which to gain another ninety days' time.[21] Three months later, however, the district adopted the controversial plan.

As is so often the case, both sides were able to marshal scientists and economists to support quite different conclusions as to the costs of the plan and also the effects on the quality of the region's air. To date no consensus has been reached on either of these issues.

But what of the process? And, for our purposes, can the role of the business community be improved? Although businesses, specifically from the oil industry, were involved from the beginning of the proceedings, were they really trying to reach some sort of accommodation? It is interesting that after the district board's vote, Southern California Edison quickly reached a compromise that seemed to satisfy both sides: the utility was granted a seven-year extension for compliance, but the standards were made tougher.[22] It is also interesting to note that in the final throes of the debate over the district's proposed plan, Unocal's chief executive officer, Richard J. Stegmeier, unfurled the old laissez-faire banner in suggesting that the oil firms themselves could solve the air quality problems: "One thing we should have learned from that experience [of government regulations in the 1970s] is that the petroleum industry can do the job if government will get off its back."[23] This contrasts sharply with George Keller's remarks on the necessity of regulation.

If the oil firms' claims are correct that the district's plan means the eventual demise of the oil industry in that area, then society can hardly expect the firms to participate enthusiastically in planning their own suicide. That is not likely to be the case, however, and while the economic cost of cleaner air may be high, it is much more probable that the oil firms will find ways to adapt to the changing rules. Their participation in the process of designing the new rules called for more consensus seeking.

The role of an industry association, WSPA in this instance, is likely to be more defensive and less bold and imaginative in searching for a reasonable solution than individual firms might be. Arco's June Lindstedt-Siva makes this same point: "Industry trade organization efforts are not likely to be daring, creative or 'cutting edge' due to the necessity of reaching consensus among member companies."[24]

CONCLUSIONS

These straws in the wind warn us that the business community's understanding of and concern for environmental issues are at best inconsistent and at worst shallow and narrow. However, the questions posed at the beginning certainly merit further study. We can also ask other questions.

Do businesses' interest in environmental matters suffer from the familiar short-run versus long-run problem? Are businesses focusing their attention on applying

Band-aids to immediate problems (cleaner emissions, waste reduction) rather than joining in the attack on root causes (global poverty and grossly uneven levels of development) as emphasized in the Brundtland commission report?

Do corporate environmental concerns become institutionalized, or do they depend on the values of individuals? Will Chevron after Keller maintain its level of spending and concern? Is Arco after Bradshaw and Anderson retreating from its environmental commitments?

An encouraging sign is that in 1987 the Conference Board reported that 82 percent of the chief executive officers of major corporations regarded environmental issues as ethical matters. When asked, "Which issues will be important over the next five years?" 86 percent of these same executives put environmental questions at the top of the list.[25] But do executives' actions match their words? Preliminary evidence suggests that corporate response to date has been minimal and aimed at the short run: what is the least we can do to get beyond the immediate environmental and public relations problems? True understanding and acceptance of the long-range and critical nature of the issues appear to be rare.

NOTES

1. The Environmental Protection Agency was created in 1970.

2. From the Enterprise series film for public television, "Not for Jeans Alone," concerning growth strategy at Levi Strauss.

3. For example, Julian L. Simon and Herman Kahn, *The Resourceful Earth, A Response to Global 2000* (New York: B. Blackwell, 1984).

4. Julian Simon, *The Ultimate Resource* (Princeton, N.J.: Princeton University Press, 1982).

5. *North-South: A Program for Survival: Report of the Independent Commission on International Development Issues* (Cambridge, Mass.: MIT Press, 1980).

6. World Commission on Environment and Development, *Our Common Future* (Oxford: Oxford University Press, 1987).

7. Ibid., p. 8.

8. *Time*, January 2, 1989.

9. "Price Tag of Impending Clean Air Measure (S. 1894) Makes It Most Expensive Environmental Package Ever," press release from the Business Roundtable, March 9, 1988.

10. Examples are "Corporate Responsibility and the Environment," *Conference Board Reports* (April 1971); "Can We Stop Acid Rain? And Who Should Pay the Bill?" *Across the Board* (February 1984); "An Environmental Agenda for World Business," *Across the Board* (March 1987).

11. Widely believed to be an important cause of ozone depletion.

12. *Chevron Corporation Annual Report 1988*, p. 5.

13. From a speech to the California Manufacturers Association on the occasion of Keller's being named Manufacturer of the Year, San Francisco, October 30, 1987.

14. From a position paper sent to the author by Arco: June Lindstedt-Siva, *Environmental Issues of the 1990s*, January 11, 1989. See also another paper by the same author,

Environmental Planning and Management—an Important Component in Maintenance of Biological Diversity, September 14, 1988.

15. A limited survey I conducted in 1983 revealed that corporate chief executive officers were unfamiliar with *Limits to Growth*—either the book itself or the environmental concerns the book embodied.

16. From personal correspondence with the author, April 7, 1989.

17. The same forces that prompted *Limits to Growth* and Kahn's *The Next 200 Years.*

18. World Commission on Environment and Development, *Our Common Future* (Oxford: Oxford University Press), p. xi.

19. See, for example, Bob Davis and Barbara Rosewicz, "Poor Track Record Marks Global Climate Predictions," *Wall Street Journal,* April 10, 1989, p. B1.

20. William E. Halal, *The New Capitalism* (New York: John Wiley & Sons, 1986), p. 85.

21. Southern California Edison was also a strong critic of the district's plan. As more claims were aired concerning the billions of dollars the plan would cost and the hundreds of thousands of jobs that might be lost, city and county governments joined with the oil and utility firms. These governmental bodies favored cleaner air but were frightened by the potential economic hardships.

22. From a conversation with Larry B. Stammer, staff reporter for the *Los Angeles Times.*

23. Donald Woutat, "Oil Executive Calls Clean-Air Proposal 'Popular Hysteria,' " *Los Angeles Times,* January 26, 1989, p. II-1.

24. Lindstedt-Siva, *Environmental Issues of the 1990s,* p. 8.

25. Conference Board, *Corporate Ethics,* Research Report 900, (New York: Conference Board, 1987), pp. 3–4. Responses came from 252 large U.S. and 48 non-U.S. companies.

II

CORPORATIONS AND THE ENVIRONMENT: CASES AND ANALYSES

6

Du Pont and Corporate Environmentalism

B. W. KARRH

Often when people in industry begin to discuss environmental issues, the discussion takes place in the rarefied atmosphere of corporate headquarters by people who sit at desks and think big-picture thoughts. But if they are the only ones with input, the agenda may not address all the concerns or uncertainties of the people who typically end up making the environmental decisions. Most of those people wear safety glasses and hard hats and operate world-scale plants, hundreds if not thousands of miles from the company headquarters. Their participation is essential if a corporate policy is going to have an impact on the way the company does business.

Recently at Du Pont we engaged in an exercise that did just that. We brought together the safety, health, and environmental managers from around the company to look at the kind of organization we hope to be in terms of safety, health, and environmental performance at the end of the 1990s. Our stated goal was not to create an ethics policy. Rather we worked to create what we call a vision statement.

In a philosophical sense, this document constitutes our company's environmental agenda for the 1990s. It does not do so by listing what we will do point by point, but it describes how we will conduct ourselves in key areas of business practice and policy relating to safety, health, and the environment. In environmental policy, stating how you would like to be perceived by your shareholders, customers, and the public boils down quickly to how you are going to act. The days of smoke and mirrors are gone in the area of environmental policy. Flowery policy statements do not accomplish anything unless the facts back them up. A company's actions are monitored carefully by government, the public and the press, and even its own employees, many of whom have deep personal commitments to environmental causes independent of the company's policy.

We said that the kind of company we hope to be as we emerge from the twentieth century will be one in which our environmental policies are understood and followed throughout our global operations. We said that we will anticipate, seek, and respond to public values about the environmental impact of our operations and audit our facilities to ensure that they are operated safely and are acceptable to the communities in which they are located. We said that we hope to be a company in which we work with suppliers, carriers, and customers to ensure public and environmental protection from product creation to final disposition.

We said more specifically that performance excellence and ethical behavior in environmental protection will be part of the company's core values at all levels of management. We said that environmental protection must be a line and business responsibility, with accountability residing with those with appropriate authority. We acknowledged that it is a responsibility of the company's management to ensure that adequate technical resources are available to sustain our commitment to environmental protection and to improve our performance. And we said that we support constructive laws and regulations in this area of policy and recognize our responsibility to work in ways that address transnational issues and lead to international consensus on environmental issues.

It is in the nature of such a vision statement to be future oriented. We do not claim to have fully developed each of those points, as well as the others included in the document. But in each of those areas we are working from a well-established base of past practice or, at the very least, of present sensitivity and awareness.

I believe that this discussion and the resulting document have broad ethical implications. To say that the company has a responsibility to ensure that the technical resources are made available to improve environmental performance is to express a fundamentally ethical value. To say that we should anticipate, seek, and respond to public values in the communities where we operate is another ethical concern. So is our desire to work with suppliers, carriers, and customers to ensure public protection throughout the life cycle of our products. These actions are not required by law. And although they make good business sense, they are not strictly bottom-line items. Rather they spring from the perception that industry's right to operate in a given community is not absolute. Our existence as a manufacturer requires at least the nonobjection and preferably the support of the people and governments in the societies where we operate around the world. To gain that support, companies ought to display an attitude and a performance commitment that place corporate environmental stewardship fully in line with public desires and expectations.

That, in fact, is how Du Pont's chairman defines what he calls corporate environmentalism. It is a fundamentally ethical imperative because it goes beyond pragmatism and indicates a sense of what is correct and responsible behavior for the corporation in relation to society and nature. This sense of responsibility must be at the heart of any environmental agenda for the next decade and beyond. An agenda that merely addresses problems and their symptoms may well be ameliorative for a while, but the systemic and attitudinal causes of our environmental problems could well remain unchanged if our work habits, research practices, and manufacturing technologies are not grounded in an environmentalist ethic.

At Du Pont, we are optimistic that this can be done, largely because we have nearly 200 years of success with our well-known safety ethic. Like the environmental imperative, the safety imperative insists on an attitude and performance that have pragmatic value but are adopted for humanitarian, that is, ethical, reasons. The Du Pont employee who knowingly allows an unsafe situation to exist in the workplace without correcting it or alerting others to the danger and seeking immediate help is likely to lose his or her job. I am not just talking about a plant ready to go haywire; a puddle of water on a linoleum floor is serious enough.

Now imagine transferring that same degree of awareness and second-nature response to an employee's environmental outlook, and you have an idea of what the basis must be for a company's environmental agenda in the future. That is what we are trying to do at Du Pont. Once such a commitment is in place, it has to be apparent throughout the organization at every level and in every business function. For obvious reasons, much of the environmental emphasis has been on manufacturing. The National Wildlife Federation publishes its Toxic 500 list each year showing the 500 plants with the most emissions of federally listed substances. Du Pont has 14 plants on that list, so there is no doubt that for the next decade we will be working aggressively to reduce the level of material that leaves our plants in the form of emissions or waste. We have cut the amount of waste our manufacturing facilities produce by 35 percent since 1982, and we will at least duplicate that by the end of the 1990s.

But environmental awareness has to extend also to the products we manufacture. For example, we are eliminating the use of lead and cadmium from pigments used in certain plastics to eliminate the accumulation of heavy metals in the incinerator ash resulting from the destruction of that portion of plastic waste that cannot be recycled. As a leading manufacturer of plastics and polymer materials, we have the expertise and the responsibility to lead in the recovery and recycling of plastic waste in general. We have embarked on a major joint venture to establish a worldwide business in this technology.

Many of our other efforts regarding the environment are not so easily classified. Perhaps they can best be summarized by what we call competitive advantage or a "win-win" approach—activities that benefit both the environment and the company. At Du Pont, we believe that environmental performance should not be viewed as a cost to be carried but rather as an advantage in the marketplace.

The ultimate competitive advantage is to remain in business when competitors are driven out. In the decades ahead, many companies that have not responded to the environmental imperative will be denied the privilege to operate. We already have examples of companies being denied permits to build new plants in the United States and in Europe because the communities in which they wanted to locate did not believe that they could operate without damaging the local environment.

Competitive advantage is not just a big ticket item. It can be lots of smaller opportunities on a more routine level. For example, at one of our plants, we are using a column in an acrylonitrile process to recover by-product acetonitrile, a hazardous material, which used to go into the waste stream. This same material is now marketed for use to pharmaceutical firms that manufacture insulin and as an extraction solvent in a petrochemical operation. The marketing effort has been so successful that the demand is pushing our supply. The total effort has resulted in the elimination of 20 million pounds per year of waste that used to be incinerated.

In Europe, one of our petroleum affiliates devised an ingenious program to recover and recycle automobile oil. In West Germany, improper disposal of used motor oil by consumers is a serious pollution concern. Our company will change the oil for the customer. We then forward the used oil to a recycler and melt down the plastic bottles for recycling or proper disposal in small furnaces built for that purpose. If customers bring in used oil, we take that and follow the same system. This program has the triple benefit of preventing pollution from used oil, minimizing a plastic waste, and conserving natural resources through recycling. The result is an increase in profitability while helping to improve West Germany's environment.

Environmental protection and competitiveness are not mutually exclusive. When environmental regulations apply to everyone, the company that meets them most efficiently has a cost advantage over those that do not. Environmental performance is a new business variable that will be with us from now on. Companies that drag their heels and view it as a burden will chase numbers from year to year and just get by. Companies that see environmental performance as an opportunity to innovate and leapfrog the competition will gain.

Once a company has decided to inculcate an awareness of environmental protection into all its activities and direct its efforts in a manner that gains competitive advantage, then efforts to address specific issues of policy will be more focused and have more credibility. This is the case at Du Pont where we have had to address several large issues relating to our business operations or products.

Chief among these is the chlorofluorocarbon (CFC) issue. We are the world's leading manufacturer of these materials. Our unilateral decision to phase out the manufacture of these compounds as soon as possible—but by the end of the 1990s at the latest—went beyond the Montreal Protocol and has set the pace for an accelerated phaseout by other manufacturers. Now when we comment on other developments in certain searches for alternatives, we tend to be heard, and our credibility has enabled us to participate in other discussions of environmental policy.

Nevertheless, we are not always viewed as environmental good guys. Some special interest groups disagree with us on particular points, but those with whom we enter into dialogue know that we are serious, that we want to be a positive force, and that we are prepared to lay enormous assets and investments on the line for the sake of environmental protection. Our CFC business is a $750 million enterprise; we have so far invested $170 million in the search for alternatives and plan to spend another $1 billion during the 1990s.

Another issue we are grappling with deals with a unit of our petroleum subsidiary Conoco, this time in South America. Conoco Ecuador Limited has been asked by the government of Ecuador to act as a contractor to develop petroleum reserves in a national park in the midst of a vast rain forest. Some people fear that roads built into the area will result in an influx of settlers and the slash and burn agriculture that typically follows. Moreover, there are native peoples in the region whose way of life could be threatened by careless development. Conoco Ecuador is well aware of these challenges and is working with the government of Ecuador to minimize the impact of oil development. In the meantime, the Sierra Club Legal Defense Fund recently complained to a United Nations subcommission that the company's activities in Ecuador will lead to the genocide of the indigenous people.

Conoco is an oil company with an admirable record of environmental concern and responsibility. The Conoco Ecuador people believe that the oil field can be developed responsibly and have proposed a model minimum-impact oil development plan for the rain forest. The cornerstone for this plan is the fact that the Ecuadorian government had the foresight in 1979 to establish the 1.7-million-acre Yasuní National Park. Laws prohibit colonization in the park, and Conoco Ecuador is working with government officials to enforce the law and to develop the park with sensitivity and respect for the forest and its native inhabitants.

Nevertheless, our dilemma is by no means resolved. Should Conoco Ecuador remain confident that it can extract the oil in a responsible and environmentally sensitive manner? Or should the company withdraw, knowing that absent its involvement the owner of the oil—the government of Ecuador—will go forward with development because oil is the financial lifeblood of that country? So far Conoco Ecuador is moving cautiously forward, but the discussions continue, along with special engineering in an attempt to meet the sweep of needs—environmental, societal, technical, and economic.

Similar situations will continue to arise, and they will be properly managed only if we succeed in accomplishing what I think ought to be the main points on the environmental agenda for industry during the next decade:

1. Management has a responsibility to set a tone and a standard for environmental awareness and protection within corporations. This commitment has to be substantiated by genuine progress and action in environmental affairs.

2. Business as usual no longer applies. Every aspect of corporate activity has to be reassessed in the light of our increased awareness of environmental degradation, our increased understanding of the environmental impact of our operations and products, and an increased appreciation for society's environmental values.

3. If we are to make quantum leaps in industrial environmental performance, the approach we take will have to be grounded in gaining competitive advantage as a result of our environmental innovations. This will not only spur radical departures from business as usual but will also satisfy the fiduciary responsibilities we have to shareholders. In short, we cannot persist in viewing profitability and environmental protection as an either-or proposition.

4. Our public stance in environmental matters has to be one of openness and receptivity to dialogue. Industry's knee-jerk response to protest and disagreement is euphemistically called "educating the public." This means making them see our side, and the assumption is that they will then agree. It does not work that way. At the same time, we hope that those with opposing points of view will refrain from their own knee-jerk response, which usually is "let's sue the pants off them." That does not work either.

Dialogue must hold a prominent place on everybody's agenda for the 1990s. The CERES Project's Valdez Principles (see appendix) proposal is a good example of what we need. Whether Du Pont ultimately subscribes to this document, we certainly want to sit down and talk about it—what it means and how it can open channels of communication. We have stated that in writing to the CERES Project, and we hope they respond.

Du Pont is generally encouraged by what seems to be taking place in industry. Major manufacturers in the chemical and materials industry such as Dow, Monsanto, and 3M have demonstrated impressive commitments to environmental improvement, but we all have a long way to go.

The most necessary ingredient in long-term success appears to be in place: an awareness by all parties that industry is not just part of the environmental problem but increasingly is part of the solution. It will be to our collective benefit and to the benefit of what the National Wildlife Federation aptly calls the "Nature of Tomorrow" to continue in that direction.

APPENDIX

The Valdez Principles were created by the Coalition of Environmentally Responsible Economics to help investors make informed decisions around environmental issues. The principles set forth broad standards for evaluating activities by corporations that directly or indirectly impact the Earth's environment.

INTRODUCTION

By adopting these principles, we publicly affirm our belief that corporations and their shareholders have a direct responsibility for the environment. We believe that corporations must conduct their business as responsible stewards of the environment and seek profits only in a manner that leaves the Earth healthy and safe. We believe that corporations must not compromise the ability of future generations to sustain their needs. We recognize this to be a long term commitment to update our practices continually in light of advances in technology and new understandings in health and environmental science. We intend to make consistent, measurable progress in implementing these principles and to apply them wherever we operate throughout the world.

1. Protection of the Biosphere

We will minimize and strive to eliminate the release of any pollutant that might cause environmental damage to air, water, or earth or its inhabitants. We will safeguard habitats in rivers, lakes, wet lands, coastal zones, and oceans and will minimize contributing to global warming, depletion of the ozone layer, acid rain, and smog.

2. Sustainable Use of Natural Resources

We will make sustainable use of renewable natural resources, such as water soils and forests. We will conserve nonrenewable natural resources through efficient use and careful planning. We will protect wildlife habitat, open spaces and wilderness, while preserving biodiversity.

3. Reduction and Disposal of Waste

We will minimize the creation of waste, especially hazardous waste, and wherever possible recycle materials. We will dispose of all waste through safe and responsible methods.

4. Wise Use of Energy

We will make every effort to use environmentally safe and sustainable energy sources to meet our needs. We will invest in improved energy efficiency and conservation in our operations. We will maximize the energy efficiency of products we produce or sell.

5. Risk Reduction

We will minimize the environmental, health and safety risks to our employees and the communities in which we operate by employing safe technologies and operating procedures and by being constantly prepared for emergencies.

6. Marketing for Safe Products and Services

We will sell products or services that minimize adverse environmental impacts and that are safe as consumers commonly use them. We will inform consumers of the environmental impact of our products or services.

7. Damage Compensation

We will take responsibility for any harm we cause to the environment by making every effort to fully restore the environment and to compensate those persons who are adversely affected.

8. Disclosure

We will disclose to our employees and to the public, incidents relating to our operations that cause environmental harm or pose health safety hazards. We will disclose potential environmental, health or safety hazards posed by our operations, and we will not take any action against employees who report any condition that creates a danger to the environment or poses health and safety hazards.

9. Environment Directors and Managers

At least one member of the Board of Directors will be a person qualified to represent environmental interests. We will commit management resources to implement these principles, including the funding of an office of vice president for environmental affairs or an equivalent executive position, reporting directly to the CEO, to monitor and report upon our implementation efforts.

10. Assessment and Annual Audit

We will conduct and make public an annual self-evaluation of our progress in implementing these principles and in complying with all applicable laws and regulations through out our world-wide operations. We will work toward the timely creation of independent environmental audit procedures which we will complete annually and make available to the public.

Total Quality: Ethics and the Environment

VAN C. CAMPBELL

Today every responsible person in business or elsewhere must be or become something of an ethicist or an environmentalist. Let me give you a brief example. Corning is a global company, and we also draw a significant part of our profits from our strategic alliances or joint ventures with other companies. A couple of years ago we found ourselves assailed in the American press for something we literally knew nothing about. A joint venture in India—we owned only a minority interest in it—was buying some supplies from a company that employed children in its factory. We found ourselves portrayed as vicious stealers of youth and supporters of an abhorrent cause. It was as if we were a company straight out of Dickens's London, using children to pick pockets and then taking the food straight out of their mouths.

After we ascertained the facts, we asked what we could have done to prevent the damage and the scandal. We were as horrified as any other Westerner would be over the use of child labor (although in India, child labor is not against the law). Nevertheless, we do not normally investigate the labor practices of our suppliers, and we certainly do not investigate them when we have little or no managerial control.

For once, we found ourselves on the other side. We are usually the guys in the white hats. For example, to help achieve the objectives of the Clean Air Act, we developed at considerable initial expense and risk the advanced ceramic technology that makes the automobile catalytic converter work. But in the case of India, we ended up telling ourselves that we would try to do better. We instructed our Indian affiliate not to buy from any supplier using child labor and stated our absolute belief that child labor is not acceptable to us in business in any form.

Let us step back from the emotion of the situation and examine what happened. First, ethics is normative and cultural. In parts of India, children are permitted to work, and they will work no matter what we in the United States think about it. For us to call it unethical, no matter how much we abhor it, is to misunderstand their situation, their culture, and their history. For us to support it, however, is unethical because it goes against our culture and situation.

Second, ethics is temporal. It was not very long ago that children were a staple in the factories of Western Europe and America. Only the materially rich societies of today can afford not to have children work, so it is now unethical in these societies for children to work. Yesterday's tea is today's poison.

Not long ago, smoking cigarettes was not only permissible; it was socially desirable. All the best people did it; it was thought to be cool and sexy. I still enjoy a good cigar, but if I light up now anywhere but in the privacy of my office or den at home, I am likely to be run out of the room to the tune of a lecture on poisoning other people's airspace. Not long ago it was considered all right to discharge industrial wastes anywhere—into field, stream, or air. The world was thought to be a big place, with plenty of capacity to absorb and neutralize the substances being poured into it. There was an overall lack of knowledge and concern for the impact of what we were doing. People have only come lately to the realization that we are poisoning not only ourselves but the entire planet— and not everyone has bought the contention yet. In Brazil, it is still all right to burn off huge chunks of the rain forest to graze cattle or farm, despite the known effects on the atmosphere. In America, it is still all right to clear-cut the Tongass National Forest. According to international convention, it is going to be all right for several years yet to continue producing the chlorofluorocarbons that destroy ozone molecules in the upper atmosphere. It has been barely a year since the chairman of a major chemical company asserted in a speech that the only acceptable goal for emissions from his company's chemical factories is zero emissions.

Why is it still all right to do all these things and more, and why are we just now attacking these problems? It is because we are caught in the warp of time and the adherence to cultural norms that are out of step with the technological and social realities. But time is growing shorter, and the world is growing smaller. That is why it is critical to systematize our behavior toward the environment and toward each other. In other words, it is now critical that all responsible leaders— political, social, and business—turn to ethics.

We need nothing short of a new ethics—one that is not American or Chinese, Eastern or Western, but an ethics that is truly transnational and encompasses the global village. Such ethics will not be laden with the values of any single nation, society, or religion. It will, of necessity, be an environmental ethics, but the environment embraced will be social as well as physical. Such ethics—as with all other successful ethical systems of behavior—will be a framework for action rather than a code of rules. Such ethics will meet the traditional tests of ethics: Does it do the most good for the greatest number of people? Does it meet the standards of justice for the individual? Where will we find the models for this new ethics?

I believe that we can find these models among the most successful organizations that today span the globe and encompass all forms of diverse culture and society: global businesses—and not just any global corporation but those that understand and practice what we at Corning refer to as Total Quality. I fully realize that given the usual image of international business as a rapacious, care-not collection of robber barons bent on global pillage, my suggestion may come as something of a shock. But if we are to succeed—to save our societies and our planet—we must transcend stereotypes and look for models of success. Clearly the old models are not serving us well. Organized religion is a good example. Although there are individual examples of dedication, selflessness, and heroism like that of Mother Theresa, it is not hard to find examples of where the paradigm breaks down: Northern Ireland, for example, Beirut, Iran and Iraq, India and Pakistan. The paradigm of the nation-state system is also insufficient. The very definition of nations presupposes other nations with different cultures, societies, and values; it presupposes ethical conflict. Throughout history, no supranational organization has been able to assume sovereignty over an unwilling collection of nations. Even the conquests of conquerors soon fall prey to internal dissension; the greatest of empires crumbles. On the other hand, the transnational success of some businesses offers a striking model of some of the characteristics that a new ethics must include: cooperation in pursuit of a common goal, or the development of specific technology to solve market needs, including environmental needs, for example. One of the most striking examples is increasing acceptance among the best global corporations of the philosophy of quality; some people call it excellence.

At Corning, we found that to be competitive in the global economy, we had to adopt a philosophy we call Total Quality. Corning's program offers valuable lessons, lessons that are ethical in nature. The successful companies that practice the discipline of quality are meeting the most rigorous tests of ethics, including doing the greatest good for the greatest number and the test of justice and participation for the individual. The list of such companies is growing longer every day, from Corning to Toyota to IBM to Milliken.

Ethics are cultural and temporal; they adhere to the values of a particular culture, articulated and changed over time. You can change a particular culture and can put into place a new ethic, but calculated cultural change is enormously difficult and time-consuming. Nevertheless, we believe that our survival as a company is at stake, so we are changing our culture and adopting a new ethic, Total Quality. Total Quality to me equals total ethics.

Total Quality encompasses four simple principles. The first is "meet the requirements." This also is the definition of quality. It means that whatever you do or make must meet the needs of all those for whom it is intended. This attitude is what ethics is about on a day-to-day basis and it is also a total quality attitude. In other words, quality is not just what we say it is; it is what the recipient of our product, service, or communication says. Like beauty, quality is in the eyes of the beholder. The mutual requirements for quality then have to be negotiated between the transacting parties. Defining a deal as fair according to our standards is not enough. We have to consider the other person's standards.

The second principle is "do error-free work." This does not mean to be perfect. Instead, it means to seek perfection: "don't have an attitude that accepts less, or you'll always get less and you'll stop striving for what you know is right."

The third principle is "manage by prevention." It means to figure out how to do what you need to do, what is necessary to stop mistakes from occurring, and then do those things.

The final principle is "measure by the cost of quality." In other words, measure what you are doing by how much it costs to fix or not fix what is wrong.

In 1983 in formal training sessions we told all Corning employees that these four total quality principles were the principles by which our business life would be governed in the future. We did not say, "These are the new principles." We said, "These are the only principles." We did not phrase the principles as a code of laws or ethics that forbids certain types of behavior. Instead each is a plea for people to act in a certain way. Along with this set of principles, we published the values we hold as a company: Total Quality, integrity, performance, leadership, technology, independence, and the individual.

Initially our employees displayed mass skepticism: "Well, it all sounds wonderful, but I bet it will go away, and I'll really be measured and rewarded on the same old things I always was. So if I just duck, this will go away, too, like all those other management flavors of the month." But they soon realized our commitment. First, we trained everyone in the corporation—from the chairman to the maintenance crews—in what the Total Quality principles mean and what actions they had to take, and we pointed to some models for success. For example, one of our plant managers had a product that did not meet the customer's specifications. "Ship it anyway," the customer said; "I'll use it." "No way," said the plant manager. "It's not quality." And he destroyed it. Then people began to change their tune. They breathed a sort of collective sigh of relief, as if to say, "They're actually going to let me do what I knew was right all along!"

A basic guideline of Total Quality is to get all people involved and to put the responsibility in the hands of those closest to the job—those who know it best. Before Total Quality we had an authoritarian way of life—telling people what to do. We did it not only in our corporations but in our churches, social groups, and governments. In short, our cultural development has lagged behind our technological development. Is it any wonder we are in an ethical fix? Is it any wonder our environment is being degraded faster than we can repair it? We have stopped listening to ourselves. We had a modern-day Tower of Babel—lots of people shouting in lots of languages and no one listening. We must start again.

Since we began to institute Total Quality, remarkable things have happened. We are now opening a plant with only three personnel layers: the manager, his staff, and everyone else. The production workers are called coworkers; they now plan and organize the production themselves. They work in teams, each trained to do every job on the team. Another example is in our suggestion system. In 1988 Corning's 25,000 employees made more than 16,000 suggestions for improvements, about ten times as many as we got in the best year under our old suggestion system where people were paid if their ideas were accepted. We implemented more than 8,000 quality improvement suggestions, some fifty times as many as before. With Total Quality, managers must respond to employees' suggestions, and there is usually some form of recognition (for example, the employee's name on a board).

We are not the only company that feels this way. Mark Pastin at the Lincoln Center for Ethics at Arizona State University studied thirty companies in Europe and the United States—companies highly distinguished for their ethics and profitability. These companies made a lot of money for a lot of years while maintaining their integrity. The study showed that, time and time again, the one attribute successful, ethical companies shared was a tradition of participation. The study also highlighted that this tradition of participation was an important part of quality management in these companies. The study stressed that participation permeates the company; in short, it means giving voice to every employee. It works for ethics because there are always people in the organization who will voice ethical concerns and raise the level of discussion. It works for quality because there are always people who take the role of advocate for quality.

Our Total Quality does exactly what other successful ethical behavior systems have done: empowers people to act properly in the cause of organizational success by providing them with a framework for that action. It does not matter what the value systems of individual employees are because Total Quality does not supplant those values; it only provides a behavioral overlay for them and for the values we actively share as members of the same organization.

I think the most important word in ethics is *candor*. It is also the most important word in quality. The basic premise is if you cannot talk about it and if the right people do not know about it, then you cannot make it better. Candor is important in ethics because most of the worst problems organizations have faced were highly preventable. A lot of people knew them, but they never told the one who needed to know. The Three Mile Island and Bhopal crises were preventable if someone had raised the problem with the right people at the right time or if people understood that they have to manage by prevention. Candor means, first and foremost, telling each other what we need to know. Employees must be able to speak up when they know something that needs to be said, and managers have to avoid "shooting the messenger." Creating a culture of candor is essential to ethics because people will fix ethical problems when they know about them. Candor is also the key to quality because it supplies information needed to do better. The great philosopher of science Sir Karl Popper said human systems tend to correct themselves if they have prompt and accurate information about what needs to be corrected.

What of the environment? Can ethics—Total Quality—help us? The environment is not a human system, but its problems are caused by humans and by human systems. It is those systems we must aim to correct. Corning's approach to Total Quality can help, primarily because it is a system that focuses on actions to get results that meet specific negotiated needs. A few years ago a Corning employee watched a television program on PCBs (polychlorinated biphenyl) and heard that used generators were a prime culprit for PCB contamination. He remembered handling old generators many years before in an abandoned warehouse. He called our engineering group, which checked the area and found PCBs on the surface. Further digging found them in the ground, and we were able to clean up the area under state supervision. Without Total Quality, would that worker have come forward? Would we have responded in the same way? I would like to think both would have happened, but empirical evidence on other issues suggests the answer to one or the other would have been "no."

When you set out to live up to the Total Quality principles, you must identify your customers—not always obvious. For example, your secretary is one customer whose requirements you must meet. The next person down the assembly line is a customer for those who precede him or her. There are the people who buy your products or services. But there also are people beyond those immediate customers. Inevitably you come to the conclusion that society at large is a customer for your products. For Total Quality, you must meet the requirements of society for safety, health, and durability.

All of the Total Quality principles can be applied in the broadest sense. The Total Quality attitude is to prove it is right, not prove it is wrong, and prove the quality every day because every day brings new information and new questions. The attitude must be, "Our job is to prove it's the best we can do," not "It's someone else's job to prove it doesn't work, that it's not the best." In short, you can never have a take-it-for-granted attitude on either ethics or quality, because both tend to sink with time. The familiar becomes the ethical.

To ensure that ethics and quality remain high, we at Corning try to remember that although both ethics and quality begin with the person, neither of them is a one-person topic. What keeps ethics and quality high is that we expect each other to maintain the highest standards. Not knowing and not being responsible are irrelevant. The first and fundamental responsibility is to know. Once you know, fix it for good.

Although Total Quality is a behavioral system that is excellent for our purposes, it is not the total answer. No system can include everything. Knowledge and flexible action do win, though, and a systematic behavioral ethics that concentrates on ethical action for results can carry us a long way. Excellence through Total Quality is a journey, not a destination. Taking that journey is the only way we can catch up with our own speeding technology and overtake the enormous needs, both social and environmental, that beset us.

8

Martin Marietta's Commitment to Environmental Protection

GEORGE SAMMETT, JR.

The Martin Marietta code of ethics states, "To the Communities in which we live we are committed to be responsible neighbors." There are no exceptions or exclusions. It does not limit that relationship only to humans but purposely was addressed to the community as a whole: the people, the birds and the animals, the earth, and especially the association of living things as a whole.

Glenn L. Martin learned his first lessons in aerodynamics from the environment. In the fields around Salina, Kansas, he noticed that the prairie chickens with their wide, stubby wings could rise rapidly but fly only short distances and at a slow speed. He also noted that the mallard ducks had short, tapered wings. They rose slowly but once underway flew rapidly and for great distances. He watched the reaction of the birds to the wind and saw that they usually took off into the wind and landed the same way. When he decided to move his airplane plant from Cleveland to Maryland, he purchased a 1,200-acre tract on the Chesapeake Bay estuary. He designated half of that tract as a wildlife sanctuary. It remains that way, though it no longer is part of the Martin Marietta holdings.

Like Glenn Martin, the corporation has attempted to maintain that awareness and understanding of the environment and also to operate at the highest level of ethical conduct. Today our ethical standards and environmental standards have been solidified through formal policies and clear-cut operating procedures. We believe that people want a sense of pride in where they work and that our stockholders feel better about having that investment when they perceive that they have invested in a company they too can be proud of.

Martin Marietta (MM) is not only concerned about but also intensely involved in managing the company's impact on the environment. Our published operating policy states, "Martin Marietta is committed to the conduct of its business activities and operations in a manner that ensures protection of the environment."

Since the early 1980s, we have increasingly responded to the environmental requirements, both legal and ethical, as they have evolved and have developed an organized commitment of people and resources to ensure our compliance.

MM believes that the pursuit of business and the protection of the environment can be joined as a single objective. As a corporation, it intends to conduct business in such a way that any potential harm to the environment is either totally mitigated or thoroughly minimized. The realization of this goal continues to be technically challenging. To date, we believe we are meeting our near-term objectives and, probably more important, that we have established the foundation necessary to meet our environmental objectives of the 1990s. The environment was not adversely affected over only a short period; neither will the solutions to the environmental problems solve those problems in a short time.

Just as MM maintains a corporate ethics office, we also maintain a corporate environmental task force. Both offices are headed by a corporate vice-president, each reporting directly to the chief operating officer. The environmental task force is staffed by experts who have helped establish an environmental management department at each operating element—Orlando, Denver, Baltimore, and New Orleans. This organizational approach is the cornerstone of our efforts to meet the environmental requirements in parallel and in concert with our ethical commitment.

In 1984 the general manager of our Florida plant sent a letter to the company's primary customer, the Department of Defense, stating that from that point forward, MM was making a commitment to excellence in every area of its daily business. This commitment applied not only to the production of quality hardware; it permeated every aspect of the way MM managed its facilities and the surrounding environment.

Commitment to excellence soon became more than just a slogan at MM. It became part of the company's dedication to perform at the highest standards. Commitment to excellence also became the foundation of an environmental management effort that has emerged as a significant force in responsible management of the company's activities.

As the corporation changed from making airplanes to one strongly involved in electronics, electroplating, and electrochemicals, we found that we were generating a significant tonnage of hazardous wastes at our three Florida plants. By 1984 we were generating almost 4,000 tons of hazardous waste annually, and we could see that growing to 6,000 tons by 1991. Clearly we needed to take decisive action. The motivation to do so was based on three chief factors: our mandate to comply with regulatory requirements, our desire to control costs and liability, and our resolve to continue to meet our environmental responsibility.

To spearhead this effort, the environmental management group in Florida, under the umbrella guidance of the corporate task force, established specific approaches:

1. To reemphasize the positive environmental culture of the company by introducing more stringent specifications for the use and disposal of hazardous chemicals.

2. To make process or procedural changes to ensure full compliance with all environmental regulations.
3. To make capital investments to change or eliminate processes necessary to eliminate or minimize hazardous waste.

No employee in Florida at that time had the knowledge or experience necessary to solve all the problems, so we solicited the support of consultants, university researchers, and engineers to form a cohesive team that is now achieving significant results.

The first project undertaken was the remediation of groundwater at several sites on our property that had been used as disposal locations when such practice was legally permissible. Extensive groundwater monitoring was put into place to measure the extent of any potential contamination. One of the sites had been used to store a sludge solution that was the by-product of our plating operations. MM agreed to remove the sludge and relocate it to a federally approved landfill. In 1988 the sludge was solidified, rendering inert, and transferred off-site. This was the first time such a project had been done in Florida.

In 1985 we began an ambitious project to achieve zero discharge of industrial wastewater at our Ocala printed circuit board production facility. The major goals of the project were to eliminate all industrial discharge to the sanitary sewer, to minimize hazardous waste generation, to process and then reuse excess water in the noncritical operations, and to develop a system to produce better hardware without adding additional risk to the environment. The system was installed in less than two years and in such a way so that it did not interrupt any manufacturing processes. The cost of the project was in excess of $5 million. The results have been spectacular from both an environmental and production standpoint. Hazardous and industrial waste has been reduced significantly. The discharge of wastewater from the plating lines was reduced from 100,000 gallons per day to zero. Although this project was undertaken to minimize the generation of hazardous waste, we discovered an excellent by-product: a significant savings in reduced scrap and rework.

The environmental management group also embarked on a full-scale effort to minimize other hazardous waste created from various operational and production processes at each facility in Florida. Although we did not know at the onset how we could technically achieve our goal, we set a goal to reduce the amount of waste manifested from our three Florida operations to under 400 tons annually by 1991. (We were generating ten times that amount in 1984 and, left alone, expected it to grow to 6,000 tons, or fifteen times that amount by 1991.) By 1987 the bill for disposing of this waste was more than $1.1 million a year. That same tonnage today would incur an annual disposal cost in excess of $4 million, not to mention the increased threat to the environment. It became apparent that our aim to assert a responsible environmental posture could not reconcile such an increase in waste generation.

Since the onset of the waste minimization program, in 1987, the recurring process hazardous waste has been reduced to less than 900 tons to date. This reduction was achieved as a direct result of several significant waste minimization projects. The zero discharge plant at our printed circuit board facility was one. And there were others (table 8.1):

1. *A closed-loop wastewater reduction system in Orlando.* This system allows for expansion of the Orlando metal finishing operations while greatly reducing the discharge of industrial waste. Industrial wastewater has been reduced from more than 180,000 gallons per day to fewer than 5,000 gallons per day of nonmetal contact water. In addition, hazardous sludge has been reduced from 115 tons per year to 7 tons per year.

2. *A hazardous waste liquid incinerator.* This project, scheduled to be operational in 1991, will be located on-site at one of our Florida facilities and will provide a means by which all liquid solvents and flammables can be dispositioned.

3. *A corrosive neutralization process.* Operational in 1987, this process uses chemical adjust agents to lower the pH of certain corrosive waste streams. Once neutralized, the corrosives are reclassified as nonhazardous waste and are no longer a threat to the environment.

4. *Reduction of solid flammable wastes.* These are wastes used in our factory with various solvent cleaners. By recycling these wastes, we achieve a 50 percent reduction in the disposal volume.

5. *Marclean development.* In response to the growing concern for the ozone layer, the MM laboratories located outside Baltimore, Maryland, have created a nonhazardous solvent cleaner capable of replacing the TCA (1,1,1–trichloroethylene) and Freon-based cleaners currently in use. Called Marclean, it is being tested on high-tech printed circuit boards as part of a pilot program to assist its overall effectiveness. The first application of Marclean as part of a production operation is expected in 1990.

6. *University research.* To address environmental technical challenges beyond our company's current capabilities, we have entered into a contractual arrangement with the University of Central Florida. With the university's College of Engineering environmental engineering department, MM is exploring solutions for a diverse array of other technical issues.

All of these efforts have set the stage for the realization of our overall annual waste minimization goal of fewer than 400 tons of hazardous waste by 1991.

Most companies are concerned with the cost of complying with stricter environmental codes. Our experience has shown that waste minimization technologies also provide a significant return on investment. Figure 8.1 shows the capital investment we have committed in order to live by our ethical code. Over the past four years, we have invested a little over $10 million.

In terms of disposal costs, the reduction of hazardous waste from the Florida operations will result in an annual cost avoidance of more than $8 million. Furthermore, many of these projects have yielded savings by permitting the latest manufacturing technology to be used on the factory floor. A large portion of this increase in productivity can be directly attributed to waste minimization efforts. The lower right-hand chart in figure 8.1 shows the payoff: by 1992, a return of over $30 million in savings for an investment of $10 million, and more savings

Table 8.1
Florida Operations Waste Minimization Projects

Project	Cost	Benefit
Zero discharge system	$5,500,000	No industrial wastewater better productivity
Closed-loop system	2,300,000	Reduced water use, better productivity
Incinerator	1,600,000	On-site disposal
Waste treatment plant improvements	300,000	Improved waste management
Waste minimization research	1,000,000	Nonhazardous cleaners
Total	$10,700,000	

Figure 8.1
Investments and Savings

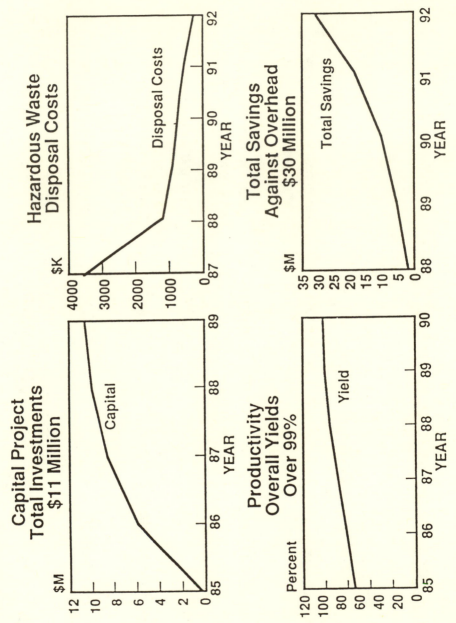

Capital Project
Total Investments
$11 Million

Hazardous Waste
Disposal Costs

Productivity
Overall Yields
Over 99%

Total Savings
Against Overhead
$30 Million

each year after. Although the pursuit of environmental compliance remains the driving force behind our thrust, we have reached the conclusion that waste minimization makes good business sense as well.

On our way to achieving our environmental goals, we have made inroads in other areas as well. A notable achievement was our effort to preserve the habitat of the red cockaded woodpecker. The woodpecker, an endangered species, was a resident on property that the company wished to develop as a testing range. In 1987 MM agreed to work with local government and the Sierra Club to develop a plan to manage and protect the habitat of the woodpecker. Today, under our watchful eye, the woodpecker population on our property has grown from twenty-two birds to over thirty-five. Jerome Jackson, a professor of ornithology at Mississippi State University and a world-renowned expert in the area of endangered species, visited our site in 1988 and reported that the red cockaded woodpecker was actually better off under MM's protection and environmental management than it had been before we got involved. Additional activities include our involvement in the state and local bodies governing the community right-to-know program and our extensive interaction with the environmental protection agency and the Florida Department of Environmental Regulation.

MM has developed a more than fully compliant and responsive environmental management program at the Florida operations. During the 1990s compliance and responsiveness to legal requirements alone will not be enough. We believe that the only ethical course is one that must go beyond the level of regulations and set its limits at the highest thresholds—eliminate hazardous waste generation wherever technically feasible and strive for technical breakthroughs.

It is our sincere conviction and experience that business, ethics and the environment are not mutually exclusive; by being sensitive to ethical and environmental issues and exposing all of our employees to the importance of those issues, the Florida operation is in fact a stronger, healthier, and more profitable business. Businesses such as ours, with all of our aerospace technology, resources, and know-how, can assume a more active leadership role in helping the government and our fellow citizens in managing the environment.

Industry is but one of the participants in the nation's environmental issue; the public at large will have to assume more responsibility for their share. It is industry and universities, though, that may have the opportunity to set the standard and blaze the trail. Industry has an obligation to make a strong commitment toward finding the technical solutions, solving today's environmental issues, and passing the solutions on to the world society to ensure a safe and healthy society.

9

The Chainsaws of Greed:
The Case of Pacific Lumber

LISA H. NEWTON

The bare facts of the Pacific Lumber Company chronicle are shortly told and widely known. Once there was a very traditional company, Pacific Lumber, based in its company town of Scotia in Humboldt County, California, home of the legendary 2,000-year old sequoia trees. It took care of its workers, conserved its giant redwood trees, turned a modest but steady profit, planned for the long term, and, in brief, made none of the mistakes that all the shortsighted lumber companies made. A California Newsreel documentary, *Mad River: Hard Times in Humboldt County,* made in 1982, excoriated the entire industry for its miscalculations of its market, its failures toward its workers, and its destruction of its trees—but mentioned Pacific Lumber as proof that good business and good citizenship could, with wise management, go hand in hand. Then came the villains, jetting in from Wall Street: the takeover artists, the sharks, Charles Hurwitz's Maxxam Inc, recently spun out of Federated, soon to be joined with MCO, who gobbled up the company's stock, bought off the management, threatened the workers' jobs and benefits, and immediately doubled the timber harvest to pay down the junk bond–financed debt. Over time pay fattened the workers' wallets but threatened long-term security; environmentalists were horrified; state and national legislatures contemplated action but took none; the courts, to whom all resorted almost immediately, tentatively fumbled through new territory, not supporting any side consistently.

Pacific Lumber crystallizes several of the most important ethical issues confronting American business, in particularly poignant and understandable form: the company is small, the trees are large and well loved, the loggers are folk heroes, the financiers are folk villains, and covering it all, the press and the senators are highly articulate commentators and critics of the whole affair, a

Greek chorus with power of subpoena. From the materials available to us chronicling this case, we recognize five familiar issues:

1. Is the traditional (paternalistic) American company worth preserving, as the traditional American family farm is held to be? Or is profit, return on investment to the shareholders, the only measure of good business practice?

2. Should hostile takeovers financed by junk bonds be outlawed in the light of the crime they invite and the injury they produce? Or are they just good business, working for the interests of the shareholders and the efficiency of the American economy?

3. What shall we do to save our national natural resources? Can we rely on business to protect them, or is state regulation essential for anything of value? If the interests of a single state are not served by conservation, does the country as a whole have a right to dictate such policies?

4. In the present structure of the judicial branch and the corporate sector, it is possible that resources might be irretrievably lost in the process of seeking legal means to protect them. Under the circumstances, are extreme and illegal tactics like those of Earth First! justified? How should a business deal with such tactics?

5. Who speaks for the worker? What courses are open to the employee in this confusion? To form a union? join with management to drive out the environmentalists? join with the environmentalists to drive out management? or try to buy the company themselves?

OLD FEZZIWIG VERSUS EBENEZER SCROOGE: HOW TO RUN A BUSINESS

No one denies that Pacific Lumber Company (PL) was an exemplar of all the virtues traditionally professed by American business. Founded a century ago, run from the turn of the century by one family, the firm undertook to protect equally the shareholders, the workers, and the natural environment and was doing very well at all of those tasks.

From the point of view of the shareholders, the firm had shown profits steadily since its founding and stood to show profits steadily into the future. Financial statements for the years through 1984 show small cyclical adjustments to demand but steady earnings on its outstanding shares.[1] Prudent management of its assets—189,000 acres of the redwood forests of Humboldt County, California, including the largest virgin redwood stands still in private hands—ensured that no more was cut each year than grew and avoided the boom-and-bust cycle endured by the rest of the lumber industry.

From the point of view of the workers, that policy worked out to steady employment, but PL was famous for employment policies that went far beyond the certainty of a job. The town of Scotia, in the center of the lumbering area, was one of the last of the company towns, wholly built and owned by PL. The houses were rented to the workers at rents that were low even for that area, and in hard times the company forgot to collect the rent. No one ever got laid off or faced retirement or medical emergency without funds to cover them. A worker's children were assured jobs with the company, if that is what they wanted, or a full scholarship to college. Company loyalty came easy, and no union ever got a foothold in PL. "They always treated everyone so well, why rock the boat?" explained a former employee. "You knew you'd retire from there, and if your kids wanted to work there, they would. . . . People cared for the company and wanted to see it prosper."[2] We hear the echoes of Old Fezziwig, Ebenezer Scrooge's first employer in Charles Dickens's *A Christmas Carol,* who ran a business as a service for customers, employees, and the community at large. People came before profits in this operation.

Those employment policies can be examined from perspectives other than that of the workers. From the point of view of the shareholders, the money paid out to meet the needs of the workers was money that could have been paid to the owners in dividends. On the other hand, in a shareholder-oriented climate, the workers would have joined a union, and paying union wages and union-obtained medical and other benefits might have been considerably more expensive. From the point of view of the society at large, PL was a real bargain. When a worker is laid off, the company saves his or her wage, but the society has to pay unemployment. When a worker is too old or sick to work, if the company does not pay, the taxpayers do. Paternalism, the bygone policy of placing the company in loco parentis for workers, at least where the satisfaction of their material needs was concerned, simply allocated a portion of all social welfare costs to the last company that employed the recipient of that welfare. Is that the proper role of the corporation? Is that an efficient way of allocating social costs? It may be from the point of overall efficiency that there is little to choose from between the paternalistic policy that picks up the costs for the worker and the new "lean-and-mean" company policy that lets the taxpayer pick up the tab. Some observations on the point, however, may be in order. First, the company is closer to the workers and their situation than are the taxpayers and is better able to meet real need and monitor for fraud. Second, union officials have to be paid, and government agencies have to be paid a great deal. Where companies administer these funds directly, there is no need to pay the middlemen, and those unproductive jobs in the bureaucracy are not added to the economy.

From the point of view of the environment, PL's record was excellent. Not only was selective cutting good for business in the long run, but it spared the hillsides the devastation wrought by clear-cutting. Since the 1930s, it has been known that cutting all the trees on a hillside leads to the immediate dispersal or destruction of the wildlife, the erosion of the soil to the point where new trees will grow poorly or not at all, the consequent silting of the streams and the destruction of the fish, and, from the increasingly rapid runoff of the rain into the silted streams, the undermining of the downstream forests. The environmental deterioration proceeds quite without limit, and in the very steep and rainy forests of the Pacific Northwest, it proceeds quickly. Most lumber companies in the area, in the rush to capitalize on the sudden demand for lumber for housing after World War II, had moved to clear-cutting as a more efficient way to get lumber out of the forest quickly and had severely degraded their lands. PL had not done this. It stood as a demonstration that prudent business practices equal sound labor relations and sound environmental practices. Beyond sound conservationist cutting policy, PL had contributed substantially to the state park system. Pursuant to an agreement with the Save-the-Redwoods League in 1928, PL set aside many of its most scenic groves for purchase by the state of California for inclusion in the Humboldt Redwoods State Park. When the money was slow collecting, PL "held on to the land it had agreed to preserve, patiently paying taxes on it, letting people use it as if it were already a part of the park," until the money finally came through and the acquisition was complete—in the case of the last parcel, forty years after the original agreement.[3]

From the point of view of the usual list of stakeholders in the operations of any corporation, PL exemplified that "excellence," of which we made so much in the early 1980s, when the new breed of management consultants started writing their best-sellers.[4] Should management be working for "excellence"? The new greed has driven anything approaching that description off the bottom line in fashionable circles. Scrooge's singleminded approach to business was not new in Dickens's time. Since Adam Smith, those who stand to profit from massive financial transactions have argued that capital is "most efficiently put to use" in that employment where it yields its highest monetary return in the shortest possible time and that therefore the general welfare is best served by leaving financiers free to seek such a return.[5] Even the notion of the stakeholder is disagreeable to Scrooge's children, the defenders of the new business orientation. John Boland, writing in the *Wall Street Journal* in February 1988, complained that shareholders have a right to protest the "diminished status" of "stakeholders" assigned to them by the community-oriented managers of the companies whose shares they hold: "the only direct, clear legal obligation of corporate fiduciaries (beyond obeying civil law and contractual constraints in general) is to corporate owners who pay them."[6] If return to shareholders can be significantly increased by management practices that are not to the advantage of the workers, the community, or the natural environment, are the corporate fiduciaries—the officers of the corporation—obliged to adopt them?

Such a question is ordinarily academic. A company that has undertaken to consider the welfare of workers, community, forests, and future in all its decisions for a century and more will not suddenly change to suit the new imperatives from the business right. But in the Reagan-era climate of hands-off regulatory policies, there arose another way to direct cash into the shareholders' pockets: the hostile takeover. In a takeover, a raider with truly astonishing amounts of cash, most of it borrowed at very high interest from investment banks that specialize in this sort of transaction, offers to buy up the stock of a corporation (the target) at a level well above the market price. The shareholders of the moment get a much better price for their stock, should they tender it for sale, than they might have expected. Where the stock is held by institutional funds (and most outstanding stock is), the fund manager is under a fiduciary obligation to the fund's owners to get that price and to tender the stock. Loyalty to the company whose shares are in question is nowhere on the manager's possible list of obligations. Having obtained a majority of the stock with rather little effort, the raider takes control of the company and then pays down the debt with the assets of the target. Once in control, he can do anything else he likes with the assets. The attractiveness of that control, especially where the assets are large and surely profitable, may tempt the raider to marginally legitimate means in pursuit of his ends. Such were the allegations in PL's case.

SHADY DEALS IN THE CANYONS: MICHAEL MILKEN AND THE SHARKS

In 1985 PL was debt free, cash rich (including a workers' pension fund overfunded by $50–60 million), resource rich beyond the knowledge of the board of directors (it had been thirty years since the last timber cruise, or inventory of its timber resources), and complacent in the knowledge that its practices were sound and well accepted by the community. But merger mania was in full swing, and Michael Milken was riding high at Drexel Burnham Lambert. On October 2, 1985, backed by Milken's junk bonds—the high-risk, high-yield notes that were Milken's specialty—the New York–based Maxxam Group, led by Charles Hurwitz, an investor from Houston, Texas, made a tender offer of $38.50 per share for the company, almost $10 more than the current market price of $29. PL's board of directors, led by chief executive officer (CEO) Gene Elam, stunned by the attack, rejected the offer as not only "inadequate" but "unconscionable." Two weeks later, they accepted a Maxxam offer just 4 percent higher than the first, at $40 per share. Many analysts were surprised by the acceptance; they had reckoned the company as worth far more than that, and indeed the entire increase from the first offer was funded, with change left over, from the pension plan. What had happened? Speculation turns on the following questions:

1. How was the board of directors taken by surprise? Were the infamous arbitragers Ivan Boesky and Boyd Jeffries involved with a scheme to "park" stock in friendly parking lots while the motives of all concerned were concealed from those who were charged with protecting the company? (Why, just as the deal got under way, did Jeffries sell about 439,000 shares of PL stock to Maxxam at $29.10 per share, when the market was closing at about $33 per share?)

2. What kind of advice did they get? They hired Salomon Brothers to advise them on a curious arrangement whereby Salomon would receive $2.25 million to keep PL independent but almost twice that if PL was sold at any bid higher than the $38.50 per share then offered. Maxxam was clearly willing to go higher. What incentive did Salomon Brothers have to oppose them?[7]

3. The major new provision in Maxxam's final offer of $40 per share included agreement to indemnify the board of directors against shareholder lawsuits and to fund severance packages of up to two years' pay for thirty-four middle managers and "key people."

When President Elam quietly left the company in June 1986, he took with him $400,000 in such severence. Were all those people really thinking about the interests of the company when they hastily agreed to a friendly merger?[8]

Lawsuit after lawsuit challenged the takeover: from Stanwood (Woody) Murphy, grandson of the last CEO, and his brother and sister, contending that the supermajority required by the company charter (80 percent of shares) had not been obtained; from shareholders, contending that the board had been negligent in failing to inform itself of the true value of the company and had sold out much too cheaply; from other shareholders, contending that Article 10 of the company charter required that the board take into account the social, environmental, and economic effects on the employees and the communities before accepting any merger agreement and that no such determination had been made. The Northcoast Environmental Center petitioned the Securities and Exchange Commission (SEC) to submit an environmental impact statement since the terms of the merger were such that, if approved, it would inevitably lead to vastly accelerated logging practices and thus would have a major impact on the environment. But the legal climate is as chilly to traditional companies as the canyons of Wall Street. By the end of February 1986, most of the claims had been rejected, and the way was open for the merger to be completed.[9] (One remains open, and when the SEC investigation of Drexel Burnham Lambert advanced to consider the PL case, another was instituted, brought again by dissident shareholders. If they are successful, the acquisition will be declared illegal, and the ownership of the company will have to be renegotiated.)

How does a financier run a lumber company? Everyone knew, by the time the last suit was settled, that Hurwitz would abandon the old careful schedule of cutting in order to raise cash. Of the $840 million he had spent for the company, $770 million was debt, $575 million of it financed through Milken's junk bonds. That debt had to be paid, with predictable results for the workers and for the environment. It is doubtful that even the board of directors foresaw the financial transformations that were to follow. Hurwitz first terminated the employees' pension plan. Of the $90 million in assets in the plan at the time of the takeover, Maxxam took $50 million for the debt and spent the remainder to buy annuities for the 2,861 plan participants. In a move that alarmed some of the executives covered by the plan, Hurwitz chose to buy those policies from the Executive Life Insurance Company of Los Angeles, which has, according to *New York Times* writer Robert Lindsey, "provided annuities to employees at several companies taken over with Drexel Burnham financing. According to investigators, that insurance company was chosen for the annuities contract despite missing a bidding deadline." The executives were alarmed because "a large proportion of its assets are in high-risk securities, among them a significant share of the bonds issued for Maxxam's takeover of Pacific Lumber."[10]

Sometimes a page of history is worth a volume of logic. Anyone who chose to investigate would have found that Hurwitz had an established career in controversial financial deals. "Indeed," chuckled *Barron's* in a review of the PL deals, "his career has been a bonanza for the legal fraternity: Everything he touches seems to turn to litigation."[11] Throughout the 1970s, his holding company, SMR Holding Corp., had been involved with questionable and sometimes disastrous deals, and he had had to defend himself from charges of improper practice and civil fraud brought by the SEC, New York State, and the Texas Securities Board.[12] In the course of his acquisitions, he had picked up Federated Development, whose financial resources he employed to take over McCulloch Oil Co., which he restructured into MCO Holdings in order to buy United Financial Group and take over Simplicity Pattern, whose cash he raided for his next ventures. Through many of these dealings, Drexel Burnham Lambert had been the underwriter, making cash available for these extensive, and very profitable, transactions. From January 1985 through the summer of 1987, Hurwitz paid Drexel "more than $48 million in fees, expenses and commissions, some $46 million of that through Maxxam."[13] Bear, Stearns also figured in Hurwitz's financial history, managing a discretionary account with $44.6 million of Maxxam's money and acting as broker for its other accounts. In fact, Bear, Stearns and Hurwitz had been partners in a run at Alamito Company in March 1986.

There were complaints when Hurwitz announced, late in the summer of 1986, that he intended to merge MCO holdings and Maxxam into one company, "in the best interests of both companies," and called in both Drexel and Bear, Stearns to help with the deal. There was, indeed, an immediate shareholder protest, arguing that the shares of Maxxam, supported by the enormous cash and resource holdings of Pacific Lumber, were worth between twice and three times what MCO was "offering" for them. It seemed to the angry shareholders that the merger was simply a device for funneling all that wealth into a shell holding company where Hurwitz could get at it more conveniently. Delaware law required that the "negotiations" for purchase be carried on by two "independent committees" of the two organizations, advised by separate investment banking firms. Such committees were formed of the only members of the boards of directors of MCO and Maxxam not on the other board or with other connections to Hurwitz, and Drexel Burnham Lambert and Bear, Stearns were retained to determine whether the deal was "fair" to all. With Hurwitz the largest shareholder of both firms and his long-term business associates advising on both sides of the table, fairness was rapidly determined all around. When, in the middle of all the dealings, Drexel (representing MCO) leaped across the table to help sell off a few pieces of Maxxam's PL holdings for about 50 percent more than their accepted evaluation, the appearance of conflict of interest—not to mention sheer double-dealing on the part of all parties—became overwhelming.[14] Despite legal protests, the merger went through, with disastrous effect on the Standard and Poor rating for Maxxam's takeover bonds.

Legal delays do not appreciably slow business operations. Hurwitz explained to his public that the cash generated from the accelerated harvest was to be used to pay down PL's debt. But tremendous amounts of cash can be generated from an established company with uncounted timber resources, and the new finance avoids such tedious uses as payment of debt when new opportunities present themselves. By early 1988, Hurwitz was on the move again, this time against KaiserTech (formerly Kaiser Aluminum), paying $224 million for a large portion of their stock. At least half that will be paid in cash, apparently (despite denials) straight from the coffers of Maxxam's biggest moneymaker, Pacific Lumber. If the shareholders' suits are successful, that cash would be taken away from Hurwitz but not if he spends it first. Plaintiffs in the suits were predictably outraged, but it is not clear what legal action is possible to block the payments.

WHO SPEAKS FOR THE TREES? THE LOGGER AND THE STATE

The law has already figured largely in this case as the vehicle for private parties to express, and attempt to validate, their conviction that their rights have been violated. There is another place for the law: not as instrument of the remedial rights of offended private parties but as creator of primary rights for the society as a whole, to protect what we value as our common inheritance and to provide for the common good in the future. Presumably our elected representatives are the authorized determiners of that public interest and ultimate protectors of the resources of the nation. Presumably when we are dealing with unique and irreplaceable resources like stands of 2,000-year-old redwoods, we might expect that the public authorities will determine what policy for those redwoods best serves the public, and private profit-oriented enterprises will operate within the guidelines set down in accordance with that policy.

That expectation is not generally fulfilled in a country dedicated to free enterprise. On the contrary, the presumption has been that anything that can be privately owned, like land, will be privately owned and that whatever owners have traditionally been permitted to do with their land (cut down trees and sell the lumber), the owners shall be permitted to do. The burden is on the public to prove that private control of the uses of land is so contrary to the public safety that the situation cries out for regulation and public control. On the question, Who speaks for the trees? the lumber industry has answered with a single voice that it does and that it needs no public regulation and environmentalist criticism to teach it how to protect its resources.

This voice has been heard in the lumber industry's publications from the origins of the industry and especially since 1970, when the nascent environmental movement descended on logging operations with renewed energy. When Maxxam took over PL, with obvious plans to go after the older stands of timber protected by the old owners, the debate over the need for state protection of the lumber took on new urgency. An ecologist with the Northcoast Environmental Center, Andy Alm, summarized the areas of danger from the new practices: depletion of the timber supply, erosion of the watershed areas, increased sediment loads on area streams (endangering the fish, all species that depend on the fish, and all species that depend on the streams), and the possible extinction of many endangered wildlife species such as the spotted owl.[15] A cautious scientist, Alm conceded that at that point the projected impact on the environment "is speculative." More assertive was Earth First!s Greg King, who advocates the complete cessation of harvest of old-growth timber. The spokespersons for PL predictably presented views in opposition to the environmentalists: statements from a consulting firm hired by Maxxam reassured that PL "could easily continue to harvest its timber at the current doubled rate for the next 20 years" and that "PL is just helping to fill in the gap left by the other companies whose capacity in production was reached shortly after World War II." The county should be happy, the consultant concluded ominously, that a company like PL was "there to fill the gaps when other companies are not only dropping off production but laying off workers."[16] David Galitz, the company's manager of public affairs, was similarly reassuring, concluding on the familiar note: "We're here to protect the land. Our resource is that land and we know it. The trees are a crop, and they keep coming back. If you want to meet a group of environmentalists, come within the Pacific Lumber Company. . . . I think we practice more environmental protection methods and have more concern for the environment than the Greg Kings of this world."[17]

The dispute inspires reflection, to be conducted in three questions:

1. Where, if anywhere, does private enterprise get the right to speak for the trees? Aren't they naturally suspect in such a case?
2. If the trees are to be guarded for the sake of the people, where do the people stand on the issue? And if the people are divided, do those on the spot have more right to vote than the others?
3. Given that the California Department of Forestry is supposed to be appointed especially to speak for the trees, what is its position on the issue, and why don't we just listen to it?

Private Enterprise

Private enterprise's claim derives from the ancient truth of Galitz's statement: "Our resource is that land and we know it. The trees are a crop, and they keep coming back." We come from a long line of farmers and herdsmen—about 800 generations probably. Only since the last century—three or four generations—has it become possible for any but a tiny percentage of us to live any other way. The imperatives of the farmer and herdsman are abundantly plain: conserve the land, the flock, the ability of the farm to produce more in future, or die. Owners and caretakers of property in land or livestock had interests in common, closely tied to obedience to those imperatives. Cultures that disobeyed the imperatives died out; cultures that obeyed them well flourished and produced us, who carry the same commands by now in all our understanding of our cultural inheritance. For the best of economic reasons, then, in that inheritance, property owners have properly been trusted with the care and preservation of their property, and barring a few municipal regulations to preserve residential peace and quiet, the legal system has incorporated few restrictions on how they may use that property.

But ancient truth does not mean present workability. The business community took note of the "separation of ownership and control" of the modern corporation earlier in this century, largely to call attention to the troubling fact that those who run the corporation (management) may, on occasion, reprehensibly deviate from the desires of the proper owners (shareholders). Of more interest to the environment, specifically to the owned land and livestock, is the fact that, once separated from control and daily management, the owners may have no interest at all in the care of the property, which will be consigned to hired stewards. Such stewardship itself has a long tradition and becomes problematic only when the steward is given responsibility not for land, stock, factory, or corporation but for a sum of money, or fund, that owns property only to use it to make more money. This is the position of the institutional funds, whose stewards must, on pain of breach of fiduciary responsibility, tender shares to raiders on evidence that they are likely to see no higher price. When the raider has no interest in the property except to drain it of cash for his next ventures, his own future welfare disappears from the imperatives above, and the property is no longer safe in its owner's hands. Ought we to take it away from him? Do we have the legal structure to do so? We know that under the doctrine of eminent domain, we can seize the redwoods for a new park; but can we seize all that land just to continue a more conservative commercial logging operation? Or is that choice necessarily owners' option, a case of "different management philosophies and needs which need to be addressed," as David Galitz put it?[18]

The People

What do the people want? Most of the people in the area are PL employees. Almost by definition, they want their jobs, and they want wages as high as possible. The rest of the people are the shopkeepers, craftsmen, and service personnel who take care of the employees and the towns in which the employees live. Their interests are as intimately tied to the company as those of the loggers. We may ask how the people affected by these policies see the issue.

One indication of the will of the people turned up in May 1987 in the California State legislature in Sacramento. State Senator Barry Keene had submitted a bill (SB1641) that would "limit sudden increases of timber harvesting and clearcutting brought on by potential change of ownership of logging companies."[19] No one who favored or opposed the bill had any doubts about whose ownership was being discussed. PL's executive vice-president was one of those who spoke against it, predicting a "whole new round of timber industry layoffs" should the bill be adopted. It was not. It had some support, especially from environmentalist groups like the Sierra Club, but was voted down in committee.

Legislatures can be influenced by persistent popular effort. As is typical in such political exchanges, the corporations organized first. The sawmills, logging, and trucking companies got their representatives to the May 1987 meetings and defeated the Keene bill. The environmental groups, all volunteer, organized much more slowly. As summer turned to fall, these groups got an unexpected publicity boost from the congressional investigations into Maxxam's tangled financial history. By spring 1988, the country had begun to notice what was happening in Humboldt County. An article by Richard Lovett in the *Sacramento Bee* in February told the PL story to a statewide audience. "While the future of old-growth forests is very much in doubt, one thing is certain," Lovett concluded. "The Pacific Lumber takeover is a frightening cautionary tale—an example of how progressive business management can be replaced virtually overnight, with decades of conservationist practices likely to be erased in only a few years.[20] Alarm went nationwide with an article by Robert Lindsey, dramatically entitled "They Cut Redwoods Faster to Cut the Debt Faster," in the *New York Times* in March, citing not only the extensive environmental damage caused by the new logging policies but also the dubious financial maneuvers behind the takeover.[21] And in April, Earth First! staged public demonstrations on PL land, getting themselves headlines in California newspapers.

By May 1988, Byron Sher, chairman of the Assembly Natural Resources Committee for the California State Assembly, was able to launch a campaign to get PL to stop clear-cutting the remaining stands of virgin redwood. The demand seems minimal, yet even this would have been impossible without the negative publicity of the previous six months. Under those circumstances, he was able to muster enough clout, he thought, to enforce a reasonable agreement. An agreement was made on May 26, 1988, and proudly announced by Sher, Assemblyman Dan Hauser of Humboldt County, and PL: "Pacific Lumber has agreed to stop clearcutting its remaining stands of virgin redwood. . . . This is the practice it followed for decades and earned it a reputation as a model timber company in the eyes of many Californians."[22] Sher's office simultaneously released a hopeful statement on the agreement, as did PL's public relations office: "The agreement reflects the Company's sensitivity to concerns expressed by Assemblymen Sher and Hauser, as well as others, over the aesthetic effect of clear-cutting in virgin old growth redwood stands." The *New York Times* found the agreement sufficiently newsworthy to record—and recorded also the skepticism of local environmentalists and Woody Murphy: "If the wolf tells you that he no longer wants to eat chickens, who are you going to believe?" Indeed, with time, the volunteers go home and the paid agents return to the saw. By January 1989, Sher was sponsoring a new bill calling for the whole industry to stop clear-cutting older trees or face $50,000 fines for each incident. "Pacific Lumber has reneged on last year's agreement," said Sher. "They are moving as quickly as they can to destroy the old-growth characteristic of their virgin redwood holdings." In hindsight, he regretted the May 1988 agreement that had ended his pursuit of similar legislation.[23]

Letters to local newspapers during the period in which it was pending overwhelmingly opposed the bill. One letter, chilling in its naiveté, shows how much the new owners relied on the old for their early support. The writer argued:

Inasmuch as the cutting of trees is the timber companies' main source of revenue, surely Senator Keene does not think that they would purposely shorten their own existence by clear cutting their timber without a definite re-forestation plan in mind. As far as the Pacific Lumber Company is concerned, they would not have been so attractive an acquisition were it not for the fact that, through careful timber management, they have built a solid reputation spanning a hundred years or more for good business practices which include long range goals benefiting both themselves and their community. In conclusion, I feel that we need to have enough faith in the experts of the timber industry to allow them to continue to make the necessary, intelligent decision regarding the future of the logging in this area.

This was four months before Hurwitz's move to merge Maxxam and MCO, stripping the cash from PL to feed more takeover attempts, was made public. Another letter, from the owner of a local sawmill that purchased logs from PL, pointed out that his sawmill would be out of business if PL stopped cutting and that "there will be less jobs!" if the sales should stop: "Instead of kicking a good neighbor and generous community supporter, let's get behind Pacific Lumber and give them all the support we can." A third had

a few thoughts on the Barry Keene "Maxxam-shutdown" bill. . . . As we all know by looking at a map of California, a majority of the land is owned by some form of government, i.e. national parks or state parks. Now that Maxxam owns The Pacific Lumber Company "private land," Maxxam should be able to use it in the way the present guidelines are set up. They were good enough for everyone else, why not Maxxam? We don't need government harassment in Humboldt County! The county has been hurting enough these past few years. Is the Barry Keene bill another "land grab" by the government? By forcing Maxxam into bankruptcy, are they going to buy the land for yet another rotting park? I am really tired of government and their "screw up of everything they touch" record. My only consolation is that when Pacific Lumber closes down, my family and I can mooch off the government instead of paying taxes, and I'll have a lot of time to get involved in demonstrations to shut down other private industries.

This letter shows clearly the agenda that the environmentalists faced in their public education activities.

Simultaneously the Fortuna Town Council convened a special meeting, ostensibly to debate the Keene bill but actually (in the absence of any supporters) to denounce it and pass a resolution to that effect. The participants in the denouncing were not, significantly, employees of PL but residents of the town and officers of local trucking companies and sawmills. The entire area's dependence on the logging industry, and on the freedom of that industry to bring in cash, could not have been more emphatically underlined.[24]

What of all the other people in the country? Don't we have an interest in the redwoods? If the people of the area only want to speak for Maxxam, can't we speak for the trees? Whose are they anyway? Can't our ownership, as Americans, be taken into account somehow? How should it be balanced against the need in Humboldt County for jobs, security, a steady economic and political setting in which to raise children and carry on communities with a hundred years and more of settled existence? Their interests are more immediate, but there are a lot more of us. Do we have a way to allot votes in such situations? Do we even have a candidate for a way?

The Government

Recognizing some years ago that redwoods were special, California had passed legislation requiring the lumber companies to file timber harvest plans (THPs) with the state, and charged its Department of Forestry (CDF) with the task of reviewing these THPs for environmental soundness and compatibility with the long-term benefit of the industry and the state of California. This the department had done, without much controversy, for years, until the takeover of PL.

The CDF made an early appearance in the PL affair as participant in the debate between Greg King and David Galitz on the wisdom of trusting private enterprise with the care of the trees. The CDF's position might surprise those accustomed to chilly relations between industries and the state agencies appointed to regulate them: "To date, the department has found no significant impacts to the various biological or environmental resources as a result of The Pacific Lumber Company timber harvesting. Whether it be clearcutting or selection, this harvesting has been ongoing since the turn of the century. Hopefully, it will continue on indefinitely into the future. The actions of The Pacific Lumber Company are not expected to deter this prospect." So said Tom Osipowich, the forest practice officer with the CDF. One wonders why Maxxam felt it had to hire private consultants to present its case.[25]

When the new PL started submitting THPs, the issue revived. Shortly after the Keene bill failed in committee, the Environmental Protection Information Center, one of numerous environmental organizations active in this case, brought suit against PL and the CDF to oppose state approval of some of those THPs. In company with other environmental organizations, EPIC was worried not only about the amount of timber that would be taken but about the old-growth-dependent wildlife that would be displaced. "You have specific species of wildlife that are dependent upon old-growth stands," explained John Hummel, a wildlife biologist attached to the California Department of Fish and Game to a public meeting on the THPs. "If their habitat is taken away from them you're going to lose a significant number of the population of certain species."[26]

EPIC wanted to send its own experts into the forests to see if matters were as the company said they were and to see if damage to the environment would be as slight as the CDF said it would be. On that issue, Judge Frank Peterson of the superior court ruled in favor of the company: no independent experts traipsing through private property second-guessing the authorized foresters. On the larger issue of the methods the CDF used to reach its determinations, the judge was unsparing:

One can conclude that no cumulative impact study or findings were adequately made and no alternative to clear-cutting was considered. It appears that the CDF rubber-stamped the timber harvest plans as presented to them by Pacific Lumber Company and their foresters. It is to be noted, in their eagerness to approve two of these harvest plans (230 and 241), they approved them before they were completed. . . . As to the effect on wildlife, there was no evidence presented except the conclusion of the Foresters that there were no *concerned* or endangered species affected. Both the Water Quality personnel and Fish and Game relied on the information provided by the professional foresters hired by Pacific Lumber and the Department of Forestry. Fish and Game's position was, if the forester saw something that needed their attention, he or she would inform them. That is not compliance with the law. That is not only naive, it was a total failure to exercise any discretion by those agencies who by law are to make findings and recommendations upon which the director is to base and exercise reasonable discretion. . . . What is most distressing to the Court is the position of the Water Quality and Fish and Game personnel, that any suggestions by them would not be considered by Forestry, and in fact Forestry would consider it to be ill advised. . . . In this case it is apparent that California Department of Forestry, the State Board of Forestry, its resource manager and director, as the *lead agency* does not want Fish and Game or Water Quality to cause any problems or raise any issues which would deter their approval of any timber harvest plan. Again it must be emphasized, this is not following the law; it is not only an abuse of discretion, but an absolute failure to exercise discretion, which the law demands.[27]

The CDF was not a little miffed by the public scolding but promised reporters that the whole matter would be straightened out soon. "We'll just change the documentation of what we do so the judge will have less difficulty in understanding it," said staff forester Harold Slack.[28]

The story of the CDF is familiar, almost a paradigm for American politics. Underfunded and understaffed, the CDF cannot monitor the forests it is supposed to monitor even if it wanted to, which it does not. Given the leghold restraints on its operation, it cannot keep the bright, young idealists who periodically pass through its doors but settles for career government people who know that satisfaction in life depends on not rocking the boat. The boat is the huge and rich industry that they minister to, source of colleagues, support in the legislature, and jobs when they retire from government work. As long as the industry is kept happy, the only threat to their existence is turf infringement by other government agencies in the same line of work. The CDF, like any other typical regulatory agency, divides its time between pacifying its legislature (to avoid scandal), adjusting its delicate relationship with its industry (attempting to balance its eager cooperation with a show of control in the public interest), and fighting turf wars with other agencies.

Why did we ever expect anything better? When we set up task forces within a company to get a job done, we know enough to structure the incentives so that it will at least be to the interests of the task force members to do the job. But in the CDF, we have an agency (and again, not an unusual agency) whose employees are rewarded both in daily dealings and in long-term career prospects for not doing their job: for ignoring what they are supposed to know, for concealing what they are supposed to reveal, for handing over for destruction what they are supposed to protect, and in general, for serving as advocate not for the people but for the industry the people hired them to control. Is there a better way to get the people's business done?

No doubt political pressure can help. The agencies, after all, have to maintain at least the public appearance of right-doing. Judge Peterson's opinion effectively tarnished that appearance. The following months show signs of diligence. The following April, the State Department of Forestry for the first time turned down two THPs proposed by PL. Ross Johnson, a program manager for the department, admitted that their decision was due to pressure by environmentalists. "Because we've had so many lawsuits, we're being more thorough in our review of these timber harvest plans," he explained to a *Times-Standard* reporter. "I guess you could give credit to these environmental groups. If we keep getting beat up on, we'll continue to do a better job." PL continued to keep the pressure on from its side; it immediately appealed the ruling to the State Board of Forestry, to which the department reports, and the board saw things the company's way, overturning the department's decision and giving PL permission to carry through the original THPs. EPIC went back into court to sue yet again to force the state to do its job.[29]

The state-appointed and taxpayer-bankrolled agencies openly admit that only public exposure and humiliation brought about by pressure from private groups will make them do their jobs; for the rest, they serve the industry. Let them actually be frightened into conscientious action for a change, and their action can be overruled by a taxpayer-financed but politically sensitive board that is well aware of where the votes are on the next election day. And so, having paid for the board and for the agency to protect the trees, if we want to save the trees, we must sue as private citizens the very same public servants and pay the tab for the private litigation as well. There has to be a better method.

DO EARTH'S ENDS JUSTIFY EXTRALEGAL MEANS?
ENTER EARTH FIRST!

Who speaks for the trees? Once the lumber companies did. Legitimately the people can, but with no single voice. Authoritatively the California Department of Forestry can, but not well. Yet the trees need protection now, not in some rosy future when we will have responsible business practices and an enlightened people and dedicated public agencies. Each day that goes by means that responsibility, enlightenment, and dedication will arrive too late for yet more groves of redwoods. A grove of redwoods is not like other things a bulldozer might accidentally run over.

Ordinarily we will stop the bulldozer if you are in front of it. The reason we will stop it is complex. It is not just a matter of law, not just a matter of prudent use of resources, and certainly not just a matter of tender feelings for you. It is more a perception of the dignity of the unique in life, and some permanent injunction against destruction of that uniqueness, an injunction to be breached only prayerfully and in strict necessity. The point is worth examining further.

It is not just a matter of law. Law forbids me to chase you down the sidewalk with a bulldozer or ram through your house on your lot. But if you should place some construction on my property, blocking the legal and appropriate work of my bulldozer, I will knock it down with no qualms at all. The law provides no protection at all for your stuff on my property against my will and precious little formal protection for your body. What legal right you might have is easily removed by legal injunction, forbidding you to block my bulldozer with your body. Yet if you defy the injunction and show up in front of my bulldozer, I will stop. Why? Certainly not because human beings are irreplaceable or even endangered. On the contrary, we are replacing ourselves faster than the biosphere can adapt, and we run the danger of flooding the surface of the earth with bodies. No matter how many we run over, we can always grow more, and we could really do with fewer. Any cost-benefit analysis of the choice to stop or to keep going when you place your body in front of my bulldozer will yield an immediate solution: keep going.

I might decide to ignore the results of the cost-benefit analysis if I were particularly fond of you, of course. But what if I am not? Typically the people who plant themselves in front of bulldozers are not the type those bulldozer drivers would even like, let alone love. In the hardest case imaginable, that might be Charles Hurwitz in front of my bulldozer. Would I stop even for him? I probably would. The prohibition against placing the bulldozer in forward gear, opening the throttle, holding the steering levers in place until the human face disappears, first beneath the scoop, then beneath the treads, of the oncoming machine, goes beyond any feelings I may have. Where does it come from?

It seems to have something to do with respect for that which we cannot create, a totally unique center of life and spirit that, once gone, is gone forever. I can grow other human beings to replace you, but they will not be the same; no combination of individuals will ever add up to or duplicate you, do what you did or be what you were. This uncreatable uniqueness properly inspires in us reverence and respect and leads us to agonize over every deliberate taking of human life, no matter how justified by law and conduct (witness, for instance, the extreme reluctance of the states to bring back capital punishment and their even greater queasiness at applying it in an instant case).

By this criterion, an old grove of redwoods has all the bulldozer- or chainsaw-stopping rights of a human being. (I will adopt as correct the environmentalists' assumption that from the point of view of the environment, it is the ecosystem as a whole, not the individual tree, that is the viable unit, including all its soil mass, wildlife, water, air, and even its insects, as well as flowers, moss, and trees. By grove, I will understand a stand of trees of sufficient size to support itself indefinitely, barring interference from outside.) It is unique and uncreatable, certainly uncreatable by us. We can plant redwoods, but we cannot plant 1,000-year-old redwoods. We can plant trees, but we cannot restore the soil that has been washed away after the last clear-cutting, and therefore we cannot replace the floral ground cover, or bring back the animals that lived on that assortment of plants dependent on the shade and moisture of that grove. It is very difficult to create any ecosystem, let alone to recreate a particular ecosystem. I think it could be argued that it is by definition impossible to recreate one that has been slowly coming to be over a millennium. When we are dealing with groves of this complexity and antiquity, we do not need to ask for the solution to a cost-benefit analysis, although some interesting analyses of the cost of extinction of species have been presented. We need only note that the grove in front of the saw can in no way be created or recreated by us, that it deserves our respect, and that we have no right to destroy it.

Earth First! is not a polite, conservation-minded group. Its specialty is monkey-wrenching—tossing monkey wrenches into or otherwise fouling up any and all activities that destroy the environment. In addition to the usual suits and injunctions, the group's program includes burning billboards, pulling up developers' landmark stakes, and crippling bulldozers with substances like maple syrup.[20] The actions of Earth First! on PL property were restricted to sitting in trees, talking to loggers, and occasionally serenading the company with guitar-accompanied renditions of "Where Are We Gonna Work When the Trees Are Gone," led by folk singer Darryl Cherney. (Cherney was at that time a candidate for the state legislature.) Occasionally arrested and sued at least once by the company, Earth First! quietly settled the suit and volunteered for community service instead of jail.[31] But they are not always so nonviolent. In their efforts to prevent other logging operations, their activities have been known to include spiking roads to cripple the logging trucks and tree spiking (driving a twenty-penny nail into a tree). The nail is easily concealed, and the operation does not hurt a living tree, but it does render the tree useless for lumber because the nail chews up the blades of the saws. If the authorities are informed that a grove is spiked and tells the logging company about it, a prudent company would not log that grove until the spikes could be removed. If the spiking is sufficiently persistent, it may be impossible to log the grove.

Is this good environmentalist activity? "They are outlaws," says Jay Hair, president of the National Wildlife Federation, "They are terrorists; and they have no right being considered environmentalists." "A terrorist organization," echoes Michael Kerrick, supervisor of the Willamette National Forest in Oregon; Cecil Andrus, former secretary of the interior, calls them "a bunch of kooks."[32] It is hard to find supporters for these tactics in the ranks of the traditional conservationist organizations and even harder in the ranks of the government agencies charged with enforcing environmental regulation. But has anything else worked for individual groves or ecosystems? Sometimes we can get trade-offs—we agree not to press the matter on 15 or 20 acres of old-growth redwoods, and they will preserve some particularly desirable stretches in Alaska. But if it is a grove of trees more than a millennium old that is slated for destruction today and the lumber company is in the hands of a Wall Street financier who wants only cash now, and local councils and legislatures are dominated by sawmill owners and the like, and the CDF approved the THP even before it was drafted, what other than terrorist tactics will work to preserve it?

Perhaps the notion of a trade-off is not entirely appropriate to the situation of the irreplaceable grove. If we trade off a grove for another today, what shall we trade tomorrow? It is impossible to grow something of equal value to satisfy the appetite of the company. Only complete preservation will preserve the status quo ante, the balance that trades try to maintain. We do not, after all, always insist on trade-offs in all matters, even in the political system. We never tried to get the Ku Klux Klan to lynch fewer blacks or only rural blacks or blacks in the Deep South states. Sometimes we had to endure lynchings, but the notion of a legal and accepted compromise on the number of lynchings never came up. It may be that when we are dealing with fragile ecosystems, as when we are dealing with human beings, the rule of compromise, applicable elsewhere in environmental matters and in political matters generally, will have to be scrapped in favor of a rule of strict preservation, and no lobbying or legislative efforts should be spent in attempts to reach compromise solutions. If this is the move of the future for the environmentalist community, we will owe perhaps more of a debt than we are willing to acknowledge to Earth First!

Meanwhile, how should a legitimate business react to terrorist tactics? If PL by now does not seem to be legitimate, the question can be raised about any other company or industry. How should we react to pro-life threats to smash all windows in pharmacies that sell abortifacients? to vegetarian threats to poison cattle herds? to Muslim threats to firebomb bookstores? The usual counsel, and indeed, my counsel, under all other circumstances, is to take the strongest possible measures to arrest and disable the terrorists while conducting business as usual to show that terrorism is unavailing. Should that be our advice to Maxxam in its dealings with Earth First!?

TELL ME, WHICH SIDE ARE YOU ON? THE TRAGIC OPTIONS OF THE LOGGERS

While the well-oiled machines of finance whir on Wall Street and the salvoes fly between environmentalists and the industry, what is the worker to do? The communications identifiably from loggers and their families in the local newspapers reveal above all a sense of loss for the destruction of the company they knew and which they expected to take care of them until retirement and beyond. Above all, they want to preserve the life-style and security they had. They cannot do that. Beyond that loss, all other options lead to more loss.

Onward and Upward with Private Enterprise

They can side with the company and applaud the wasteful acceleration of the logging. After all, it leads to plenty of work now, including overtime, and that feeds the wallet enough to block out that empty feeling in the soul when the clear-cut hillside is finished and abandoned. Loggers prefer to drive pickup trucks; now the PL loggers drive new pickup trucks. It could be argued that the job, now so secure, will evaporate twenty years down the road, just as the jobs did at other companies, when the timber is gone. But twenty years is a long time; indeed, for a young father, raising four children between the ages of two and seven, twenty years is forever, or as long as you need, which is the same. In many respects, this is the most rational option for the logger, and certainly it was the one most taken. By June 1988, PL employees had even founded a proindustry, antienvironmentalist newsletter, "a cooperative effort to gather support against radical environmentalists that are attempting, and in some cases succeeding, in halting our attempt to make a living." The editors maintained that the publication was "not company supported," inviting cynicism. The first accomplishment claimed for the effort was a successful letter-writing campaign to the State Board of Forestry that brought about the approval of those THPs temporarily held up by the CDF.[33]

Save the Trees

The loggers can side with the environmentalists and try to get the trees, especially the old growth, preserved forever under some state umbrella. This course is not so immediately unlikely as it sounds. Most loggers genuinely love the woods and streams among which they live and enjoy outdoor recreation by choice. But it was never a real option for the PL loggers. First, there was the visceral hatred of the environmentalists: long haired, dirty, foul mouthed, middle class, and instinctively contemptuous of workers, to all appearances communists and drug abusers. These hippies repelled the loggers from the day they bumped into town in their Volkswagens. Even Stanwood Murphy, their natural ally, found them repulsive. "I agree with them that the accelerated harvesting is the wrong way to go at it," he told *L.A. Times* staff writer Ilana DeBare. "But Earth First! is a radical group, and a lot of that I just can't associate myself with. [They look like] a bunch of college kids with ponytails. . . . You've got to look like the people you're trying to convince."[34] Second, and more enduringly important, saving the trees meant instant unemployment and the necessity of leaving the area for a very uncertain future elsewhere. The loggers were never for one minute unaware of this. PL spokespeople never opened their mouths without reminding the workers that if the environmentalists had their way, there would be no jobs. To a young head of a family without any educational qualifications, forced relocation is equivalent to suicide; environmentalism had very few friends among the loggers.

Solidarity Forever

There had never been a union at PL. Was it worth a try after the takeover? One article, filed two weeks after the takeover was announced, reported that Local 3-98 of the International Woodworkers of America, AFL-CIO, was considering an organizing effort in response to a few requests from frightened workers. About all the union could do, its business agent conceded, was make sure that layoffs took place in an orderly manner, respecting seniority. Given the way the company had always been run, he foresaw a great deal of difficulty in convincing the workers of the need for a union: "The employees have to understand they can't deal with management as individuals anymore, particularly if they find themselves with an owner who lives thousands of miles away and doesn't know the lumber business. . . . They're going to have to deal with the company as a group with some power."[35]

Unions were established in America because men like Hurwitz took over industry from men like Stanwood Murphy. In the vast impersonality of the factory, reduced to an impersonal cog in an impersonal machine, laborers found support, identity, and confirmation of their own worth, as well as political and economic power, in the union. Is it too late for PL workers to go that route? I suspect it is. I found no follow-up to 3-98's "consideration" of their case.

The Dream of Ownership

By September 1988, the extent of the destruction of the timberlands was evident to everyone, and the workers had begun to talk about alternatives to unwavering support of present management. Could they take over the company? The Employee Stock Ownership Plan (ESOP) was a new idea for the workers, but organizer Patrick Shannon assured them it was feasible. The appeal was undeniable: to be the boss, to be the owner, to be in control of one's destiny. Woody Murphy immediately came out in favor of it but pointed out that with the large, and undiminishing, debt accumulated by Maxxam, there might not be enough money in the company any more to afford it. Hurwitz and William Leone, his chief executive officer, immediately published an ad in the *Eureka Times-Standard* insisting that the company was not for sale—but, Shannon pointed out, it had not been for sale when Hurwitz and Maxxam acquired it in 1985.

It is not actually an ESOP that is contemplated; such plans are usually initiated by management and never give the workers actual control. Shannon is urging a hostile takeover by workers, requiring that they raise hundreds of millions of dollars to buy up shares on the open market until they have a majority. Is this even remotely possible? Hurwitz did it in 1985. But he had access to Drexel Burnham Lambert, Boesky, Jeffries, Michael Milken, and all of the creative financing of which Wall Street is capable. Above all, he had the assets of Pacific Lumber—the corporate headquarters in California, now sold; a valuable welding company, now sold; the extensive virgin timberlands, now stripped or soon to be so; and all the goodwill in the world—to serve as equity for those loans. "Employees who want to pursue the dream of an ESOP takeover have every right to do so," editorialized the *Times-Standard* in October 1988. "Circumstances, however, suggest it's an impossible dream—one fraught with the potential for great disappointment and financial loss."[36]

CONCLUSION

Whatever facet of this case we have under consideration—the traditional company, with its rich inheritance of social responsibility and compassion for its workers and its land; the loggers, once secure in a relatively carefree existence; the community, once assured of a prosperous future; the financial institutions, once reliable custodians of conservative fiscal practices; or the giant redwoods themselves, which we always assumed would last forever—great disappointment and financial loss seem to be among the outcomes. At this point it is not clear whether criminal acts were involved in the takeover that opens the story, whether shameful betrayal is the correct characterization of the acts of the board of directors, whether the government agencies charged with regulating the timber industry are up to the job, whether the radical environmentalists are right in their employment of extreme measures, and whether, eventually, the workers will be able to and take control of their situation. In these and other unclarities, the case raises questions about the conduct of a business in every one of its areas of constituent relations and serves as a prism through which a multitude of issues may be seen in exemplar.

NOTES

1. In the third quarter of 1984, for instance, less than a year before the takeover, PL reported that its net earnings rose 50 percent over the previous year ($11,337,000, or 47 cents per share, compared to $7,547,000, or 31 cents per share, for the third quarter a year ago). Sources include annual reports from the years 1981 through 1984.

2. Ilana DeBare, "Old Redwoods, Traditions Felled in Race for Profits," *Los Angeles Times,* April 20, 1987.

3. The source for this statement is a brochure published by Pacific Lumber, n.d.

4. See Thomas J. Peters and Robert H. Waterman, Jr., *In Search of Excellence* (New York: Harper & Row, 1982); Terrence E. Deal and Allan A. Kennedy, *Corporate Cultures* (Reading, Mass.: Addison-Wesley, 1982); John Naisbitt and Patricia Aburdene, *Re-inventing the Corporation* (New York: Warner Books, 1985); Tom Peters and Nancy Austin, *A Passion for Excellence* (New York: Random House, 1985); Buck Rodgers, *The IBM Way* (New York: Harper & Row, 1986); Robert H. Waterman, Jr., *The Renewal Factor* (New York: Bantam Books, 1987).

5. The orthodox capitalist approach is possibly best captured by Milton Friedman in his oft-reprinted "The Social Responsibility of Business Is to Increase Its Profits," *New York Times Magazine,* September 13, 1970.

6. *Wall Street Journal,* February 10, 1988.

7. Testimony of William G. Bertain, attorney at law, attorney of record for the Murphy great-grandchildren in the suit to retain control of the company, before Congress, on October 5, 1987; investigation of Drexel Burnham Lambert's major customers.

8. "Pacific Accepts Maxxam Bid," *New York Times,* October 24, 1985; "PL Agrees to Buyout Deal: New York Firm's Offer of $40-a-Share Accepted," *Eureka Times-Standard,* October 23, 1985; "Money Talks," *Wall Street Journal,* November 13, 1985; "PL Chief Quits; Gets $400,000," *Eureka Times-Standard,* June 10, 1986.

9. "PL-Maxxam Merger Hit by Second Lawsuit," *Eureka Times-Standard,* November 1, 1985; "One PL Suit Dismissed, Another Filed Locally," *Eureka Times-Standard,* November 2, 1985; "Pacific Lumber Bid Is Studied," *New York Times,* November 8, 1985; "Ecology Interests Question PL Deal," *Eureka Times-Standard,* November 11, 1985; "Pacific-Maxxam Link Is Fought by a Family," *New York Times,* November 11, 1985; "Maxxam Gets 60% Of Pacific's Shares," *New York Times,* November 12, 1985; "Judge Clears Way for Merger of Maxxam, PL," *Eureka Times-Standard,* February 13, 1986; "Another Suit Filed to Block PL Takeover," *Eureka Times-Standard,* February 23, 1986.

10. Robert Lindsey, "They Cut Redwoods Faster to Cut the Debt Faster," *New York Times,* March 2, 1988. Attempts to secure PL comment on the allegations were unsuccessful; Mr. Hurwitz was "not available" for comment. The company lawyer, however, Howard Bressler, "said the company had complied 'meticulously' with all applicable laws in the merger" and that there was "nothing improper" about the handling of the pension plan.

11. Diana Henriques, "The Redwood Raider," *Barron's,* September 28, 1987, pp. 14ff.

12. Ibid., p. 14.

13. Ibid., p. 34.

14. Ibid., p. 34.

15. Enoch Ibarra, "Pacific Lumber Timber Harvest Causes Concern," *Fortuna* (California) *Humboldt Beacon,* January 27, 1987.

16. Ibid.

17. Ibid.

18. Ibid.

19. *Eureka Times-Standard,* May 5, 1987.

20. Richard A. Lovett, "The Real Costs—to All of Us—of a Corporate Buyout," *Sacramento Bee,* February 21, 1988.

21. Lindsey, "They Cut Redwoods Faster."

22. Statement on Pacific Lumber Old-Growth Agreement, Governor's Press Conference Room, State Capitol, Sacramento, May 26, 1988.

23. See also "Company Eases Its Policy on Logging of Redwoods," *New York Times,* May 27, 1988; PALCO news release, Pacific Lumber Company, May 26, 1988; "Bill to Stop Clearcutting in the Works," *San Francisco Chronicle,* January 28 1989; "Bill Would Restrict PL Clearcutting of Virgin Redwoods," *Eureka Times-Standard,* January 31, 1989.

24. Letters to *Eureka Times-Standard,* May 5, 13, June 4, 1987. "Timber Bill Opposed," *Eureka Times-Standard,* May 2, 1987.

25. Ibarra, "Pacific Lumber Timber Harvest Causes Concern."

26. Greg King, "Fish and Game Says Pacific Lumber/CDF Eliminating Wildlife," *Humboldt News Service,* May 11, 1987.

27. Superior Court of the State of California for the County of Humboldt, case 79879, Ruling on Petition for Writ of Mandamus, November 5, 1987.

28. "Judge Sides with PL and CDF," *Eureka Times-Standard,* July 10, 1987; "Suit against Pacific Lumber to Be Fought on PL Terms," *North Coast News,* July 16, 1987; "CDF Won't Appeal Ruling," *Eureka Times-Standard,* November 13, 1987; "CDF Upset by Court's Decision," *Eureka Times-Standard,* November 15, 1987.

29. "Pacific Lumber Harvest Denied," *San Francisco Chronicle,* April 21, 1988; "P-L Plans for Cutting Old Growth under Fire," *Eureka Times-Standard,* April 22, 1988; "PL Temporarily Blocked from Harvesting Old-Growth Again," *Eureka Times-Standard,* April 28, 1988; "Protecting Redwoods," *Los Angeles Times,* April 26, 1988; "PL Appeals Ruling on Timber Harvests to Forestry Board," *Eureka Times-Standard,* May 6, 1988; "Judge Lifts Restraining Order; PL Allowed to Log Old Growth," *Eureka Times-Standard,* June 3, 1988; "Environmentalists File New Suit over PL Logging Plans," *Eureka Times-Standard,* June 16, 1988.

30. David Foreman, *Ecodefense: A Field Guide to Monkeywrenching,* cited by Jamie Malanowski, "Monkey-Wrenching Around," *Nation,* May 2, 1987.

31. *Eureka Times-Standard,* April 8, 14, May 1, 1988; publications from Darryl Cherney for Congress.

32. Malanowski, "Monkey-Wrenching," p. 569.

33. Save the Employees Newsletter, June 13, 1988.

34. DeBare, "Old Redwoods."

35. Lewis Clevenger, "Local Union Considers Trying to Organize at Pacific Lumber," *Eureka Times-Standard,* November 8, 1985.

36. *Eureka Times-Standard,* October 11, 1988.

___ 10 ___

The *Exxon Valdez* Crisis

JOAN WHITMAN HOFF

On March 24, 1989, Captain Joseph Hazelwood, allegedly drunk, steered the *Exxon Valdez,* a 987-foot ship carrying 50 million gallons of oil, onto an incorrect course and went below deck. The *Valdez* missed a deepwater dogleg in the shipping lanes and went into shallow water. At 12:05 A.M. the ship wrecked when snagged on a pinnacle approximately 50 feet below the surface. The crew tried to correct the course but failed. The impaled ship fishtailed around the rock fulcrum and grinded to a halt as the stern rode up onto a submerged shelf on Bligh Reef. By March 25 the spill had spread to nearly 50 square miles: 7 miles long and 7 wide. At least eight of the ship's fourteen tanks were punctured. It was estimated that 1 million barrels of oil—42 million gallons—remained on board. By March 26 the slick had spread to 100 square miles. At that time Exxon had recovered only 3,000 of the 240,000 barrels spilled. By March 27 overnight winds raged up to 73 miles per hour, smearing oil 30 miles out into the sound. By March 28, the slick was estimated at 500 square miles. As of May 1989 the slick had covered more than 2,500 square miles.[1]

Attempts to clean up the oil spill were slow coming. Exxon blamed Alaska, and Alaska blamed Exxon for its lack of quick action. The Alyeska Pipeline Service Company's oil spill emergency contingency plan, required by the state of Alaska, claimed to be able to contain any spill within 50 miles in 12 hours. It is believed that had quick action been taken, the spill could have been contained, but the slow start and subsequent weather conditions created conditions that added to the volume of the spill. The consequence was a badly damaged environment (Prince William Sound) and dead wildlife. The effects will have an impact for an undetermined amount of time.

Boycotts have been enacted against Exxon for its lack of promptness in containing the oil spill, for the alleged drunken skipper of the ship, for hesitating to pay the transportation bill for the booms, and for the mere surface cleanup, which residents claim is inadequate for a healthy environment. Exxon has also reacted. During the week of October 22 it filed suit against the state of Alaska. As the legal ramifications are yet to be determined, Prince William Sound, the community, and the people are lamenting their fate. One can only wonder if the area will be the same again.

Peter French discusses in chapter 1 the moral status of such an event as the tragedy at Prince William Sound. French refers to Celtic mythology and inquires about the nature and status of the defender of the land. He discounts the reliability of the individual as defender of the land since, he claims, the individual becomes "grossly sentimental" in feeling the need to protect the environment and gets frustrated in the futile attempt of doing as an individual that which must be done by a collectivity. According to French, this "atomistic individualist" approach is nonsense because it is impossible to know what future generations might need and desire (hence discounting arguments in support of moral responsibility for the environment because one must consider future generations). Besides, people live and act in collectivities. It is corporations (all kinds of collectivities) that can act morally and guard the sacred land to protect it from becoming a wasteland. It is corporations, therefore, on whom people must rely for environmental protection and not individuals, especially not for reasons concerning future generations.

French claims "that only those persons who stand in a responsibility relationship can ascribe responsibility to each other." For example, according to French, one is not responsible to sea otters but to others for the protection of the sea otters. Also, while one might be responsible for one's immediate family, one is not responsible for generations that might exist in the "remote future." Similarly one's actions toward such things as flora and fauna are "matters of charity, not obligation." His argument focuses on who the gatekeeper is for the environment as opposed to who is responsible in the *Exxon Valdez* spill, and it seem that his conclusion is that corporations, which have corporate internal decision structures, can act morally and these actions are "redescriptions of the actions of humans." As French argues here and elsewhere, corporations are moral agents; although they do not have the sentient qualities of humans, they are moral persons just the same. In fact, they can do things such as "join cartels, manufacture automobiles, enter bankruptcy, set the price of goods and services . . . [and] have rights and duties in law . . . carry on non-legal relationships with other corporations and with human persons . . . are historical entities with births, lives, and deaths."

I agree with French that corporations are moral entities although not with the claim that they are the same type of moral entities as humans. However, I will not focus on the rebuttal of that claim here. Rather I focus on some reasons that sometimes it is essential for humans to act morally, independent of a community of people. I shall address some particular claims French makes concerning the individual person, future generations, and community.

I cannot deny that there may be some sentimentalism felt by atomistic individualists who want to guard the environment and "all creatures great and small." Most certainly, attempting to protect the land by oneself often seems futile, leaving one frustrated. However, the attempt of the individual to act morally toward others or toward one's environment is fundamental to moral corporate activity. The corporation may have an internal decision structure, but this rests on individuals within the corporation. For example, Exxon's moral integrity rests on the integrity of the "members" of Exxon, such as Joseph Hazelwood. The corporation's lack of "humanhood" leaves the corporation unable to process ideas and act morally in the same way humans do. Perhaps more important, the corporation does not have any emotions, and while emotions do not necessarily serve as the foundation for ethical behavior, they can. For example, one often acts morally toward one's children out of caring. Literature suggests that if caring is not present, the health of the child may suffer. Similarly, it is my contention that caring for one's environment—because it has a certain integrity, because it is one's own, or because it belongs to others in a community—often helps one to make difficult ethical decisions about the environment. This is not to say that one must be emotional in order to act morally. People are both rational and emotional. While the parts can be analyzed somewhat individually, the human being is a whole. The parts are interactive. Literature suggests that this may also be true of other animals too. Without developing an argument in support of such a "caring morality" here, it at least seems important not to dismiss the sentimentality of the atomistic individual or the individual's attempts at securing a safe and healthy environment for today or the future. For example, one must consider what will be the future of Valdez without caring individuals.

In terms of future generations, the caring consideration can also be applied, although there is another dimension that should be considered as well. While one may be quite removed from one's future relatives—one's great, great, great, great, great grandchildren, let us say—person A (present generation) is at least causally responsible for person Z (future generation). While one is not necessarily morally responsible for actions for which one is causally responsible, if the initial relationship with person or event A has a moral aspect to it, it might well be argued that there also exists a moral aspect to the causal relationship with person or event Z. One might not know what the needs or desires of future generations will be, but I cannot imagine things being such as they turn out to be in Woody's Allen's *Sleeper,* in which, after a long sleep, a man awakens in a world where what was once good for him is now bad for him and vice versa. The lack of knowledge about distant future generations does not let one off the moral hook.

I support French's claim that in many respects community is stronger than individuality. It is the actions of a community that help the individuals within it to secure their needs and desires, but without the initial interests of the individuals, the community fails. Similarly the community may develop interests different from those of individuals, as often happens in corporations. People might have very different morals than the corporation as a whole might have. While humans are merely potential persons, according to French, (and I do not disagree with this claim), and while humans act morally in a community, the community of nature is just as important as the community of humans and/or persons. In response to French's claim that some corporations are around longer than some people, it is my guess that my great, great, great, great grandchildren will be around longer than most, if not all, corporations existing today. Besides I fear leaving moral decisions and actions up to corporations, many of whom fail in every respect to act on behalf of people and their environmental community.

Where does this leave the *Exxon Valdez* spill? I think that French clearly would assign moral responsibility to Exxon for the spill (as he suggests in his earlier literature concerning intending and willing) and I believe rightly so. First, I believe that it is important to examine the situation and, if not blame, assign moral responsibility to agents for their actions or failure to act in the situation. Captain Hazelwood failed to act responsibly by being drunk and going under- deck. One might also argue that his "carelessness" prompted the accident. In addition, Exxon failed to respond appropriately, and perhaps the state of Alaska did too. When people in the community were asked to bring linens to help clean up the spill, they responded in small numbers. The problem then, it seems, is that individuals in the community, as well as the community-corporation-collectivity of Exxon, failed to assume their responsibility in various facets of the spill. The fact is that the environment, the area of Prince William Sound included, is a community in which all people live. Ironically it belongs to us but does not belong to us. Individuals cannot choose to desecrate it without infringing on other individuals in the community. Neither can corporations. Whether it is because of health factors, damage to the parts of the ecosystem, the ecosystem itself, or pure aesthetics, how individuals act toward the environment affects the whole. I fear leaving moral decisions solely up to corporations. Many do not have a good track record when it comes to moral activity in the community.

Regarding Exxon and the oil spill in Alaska, Joseph Hazelwood and the corporation of Exxon itself might not have intended to harm Alaska, but care- lessness prompted what became the neglect of the responsible agents. Hence, they were at least willing to allow the consequences that prevailed.

The concept of caring must be further examined, particularly with respect to the environment. To quote Nell Noddings, "The problems we struggle with as we do so shed further light on the questions we have already considered, and we may find deeper support for our contention that the ethical impulse or attitude is grounded in the caring relationship."[2]

NOTES

1. This and subsequent quotations and information concerning the events of the spill were taken directly from *Outside* (June 1989).

2. Nell Noddings, *Caring* (Berkeley: University of California Press, 1984), p. 148.

— 11 ——————————————————

Rational Risk and Moral Outrage: Arthur D. Little, Inc., and the Toxic Alert

JOHN A. SEEGER

In disputes between businesses and environmental activists, tempers commonly rise faster than does understanding. In a typical scenario, each party assumes the other fits a stereotype; each therefore acts in ways that evoke stereotypical responses, thereby confirming the original assumptions. As original prejudices are reinforced, the willingness to question them diminishes. As if by tacit agreement, an escalating war of mutually determined misunderstandings leads to a final act where one side or the other may claim victory but where any objective view of the public interest has been left behind.

Insight into the origins of some of these misunderstandings is offered by analysis of a business school teaching case describing the 1983–1985 conflict between Arthur D. Little, Inc. (ADL), the international consulting firm, and a community action group, the North Cambridge Toxic Alert Coalition (Seeger, 1987). The conflict arose over whether ADL could use a newly constructed laboratory at its Cambridge headquarters to work with chemical warfare agents ("nerve gas") under contracts with the U.S. Army.

The analysis draws also from the more recent conflict over use of the chemical Alar in the cultivation of apples, as reported primarily in *Science,* the journal of the American Association for the Advancement of Science. Here the editor (Koshland, 1989) criticized the Natural Resource Defense Council (NRDC), for sensationalizing its report on the increased risk of cancer in children. NRDC, said Koshland, contributed to a "cacophony of false or exaggerated" scares with its "scare of the week" report. In response, Edward Groth III, of Consumers Union of the United States (1989), observed that the Alar risk was inherently outrageous, whether it was tiny or not. "It is not the size of the risk but its moral offensiveness that makes the public respond so strongly," Groth said. "However big a risk may be, whether it is acceptable or not is a value judgment and is heavily influenced by moral dimensions of the risk."

THE "NERVE GAS" CONTROVERSY

In January 1983, ADL informed the Cambridge, Massachusetts, police and fire departments that work in a planned new laboratory facility "would involve highly toxic materials of particular interest to the Department of Defense." The city officials did not ask for specific chemical names but reviewed the plans and suggested several modifications. By September 1983 the laboratory was finished, at a construction cost of some $800,000. Cambridge fire officers, acting under reciprocal public safety agreements with neighboring towns, asked ADL to inform the authorities in Arlington and Belmont. The Arlington town manager, after touring the laboratory, told ADL he could not in good conscience comply with their request for confidentiality; he would raise the issue at the next meeting of his selectmen.

After a *Boston Globe* story about the Arlington meeting, the Cambridge City Council asked ADL for information. The laboratory was the safest conceivable facility for its purpose, ADL reported, and its purpose was in the public interest: detecting chemical nerve agents, neutralizing them, and developing improved protective clothing. The council called for creation of a Scientific Advisory Committee to advise it on the environmental hazards of ADL's work. The laboratory had already received its first consignment of the materials and continued with its testing work, through the fall of 1983 and the winter of 1984 in spite of complaints by some council members and efforts to impose a moratorium.

On March 13, 1984, the city's commissioner of health and hospitals issued an emergency order barring the testing of the five nerve and blister agents involved in ADL's work. Three days later ADL won a court order restraining the city from enforcing the commissioner's order. Tests continued at the laboratory.

Cambridge's Scientific Advisory Committee (SAC) convened on April 12, 1984, beginning a five-month investigation that concluded in September that even though the risks of handling these materials in densely populated areas might be very small, the consequences of any mishap were too severe to justify the work's presence in Cambridge. Tests continued at the laboratory, however, pending court resolution of two legal issues.

Through the summer of 1984, while the SAC deliberated, three of its members and several outside paid professional organizers had worked to raise public consciousness of the environmental issues. When the SAC decision was published, these activists scheduled a public meeting to organize the North Cambridge Toxic Alert Coalition (NCTAC) and call for a large-scale public debate on ADL's work. Television coverage of the November "debate," which ADL did not attend, included a crew from ABC's "20/20" news show. The next day this crew filmed a group of Toxic Alert members releasing a cloud of black balloons near ADL's headquarters to demonstrate how the wind might carry any chemical fumes toward the houses a quarter-mile away. Four days after the NCTAC public meeting, the Bhopal tragedy in India made poison gas a common topic and a credible threat. ABC News aired its ADL protest segment on "20/20" the following week.

In December 1984 the superior court ruled for the city on one legal question but kept in force the injunction permitting ADL to conduct its testing work. Negotiations continued between Toxic Alert leaders and ADL management to schedule a public debate on the issues, finally settling on March 7, 1985.

At the end of January 1985, 61,000 residents in North Cambridge, Arlington, and Belmont received by first-class mail a package of materials containing a three-page letter from ADL president John Magee and eight pages of materials describing the company and the new laboratory. Toxic Alert members called the mailing condescending and patronizing. Letters to the editors of local weekly newspapers were unanimously negative toward ADL.

On February 26, 1985, the superior court found the city's order against nerve gas testing "valid and enforceable." Although he expressed reservations about the fairness of his action, the judge permitted enforcement of Cambridge's order. The testing stopped, and ADL began its appeal to the state supreme judicial court. The *Cambridge Chronicle* took an editorial stand against ADL's "quixotic battle."

In preparation for the March 7 public meeting, Toxic Alert invited the directors of ADL to attend in order to inform themselves, independently of management, on the issues and their impact on ADL's name. They also appealed for formation of a board-level Committee on Social Responsiveness. They noted that ADL's relationships with the community had always been so positive that board inputs to management had not been necessary. Now those inputs were needed, but "it seems unlikely such a committee would be organized at Mr. Magee's own request, given his level of commitment to continued testing." One director acknowledged the Toxic Alert letter; none attended the March 7 meeting.

Television crews, reporters, and some 300 citizens attended the March 7 meeting. Executive Vice-President D. Reid Weedon III presented the ADL case, stressing the safety of the new facility and the precautions taken in transporting the nerve agents. He showed the audience a gray steel canister, called a "pig," so strong it could withstand dropping from an airplane without damage to its glass vial contents. Further, he said, voluntary limits on the quantity of each nerve agent to be kept in Cambridge would make large-scale accidents like those feared by the SAC impossible. The SAC report, he said, was based on totally unrealistic assumptions. It was not fair to postulate impossible risks.

Weedon described both the military and the medical needs for the knowledge their research might produce and listed a variety of common chemicals, available in hardware stores, that posed greater threats of exposure than did the army's nerve agents. He appealed for freedom of research. "We're often asked, 'Why locate chemical warfare work in Cambridge?' " Weedon said. "The appropriate answer is, 'Because it is safe and Arthur D. Little is here.' " Doing the testing elsewhere would require duplicating ancillary services available at the headquarters site, he said, and "duplication, while possible, would price us out of the competition." Weedon concluded with an appeal for the city to regulate all toxic agents, not just those in question at ADL. The company, he said, stood ready to use it substantial talents to help the city in that effort.

Five speakers presented the Toxic Alert case. Four were professional organizers and one a neighborhood canvasser for NCTAC. The first speaker, using slide projections to illustrate his points, expressed skepticism about corporate reassurances of safety. His examples were the captain of the *Titanic;* the president of the pharmaceutical firm selling thalidomide; the management of Hooker Chemical, expressing concern for the environmental well-being of Niagara Falls; employees at Three Mile Island, expressing confidence in the safety of their plant; and the state labor minister in India, saying, "There is no danger to Bhopal, nor will there be." The speaker said all were highly trained, competent people who probably believed that their operations were entirely safe—just as ADL's people believed what they were saying.

The second speaker described her reactions to ADL's presentations at the City Council and elsewhere, characterized as evasive and deceptive use of technical jargon. She went on to a graphic description of the effects of these gases on their human victims. The third speaker, a physician, dealt with the concept of acceptable risk, noting that asbestos in schools and cyanide in Tylenol capsules were also small risks but had been judged unacceptable. The fourth speaker argued this was too important an issue to let businesspeople or scientists decide because they were typically unable to deal with being wrong, and that made them dangerous. Informed citizens, he said, have a right to decide for themselves what risks they will take.

The fifth Toxic Alert speaker summed up with an emotional defense of the people's right to say "no" and a threat to take to the streets if necessary to stop ADL. ADL president John Magee summed up for the company, reiterating his points on the laboratory's safety and attacking the bias of those who opposed any kind of defense research on chemical or biological warfare agents. He appealed again for the development of comprehensive regulations for all toxic substances, wherever they were used.

Through the summer of 1985, assorted pickets and public hearings and meetings took place as the issue simmered, waiting for a ruling from the Massachusetts Supreme Judicial Court. In September the court held for the city, and testing stopped again. The company, in consultation with its research sponsors, decided against appeal to the U.S. Supreme Court. In a nonbinding referendum vote in November, Cambridge citizens voted by a margin of 18,952 to 3,459 to bar any further work on the nerve agents.

At the annual stockholders' meeting in April 1986, John Magee said in response to a question that ADL had placed too much confidence in its relationship with the city and that it might be necessary to reevaluate whether Cambridge was an appropriate site for a company needing an environment supportive of freedom of research. At the ensuing meeting of the board of directors, Magee was named chairman of the board in addition to his position as president and chief executive officer.

ANALYSIS

Written into the business school case are direct quotations from leaders of both the Toxic Alert and ADL. Analysis of these quotations shows a number of areas where management's assumptions, perceptions, and values hindered ADL's ability to respond to its attackers or to communicate with its stakeholders in a common language. ADL chose to consider this environmental conflict solely in scientific terms and to regard its own people as the only qualified judges of the science involved.

ADL's concept of the stakeholders in the conflict appeared to include only its own employees, the civil servants of the Cambridge municipal government, the sponsors of its research, and society at large (as the benefactor of its research). Missing from the firm's worldview were the citizens living near its headquarters (in the towns of Cambridge, Arlington, and Belmont), the professional organizers who were attracted to the conflict, and local politicians.

The community organizers saw the issues as political and promoted fear of environmental risks and corporate greed to build support for their David-versus-Goliath campaign. The relative success of the activists may be measured by the results of the referendum vote in the Cambridge elections of November 1985: by a 5.5-to-1 margin, the people voted to bar ADL from further testing work.

Management Assumptions

Consistently through the two-year process of this battle, ADL management displayed five underlying assumptions:

1. ADL's staff had a right to do whatever work they chose.
2. Science could accurately measure risk levels and apply the results to determine the work was safe.
3. ADL's people were better judges of the science and the safety than any of its opponents.
4. By using precise language, ADL could maintain rationality in the debate.
5. ADL's history of responsible citizenship in Cambridge entitled the company to a fair hearing and a positive outcome.

The first assumption led to ADL's belief that its right to a competitive advantage—or at least a level playing field with the fourteen other laboratories doing this kind of work—took precedence over any local opinion. The laboratory was sited in Cambridge because the required ancillary services existed there. Placing the laboratory in an isolated area would increase its operating costs greatly, pricing ADL out of the market. That external costs might be borne by its neighbors in order to allow the firm a competitive cost structure was not considered.

The second assumption—that risk is a scientific, objective, measurable variable—led to ADL's conclusion that safety was not a real issue in the dispute. "It just never occurred to us that this would be a safety concern to the community," one manager said. "We made the assumption, perhaps naively, that since it *was* safe, people would recognize that."

The third underlying value—supreme confidence in its own judgment—put management in the position of equating agreement with its views to rationality. All rational people, the view seemed to hold, agreed with ADL or would agree if they were fully informed. Any disagreement therefore must stem from either lack of full information or deliberate malicious intent.

Repeatedly in their comments, ADL's managers demeaned the competence or the motives of anyone who criticized the nerve agent research. Toxic Alert's negotiators, the city council, the SAC, local newspapers, the commissioner of health and hospitals, and even the League of Women Voters were characterized as ignorant of the facts, biased, belligerent, politically weak, or morally corrupt. Mr. Magee attributed pacifist motives to the Toxic Alert leadership, assuming that two prominent antiwar activists were involved; they were not, and NCTAC's professional organizers carefully avoided any hint of an antiwar appeal in their arguments.

A fourth underlying assumption of ADL management was that it could control the debate through language. From the very beginning, ADL avoided the word *gas,* calling its use an effort to inflame the debate with emotional language. They did not work with gases, ADL said in every venue; the surety agents in their laboratory were liquids—no more volatile than water—and were therefore safe to handle. What this meant to ADL management was that they did not work with aerosols—the mixed state of gas and very small droplets of liquids in which chemical warfare agents were dispersed on the battlefield. But what ADL's language meant to the public—pointed out by the community organizers on many occasions—was that ADL was lying: their contracts called for them to detect gases and that must imply the presence of these agents in a gaseous state. In private, ADL staff admitted the use of vapors, but management steadfastly denied any presence of gas on the site.

A fifth factor in the mindset of ADL management was its conviction that it knew the city of Cambridge and was a highly regarded member of the city's establishment. There is little doubt that Mr. Magee was well respected by university presidents, bank presidents, and others. But the Toxic Alert's organizers were knocking on the doors of blue-collar workers, welfare clients, and politicians, segmenting the population in a political campaign.

As a result of its implicit values and confidence in its own views, ADL management was unable to question its position or its assumptions. Outside

ADL's vision were the local weekly newspapers, which were assiduously cultivated by the Toxic Alert organizers. ADL recognized the *Boston Globe* as a communications medium, but most of the news stories about the controversy appeared in the *Cambridge Chronicle,* the *Cambridge TAB,* the *Arlington Advocate,* and the *Belmont Citizen.* John Magee was asked directly about the effect of coverage and editorial stands in the local press. "Do they cause us to stop and ask ourselves whether we're doing the right thing?" he asked. "No."

Toxic Alert Perceptions

On their side, the Toxic Alert organizers also displayed a set of underlying assumptions, centered generally around an image of the public as needful of defense against an exploitive business community. The leadership appeared to assume:

1. The public at large is naive and defenseless against corporate or government exploitation.
2. Business takes advantage of this naiveté to transfer costs to the public sector.
3. Organizational skills can mobilize the public to exert political pressure to protect themselves.

These assumptions led to a belief that organization is a worthy effort, regardless of the issues at hand. In North Cambridge, two of the principal activists (one later appointed to the SAC) had "scoped out an organizing plan for the neighborhood a year before" the ADL work became known. Residents were frightened and angry about chemical wastes on a local W. R. Grace plant site. "The discovery that ADL was testing nerve gas came as the last straw," one Toxic Alert leader said. "Things crystallized. We sat down and planned it. There were already good people in the neighborhood. We brought in skilled, professional, paid organizers beginning in the summer of 1984."

The paid organizers included door-to-door canvassers who took the issues to the people, asking for financial support as well as political action. These canvassers were paid half the money they collected; dedication to the cause was not their only motivation for pounding the sidewalks.

The activists appeared sincerely convinced that the public needed help to defend itself against a rapacious business establishment, which, without the presence of the organizers, would run roughshod over the people. Normal political and regulatory processes could not be trusted to defend the public interest; they were seen as controlled by the business establishment. The organizers themselves were part Robin Hood, part paladin, part knights errant—equipped with the weapons to bring justice to the world and competent in their use. The public media were seen as tools to be used, through education and persistent cultivation, to bring truth to the people. One activist spoke of spending an hour a week with one weekly newspaper and two hours per week with another.

Contrasting Views

The organizers' view of the world seemed broader than that of ADL management, perhaps because their politically oriented outlook required them to identify sources of both support and resistance in their environment. Their understanding of business management and corporate decision making often seemed naive, but their knowledge of the opposition was much better developed than was ADL's knowledge of the organizers. A summary of the contrasting views of the parties follows:

	ADL Management View	*Toxic Alert View*
Basic value	freedom of research	control of environment
Central issue	primacy of science	public safety
Source of power	informed bureaucracy	political processes
Self-image	Galileo	Robin Hood's band
Other's essence	small group of activists	monolithic corporation
Own motivation	continue good work	beat the bad guys
Other's motivation	antiwar pacifism	profit maximization
Dominant mood	rational	inflammatory
Pertinent audience	civil service, courts	naive populace
Communication media	mail, *Boston Globe*	local press, TV, meetings

Ethical Questions

A number of ethical questions are posed by the views of both sides in issues such as this one and the Alar controversy.

1. Do business organizations have a right to compete on an equal footing with all comers? Does the community that is home to a business have a right to constrain its operations more severely than its competitors are constrained?

2. Is it ethical for management to transfer some part of its costs to the neighborhood in which it operates or to the consuming public, without the understanding and consent of its neighbors or customers?

3. What are the ethical implications of the view that community activism is justified, whenever and wherever a central cause emerges, that any fight is worthwhile, or that any fear or uneasiness in a neighborhood may be justifiably blown up into a major conflict?

4. Is it ethical for door-to-door canvassers to solicit contributions for a cause, knowing that a major portion of the proceeds is going to their own pockets?

INSIGHTS FROM THE ALAR CONTROVERSY

Daniel Koshland of *Science* magazine argues that public interest groups and activists themselves are subject to conflicting interests. By waging battles, they

attract new members, so they are inclined to
writes:

Because they are selling products in the marketplace
hazards. Because public interest groups acquire m
hazards. Each group convinces itself that its worthy
"ignorant" public. Businesses today have product lia
they place a dangerous product on the market. P
constraints at the moment; it may be time to develop
irresponsible information have redress.

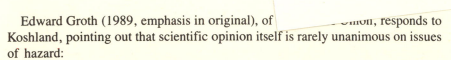

Edward Groth (1989, emphasis in original), of ⌐⌐⌐⌐⌐ ⌐⌐⌐⌐on, responds to
Koshland, pointing out that scientific opinion itself is rarely unanimous on issues
of hazard:

For instance, most people probably do not know whether Alar poses a real cancer threat or
not, but they know some experts think it *may*. And they prefer not to gamble with their
own or their children's health. The fact that Alar is present in apple products without their
consent or knowledge and that consumers can do nothing on their own to detect or remove
it makes this sort of risk inherently *outrageous,* whether it's a tiny risk or not. As Slovic
[1987], Sandman [1987], and others have pointed out, public response to risk depends far
more heavily on such value and ethical dimensions of the risk than it does on the
quantitative magnitude of the hazard.

Risk management must balance values and ethical choices and is unavoidably a political, not a scientific process. . . .

The nub of the issue . . . is how we should respond to public outcries over problems
like Alar. Yes, we must teach people to see risks in perspective. At the same time, we
must *listen* to what people say about risks. It is not the size of the risk but its moral
offensiveness that makes the public respond so strongly. People are not just frightened,
they are angry—in large part, because they believe industries, the government, and now
even the editor of Science, have not told the truth.

THE CHALLENGE FOR MANAGEMENT

The central challenge for managements facing public issues like the
Cambridge nerve gas controversy is to identify the stakeholders involved, including those whose view of the truth is different from management's, and to listen to
those people. The challenge is difficult: it requires rejection of stereotypes and
the central tenet that management already knows all-important aspects of the
truth.

Perhaps Groth's admonition—that we look beyond the size of the risk or
impact to see its moral dimensions or its inherent outrageousness in the eyes of
the disaffected—can help. If public anger at perceived untruthfulness lies at the
heart of the organizers' success, then management must strive to see how its
actions play into the image of mendacity. Management must be willing to see and
sympathize with the outrage if it hopes to influence the public's perceptions.

. (1989). "Alar in Apples." *Science* 244:755.

, D. E., Jr. 1989. "Scare of the Week." *Science* 244:9.

an, P. M. 1987. *EPA (Environmental Protection Agency) Journal* 13, no. 9:21.

ger, J. A. 1987. "Arthur D. Little, Inc. and the Toxic Alert." *Case Research Journal* (1986): 1–26. (Revised copies available from the author at Bentley College.)

Slovic, P. 1987. *Science* 236:280.

Union Carbide Limited and the Bhopal Gas Incident: Issues and Commentary

ARTHUR SHARPLIN

CASE SUMMARY

December 2, 1984, began typically in the central Indian city of Bhopal. In the shadow of a Union Carbide India Limited (UCIL) pesticide factory, tens of thousands of India's poorest citizens milled about the shantytown they called home. Inside the plant, an all-Indian crew operated the systems that produced the mildly toxic Sevin and other patented pesticides of Union Carbide Corporation (UCC), UCIL's Danbury, Connecticut, parent. In a failing market, the plant had been allowed to run down. Some of the safety equipment was in disrepair, and personnel standards had been lowered substantially. Officials of UCIL and its U.S. parent had discussed selling the plant or dismantling it and shipping it to Brazil or Indonesia.

The Gas Incident

Poisonous methyl isocyanate (MIC) was used in making Sevin. MIC is a liquid that boils at well above usual daytime temperatures. Two tanks in the plant, numbers 610 and 611, respectively contained 41 and 20 metric tons of the liquid. Sometime before midnight, several hundred gallons of water entered tank 610, which had been on standby for several weeks. UCC would later say the water was injected by a "disgruntled employee"; the Indian government would blame faulty procedures and design. The water reacted violently with the MIC, producing heat and gases. Several workers' eyes started to water and sting, a signal they knew indicated an MIC leak. They found what they believed was the source and took minor corrective action. It was 12:15 A.M. then, time for tea, and the supervisors retired to the company canteen—in violation of instructions not to take their breaks together.

An operator soon called the supervisors back. Pressure was up in the tank 610, it was rumbling, and the concrete mounded over it had cracked. Someone rang the alarm and summoned the fire squad. The crew frantically sought ways to correct the problem but soon had to evacuate upwind, some scaling the high fence at the plant perimeter. A relief valve had lifted, and MIC vapor could be seen billowing from a vent line 120 feet in the air. Practically the entire contents of tank 610 was converted to gas and escaped.

The deadly white cloud drifted and settled toward the shanties. As the gaseous tentacles reached into the huts, there was panic and confusion. Many of the weak and elderly died where they lay, blinded and smothered by the acrid fumes. "It was like breathing fire," one survivor said. The affluent were generally able to flee in their cars. Most of the poor were left behind.

About 2,000 died and tens of thousands more were injured that night. Nearby towns were woefully unprepared to accept the gasping and dying masses. Screams and sobs filled the air. Confused crowds waited outside hospitals. No one was sure how to treat the gas victims, and medical supplies quickly ran out. Safe food stocks were soon exhausted. People were afraid to drink the water.

Disposing of the dead was a major problem. Bodies were cremated or piled in hurriedly dug graves. A cholera epidemic was feared. Bhopal's mayor said later, "I can say that I have seen chemical warfare. Everything so quiet. Goats, cats, whole families—father, mother, children—all lying silent and still. And every structure totally intact. I hope never again to see it."

Historical Background

UCIL's history can be traced to 1926 when the Ever-Ready Company, Ltd. (of Great Britain) began manufacturing flashlight batteries in Calcutta. In the late sixties, UCIL began marketing Sevin and other pesticides in India. A simple plant to dilute and package mildly toxic Sevin powder was started at Bhopal. Under pressure from the Indian government, UCIL later built a plant to manufacture Sevin, which required using large quantities of MIC. UCIL's pesticide sales collapsed after 1981, and the plant was operating at only one-fifth of capacity by 1984.

By the early eighties UCIL was involved in five product areas: batteries, carbon and metals, plastics, marine products, and agricultural chemicals. In 1982 the company expanded its battery-making operation to Nepal. UCIL got out of marine products in 1984.

The Legal Battle

After the gas incident, UCC chief Warren Anderson rushed to India, only to be arrested and briefly detained. He said UCC took moral responsibility and offered medical and financial aid, but the offers were rejected. The Indian Central

Bureau of Investigation (CBI) took control and began a criminal investigation. It barred UCC investigators from the plant for several weeks and prohibited them from interviewing employees for an extended period.

Several American lawyers flew to Bhopal to recruit clients and quickly brought lawsuits in the United States. But the Union of India (UOI) declared itself the representative of all the victims. The cases were soon consolidated in a New York court.

UCC sued to return the consolidated case to India. It said UCIL was independent, managed by Indians in India, and that the parent had never even "had a presence in India." After 1982 and aside from infrequent safety audits, UCC had in fact generally refrained from direct involvement in UCIL affairs. At the time of the gas incident, all the employees of UCIL were Indians. Few Americans ever worked at Bhopal; the last one had left in 1982. The plant was built by a Bombay contractor, who also prepared the working drawings.

On the other hand, the UOI argued, "In reality, there is but one entity, the monolithic multinational [UCC], which is responsible for its subsidiaries." UCC owned 50.9 percent of UCIL's common stock. A UCC executive vice-president was on UCIL's eleven-member board. Union Carbide Eastern, Inc. (UCE)—a wholly owned subsidiary of UCC—and UCIL had four common directors, including the chairman of the UCE board. Also several senior UCIL officials had previously been employed by UCC. Finally, the MIC plant was based on UCC technology, and UCC engineers designed the plant and checked it before startup.

The U.S. courts concluded the plant was built and managed by Indians in India and that Indian courts were competent to hear the case. The UOI commenced suit in India in September 1986. UCC continued to claim the plant had been sabotaged by a "disgruntled employee," although it refused to name the alleged culprit. The UOI blamed faulty operating procedures and design and had said damages could reach $3.1 billion. UCC offered $70 million at first and $350 million later. The Indian government suggested $615 million.

Financial Impact of the Gas Incident on UCIL and UCC

Much of the financing for the Bhopal plant had come from government-sponsored loans. UCC loaned UCIL no money and guaranteed no UCIL debt. From a financial standpoint, the gas incident seems to have had modest, and perhaps salutary, effects on UCIL. UCIL's common stock had traded between 20 and 30 rupees (Rs) for several years before the incident. The average of highs and lows in 1983 and 1984 was Rs. 24.5. For 1985 and 86, the average was Rs. 29.3. The 1987 high was Rs. 43. Revenues were up each year from 1981 to 1985—9 percent in 1985 alone—but 1986 brought a 10 percent drop. Then revenues were stable at about Rs. 2.1 billion a year through early 1989. Net profits fell from an average of Rs. 92 million in the four years before the gas incident to Rs. 13 million in 1985. Then profits were stable at about Rs. 50

million a year through early 1989. Dividends were reduced from Rs. 49 million a year over 1981–1983 to Rs. 16 million in 1984. No dividends were paid in 1985, but they were restored to Rs. 39 million a year in 1986 and 1987.

Although the gas incident produced a substantial financial blip for UCC, the company and its executives made large gains thereafter. UCC stock traded in the low fifties just before December 1984, having fallen back from its high of $74, reached in 1983. After the gas incident, the stock fell to the low thirties. When GAF Corporation tried to take over UCC in mid-1985, the stock shot up. UCC adopted golden parachutes worth at least $8.8 million for forty-two top executives, $500 million was extracted from the employee pension funds, and the company was reorganized and financially restructured. GAF's attempt failed. UCC's shares were split three for one in 1986 and would trade near $30 ($90 adjusted for the split) in 1989. For 1985 UCC reported a $581 million loss after $1.2 billion in charges related to restructuring. Over 1986–1988 net profits averaged $463 million, up from an average of $237 million in the three years before the incident.

The Settlement

After more than four years of legal wrangling, the Indian Supreme Court ordered a $470 million settlement. UCIL paid 10 percent and UCC the rest. The money was held in escrow by the government. By late 1989, there were about 500,000 relief claims, although only about 100,000 persons had been in the disaster area. Before the settlement, the Indian government had already given some survivors $800 for each family member who died, but it was uncertain when, or if, the $470 million would be distributed. A GOI attorney said all of it would go to victims.

After the incident, UCC established a corporate policy that it would take responsibility for safety "wherever we have an interest." A company executive said even contracts for distribution of UCC products through facilities owned by others would thereafter have provision for safety inspection by UCC. The cost of such inspection would be paid by UCC and would be included in the contracts. The official said UCC could have conducted frequent safety audits at Bhopal and even kept safety personnel there but that UCIL was not allowed to pay for such service.

The controversy surrounding Bhopal continued in 1989. In its 1989 proxy statement, UCC reported it was still spending $7 million to $8 million a year on "Bhopal-related litigation." The Supreme Court of India was reviewing the constitutionality of the Bhopal Gas Leak Disaster Processing of Claims Act, under which it had ordered the settlement. The Central Bureau of Intelligence continued its criminal investigation. A reporter asked a top UCC official, "You have said when the time is ripe you would reveal the name of the alleged sabateur; when will the time be ripe?" "Never," replied the official. "The case has been settled." Bruce Finzen, attorney for the UOI, termed it "outrageous" that UCC would "claim to know the name of a person who killed more than 2,000 people and refuse to identify that person to criminal investigators."

ISSUES RELATED TO MULTINATIONALS IN GENERAL

The Bhopal tragedy and its aftermath raise a number of ethical, legal, and public policy concerns:

1. Should a multinational have or assume cradle-to-grave and absolute responsibility for dangerous technology it exports (for example, the pesticide technology developed by UCC and transferred to UCIL)?

2. Under what circumstances should multinationals be morally or legally accountable for the acts and omissions of subsidiaries (for example, UCC's claim that a corporation is not responsible by virtue of owning stock)?

3. Should, or can, a multinational accept moral responsibility beyond its legal responsibility in the event of a disaster (for example, Anderson's statement shortly after the incident that UCC accepted moral responsibility)?

4. What compensation standards should apply to torts committed in developing countries: those of the parent country or the host country (for example, the compensation levels in the United States compared to the much lower ones in India)?

5. What safety and environmental standards should apply to subsidiary operations of multinationals: those of the parent country or of the host country (for example, the standards at Bhopal in comparison to those at UCC's Institute, West Virginia, plant)?

6. How do legal attacks, such as criminal charges or numerous large lawsuits, affect the moral imperatives of managers in event of a disaster such as Bhopal (as in the arrest of Anderson and massive suits by Belli and others)?

7. Does the threat of a takeover narrow a company's options in social responsibility areas (for example, the GAF raid)?

8. In the event of a disaster involving a subsidiary of a multinational, should the host country accept offers of medical and financial aid from the multinational (for example, Indian's rejection of UCC aid)?

9. What should be the response of a multinational urged to make suboptimal new investments in order to keep older, profitable operations (for example, UCIL's decision to make pesticides in relation to keeping its profitable battery operations)?

10. How should a multinational respond when a host country demands backward integration of manufacturing that will involve production and handling of toxic substances (for example, India's insistence that UCC manufacture constituents of Sevin domestically)?

11. How should a multinational respond when a host country resists its efforts to provide technical assistance and supervision to a subsidiary, especially one involved in hazardous operations (for example, India's insistence that no Americans work at Bhopal)?

12. Does the occurrence of a disaster involving a company's operations or products affect the ranking of company stakeholders in terms of management's responsibility to them

(for example, UCC's attention to protecting management and shareholder interests while accused of staving off victims' claims)?

13. Is it acceptable that corporations or their executives or shareholders benefit from a mass disaster (for example, UCC and UCIL before versus after the Bhopal disaster)?

No attempt will be made here to address all these issues; however, the first seems to capture the central thrust of the case.

CRADLE-TO-GRAVE AND ABSOLUTE RESPONSIBILITY?

It is clear that Union Carbide transferred dangerous pesticide technology to India and relinquished direct control of it. This was done under pressure from the Indian government, however, and UCC did take seemingly appropriate steps to insulate itself from legal liability for actions of UCIL. It seems clear UCC would not have been willing to transfer the technology to India under conditions of absolute liability.

UCC asserted three layers of legal, and moral, defense: (1) ownership of stock in a company does not make the owner responsible for that company's acts; (2) even if a majority owner is considered responsible, the liability is diminished if the owner cannot, or does not, exercise control; and (3) no liability exists anyway since no company can be held accountable for damages caused by an act of sabotage.

Only the third of these could be a defense for UCIL, and the concept of cradle-to-grave and absolute responsibility would overcome any and all of these defenses as they apply to either company. Moreover, if UCC had assumed it had such responsibility before the incident, it would probably have conducted more frequent safety inspections at the plant and undoubtedly would have taken actions that could have prevented the incident or at least diminished its severity. In fact, UCC's post-Bhopal policy of doing safety inspections at its own expense is a clear step toward the assumption of cradle-to-grave responsibility for dangerous technology.

There were several steps in UCC's relinquishment of control over the MIC technology; each might have been prevented if UCC had assumed cradle-to-grave responsibility for its pesticide technology. First, the technology was transferred to India, where distance, cultural differences, and communications and transportation limitations made effective control practically impossible.

Second, UCC gave in to India's desire that only Indians build, manage, and operate the Bhopal factory. Certainly UCC could have chosen not to build the plant and could have conducted frequent audits on all aspects of the operation. The choices appear to have been mainly economic ones.

Third, UCC continued its hands-off practices concerning UCIL after sales collapsed and the technology consumed, rather than produced, cash. The ownership structure of UCIL complicated this problem. As only half-owner, UCC might be excused for refusing to subsidize the operation, and there was no

Indian deep pocket to tap. Besides, standard corporate practice in most companies is to require a subsidiary, such as UCIL's pesticide division, to fund its own cash flow. The Bhopal operation ran down, creating a propensity to fail in the human system as well as the physical one. The distressed condition of the plant and rumors of dismantling it could even have helped create an atmosphere where sabotage was thinkable.

At the risk of unduly vilifying UCC, which by all accounts is more socially responsible than most other multinationals, it is interesting to consider a cynical interpretation of UCC's relationship to Bhopal: UCC may have given in to Indian demands for autonomy of UCIL in part because that would allow UCC to disclaim responsibility for just such an incident as occurred or failure of any other kind, such as financial collapse.

What is the rationale for such a view? UCC officials say they and UCIL agreed the plant would be built only because the Indian government demanded it as a price of UCC's continuing to do business in India. Certainly UCC might have lost its most-favored-company status if it had refused to go along. India's threat, though perhaps only implied, was credible. Several operations of international oil companies had been nationalized earlier. And in about 1977 IBM and Coca-Cola had pulled out under pressures similar to those UCC was apparently experiencing.

Having decided not to pull out but to help UCIL build the plant, UCC might have faced this dilemma: it knew the technology was dangerous if not competently and carefully managed; on the other hand, even if UCC employees could stay at Bhopal the company knew problems of distance and culture would limit their ability to stay in control of plant maintenance and safety. UCC had an incentive to give in to Indian demands that the plant be built and run by Indians. If an Indian construction firm built the plant and Indians ran it, with no American on site, how could anyone hold UCC responsible in case major problems did crop up? Maybe they never would. No overt act by UCC was required to effect such a transfer of the MIC technology, only acceding to the Indians' escalating demands, surely a pardonable sin if a sin at all.

The most important evidence that this rationale may be correct is the same evidence UCC cited as supporting defense number 2. That defense was stated by the UCC attorney who said, "UCIL has been subject to less control by Union Carbide than any subsidiary I know of anywhere in the world." Despite the fact that UCC was a world leader in MIC technology, it seems to have contrived to distance itself in designing, building, and operating the plant. Only five Americans worked at Bhopal from 1979 to 1980; only one stayed until 1982, that one an employee of UCIL, not of UCC; and no American remained after December 1982. Even safety inspections by UCC personnel were infrequent, and corrective actions were apparently left to UCIL. Despite UCC's ownership of majority interest in UCIL, it could truthfully state that seven of eleven UCIL directors, including the chairman, were Indians starting in 1987. And the Bhopal plant apparently made no operating or safety reports directly to UCC.

It is hard to imagine that such an extreme hands-off policy could exist without strategic intent. And even if the intent was not to build a defense in advance of the improbable incident, the result was the same. The freedom of the Bhopal operation from control by UCC certainly was a factor in limiting the American parent's accountability and allowing it to settle all Indian claims against it for less than $500 million.

Still, it is an odd concept of noblesse oblige that would assign UCC responsibility beyond that of the sovereign Indian government. Some may consider the Indian government corrupt, incompetent, and unresponsive to the needs of its subjects. But it is the government and should be accountable for the harm to its own people caused by any coercive treatment of international companies.

Of course, it is unlikely that many managers at UCC comprehended the strategy described and perhaps none did. No one can ever be sure if such a strategy even existed. Whatever the truth of that matter, assumed or enforced cradle-to-grave responsibility for dangerous technology by multinationals could limit such disasters in the future. Multinationals would more strongly resist pressures to violate home country standards of safety in Third World operations. In particular, it seems unlikely that the gas incident would have happened had UCC been forcefully concerned with matters of safety at the plant in 1983–1984.

ISSUES RELATED DIRECTLY TO UCC

UCC Responsibility

The argument by Indian attorneys that there is but one entity, the monolithic multinational, is compelling. While UCC attorneys were able to build a strong case that UCC did not exercise effective control over the Bhopal plant, this begs the question of whether the company should or could have controlled its technology. Clearly majority ownership has some relevance, and the interlocking directorates of the UCC subsidiaries along with the multicompany career patterns of UCIL officials indicate some measure of control by UCC.

Certainly UCC had the knowledge and capability to ensure a higher degree of safety than existed at Bhopal, and it could have prevented construction of the plant. The company's choice to go ahead in the light of the obvious risks can be seen only as a conscious, strategic one. UCIL's decision to let the plant run down, in physical and human terms, and UCC's choice largely to ignore that decision, seem to have been based largely on economic factors. To excuse UCC for the final outcome is to portray the company merely as a pawn. Warren Anderson, at least, accepted moral responsibility for the incident.

On the other hand, UCC officials might believe the Indians' desire for economic activity at any cost justified some relaxation of U.S. standards in every area. Indian workers are not paid nearly as much as U.S. workers. They neither demand nor expect the kinds of working conditions U.S. workers have.

Three other reasons may absolve UCC of some responsibility. First, UCC washed its hands of the matter by allowing itself to be distanced from the Bhopal operation. Second, UCC officials say the Indians were fully competent to manage the plant. Third, UCC officials say the real cause of the incident was sabotage by a disgruntled worker, a factor some might believe is uncontrollable.

Rule of Strict Liability

Black's Law Dictionary defines strict liability as "a concept applied by the courts in product liability cases in which a seller is liable for any and all defective or hazardous products which unduly threaten a consumer's personal safety." Strict liability does not require the showing of intent to harm or negligence.

Warren Anderson apparently felt strict liability in a moral sense, but his company disclaimed legal responsibility and tried to prove it was not in control of the offending operation and the incident was caused by sabotage, not negligence or any other failure by UCC or UCIL. A manager who accepted strict liability might have said, "An operation which was managed largely for our benefit (as 51 percent owner) damaged third parties, so we assume responsibility for that damage."

Managers committed to accepting responsibility for any harm caused by their operations are less likely than others to take risks with the lives or health of third parties. On the other hand, such managers might avoid many investments others deem desirable, such as the Bhopal plant.

Accepting responsibility that is not legally imposed could subject managers to lawsuits by shareholders. One gets the clear impression from the case that GAF would have been less likely to do this than was UCC. When UCC's stock price dropped, in part because of Anderson's expressed assumption of responsibility for the incident, arbitrageurs and speculators began to accumulate shares. GAF eventually mounted a takeover offensive. UCC then hardened its position and aggressively defended the claims. Without a legally imposed rule of strict liability, which would have applied to GAF after any takeover, management may not have the power to assume moral responsibility for incidents such as Bhopal.

Host Country or Developing Country Safety Standards

If one accepts the view that UCC had or could have retained enough control of the situation to impose safety standards, the question remains, Which standards? There is a growing sense that multinational companies should refuse to compromise on human safety. Clearly the level of safety at Bhopal was lower than at UCC's U.S. plants. In fact, the cost of imposing U.S. safety standards in India might have been prohibitive, in the sense that the project would not have been economically feasible if such standards had been applied. Related questions involve standards for air and water pollution and corporate social performance in many other areas.

UCC's policies, some quoted in the case, require high standards of safety in operations of subsidiaries. In fact, UCC officials have stated the higher of home country or host country safety standards should apply. It is hard to defend any other position.

Effect of Legal Attacks on Moral Imperatives of UCC Managers

Shortly after the incident, UCIL and UCC managers were under attack from all sides, so something of a siege mentality was unavoidable. As is often the case, some of the attackers were subject to criticism themselves. The attorneys who rushed to sign up victims were seen as ambulance chasers. Many of the supposed victims were opportunists who saw a chance to collect money. Some feigned illness, and others exaggerated the problems they did have. The Indian government could be viewed by Westerners as "corrupt, uncivilized, and incompetent." Besides, any consideration given to actual or supposed victims was an assumption of responsibility, likely to work against the companies in court.

Corporate lawyers took charge of matters related to the lawsuits. The adversarial approach of the courtroom surely affected management strategy, although UCC claims otherwise. Every move had to be considered in terms of its effect on the burgeoning legal battle. Still, the team Anderson formed to manage Bhopal-related matters focused on humanitarian as well as legal concerns.

In summary, it can be argued that the attacks weakened the moral imperatives of the managers. On the other hand, the attacks were often moralistic and undoubtedly had some tendency to heighten management's moral sensibilities.

The GAF Raid and Concern for Nonowner Stakeholders

Nonowner stakeholders of the companies included employees, the gas victims, and Bhopal residents. UCC's early initiatives regarding the tragedy suggested stockholder value would be diminished to compensate the victims and benefit the Bhopal society beyond what was legally required. Anderson's expression of responsibility and concern certainly indicated that, so the common stock of UCC, and of UCIL, would be worth more under other management, if that management had a weaker commitment to nonowner stakeholders. Further, there is reason to believe involvement in a mass disaster makes any company ripe for a takeover. New owners and managers can act without the burden of guilt felt by and assigned to their predecessors.

GAF management filed that bill well. GAF managers would have been unburdened by any guilt related to the disaster, not having been involved, even arguably; they were experienced in handling tort claims, having been defendant in many asbestos health cases; so GAF would have probably had little commitment to the victims.

To fend off the takeover, UCC managers seemed to become more like those at

GAF were assumed to be. They extracted $500 million from the employee pension fund, decreasing the security of that fund. They hardened their resolve to defend the lawsuits. In the end, UCC allowed the settlement money to go the Indian government, where some think some it may be consumed by corruption, delay, and mismanagement. Further, it seems likely UCC managers now feel absolved of any responsibility to furnish safe and profitable employment in the Bhopal area. In short, takeover threats reduce the feasibility of representing nonowner stakeholders, and this applies to the GAF initiative toward UCC.

Managers' and Stockholders' Gain from Mass Disaster

Clearly by any objective measure, UCC and its managers benefited from the Bhopal incident, as did UCIL. They were politically able to close a burdensome plant, take aggressive actions to restructure both companies, and improve management benefits.

The GAF takeover attempt, apparently initiated by the share price drop following the Bhopal incident, gave UCC an excuse (or reason) to vote top managers improved golden parachutes (2.99 times the five-year average compensation, plus better benefits), to raid the employee pension fund ($500 million), and to build a shark-repellent wall around themselves. Later managers' and directors' compensation and benefits were increased even more.

UCC was restructured, and unwanted divisions were divested. UCIL and UCC were able to get rid of the failing Bhopal pesticide division, which neither had wanted in the first place. UCC stock doubled in value, as compared to the price before the incident. And UCIL stock reached historic new highs in 1985 and 1986.

It is ironic, at best, that a disaster such as Bhopal might leave its victims devastated and other corporate stakeholders better off.

CONCLUSION

The entire U.S. chemical industry, with active leadership by UCC, moved toward heightened responsibility after Bhopal. In 1988, the Chemical Manufacturers Association (CMA) adopted ten "Guiding Principles for Responsible Care." Five of these principles seem particularly applicable:

- To develop and produce chemicals that can be manufactured, transported, used and disposed of safely.
- To make health, safety and environmental considerations a priority in our planning for all existing and new products and processes.
- To report promptly to officials, employees, customers and the public, information on chemical-related health or environmental hazards and to recommend protective measures.

- To operate our plants and facilities in a manner that protects the environment and the health and safety of our employees and the public.
- To participate with government and others in creating responsible laws, regulations and standards to safeguard the community, workplace and environment.

Commitment to the principles was made a condition of membership in CMA. UCC chief Kennedy was the 1989 chairman of CMA.

NOTE

The factual information presented here is documented in an extensive case study available from Professor Sharplin at McNeese State University, Lake Charles, LA 70609. The assistance and support of the Center for Business Ethics at Bentley College are gratefully acknowledged. Union Carbide Corporation provided invaluable assistance. Special thanks also go to the government of India, through its U.S. attorney. Finally, I am grateful to certain anonymous Indian nationals without whose help this project would not have been possible.

Business Ethics When a Crisis Occurs

_____

RONALD S. WISHART

Much of the literature about Bhopal is centered on two aspects of the disaster: crisis management, a topic of great interest in business schools and boardrooms, and the question of corporate liability for the acts of a separately incorporated affiliate company in which it owns shares, an aspect of the disaster understandably most intriguing to lawyers. The tragedy is less often examined in the context of the ethical issues it raises. My purpose in this chapter is to place Carbide's response to the tragedy in such a context, to comment on the company's view of its ethical obligations, and to review Carbide's effort to do the right thing.

That effort began at once when Carbide's chairman, Warren Anderson, declared that the company would assume a moral responsibility for assisting the victims. This left the question of liability for the courts and allowed Carbide to move quickly on several fronts: for the chairman to travel to India to try to arrange aid for the victims, to see what medical expertise would be needed and to try to provide it, and to send a team of technical experts to India to determine the cause of the tragedy.

Is it advisable for a corporation to go beyond its legal responsibility in responding to a disaster? Although Carbide tried repeatedly to do so, it accomplished little in this instance because the tragedy took on a political dimension in India that for a long time blocked a settlement and prevented the company from giving other forms of aid. But where there is even a chance that moving into the breech as Carbide did might facilitate the relief effort, there is strong reason to go ahead and let the lawyers fight it out in court.

Some have noted that lawsuits are adversarial by nature and can affect other decisions if management allows that to happen. Carbide management did not allow itself to be distracted or dissuaded from following through on moral commitments it had made simply because lawyers and others were on the attack. By the time of the Bhopal settlement, virtually all offers of aid unrelated to the settlement, totaling $20 million, had been rejected, and a rehabilitation center was bulldozed to the ground when authorities learned that Carbide money was behind it. Nevertheless, the company persisted in its efforts to aid the victims.

Should the Bhopal plant have been there in the first place? Did it employ technology that was beyond the capabilities of Indians to manage? A foreign affiliate receiving potentially hazardous technology should consider the prospects for its success from a business standpoint and also decide whether it is capable of safely designing, building, and operating the new facilities. The parent company also should consider safety and provide sound technology.

Both Union Carbide India Limited (UCIL) and Union Carbide Corporation considered these and other issues carefully, and UCIL saw no problem in acceding to the Indian government's insistence on back integration into pesticide manufacturing or in accepting the government's choice of a site, at the time a lightly populated area.

Some suggest that responsibility for the safe operation of any technology transferred to a developing country attaches forever to the transferor. It is a position that would deny developing countries the very technology they require to move forward, for it is not reasonable or feasible to hold a company responsible for technology that for reasons of local pride or regulation it may not control. Any company required to accept responsibility for technology at the same time it is asked to renounce control of that technology would have to think very hard about parting with it.

The point is underscored in the case of Bhopal. Investigation of the cause has established that it was an act of sabotage by a disgruntled employee who may have believed that he was simply spoiling a batch of chemical. A novel theory of multinational responsibility was promoted in this case to create responsibility where control did not exist. It purports to make any non-Indian company transferring technology responsible for any mishap in India involving that technology regardless of the circumstances. Few believe such a theory could be sustained in court.

Early in 1989 Carbide entered into a settlement with the government of India that is generous by any standard. That almost any settlement would be challenged in some quarters became inevitable once lawyers from the United States took to soliciting clients in India by promoting visions of multibillion-dollar judgments. But the $470 million settlement will literally change the lives of the victims and the families of those who died. The continued squabbling simply delays the day; it cannot change the outcome.

With the settlement, the chairman of Union Carbide India says his company will now be free to go about the task of restoring its place in the Indian economy and society—good news for the Indian company and for India. For our part at Union Carbide Corporation, we are secure in the knowledge that our response to the crisis reflected the decency and integrity that our constituencies—employees, stockholders, customers, and suppliers—expected of us. The tragedy also had a major impact across the board in our industry, which has redoubled the intensity of its risk management efforts to see that there are no more Bhopals. One is reluctant to talk of the tragedy in terms of benefits, but that is surely one.

14

Union Carbide Corporation's Liability for the Bhopal Disaster: Multinational Enterprise Liability

BRUCE A. FINZEN AND
ROBERTA B. WALBURN

A multinational corporation has a primary, absolute and non-delegable duty to the persons and country in which it has in any manner caused to be undertaken any ultrahazardous or inherently dangerous activity. This includes a duty to provide that all ultrahazardous or inherently dangerous activities are conducted with the highest standards of safety and to provide all necessary information and warnings regarding the activity involved.

With this pleading, the Union of India in its complaint against Union Carbide Corporation asserted a new cause of action: multinational enterprise liability.[1] This cause of action represents the natural evolution of well-established principles of law adapted to meet the economic and functional realities of multinational corporations. By imposing liability on the parent corporation at the apex of the enterprise, the doctrine of multinational enterprise liability begins to fill the void in the regulation of multinational corporations, which, although ever more prevalent and powerful, are too often insulated from the consequences of their actions.

Union Carbide's liability for the Bhopal disaster did not rest solely on this doctrine. Its direct actions in designing, constructing, maintaining, and operating the Indian plant were clearly sufficient to establish direct liability against the parent corporation under more traditional legal doctrines. Union Carbide engineers in the United States developed the technology for producing pesticides using the methyl isocyanate (MIC) process and implemented this process initially at the corporation's plant in Institute, West Virginia. Union Carbide's Management Committee, a high-level panel whose membership included the corporation's chief executive officer, reviewed and endorsed the decision to transfer this technology to India. Union Carbide prepared the design plans for the Bhopal plant and entered into a technical service agreement to provide continuing tech-

nical expertise to its Indian subsidiary. Union Carbide sent key technical personnel to India to monitor construction and start-up activities in Bhopal and to
manage the plant on-site during the early years of operation, and it trained other
Bhopal technicians at its facilities in Institute. Union Carbide conducted several
safety audits of the Bhopal plant, including a 1982 investigation, which found a
number of "major" concerns and possibilities for "serious personnel exposure."
Union Carbide also controlled key financial decisions in Bhopal. In fact, on the
eve of the Bhopal disaster, Union Carbide was contemplating dismantling the
Bhopal plant and shipping it to another country.[2]

It is clear that Union Carbide—with 50.9 percent ownership—controlled all
of the actions of Union Carbide India Ltd. (UCIL), its Indian subsidiary. Although Union Carbide attempted to deny this control for purposes of the Bhopal
litigation, there could be no genuine dispute as to the realities of the corporate
organization, as demonstrated by the following testimony of a Union Carbide
executive vice-president who also served as a UCIL board member at the time of
the Bhopal disaster:

Q: In order to secure effective management control of an affiliate, Union Carbide need not
have 100 percent say on the board of directors, correct?

A: Union Carbide does not control its affiliate companies, period.

Q: Sir, who controls an affiliate company?

A: The board of that company.

Q: Who is the board elected by?

A: The equity participants.

Q: And who's the majority equity participant in UCIL?

A: Carbide's 50.9.[3]

Given Union Carbide's direct actions and direct control over UCIL and the
Bhopal facility, the Union of India asserted direct causes of action against the
parent corporation for absolute liability, strict liability, negligence, breach of
warranty, misrepresentation, and punitive damages. In addition, the Union of
India asserted a cause of action for multinational enterprise liability.

Multinational enterprise liability, as delineated in the complaint filed by the
Union of India, eliminates many artificial barriers imposed by antiquated legal
theories. The rationale for this cause of action was summarized in the Union of
India's complaint:

Multinational corporations by virtue of their global purpose, structure, organization,
technology, finances and resources have it within their power to make decisions and take
actions that can result in industrial disasters of catastrophic proportion and magnitude.
This is particularly true with respect to those activities of the multinationals which are
ultrahazardous or inherently dangerous.

Key management personnel of multinationals exercise a closely-held power which is neither restricted by national boundaries nor effectively controlled by international law. The complex corporate structure of the multinational, with networks of subsidiaries and divisions, makes it exceedingly difficult or even impossible to pinpoint responsibility for the damage caused by the enterprise to discrete corporate units or individuals. In reality, there is but one entity, the monolithic multinational, which is responsible for the design, development and dissemination of information and technology worldwide, acting through a forged network of interlocking directors, common operating systems, global distribution and marketing systems, financial and other controls. In this manner, the multinational carries out its global purpose through thousands of daily actions, by a multitude of employees and agents. Persons harmed by the acts of a multinational corporation are not in a position to isolate which unit of the enterprise caused the harm, yet it is evident that the multinational enterprise that caused the harm is liable for such harm. The multinational must necessarily assume this responsibility, for it alone has the resources to discover and guard against hazards and to provide warnings of potential hazards. This inherent duty of the multinational is the only effective way to promote safety and assure that information is shared with all sectors of its organization and with the nations in which it operates.

The doctrine of multinational enterprise liability recognizes that multinationals can be regulated effectively only by requiring some measure of accountability by the parent corporation. This principle simply recognizes the basic economic realities of multinational corporations.

Yitzahak Hadari provides a detailed analysis of the structure of multinational enterprises in "The Structure of the Private Multinational Enterprise."[4] He states that the major identifying criterion is the "implementation of a global strategy involving all the units of the enterprise and directed by a single top management."[5] He points out two distinctive features of a multinational enterprise: it transacts a sufficient amount of business abroad so that its financial status is dependent on operations in several countries, and management decisions are made on the basis of multinational alternatives. In short, multinational enterprises centralize control of basic strategies in order to operate in the most efficient manner and to exploit opportunities on a worldwide basis.

Hadari notes that "the separation of control from the situs of the subsidiaries or affiliates raises some difficult political as well as business and legal problems."[6] He cautions that "national policies may well be frustrated if states treat a local affiliate of [a multinational enterprise] as a wholly independent entity without regard to the actual location of authority and control over the particular subject matter sought to be regulated."[7]

Numerous courts and commentators have also recognized the lack of effective legal regulation of multinational enterprises. For example, the International Court of Justice has stated that "no generally accepted rules in the matter have crystallized on the international plane."[8] One of the best-known authorities on multinational enterprises has stated:

Because of the worldwide empire which they are carving out for themselves, the n.ultinational corporations are able to create a new jungle, widely spread out in component parts and commanded from geographically remote bases. They account to no single national authority, and since international law is feeble or non-existent, they are free of international authority as well.[9]

Another commentator wrote:

Current frameworks for resolution of issues of transnational veil-piercing are inadequate to provide consistent judicial decisions and uniform legal standards. . . . An enterprise framework will help to develop a more consistent body of law based upon economic reality and should result in more effective legal risk assessment by multinational enterprises.[10]

The principle of holding a parent corporation of a multinational enterprise liable for harm caused by an inherently dangerous activity serves as an important step in the common law's evolution. Indeed, by imposing liability on the parent corporation, multinational enterprise liability furthers the basic principles that have shaped the development of common law in the United States:

- The risk of loss is placed on the legal entity best able to bear and distribute that risk. The parent of a multinational enterprise not only has the most financial wherewithal to bear the risk but also can distribute the risk among all customers of the enterprise and is in the best position to purchase insurance.
- The parent corporation is in the best position to prevent injury by minimizing the risks inherent in the creation of a dangerous activity. The parent typically has superior engineering and technological resources to identify the risks and implement safety procedures. The doctrine of multinational enterprise liability provides the parent corporation greater incentive to devise and distribute to its subsidiaries and affiliates the safest technology possible, thereby avoiding injury and damage altogether.
- Fair and adequate compensation of the innocent victims is best achieved, and indeed in many cases can only be achieved, by holding the parent company liable for the inherently dangerous activities of the enterprise. The parent has at its disposal, and can effectively allocate, the necessary resources of the entire enterprise to compensate innocent victims.
- Justice is efficiently administered. Neither the victims nor the courts need to sort out the tangled web of cross-connections between the parent and the various subsidiaries and affiliates for the purpose of assessing liability.
- The courts and the victims are not required to struggle factually with obsolete legal theories designed to limit liability, such as "piercing the corporate veil." Many of these theories were created decades ago to protect individuals from personal liability and have become so outdated as to constitute at best a legal fiction, and at worst an outright fraud, in view of the realities of international corporate enterprises.

These same principles and considerations have played an instrumental role in the development and evolution of other doctrines of liability under the common law.[11] For example, strict products liability was a common law response to hazards created by the modern industrial age. U.S. courts recognized the need for the law to evolve beyond the confines of a pure negligence theory of recovery, which frequently left innocent victims uncompensated. Thus, under the doctrine of strict liability, a defendant is held liable even if its conduct does not fall within the traditional boundaries of negligence. Instead it is sufficient that the defendant acts out of a profit motive to place a defective product into the stream of commerce. Indeed the doctrine of strict liability is a form of enterprise liability that reaches all companies in the chain of distribution of a product.

U.S. Courts have recognized enterprise liability in a variety of other contexts. For example, courts have adopted a form of enterprise liability to hold an entire industry liable for acts involving industry-wide cooperation.[12] Market share liability, in which each manufacturer of an identical product may be held liable in proportion to its share of the market, is another form of enterprise theory.[13] Another enterprise concept is concert of action, which rests on the principle that "all those who, in pursuance of a common plan or design to commit a tortious act, actively take part in it, or further it by cooperation or request, or who lend aid or encouragement to the wrong-doer, or ratify and adopt his acts done for their benefit, are equally liable with him."[14] U.S. courts have also recognized the liability of principals for the acts of independent contractors carrying out hazardous and inherently dangerous activities.[15]

Courts in other countries also have recognized enterprise theories of liability in a variety of contexts. For example, the Court of Justice of the European Economic Community upheld the liability of a parent corporation for the price-fixing activities of its subsidiaries, noting that "the fact that the subsidiary has a distinct legal personality does not suffice to dispose of the possibility that its behavior might be imputed to the parent company."[16]

Finally, the Supreme Court of India recognized the absolute and nondelegable duty of an enterprise engaged in an inherently dangerous activity in a case decided while the Bhopal litigation was pending in the Indian courts. In *M. C. Mehta v. Union of India,* a case involving another toxic gas leak, the Supreme Court of India stated:

We would therefore hold that where an enterprise is engaged in a hazardous or inherently dangerous activity and harm results to anyone on account of an accident in the operation of such hazardous or inherently dangerous activity resulting, for example, in escape of toxic gas *the enterprise is strictly and absolutely liable* to compensate all those who are affected by the accident.

We are of the view that an enterprise which is engaged in a hazardous or inherently dangerous industry which poses a potential threat to the health and safety of the persons working in the factory and residing in the surrounding areas owes an *absolute and nondelegable duty to the community* to ensure that no harm results to anyone on account of hazardous or inherently dangerous nature of the activity which it has undertaken.[17]

This decision had obvious significance for the Bhopal litigation. However, the issue of the applicability of the doctrine of multinational enterprise liability was never decided because Union Carbide and the Union of India reached a settlement prior to a decision of this issue.

Although unresolved in the Bhopal litigation, it is clearly time—indeed long past time—for courts to implement the doctrine of multinational enterprise liability. The doctrine is not a radical concept in the fields of either law or economics but rather a natural development of the common law and an initial response to the general recognition of the necessity for regulation of multinational enterprises.

NOTES

1. The Union of India v. Union Carbide Corporation, No. 85 Civ. 2696 (JFK), U.S. District Court, Southern District of New York, April 8, 1985.

2. A detailed factual analysis of Union Carbide's liability is beyond the scope of this chapter. For a further discussion of the factual basis of liability, see Memorandum of Law in Opposition to Union Carbide Corporation's Motion to Dismiss These Actions on the Grounds of Forum Non Conveniens, filed by the Plaintiffs' Executive Committee on December 6, 1985, in the U.S. District Court, Southern District of New York.

3. Deposition of James M. Rehfield, at pp. 228–29. "The Structure of Private Multinational Enterprise."

4. *Michigan Law Review* 71 (March 1973): 731–806.

5. Ibid., p. 742.

6. Ibid., p. 749.

7. Ibid., p. 752.

8. *Barcelona Traction, Light & Power Co. (Belgium) v. Spain* [1970], I.C.J.3.

9. Testimony of Jean-Jacques Servan Schreiber, *Hearings before the Subcommittee on Foreign Economic Policy of the Joint Economic Commissions,* 91st Cong., 2d sess., 1970, p. 935.

10. David Aronofsky, "Piercing the Transnational Corporate Veil: Trends, Developments and the Need for Widespread Adoption of Enterprise Analysis," *North Carolina Journal of International Law and Commercial Regulation* 10 (1985): 31, 86.

11. The best-known work on tort law in the United States concludes that the following similar factors have shaped the development of tort law: a recognized need for compensation, historical development, moral aspect of defendant's conduct, convenience of administration, capacity to bear or distribute loss, and prevention and punishment. *Prosser and Keeton on Torts,* 5th ed. (St. Paul, Minn.: West Publishing, 1984), pp. 20–25.

12. *Hall v. E. I. Du Pont de Nemours & Co. Inc.,* 345 F. Supp. 353 (E.D.N.Y. 1972).

13. *Sindell v. Abbott Laboratories,* 26 Cal. 3d 588 (1980).

14. *Bichler v. Eli Lilly & Co.,* 55 N.Y.2d 571, 580 (1982).

15. The Restatement (Second) of Torts, Sec. 427A, provides: "One who employs an independent contractor to do work which the employer know or has reason to know involves an abnormally dangerous activity is subject to liability to the same extent as the contractor for physical harm to others caused by the activity."

16. *Imperial Chemicals Industries, Ltd. v. Commission of the European Communities,* 1972 E.C.R. 619, 661.

17. 1986(1) SCALE (*Statutes and Cases Automated Legal Enquiry*) 199, at 1202, 1203 (emphasis added).

The Proposal of Multinational Enterprise Liability in the Bhopal Litigation

ROBERT A. BUTLER

During the course of the litigation arising out of the Bhopal disaster, the government of India attempted on several occasions to introduce a new concept of liability into the case that no court in the world had ever sanctioned. Throughout this century, one of the most important tenets of the world economy has been the principle of limited liability—the concept that owning shares of a company does not make the shareholder liable for the debts or activities of the corporation. Nicholas Murray Butler, president of Columbia University, thoughtfully stated:

I weigh my words when I say that in my judgment the limited liability corporation is the greatest single discovery of modern times, whether you judge it by its social, by its ethical, by its industrial or, in the long run—after we understand it and know how to use it—by its political effects. Even steam and electricity are far less important than the limited liability corporation, and they would be reduced to comparative impotence without it.[1]

In the Bhopal litigation, the Indian government attempted a direct attack on the principle of limited liability by alleging a new theory, multinational enterprise liability, that postulated that so-called multinational corporations are not entitled to limited liability and are directly liable for any actions of companies whose shares they own. As articulated by the government in its pleading in the Bhopal case, the theory states:

Key management personnel of multinationals exercise a closely-held power which is neither restricted by national boundaries nor effectively controlled by international law. The complex corporate structure of the multinational, with networks of subsidiaries and divisions, makes it exceedingly difficult or even impossible to pinpoint responsibility for the damage caused by the enterprise to discrete corporate units or individuals. In reality, there is but one entity, the monolithic multinational, which is responsible for the design, development and dissemination of information and technology worldwide, acting through a forged network of interlocking directors, common operating systems, global distribution and marketing systems, financial and other controls.[2]

There are many problems with the proposed doctrine, not the least of which is that it did not even apply to the facts of the case in which it was being espoused. Since at least the 1960s, India has been concerned about the impact of foreign investment on its industry and people and has developed a vast array of laws, regulations, and agencies to ensure that Indian companies were controlled and managed by Indians and that foreign companies could exercise virtually no control over Indian companies in which they had invested. Indeed every sentence in the portion of the government's pleading was specifically not the case with respect to Union Carbide India Limited (UCIL).

At the time of the tragedy, all of the employees and officers of the company, including its managing director, were Indians. None of Union Carbide Corporation's directors were on the board of the Indian company. UCIL had numerous sales offices, over fifty warehouses, and fourteen manufacturing plants, which manufactured chemicals, plastics, pesticides, fertilizers, and dry cell batteries, all for use in India.

The Bhopal plant employed approximately 650 people, all Indians. The products manufactured at the plant were sold only in India. Each phase of the Bhopal plant's construction was financed entirely by the Indian company, borrowing solely on its own credit. At no time did Union Carbide Corporation participate in the financing of the Bhopal plant, nor did it directly or indirectly guarantee any loans extended to the Indian company.

Methyl isocyanate (MIC), the gas that was released, is an intermediate in the production of certain pesticides manufactured at the Bhopal plant. Although it would have been far more economical for UCIL to have imported the pesticides from Union Carbide Corporation and sold them in India, and UCIL would have preferred that, the Indian government required the Indian company to manufacture MIC in India if it wished to sell pesticides in India. But for the government's insistence, MIC would never have been manufactured by UCIL in India.

The Bhopal site was selected by the Indian company with the concurrence of the government. The property on which the plant is situated is owned by the government and leased to the Indian company. The financial plans for the construction and development of the plant were presented to and approved by the Indian government. Much of the funding for the plant was provided by financial institutions controlled by the Indian government. Before the Indian company could make any purchase abroad, it had to demonstrate to the government that the materials and equipment sought were not available from any Indian supplier.

The government drastically limited Union Carbide Corporation's involvement in the plant. Union Carbide Corporation was allowed—ten years before the disaster—only to transfer preliminary process design packages to the Indian company for the Bhopal plant. The blueprints and detail design plans for the plan were required to be prepared entirely in India by Indian engineers. An Indian company had to be the general contractor for the plant, and subcontractors had to be Indian concerns. The designs, drawings, and blueprints were all approved by agencies of the government of India. In addition to pervasive involvement in the construction of the plant, over two dozen Indian governmental agencies were involved in regulating every activity at the plant after it started operating.

As the U.S. Second Circuit Court of Appeals said when it affirmed the dismissal of the government's case in favor of an Indian court, "UCC's participation was limited and its involvement in plant operations terminated long before the accident," and "in short, the plant has been constructed and managed by Indians in India."[3] Accordingly, one of the central difficulties confronting the American attorneys for the Indian government, who had developed the multinational enterprise liability theory, was the fact that their own client's laws and regulations for over twenty years, as well as its specific actions with respect to the Bhopal plant, were directly inconsistent with the novel theory they were proposing should apply to the case. For twenty years, the government had treated UCIL as a separate, self-contained, wholly Indian entity, and yet it was now claiming in court that the company was in fact merely a piece of a much larger foreign entity.

In addition to its inconsistency with the facts of the case, the multinational enterprise liability proposal was also contrary to well-established law. Under principles intended to allow a corporation to raise investment capital, the law has long exempted shareholders from liability for the debts or other acts of the corporation they invest in. It is only in the rare instance where a corporation is the "mere instrumentality" or "alter ego" of a shareholder that the law imposes liability on the shareholder. Holding a majority or all of the stock and using the voting rights to elect the officers and directors does not make a shareholder liable. For a parent corporation to be liable for the acts or debts of a subsidiary, there must be complete domination, and the subsidiary must be operated as a mere department of the parent. By proposing automatic, unlimited liability for parent companies, multinational enterprise liability theory would have upset long-settled law.

The multinational enterprise liability theory was also directly at odds with the efforts India and other Third World countries were making to attract foreign investment. In a world rapidly evolving into a single market, countries, particularly developing ones, are more than ever competing with other countries for investment. If the rest of the world is offering foreign investors the traditional limited liability while India is proposing to subject them to unlimited liability, investors will naturally be more inclined to seek other opportunities. India badly needs foreign investment, and developing new bases of liability for foreign investors clearly undermines that effort.

There is also a practical problem with the multinational enterprise liability theory. Inasmuch as it was concluded that the Bhopal tragedy was the result of sabotage, how is a so-called multinational corporation, which has been denied by

Indian law virtually any ability to control events in a subsidiary, supposed to protect itself against that possibility? Under such circumstances, it makes little sense in either logic or law to postulate that all of a parent company's assets should be available to satisfy claims caused by an act of sabotage.

It is similarly difficult even to discover any need for such a theory. Countries that wish to control the activities of foreign investors have ample regulatory means at their disposal to do so, and disasters where the liability exceeds a subsidiary's net worth are exceptionally rare. As the current tort liability crisis in the United States shows, developing new liability doctrines is a clumsy and inexact method of accomplishing social goals, with often unwanted consequences. The reasons no court in the world has adopted the multinational enterprise liability theory are not difficult to understand. No particular need for such a doctrine has ever been shown; there are other far more precise means of accomplishing the goals it seeks to promote, and, most significant, it would undermine one of the most important tenets of the world economy.

NOTES

1. W. Fletcher, *Cyclopedia of the Law of Private Corporations* (1917), p. 21.
2. *In re Union Carbide Corporation Gas Plant Disaster at Bhopal India in December 1984*, 809 F. 2d 195, 200 (2d Cir. 1987).
3. Ibid.

III

NEW CORPORATE STRATEGIES FOR CONTROLLING ENVIRONMENTAL RISKS

Environment and Business in the 1990s: Threats, Opportunities, and Prospects for Cooperation

RICHARD SEIBERT

At a recent National Association of Manufacturers' joint meeting of its Energy/Natural Resources and Environmental Quality committees, one of the speakers, Robert Berrier of the Wirthlin Group, related some of their polling data concerning the environment. According to the Wirthlin Group, in 1981 45 percent of the American population believed that protecting the environment was so important that environmental standards could not be set too high. By 1989 80 percent of the public agreed with that statement. In 1976 40 percent of the population agreed that economic growth should be sacrificed in order to protect the environment. By 1986 that figure had risen to 60 percent.

In the last ten years or so, a change has come over the United States. Environmentalists no longer consider themselves out of mainstream America. This is equally true for those who work for industry. Unfortunately, when the American public looks at business, it rarely sees environmentalists.

To indict business as being callous and unfeeling about the environment is not only unfair but loses sight of the very nature of business in a free enterprise system. Is it advantageous for a company to be perceived by the public as damaging the environment? Can a company with a bad environmental reputation expect to attract loyalty and support from the consumers? Can it expect to survive, let alone profit and prosper? It is not in any company's interest to ignore the public's commitment to improving environmental quality. A company that neglects or abuses the environment can expect high employee turnover, dwindling customer loyalty, and unhappy stockholders.

It is important for everyone to recognize that while much remains to be done, and must be done, great progress has been made during the twenty years since the first Earth Day. The Clean Air Act, the Clean Water Act, the Resource Conservation and Recovery Act (RCRA), and Superfund are the highlights of a lengthy list of environmental laws and regulations passed over the last twenty years. The Environmental Protection Agency (EPA) also is twenty years old.

It would be foolish not to recognize that many serious environmental problems remain, but it would be equally foolish and shortsighted to ignore some of the great strides made since 1970. Lakes and rivers once given up for dead are not only cleaner today but giving birth to plentiful new marine life. Fifteen or twenty years ago in cities like Pittsburgh and New York, smog was so thick it was almost impossible to see the tops of buildings, let alone the skyline. We enter the 1990s sobered by the seriousness of our attainment problems, but by and large air quality in most of our cities is far better today than it was in the 1960s and 1970s. In spite of a national debate over what standards should be adopted and how quickly ambitious goals can be reached, we should not allow that debate to cloud the fact that the United States has seen substantial environmental progress over the past twenty years—most of it achieved despite dramatic and continuing increases in the number of people, cars, buses, and planes located in major urban areas.

No one would claim this progress has been unnecessary, but the price for this progress has been high. It is estimated that industry currently spends upwards of $34 billion per year on environmental controls. According to the August 1989 DRI/McGraw-Hill survey of pollution control expenditures for 1988–1990, investment by all businesses for new plants and equipment for pollution abatement is running above $10 billion per year. This is investment for new pollution control facilities and does not include the billions of dollars spent annually to operate and maintain the many billions of dollars worth of pollution control facilities already in place.

Two important points must be kept in mind. First, the cost for environmental improvement has mostly been absorbed by industry, and despite the criticism heaped on it, industry has been a major force behind environmental progress. Second, many foreign competitors are not faced with as strict environmental regulations in their production processes as U.S. companies are. Therefore, it costs more for U.S. companies to manufacture a product, thus making them less competitive in the world marketplace.

Related to this second point, we need to be mindful that despite all the criticism, editorials, commentaries, and lectures aimed at American business, the United States leads the world in environmental progress. While some other countries may have stricter controls in one area—air, land, or water—overall environmental laws are more stringent in the United States than anywhere else. We in the United States all too often seem to enjoy needless self-flagellation, particularly with the environment. The popular myth is that our environmental policies are inferior to those of other countries. Although some other countries use technology-driven programs, there is no proof that they are more protective of human health than the health-based standards in the United States.

Nevertheless, some major environmental issues face the country. There currently rages a fierce debate on Capitol Hill over reauthorization of the Clean Air

Act. Once that debate is finished, Congress will begin reauthorizing RCRA and setting a comprehensive waste minimization goal. After that, attention will turn to Superfund, the Clean Water Act, and others. These debates will mostly center around setting more stringent standards and how quickly or if these standards can be attained. We in industry are concerned, however, that too often standards are not health based or even based on good science but rather on emotion. We need to recognize that scientific advances allow us to detect incredibly small traces of substances in air, water, and food, but just because something is there does not necessarily mean that we are at risk. We need to work together to develop stringent but realistic standards.

In the past, the United States has focused on "command-control" legislation, focused primarily on industry. One of the major environmental issues to be debated in the 1990s will be surface water and groundwater. Clearly this is an issue of quantity and quality that concerns everyone. Whereas the focus of improving the nation's water quality in the past has been on industry, with groundwater we acknowledge that the major culprit is nonpoint source pollution. Here we are talking about changing our farming practices and making some changes by our municipalities. Living on the Chesapeake Bay, I can assure you that controlling nonpoint source pollution is difficult.

The command-control approach on the bay has probably made about as much difference with industrial sources as it can, and still the bay suffers. We need to look for new solutions (and changes in thinking) to our problems. With the Chesapeake Bay, one of the major problems is a lack of dissolved oxygen in the water. When the EPA and others were unwilling or unable to help my community, we began our own aeration program, which has raised the dissolved oxygen level in the water. We are now noticing the return of schools of fish and have seen increasing numbers of crabs in the water. We have to shift from our old command-control mindset and look for new approaches to environmental problems.

Another shift in the future will be to the municipalities, which will face major environmental and financial headaches in the 1990s. When the Clean Water Act was originally passed, the country's goal was to build as many wastewater treatment facilities as possible. It was also believed that these facilities would last twenty-five years or longer. The experience has been something else. We never anticipated the growth that has occurred in coastal urban areas. While we were able to build such facilities in most large and medium-sized cities and towns, hookups have outstripped our treatment capacity. In many cities, raw or only partially treated sewage is being dumped in water during heavy rainstorms. Some estimate that the cost just to repair the current wastewater infrastructure system will be close to, if not in excess of, $100 billion. This does not include the cost of bringing new systems on line or dealing with additional secondary treatment systems as cities expand.

Another municipal problem growing more acute is landfills. Available space is shrinking. There are no perfect solutions, and population growth will continue to multiply the solid waste dilemma. We are the generation that will determine whether the next generation will inherit a cleaner, more livable environment. Clearly we must do more recycling and waste prevention. As far as pollution prevention, companies like 3M, Du Pont, and Polaroid have set excellent examples for the rest of industry. We at the National Association of Manufacturers, in cooperation with ENSR, a consulting engineering firm, have published a booklet on waste minimization to give encouragement to and examples of how companies can reduce their waste load into the land, air, and water. We need to shift our focus from the end of the waste stream and learn to reduce the waste produced by manufacturing processes.

One area where the United States falls short of many foreign nations is recycling. It is estimated that we recycle only 7 to 9 percent of waste; some other industrialized countries recycle in excess of 45 percent of their waste. While we can and must do a better job of recycling, the reality is that we will not live in a waste-free society. We will need to do something with our waste, whether we recycle it, put it in a landfill, or incinerate it. But as space runs out in existing landfills, it is difficult to get approval for a new landfill or incinerator site. We need to develop a public consensus on what to do with our waste. Until we do, municipalities will be caught in the middle. We also need to expedite the permitting and building of recycling centers.

The price we will pay for solving many environmental problems will also include changes in life-style. Many of the costs of environmental improvements to date have been hidden from the public. But as we ratchet standards tighter, the public will need to make life-style changes. For example, the Southern California Air Quality Commission has recommended paying to park in grocery store lots, no more barbeques using lighter fluids, driving only four days a week; telecommuting jobs, and paying up to four dollars to dry clean a shirt. We must look at the impact these economic changes will have on low-income persons.

Perhaps the most positive development in the 1980s was the realization that global problems demand global solutions. Americans now seem to recognize that we cannot solve the global climate issue by ourselves; we need the cooperation of all countries. While having a major impact on the economy, a unilateral U.S. reduction in carbon dioxide emissions could have little effect in reducing greenhouse gases if one considers the amount of coal China and India plan to burn, apparently without any pollution controls, into the next century.

Economic growth and strength can only expand the available resources and technology available to utilize in tackling environmental challenges. Economic strength can enhance environmental commitment. It is not just industry but families and individuals who must make sacrifices and choices. Those choices must reflect a commitment but in day-to-day life-styles and habits.

Free enterprise has provided us with much to be thankful for in the United States. Most of the rest of the world still hungers to attain our standard of living. It is perhaps because we are so spoiled by the fruits of our progress, conveniences, and creature comforts that we find it so easy to criticize and argue about how much more might have been done instead of agreeing on what realistically can be done. Americans have not solved great problems or won great challenges by fighting among themselves. Whether those challenges have been world wars, the race to the moon, or breathing new life into a stagnant economy, the United States always manages to succeed when it pulls together, not apart. If there is a lesson to carry into the 1990s it should be not to turn the debate over environmental problems into a costly fight no one will win.

Imposing additional heavy regulatory and financial burdens on business may pacify some environmental activists but will not solve our problems any sooner and may extract a heavier price in the long run. Every American has a stake in meeting the environmental challenge.

I have been impressed with much of the progress, initiative, and leadership that industry has provided in the effort to improve the quality of the environment. These success stories must be told—not only because it is fair to keep a proper perspective but because success breeds success. Other companies can learn from successful examples.

No company that deliberately ignores environmental laws, regulations, and public fervor today deserves to be spared from proper accountability or appropriate penalties. However, citizens and politicians must recognize that environmental problems cannot be laid at industry's feet alone. Political leaders must focus on workable, intelligent solutions, not emotion and political pandering to make industry the scapegoat for a problem it was not exclusively responsible for and alone cannot solve. Everyone must do their part to ensure a cleaner and safer environment for succeeding generations. Just saying you care is not enough today and certainly will not be enough in the 1990s. Actions speak louder than words.

The Development and Implementation of Industry-wide Environmental Codes of Practice

DAVID POWELL

A code of conduct, business practice, or ethics is commonly used by a business to define a commitment to lawful and ethical business practice and to guide employees in appropriate business behavior. The focus is usually on the business activities commonplace to the company, such as marketing and relations with customers and governments, although an important variation, the code of environmental practice, has emerged within Canadian industries whose operations affect the environment.

A business code is normally promulgated by a corporation and enforced by it. Sanctions and punishments administered for code infractions are within the authority of the organization in its capacity as employer. The corporation has the power and authority to enforce its code, the observance of its prohibitions serving as a condition of employment.

In trade associations, the situation has been completely different. Membership is voluntary, dues are determined according to formulas developed by the membership, and minimal authority is ceded to the management of the association. This chapter reports on a new and important development: the development and enforcement of mandatory codes of practice for the environment and occupational and public health and safety by the membership of the Canadian Chemical Producers' Association (CCPA).

The climate for the introduction of environmental codes of practice has been created by a number of factors. In recent years, the public has become increasingly more aware of and knowledgeable about environmental concerns and is placing increasing demands on industry and government to improve the prevention and cleanup of environmental problems. Governments in Canada are responding with much tougher environmental legislation and regulations governing industrial activity. Although industry usually objects to increased regulatory control, more progressive and aware industries recognize that this is often necessary. In order to minimize negative impacts resulting from inappropriate or unnecessary regulation, some companies and industries respond by taking a proactive role in setting the regulatory agenda. They get involved as partners with governments early in the development of new legislation and regulations and establish self-regulatory activities designed to reduce the need for government regulation and influence the nature of regulations that are introduced. Environmental codes of practice are an important self-regulatory tool for achieving this goal.

The costs of environmental incidents and ongoing environmental problems are becoming increasingly too expensive in terms of both cleanup and negative public and customer perception, which results in lost business or consumer boycotts. Environmental codes of practice can be a useful mechanism for preventing environmental problems and providing effective response to environmental incidents.

Finally, environmental advisory bodies at the international and national level are recommending developing codes of practice for industry. In 1987 the United Nations' World Commission on Environment and Development, commonly referred to as the Brundtland commission, recommended that "all industrial enterprises, trade associations and labour unions should establish company-wide or industry-wide policies concerning resource and environmental management."[1] Later that year in Canada, the National Task Force on Environment and Economy, composed of Canada's environment ministers, senior executive officers from Canadian industry, and representatives from environmental organizations and academia, recommended in its final report that industry associations develop environmental codes of practice for their members.[2]

THE CCPA CODES OF PRACTICE

The CCPA has a membership of seventy-three companies that produce a broad range of chemicals and whose annual sales represent about 90 percent of the Canadian market. In the late 1970s the CCPA adopted the Statement of Policy on Responsible Care, which includes a set of Guiding Principles pertaining to the protection of people and the environment from the hazards of operations; the understanding of the hazards associated with new and existing products, processes, and plants; the provision of information on hazards to those affected by operations; responsiveness to the concerns of the community; and proactive involvement with governments and others in developing standards.

In the aftermath of Bhopal in December 1984, the CCPA board of directors (senior member company executives) made the following decisions to strengthen responsible care:

• To make membership in the association contingent on signature to the Guiding Principles.

- To create a safety assessment program to be carried out at each member plant site involving a safety assessment of plant operations and a determination of its emergency response capability (the first series of assessments was completed by late 1986).
- To follow up this program with a Community Awareness and Emergency Response Program (CAER) at each site.
- To initiate a process to examine environmental and health and safety concerns in the full chemical life cycle and to conceptualize a program response to be carried out in consultation with its members.

At the annual meeting of June 1986, the membership approved the following components of this program response:

1. A research survey of public opinion of the environmental commitment and performance of the industry.
2. The development of a chemical referral center to answer public inquiries about chemicals and their associated hazards (it was in operation by August 1988).
3. An ongoing advisory panel of environmental and consumer activists (instituted in the fall of 1986).
4. The development of codes of practice to address environmental and occupational and public health and safety concerns throughout the full chemical life cycle from research and development to management of wastes.

The results of the public opinion research survey, made public in November 1986, indicated strong public distrust of the industry, public concern about unacceptable environmental risks associated with the industry, and a lack of industry openness with communities. The CCPA made a public commitment to respond to these concerns through the programs under responsible care.

The focal point of responsible care is the codes of practice. To date six codes have been developed covering the full chemical life cycle. There are separate codes of practice for research and development, manufacturing, community awareness and emergency response (CAER), distribution, transportation, and hazardous waste management. The CAER code incorporates the CAER program begun in June 1986, and there is a related Community-Right-to-Know Policy. The Safety Assessment Program is being subsumed under the Manufacturing Code of Practice.

The development and implementation of the codes was carefully planned. The CCPA hired a responsible care coordinator to administer this process who had extensive experience in the industry. A responsible care management committee of the CCPA board oversaw the process. Each code was developed by a task force composed of member company representatives with expertise relevant to the code in question. A draft of each code was circulated to the Advisory Panel for comment at least twice before being finalized by the code task force. Panel comments on existing code content and omissions were given serious consideration by each task force, and recommended changes or additions were either made or reasons for not doing so were conveyed to the panel. Drafts were circulated to the responsible care management committee for comment, and the final version was approved by this committee and then the full board. Once the six codes were completed, they were given to me, a member of the Advisory Panel, to ensure there were no significant inconsistencies in language or content among the codes. I worked with the responsible care coordinator and consulted with each task force chairman during this process, as well as with the Advisory Panel. The codes were then submitted to the responsible care management committee and the board for approval in April 1989.

The implementation program for the codes of practice is currently being under-taken. Member companies are expected to complete this implementation pro-cess, including the first evaluation of procedures developed under the codes, by December 1992. The senior executives of member companies are strongly com-mitted to implementing the codes.

For each code, an implementation subcommittee is creating implementation support materials. These include a standards guide containing operational defini-tions of code statements and a detailed description of the operational implications of the code on which each member can build its own detailed implementation plan. The CCPA has developed programs for training member company person-nel about the purpose and implementation of each code. These programs include introductory seminars, an introductory video, which has also been distributed to each member company senior executive, and detailed training seminars.

The adoption of the codes of practice is a condition of membership in the CCPA. The senior executive of each member company must formally agree to implement each code within a company-specific milestone timetable, which was submitted to the CCPA by October 1989. The CCPA will be monitoring this process through aggregate data on member company implementation perfor-mance to ensure that members are meeting their implementation timetables and to identify any problems. The implementation subcommittees are also a forum for identifying and discussing implementation problems of a technical nature. Implementation problems at the policy level will be discussed in the responsible care leadership groups, composed of the senior executives of member com-panies. Those in companies with implementation successes will encourage and offer support to their counterparts in other member companies that may be experiencing implementation difficulties.

The CCPA has also created ongoing national and regional task forces that bring together representatives from member companies, the transportation indus-try, governments, and public agencies, such as police, fire, and transportation regulation, to facilitate and coordinate the integration of the transportation code with existing transportation, regulatory, and emergency response systems. The CAER code requires members to integrate their emergency response plans for each site with those agencies involved in emergency response at the community level.

Once the codes have been implemented, the CCPA will not formally audit its members to determine code compliance. It does not believe that such a policing action is appropriate. It believes that noncompliance will be manifested in the behavior of a member and be obvious to the CCPA, which will respond by inquiring about compliance problems that a member may be having and by offering assistance. A member failing to alter its behavior will be expelled from the organization.

The CCPA has ongoing communications with other industry associations involved with chemicals through member companies represented on the boards of these associations to encourage them to adopt similar codes of practice. For example, the Canadian Association of Chemical Distributors is adopting the CCPA Distribution Code of Practice for its members, with the CCPA providing implementation support to this effort.

The codes of practice themselves expand on the original guiding principles of responsible care. Each begins with a reference to the objectives of responsible care and to the guiding principles. The codes require that member companies meet or exceed the letter and the spirit of the law. They require that policies and procedures are created that identify risks to people and the environment, eliminate or minimize those risks, provide information to all stakeholders about these risks, provide effective emergency response, and train and evaluate company personnel in risk management. They require that policies, procedures, and performance be periodically audited and updated by each member and that necessary corrective action be taken. Operations are not to be undertaken unless they meet code requirements. The codes make certain requirements of contractors, suppliers, distributors, and even customers. Finally, they require that, when possible, member companies work with other affected stakeholders to assist governments in the development of relevant public policies, legislation, and regulations. The codes themselves will be periodically improved over time in the light of the experience of member companies in their implementation and practice.

Although each code is written to stand on its own, the complete set of codes has been published as a package with the Statement of Policy on Responsible Care and a preamble outlining the objectives of the codes and their implications for member companies and their employees.[3] The preamble emphasizes the importance of ethical thinking, decision making and performance in meeting code requirements, and the need to give consideration to the concerns of all affected stakeholders in decision making. This package has been given to those within member companies who have responsibilities under the codes and is available to the public.

Chemical industry associations in other countries are following the CCPA's lead. Some are now developing codes of practice (the United States, the United Kingdom, New Zealand and Australia), and others have made inquiries of the CCPA (Japan, Sweden and the European association).

SUCCESS FACTORS

The process the CCPA employed provides a useful case study of the effective development and implementation of environmental codes of practice for an industry.

Having the process originate from within a major industry association is important for achieving broad and consistent environmental practices across an industry, for ensuring individual company adoption of codes, and for facilitating the implementation process within each company through association support services. In effect, the association provides a channel for more committed association members with greater resources to assist other members that might be unable to develop or implement such codes on their own. Although not necessary in the case of the CCPA codes, the process also allows senior executives of committed member companies to encourage code adoption by less committed members through peer pressure. The use of task forces composed of member company representatives to develop the codes ensures technical comprehensiveness and encourages code adoption through a sense of ownership at the company and individual levels. The use of a coordinator for code development and implementation who has extensive industry experience increases the credibility of the process to task force members and improves the effectiveness and efficiency of the program. Consultation with the concerned public through a mechanism such as the advisory panel ensures that public concerns are understood and addressed, and increases public credibility in the codes. A public commitment by the industry to the codes also increases credibility, as does making them public documents.

Adoption of the codes is ensured because it is a condition of membership in the association. In addition to the implementation support materials and program, effective code implementation is enhanced through the visible commitment of senior company executives and the milestone timetables, which facilitate timely implementation and identify companies with implementation problems to the association. Code compliance is ensured through ongoing assistance from the association and the ultimate sanction of expulsion and enhanced through the ongoing evaluation of personnel, policies and procedures, and operations within member companies. The integration of the codes with outside agencies involved in emergency response is also important in facilitating code compliance.

The ongoing revision of the codes in the light of member company experience with them is made more effective because the revision can be based on the collective experience of the association's members.

In terms of content, the CCPA codes are comprehensive in meeting the essential requirements of such codes. Environmental codes of practice should be linked to a general mission statement on responsible environmental practices. The use of a preamble explaining the objectives and implications of the codes is important for ensuring understanding and acceptance by those responsible for implementing them and for gaining the understanding and trust of the public.

Codes should require that companies subject to them meet or exceed the letter and the spirit of the law. This commits the companies adopting them to ethical thinking, decision making, and practice. The codes should be comprehensive in their content by addressing the identification and control of risks, the needs of affected people and communities for protection and information, and the evaluation of personnel, policies and procedures, and practices. Where appropriate, they should make requirements of suppliers, distributors, and customers. They should restrict operations that cannot be carried out in compliance with the codes. Finally, they should address the importance of involvement with government in developing environmental public policies, legislation, and regulations.

OTHER CANADIAN EFFORTS

There are several other cases of environmental codes of ethics or practice being implemented or developed in Canada on an industry-wide basis. To date, none of these is as comprehensive as the CCPA's program.

The Canadian Petroleum Association (CPA) has developed a code of practice for its sixty-five members that contains many of the essential requirements of the codes as discussed, although there is no requirement to exceed the law in letter and in spirit. The code was developed by a committee of technical people from member companies. The public was consulted during the development process. There are related support materials and an initial seminar was held to provide implementation guidance. The CPA does not require code implementation and compliance as a condition of membership but only recommends adoption. There is no procedure to monitor implementation. Although the code is a public document, there has been no general effort to publicize it.

The Crop Protection Institute (CPI), the Canadian association for pesticide manufacturers, is in the process of developing and implementing the Code of Warehousing Standards for its members, distributors and retailers. The standards will act as a building code for new warehousing facilities and a guide for upgrading existing facilities. The CPI is providing implementation training and support to its members and will informally monitor member compliance. A member could be expelled from the CPI for failure to comply.

The Mining Association of Canada issued a Mining Policy on Environment in May 1989 and is planning to develop and implement related codes of practice governing mining activities. Members are not required to sign off against the association's policy, but there is moral suasion for each member to adopt a comparable company policy.

The Taskforce on Churches and Corporate Responsibility (TCCR) is developing a comprehensive model code of practice on forest land management for the Canadian forest industry through consultation with professional foresters, environmentalists, and representatives from the few forestry companies that already have some kind of a code of practice for forest land management. No forest industry association has taken the lead here, so code adoption beyond a company-by-company basis seems unlikely unless the TCCR can convince an association to promote it.

The Canadian Pulp and Paper Association issues an environmental statement in June 1989 similar to the guiding principles of the CCPA. Although there has been no decision to follow up with a code(s) of practice, one is under consideration. Members are not required to adopt the statement, but they are expected to adopt policies and practices reflecting the intent of the statement. The CPPA and provincial associations are providing implementation support to members for developing such policies and practices.

The Ontario Waste Management Association, which represents the private waste management industry, adopted the Membership Code of Ethics in 1986 that contains statements on environment and occupational health and safety. Members must sign off against the code and can be disciplined for noncompliance or criminal convictions. This disciplinary action can be dismissal from the association.

The Ontario Liquid Waste Haulers' Association has a code of conduct that includes consideration of the environment. The code sets a minimum standard of practice for members. Noncompliance could result in dismissal from the association.

CONCLUSIONS

The development and implementation of mandatory environmental codes of practice through industry associations can be an effective approach to better environmental practice and performance by industry. Well-designed codes promote and improve ethical business thinking and behavior. They also encourage the involvement of business with other affected stakeholders in the development of effective and efficient public policies, legislation, and regulations. Successful code implementation and compliance improve the credibility and moral authority of industry. In Canada the courts are using the standard of best environmental practice within an industry in making judicial decisions. Environmental codes of practice set such industry-wide standards of best practice. This means that companies within an industry that are not members of an industry association that has adopted such codes are effectively bound by these codes as far as the courts are concerned.

Environmental codes of practice help to protect people and the environment, as well as companies that adopt them.

NOTES

I am indebted to Professor Max Clarkson, director of the Centre for Corporate Social Performance and Ethics, Faculty of Management, University of Toronto, for his advice, and to J. A. O'Connor, vice-president and director of public affairs for the CCPA for providing information about the programs under responsible care.

1. World Commission on Environment and Development, *Our Common Future* (Oxford: Oxford University Press, 1987), pp. 222–23.

2. National Task Force on Environment and Economy, *Report of the National Task Force on Environment and Economy* (Ottawa: Canadian Council of Resource and Environment Ministers, 1987), p. 9.

3. Canadian Chemical Producers' Association, *Codes of Practice Commitment Package* (Ottawa: CCPA, 1989).

Dilemmas of Disclosure: Ethical Issues in Environmental Auditing

KAREN BLUMENFELD

Environmental auditors occasionally face conflicts between competing moral demands. Situations may arise where an environmental auditor's duty to his or her employer appears to conflict with the duty to protect innocent third parties from harm. This chapter explores a fundamental question of environmental auditing ethics: what is an environmental auditor's ethical responsibility when he or she has identified a potentially serious environmental risk and, after reporting the risk through appropriate company channels, feels that the company is failing to take responsible action? Does the auditor have a moral duty to disclose the potential problem to outside representatives (e.g., the government, the plant's neighbors, or the press), or is any public duty superseded by an obligation to protect the employer's confidentiality?

I will argue that an environmental auditor does not have a special professional duty to protect third parties from harm, but the auditor does have an ordinary moral duty to do so. In the situation described, this ordinary moral duty conflicts with the auditor's fiduciary duty to protect the employer's confidentiality.[1] Both duties represent legitimate moral expectations. A principle for their reconciliation must be defined. In the absence of environmental auditing professional standards or codes of ethics, I propose a series of tests for evaluating auditors' ethical obligations when their duty to the public conflicts with their duty to their employer.

The scope of this chapter is limited in two ways. First, it is limited to ethical issues involved in the disclosure dilemma; legal issues are outside its scope. Second, it focuses exclusively on internal environmental auditors. Because special issues of professional responsibility and liability may arise with outside auditing consultants, I chose to limit the paper's scope to internal environmental auditors.

THE SCENARIO

Ed Anderson is a seasoned environmental auditor. He is a chemical engineer by training and has been with the Western Manufacturing Company for nineteen years. Prior to 1985, Anderson held increasingly responsible positions in three different plants. In 1985, while Anderson was manufacturing engineering director at the Alameda plant, he was offered the opportunity to head the new corporate environmental auditing program. Anderson accepted the offer and now heads a group of four drawn from various company operations. As director of the Environmental Audit Department, Ed Anderson reports to the company's vice-president for health, safety, and the environment. He is responsible for planning, managing, participating in, and ensuring the proper reporting of periodic environmental audits of company operations.

Western Manufacturing Company established its corporate environmental auditing program in response to a series of small but embarrassing penalties by the Environmental Protection Agency (EPA) for violations of hazardous waste regulations at two plants. In spite of the company's substantially increased investment in environmental controls, the chief executive officer (CEO) did not feel comfortable that he or his senior management team understood the firm's potential environmental exposures. On hearing about the practice of environmental auditing among nearly all his competitors by 1984 and spurred by the Bhopal tragedy, the CEO decided to establish a corporate environmental auditing program. The program would provide top management with independent assurance that company operations are in compliance with applicable environmental laws and regulations. In initiating the program, the CEO made clear to all corporate staff and line managers the company's commitment to protecting the environment and complying with the law. He clearly articulated his intent that compliance problems identified during environmental audits would be remedied. After all, he observed, the company would be foolhardy to identify and document environmental problems if it did not have a serious commitment to fixing them.

Ed Anderson and the vice-president for health, safety, and the environment designed the audit program based on discussions with other environmental professionals and a detailed review of the environmental auditing literature. Figure 18.1 illustrates the principles of environmental auditing that Anderson and his boss established for the company. Western's environmental auditing program is now running smoothly. The program has virtually full cooperation from plant personnel who generally understand that the program is not designed to punish the plants but rather to protect the company and the plants from unreasonable environmental risks and associated liabilities.

THE AUDITOR'S DISCLOSURE DILEMMA

In January 1989 Ed Anderson and two fellow auditors are on a routine audit at the Columbia plant. At the audit close-out meeting with the plant manager and

Figure 18.1
Western Manufacturing Company Environmental Auditing Principles

1.   Environmental Audit Definition:

Environmental auditing is a methodical and documented examination of our facilities' operations and practices to evaluate the extent to which they meet environmental laws and regulations.

2.   Environmental Audit Program Objective:

The primary objective of Western Manufacturing Company's environmental audit program is to provide assurance to top management that facility operations are in compliance with environmental laws and regulations, and that reasonable steps are being taken to correct identified environmental problems.

3.   Environmental Audit Program Direction:

Western Manufacturing Company's environmental audit program is sanctioned by the Chief Executive Officer and the Board of Directors. Top management support is demonstrated through our corporate environmental policy statement, which articulates management's desire for Western Manufacturing Company to be in full compliance with environmental requirements and management's commitment to follow-up on audit findings that require corrections.

4.   Environmental Audit Organization:

The environmental audit function is independent of all line operations being audited. To assure operational independence, the Environmental Audit Department reports to the Vice President for Health, Safety, and the Environment who reports to the CEO through the Executive Vice President for Corporate Affairs.

5.   Environmental Audit Program Staffing:

The Environmental Audit Department is staffed by experienced individuals drawn from company operations. These individuals are drawn both from plant operations and from plant environmental staff positions. All environmental auditors receive initial training in audit skills, knowledge and techniques, as well as continuing education and training during their tenure as auditors. It is expected that some number of auditors will return full-time to plant operations after 3-5 years in the Environmental Audit Department. In addition to providing an important corporate assurance function, the environmental auditing program is also considered to provide a useful training ground for rising professionals in the corporation.

6.   Environmental Audit Program Design:

Typically, an audit begins with pre-audit planning which involves notifying the plant being audited, arranging trip logistics, and reviewing background information. The on-site audit activities normally are conducted in four steps: (1) understand and evaluate internal environmental management systems; (2) collect relevant information; (3) evaluate information collected; and (4) report audit findings. Following the on-site visit, the audit concludes with formal reporting and ensuring that identified deficiencies are corrected. These steps are codified in a series of written audit protocols. The scope of each audit is determined in advance and may include air pollution control and/or water pollution control and/or hazardous and solid waste management. A system has been established for determining audit frequency, but in no case will any plant be audited less than once every 4 years.

7.   Quality Assurance:

Program quality assurance will be ensured by periodic independent reviews of Western Manufacturing Company's program by an outside consultant.

environmental coordinator, Ed Anderson presents the audit team's findings. He notes that the plant appears to be largely in compliance with applicable laws, regulations, and permit conditions; however, the most serious finding, in his judgment, is a situation that goes beyond compliance. The audit team has observed that the plant has limited preventive maintenance programs and aging physical facilities. Failure of any of several hazardous chemical storage loading and transfer systems could result in contamination of a water supply serving

750,000 people. Ed Anderson is convinced that a major spillage is imminent. He agrees not to document this issue in his audit report since no compliance problem is involved; however, he asks the plant manager to study the problem further to determine the degree of risk posed to the community.

The following week, Ed Anderson prepares the draft audit report and sends it to the Columbia plant manager with copies to the specialty chemicals division manager, the vice-president for health, safety, and the environment, and the office of general counsel. Four weeks later, the Columbia plant manager's response arrives. Follow-up actions have been specified for each of the audit findings with reasonable timetables for their implementation, but no mention is made of the potential spillage risk. While legally the company is not obliged to take action, Anderson feels that from a risk management standpoint, at least a study of the problem should be undertaken. He telephones the plant manager, who disagrees.

Anderson is unable to find support for his position in the company. The cost of corrective action and the company's plan to close the plant in three years have resulted in a management decision to accept the risk that the plant poses, a risk that management believes to be small. "Drop it," Ed Anderson is told. This is the first serious conflict Anderson has faced since joining the corporate staff. He feels strongly that the problem, if not fully addressed, could cause a major spillage, which would almost certainly contaminate the local water supply; however, it is not his job responsibility to fix environmental problems, only to identify and report them truthfully to company management. Plant management is responsible for fixing the problems. Worse, Ed Anderson is not entirely sure of the probability that a spill may occur. A cursory analysis was equivocal; it would take a considerable amount of effort to evaluate the risk fully.

Anderson feels he is in a moral bind. He believes that as an environmental professional he has a public duty to protect human health and the environment. He views the environmental auditor role as, at least in part, an environmental stewardship responsibility. He suspects he should notify the community about the potential danger even at the risk of losing his job. On the other hand, as a nineteen-year loyal employee of the Western Manufacturing Company, Anderson feels he has a general professional obligation to maintain the confidentiality of information that he obtained during an audit, under the good faith assumption that his findings would be kept confidential. He also wants to be careful not to undermine the audit program, to which the company is firmly committed, and which has important social value.

THE DILEMMA IN ETHICAL TERMS

Underlying Anderson's disclosure dilemma are two legitimate but opposing assumptions. First, he assumes that environmental professionals have a general duty to protect human health and the environment. Second, he assumes that professionals of all kinds have an obligation to protect the confidentiality of their

Figure 18.2
The Dilemma in Ethical Terms

Assumption	Underlying Principles	
	Fundamental Duty	Consequences
1. Failure to disclose a hazard which could potentially cause serious harm to human health or the environment is unethical.	There exists a fundamental moral duty to protect innocent third parties from harm.	Disclosure of the hazard might prevent significant human health or environmental damage.
2. Failure of an internal auditor to protect the confidentiality of his or her employer is unethical.	The auditor has a fundamental moral obligation not to disclose company information collected on the assumption that it would remain confidential.	Disclosure of confidential information jeopardizes the trust which underlies all current and future audits.

employers. He feels the second obligation keenly in a situation such as his, where, without the assumption of confidentiality, a socially responsible voluntary corporate activity—environmental auditing—would not exist.

Although Ed Anderson is an engineer, not a philosopher, his assumptions each contain two driving principles: one relates to the fundamental duty underlying his actions and the other to the consequences of his actions. The fundamental duty principle assumes that the ethical value of an action is strictly a function of the inherent moral duty from which the action derives. The consequentialist principle assumes that the ethical value of an action is strictly a function of its consequences. Figure 18.2 illustrates the fundamental duty and consequentialist principles underlying Ed Anderson's dilemma. In practice, these two principles complement and inform each other; however, for the sake of discussion, the two principles are treated separately.

DISCUSSION

This discussion centers on two questions: (1) Is Ed Anderson morally obliged to protect human health and the environment, and if so, on what basis? (2) Is he morally obliged to protect his employer's confidentiality, and on what basis? The discussion is organized around the fundamental duty and consequentialist principles underlying each question.

Is the Environmental Auditor Morally Obliged to Protect Human Health and the Environment?

The first question has to do with Ed Anderson's obligation to protect human health and the environment. His concern is that failure to disclose a hazard that could potentially cause serious harm to human health or the environment is unethical.

The Duty

Ed Anderson believes he has a basic moral duty, derived from his position as an environmental auditor, to protect human health and the environment. I will argue that he does have such a duty, but it is the same ordinary moral duty held by any individual, not a special duty derived from his position as environmental auditor.

The environmental auditing field is still emerging and is not yet fully professionalized. As a result, environmental auditors do not, in my judgment, currently have a special professional duty to protect the public—analogous, say, to the duties of public accountants.

The ethics literature is rich with descriptions as to what constitutes a profession. Three examples provide a sense of range of definitions:

Succinctly put, all professions seem to possess: (1) systematic theory, (2) authority, (3) community sanction, (4) ethical codes, and (5) a culture. (Ernest Greenwood in Baumrin and Freedman, 1983, p. 21).

[A profession has] three necessary features. . . . First, a rather extensive training is required to practice a profession. . . . Second, the training involves a significant intellectual component. . . . Third, the trained ability provides an important service in society. . . . Other features are common to most professions although they are not necessary for professional status. Usually a process of certification or licensing exists. . . . Another feature common to professions is an organization of members. . . . A third common feature of the professional is autonomy in his or her work. (Michael Bayles in Callahan, 1988, p. 28).

In general, we can agree that a profession has the following:
1. a clearly defined field of expertise, which distinguishes members of the profession from all other careers;
2. a period of prescribed education or training which precedes entry into membership;
3. a selective process of entry into the profession, restricting its membership to those qualified;
4. a procedure for testing and licensing, generally approved by a state agency under guidance from the profession itself;
5. a dedication of the profession to social service, meeting obligations to the society and performing services other groups are not capable of offering;
6. correlatively, substitution of service for income and wealth as the primary motivation of members, plus high-quality service regardless of fees received;
7. provision of adequate services for the indigent or those in extremis generally with charge;
8. the application of differential fees for the same service to different clients, according to circumstances or ability to pay; and
9. a set of self-governing rules, inculcating a high code of ethics in relationships among members and in behavior toward society, and requiring provision of service at high levels of competence. (Behrman, 1988, p. 97)

By almost any definition, environmental auditing is not yet formally an established profession. It has no professional standards or self-governing rules, no ethical codes, limited community understanding or sanction, no prescribed training or education, no commonly agreed intellectual component, and no certification of licensure (except in California). Unlike public accountants, who have a rigorous and disciplined set of professional principles and practices, environmental auditors lack a commonly understood mission. As a result, the environmental auditor lacks the financial auditor's recognized position of public trust.

In the absence of explicit professional principles and practices, and an explicit, broadly understood covenant with the public, environmental auditors have no more moral obligation to protect the public than does any other individual.[2] But what is the ordinary obligation to protect the public? Let us look at an example.

Suppose an unemployed bricklayer sitting on the subway overhears a conversation in which a man tells a companion he plans to kill his employer because the employer has discriminated against him. Suppose further that the listener has every reason to believe that the speaker genuinely intends to carry out his threat. The listener has an ordinary moral duty to inform someone, say the police, who may be able to protect the man's employer. His obligation is not derived from any professional duty (indeed the listener is unemployed) but rather from an ordinary moral duty to protect innocent third parties.

One way to derive this ordinary moral duty is to apply a basic test, developed by the philosopher John Rawls, called the "veil of ignorance" test. By situating a person behind a hypothetical veil of ignorance, this test ensures that an individual evaluates various alternatives without regard to how he or she personally would be affected.

The veil of ignorance test is as follows. If one did not know one's position in a matter (e.g., in Ed Anderson's situation, whether one owns Western Manufacturing Company, is one of the 750,000 residents who rely on the local drinking water supply, etc.), what moral rule would one accept? Without knowing one's position in the unemployed bricklayer's case, one would certainly choose a moral rule that required disclosure since, when the veil of ignorance was lifted, one could turn out to be the potential murderer's boss with a gun to her head. Without knowing one's position in Ed Anderson's situation, one would similarly choose a rule that required disclosure since most people would not voluntarily increase their cancer risk by drinking from a contaminated water supply. Because a veil of ignorance test prevents the auditor from knowing whether he will be the auditor, who leaves on the next outbound flight from Columbia, or a local resident who will unknowingly continue to drink from a contaminated water supply, he must choose disclosure.

Suppose the auditor is not certain that a spill is imminent or is not sure that a spill would actually contaminate the local water supply. Is he still obliged to disclose? At this point, the fundamental duty principle and the consequentialist principle overlap, since one can rightfully question whether an auditor has a fundamental moral duty to protect innocent third parties from harm if the harm is insignificant (e.g., the contamination is minuscule and not likely to increase the community's cancer risk). Here we must turn to the consequentialist principle, which complements the fundamental duty principle by adding a significance test.

The Consequences

Ed Anderson believes that if he does not disclose the potential hazard to the public, significant contamination of a water supply could occur, causing harm to the community. From a moral standpoint, the consequentialist principle is persuasive; if his failure to act could cause dire consequences, then not acting is unethical. From a practical standpoint, however, there must be a high threshold for this principle to be adduced.

In a consequentialist analysis, the auditor must consider—in addition to the potential harm that could be prevented by disclosure—the potential harm that disclosure could cause. For example, the costs to the community and company of raising a potential false alarm could be significant. Psychological distress, depressed property values, lost production, and other negative consequences of disclosure need to be balanced against the potential harm that could result if the hazard is not disclosed. Because the costs of disclosure could be quite high, the costs of remaining silent must be even higher in order to justify disclosure.

Viewed another way, the consequentialist argument can be supported by Rawlsian reasoning. Using the veil of ignorance test, one can evaluate the auditor's fundamental duty to disclose in relation to the consequences of the hazard. The reasoning is as follows: An environmental auditor typically is able to make a general judgment as to the type of consequences that might occur if a problem is uncorrected and the general likelihood of its occurrence. He or she is unlikely to know with precision, however, the probability of such an event's occurring or the exact nature of the consequences.

Assuming for the sake of argument that an auditor were able to know, without doubt, the probability and consequences of an environmental event, there are four possible scenarios for the event's occurrence (figure 18.3). In my judgment, only the first of the four risk—the high probability–high harm scenario—scenarios clearly justifies the auditor's duty to disclose. In this scenario, the auditor knows with a high degree of certainty that the environmental hazard will cause significant harm to human health and/or the environment. The veil of ignorance test suggests that most people, not knowing whether they were the auditor or a local resident, would prefer to be informed about imminent and severe contamination of their drinking water supply.

Figure 18.3
Four Environmental Risk Scenarios

	Severity of Harm to Health or the Environment	
	High	Low
High (Probability of Occurrence)	1 — High Probability High Harm	3 — High Probability Low Harm
Low (Probability of Occurrence)	2 — Low Probability High Harm	4 — Low Probability Low Harm

In the second risk scenario (low probability–high harm), people might well choose not to be informed of the potential risk, since we face so many of these risk situations in life (e.g., flying in an airplane) that we often feel better off not being confronted with information about every possible risk. Applying the veil of ignorance test to the third and fourth risk scenarios, both of which involve nonsignificant harm to human health and the environment, I would argue that people do not necessarily want to be informed of these low consequence risks. Clearly risks that are defined by scenarios 2–4 must be characterized and appropriately managed by a corporation. However, public disclosure of such risks is not necessarily dictated by moral obligation.

Summary

The analysis suggests that Ed Anderson's assumption—that failure to disclose a hazard that could potentially cause serious harm to human health or the environment is unethical—is justified by the fundamental duty principle and possibly by the consequentialist principle. More information is needed about the consequences of disclosure and nondisclosure to determine whether the latter principle can be adduced.

The fundamental duty principle states that an auditor has an ordinary moral duty to protect innocent third parties from harm. This duty does not arise from the auditor's occupation. However, since environmental auditors are likely to be exposed to more opportunities than most other people to exercise this duty and since auditors are better trained to evaluate environmental risks than the general public, it can be argued that auditors at least have greater opportunities than other people to protect human health and the environment from harm. The consequentialist principle adds a significance test to the disclosure decision by stating that the consequences of the identified hazard must be significant to justify the auditor's obligation for public disclosure.

Is the Environmental Auditor Morally Obliged to Protect His or Her Employer's Confidentiality?

The next question has to do with Ed Anderson's obligation to protect Western Manufacturing Company's confidentiality. His concern is that failure to protect the confidentiality of his employer is unethical.

The Duty

Ed Anderson believes he has a basic moral duty to protect Western Manufacturing Company's confidentiality. I will argue that he does have such a duty and that it is fundamental to the internal auditor-employer relationship.

Because environmental auditing is only an emerging profession, we cannot look to environmental auditing standards or codes of ethics to define the auditor's obligations with respect to protecting an employer's confidentiality. On the other hand, when a company empowers an environmental auditor to conduct audits, the company does so on the basis of trust and confidence that the auditor will protect its interests. Indeed, the environmental auditor-employer relationship is fundamentally a fiduciary relationship: "A fiduciary relation[ship is] the relation existing when one person justifiably reposes confidence, faith, and reliance in another whose aid, advice, or protection is sought in some manner" (*Webster's Third New International Dictionary, Unabridged,* 1981).

When a company voluntarily creates an environmental audit function, it does so with a view toward the social good as well as with its financial interests in mind. To preserve the integrity of the audit program, management expects that environmental auditors will protect the confidentiality of information obtained during the course of conducting audits. If management thought otherwise (in the extreme, that auditors would freely disclose confidential information to the outside), audit programs would not voluntarily be undertaken. The purpose of an environmental audit program is to identify and solve problems before they become public threats, and the success of the environmental audit function is predicated on the auditor's ability to elicit sufficient cooperation from plant personnel to be able to identify environmental problems.

How does the presence of a fiduciary relationship govern the environmental auditor's moral behavior? The dictionary offers further guidance: "[In a fiduciary relationship] good conscience requires one to act at all times for the sole benefit and interests of another with loyalty to those interests" (*Webster's Third New International Dictionary, Unabridged,* 1981). Plainly the fiduciary (the environmental auditor) is expected to act at all times in the interests of the beneficiary (the employer). The notion that an auditor should not publicly disclose information obtained during audits is supported by a fundamental moral principle of keeping promises. The company can undertake a self-auditing program only if it trusts its employees to maintain the confidentiality of audit findings. The foundation of a voluntary audit program rests on the principle of keeping promises, with the implicit assumption of reliance and expectation.

With respect to the auditor's fiduciary relationship, the fundamental duty to protect the employer's confidentiality is closely tied to the consequences of breaching that confidentiality. Indeed the fundamental duty and consequentialist principles are almost inseparable.

The Consequences

Ed Anderson believes that if he discloses the hazard to the public, he jeopardizes the trust that underlies all current and future audits. I will argue that he is correct.

A voluntary environmental audit program rests on the trust between auditor and employer. It is difficult to imagine a company that would deliberately ask its employees to identify and document problems and then report those problems to government authorities or the media without the company's permission. It is equally hard to imagine a plant manager or plant environmental staff cooperating with an auditor (by providing the auditor with access to documents, in-plant interviews, and other sources of information) if it was believed that the auditor would publicly reveal potentially embarrassing information collected during the course of the audit.

Since environmental audit programs serve a public good (because they are designed to identify and correct environmental problems before they cause harm to human health or the environment), protection of the trust on which they are based also serves a public good. A breach of this trust would be discreditable to the company and the auditor and could undermine the basic foundation of the audit program, causing management to reconsider whether to continue with the audit program and causing other companies to question their audit programs. This result would serve neither the company's best interest nor the public's.

The obligation to protect the company's confidentiality is based not only on a fundamental moral duty to keep promises but also on a broader notion of protecting the general public interest. Ironically, the principle of protecting the general public interest (by maintaining the integrity of audit programs) may be in direct conflict with the principle of protecting specific members of the public (e.g., the local community served by the Columbia public water supply). In this respect, the auditor faces an almost insoluble dilemma between protecting the greater public good and protecting a specific public good. Clearly some kind of balancing test is needed.

Before concluding the consequentialist evaluation, the auditor must consider the potential negative consequences of not protecting the company's confidentiality. Here the auditor must balance the harm done by violating the company's confidence (e.g., undermining future audits) against the harm done by remaining silent. One could argue, for example, that protecting the company's confidentiality is not necessarily in the company's best interest when such protection could ultimately result in lawsuits, fines and penalties, or public embarrassment to the company. Depending on the circumstances, either choice (to disclose or not to disclose) could be interpreted as fulfilling the auditor's moral obligation to protect the company's relevant interests.

Summary

The analysis suggests that Ed Anderson's second assumption—that failure to protect the confidentiality of his employer is unethical—is justified by the fundamental duty principle and by the consequentialist principle. The fundamental duty principle states that the auditor, because of his fiduciary relationship to the company, is obliged to protect confidential information obtained during the course of an audit. This obligation is inherent in the nature of the fiduciary relationship. The consequentialist principle adds that public disclosure of the hazard would jeopardize the trust on which all present and future audits are built.

CONCLUSIONS

Ed Anderson plainly has a conflict between legitimate moral obligations. If he exercises his ordinary moral duty to protect human health and the environment, he abrogates his fiduciary responsibility to his employer. If he strictly interprets his fiduciary responsibility to his employer and fails to disclose the potential hazard to the public, he abrogates his duty to protect a segment of the public. It is impossible for him to honor both duties at the same time. A method is needed to resolve conflicts between an environmental auditor's obligations to his or her employer and to others. The approach I suggest offers six proposed tests to evaluate when an auditor's duty to the public outweighs his or her duty to the employer.

I begin by assuming that the auditor's primary obligation is to the employer. I make this assumption for two reasons. First, the auditor has a fiduciary responsibility to the employer. This responsibility grows out of a basic trust that is essential to the integrity of voluntary corporate environmental audit programs. In addition, the fiduciary responsibility serves more than just the employer since audit programs ultimately serve the general public good. Second, because the environmental audit occupation does not hold an explicit position of public trust and because there are no environmental auditing standards or codes of ethics specifying an auditor's obligation to the public, the auditor has no special obligation to protect the public.

The question then arises, Under what circumstances does the auditor's ordinary moral obligation to the public outweigh the fiduciary obligation to his or her employer? Six tests can be used to balance these obligations:[3]

1. The potential human health or environmental harm that could result from the hazard is significant.
2. Peer environmental professionals agree that the hazard is potentially significant and is not being ad~quately addressed by the company.
3. The potential negative consequences of remaining silent outweigh the potential negative consequences of disclosure.
4. The auditor has exhausted all reasonable internal reporting channels.
5. The hazard is not on a reasonable timetable for remediation.
6. The auditor is not primarily motivated by personal gain.

These tests are especially tailored to the environmental auditor. If all six tests are met, the auditor may be justified in making public his or her concerns.

The first test is that the potential human health or environmental harm that could result from the hazard is significant. Granted, reasonable people could disagree about how to define significant (for example, is one death significant, or must multiple deaths occur in order for the consequences to be considered significant?). But the goal here is to determine the potential severity of the problem so the auditor can properly weigh its overall importance.

In Ed Anderson's case, several basic questions must be answered in order to determine the significance of the risk—for example:

* Is Ed Anderson correct in his assessment of imminent (i.e., high probability) spillage?
* Is he right in believing that such spillage would contaminate the local drinking water supply?
* Would the community's excess lifetime cancer risk substantially be increased as a result of the contamination?

In all likelihood, Ed Anderson will not be able to answer these questions alone, nor is it desirable that he do so, since even reasonable people may disagree about probabilities and consequences. This gives rise to the second test: a peer environmental professional must agree that the hazard is potentially significant. Ed Anderson needs to obtain corroboration for his beliefs, as well as supporting data. Ideally he should obtain corroboration from an environmental professional within the company. But if necessary, he should talk to a trusted peer outside the company. This test is to ensure that the auditor is squarely in the midst of a genuine dilemma. No doubt reasonable people could disagree about the seriousness of an environmental hazard or the appropriateness of public disclosure; however, some level of peer corroboration is important for validating the auditor's judgment.

The third test is a balancing test: the potential negative consequences of remaining silent must outweigh the potential negative consequences of disclosure. The auditor has to weigh the negative consequences of disclosure carefully. These may be societal—for example, the costs to the community and the company of a false alarm—or personal—for example, the financial or emotional cost of disagreeing with one's management, jeopardizing a job because of a breach of fiduciary duty to the company, or being harassed or humiliated by people in the company who disagree with the judgment. This test is to ensure that the auditor considers all the consequences of disclosure, not just the potential harm that can be prevented by disclosure.

The fourth test is that the auditor has exhausted all reasonable internal reporting channels. This is critical; the auditor must attempt to give the company every possible opportunity to understand and address the problem. This could mean reporting as high in the company management structure as the company president or even the board of directors. In extreme cases, where an auditor believes that he or she is not being heard by immediate management, the auditor must make every effort to work through the company's internal management before turning to outside authorities. The purpose of this test is to ensure that the auditor has attempted to the fullest extent possible to honor the company's confidentiality while at the same time attempting to ensure correction of the identified hazard.

The fifth test is that the hazard is not adequately being remediated, nor is it on a reasonable timetable for remediation. This is to ensure that the auditor is fully aware of the steps the company is taking (if any) to address the problem.

Finally, the last test is that the auditor not be motivated primarily by personal gain. This test is to ensure that the auditor properly respects his fiduciary obligations and is not acting primarily in a manner to aggrandize himself or herself at the employer's expense.

Determining whether a situation meets the six proposed tests is not simple. In Ed Anderson's case, the most problematic tests are the first two. He does not know with certainty the probability or outcome of a major spill and has not discussed the problem with peer environmental professionals. Ed Anderson would probably elect to disclose the problem publicly if he determined that tests 3–6 were met and that the probability of a major spillage was high, the spill would result in major contamination of the water supply, increasing the community's excess lifetime cancer risk from, say, 10^{-6} to 10^{-5}, and a trusted audit colleague agreed with Ed Anderson's assessment.

In reality, however, environmental risk situations normally are more gray than black and white. Auditors generally do not have the luxury of knowing precisely the probability or outcome of an event. Moreover, there is no guarantee that reasonable people using these tests would draw the same conclusions. The audit practitioner operates in a world of enormous uncertainty. Nevertheless, the six tests offer a way of evaluating a highly complex ethical situation that is quite typical of the kinds of situations faced by environmental auditors.

To elevate the resolution of these dilemmas from the individual to the societal level requires that environmental auditing become more professionalized. Extensive progress already has been made toward environmental audit professionalization. Three environmental audit professional groups exist, and two of them have actively studied the issue of professional standards.[4]

Over the long run, ethical issues will best be addressed through formal professional standards and codes of ethics devoted to environmental auditors. The codes of ethics that exist for engineers, who comprise a large portion of the environmental audit work force, are not quite tailored to environmental auditors' needs because they do not address in depth certain issues unique to the auditor or employer situation, such as the importance of confidentiality to the effectiveness of the audit function. The Institute of Internal Auditors' and Certified Public Accountants' codes of ethics come closer to addressing the special environmental auditor–employer relationship but do not address the substantive issues unique to the environmental audit function, such as the fact that environmental auditors deal with information relevant to human health and welfare. Until professional standards are developed for environmental auditors, tough dilemmas of disclosure will have to be addressed by individual auditors without recourse to written guidance.

NOTES

I am grateful to the following individuals for their thoughtful input to this chapter: Al Alm, Greg Dees, John Palmisano, Steve Poltorzycki, Ralph Rhodes, Ann Smith, and Bill

Yodis. They challenged my thinking and generously offered suggestions for improvement. Any errors, omissions, or misconceptions that remain are solely my responsibility.

1. The environmental auditor's duty to protect the confidentiality of audit findings may be overridden by certain legal circumstances, such as a subpoena requiring the disclosure of such information. However, this chapter assumes no legal obligations to disclose audit findings.

2. Environmental auditors usually have training in a specific field (e.g., chemical engineering, environmental sciences). Because of their training and background, many have professional affiliations with groups that have well-established ethical standards, for example, professional engineers. Membership in such a professional association confers special ethical obligations on an auditor. However, this chapter centers on the auditor's obligations qua auditor. Thus, the auditor's ethical obligations that arise from other affiliations are not dealt with here.

3. In the course of evaluating how an auditor might properly weigh his or her ethical obligations, I arrived at the six tests described. A literature search confirmed that several of these are the types of tests ethicists are likely to apply at a more general level to ethical dilemmas. See, for example, Sissela Bok or Gene G. James in Callahan (1988).

4. Three environmental audit professional groups exist as of this writing: the Environmental Audit Roundtable, the Institute for Environmental Auditing, and the Environmental Audit Forum. The first two groups have addressed the issue of professional standards.

REFERENCES

American Institute of Certified Public Accountants, Inc. 1978. *Ethics in the Accounting Profession*. New York: John Wiley & Sons.

Barry, Vincent E., 1986. *Moral Issues in Business*. Belmont, Calif.: Wadsworth Publishing Company.

Baumrin, Bernard, and Benjamin Freedman, eds. 1983. *Moral Responsibility and the Professions*. New York: Haven Publications.

Bayles, Michael D. 1981. *Professional Ethics*. Belmont, Calif: Wadsworth Publishing Company.

Beauchamp, Tom L., and Norman E. Bowie, eds. 1988. *Ethical Theory and Business*. Englewood Cliffs, N.J.: Prentice-Hall.

Behrman, Jack N., 1988. *Essays on Ethics in Business and the Professions*. Englewood Cliffs, N.J.: Prentice-Hall.

Bureau of National Affairs., 1986. *Codes of Professional Responsibility*. Washington, D.C.: BNA.

Callahan, Joan C., ed. 1988. *Ethical Issues in Professional Life*. New York: Oxford University Press.

Hoffman, W. Michael, and Jennifer Mills Moore, eds. 1984. *Business Ethics*. New York: McGraw-Hill.

Anthropocentric Ethics in Organizations: How Different Strategic Management Schools View the Environment

THIERRY C. PAUCHANT AND
ISABELLE FORTIER

The end of the 1980s will be perhaps remembered in the future as the period when the general population became aware of some of the environmental issues associated with industrial activities. As an example of this phenomenon, major television channels and popular magazines in the United States, Canada, and France such as *Time, Newsweek, MacClean's, Le Point*, and *l'Express*, published during this period in-depth cover stories on issues such as acid rain, the greenhouse effect, the depletion of the ozone layer, the deforestation issue, toxic waste problems, and major industrial disasters.

Historically the philosophical ecology literature has argued that one central phenomenon, anthropocentrism, with its corresponding code of ethics, is at the root of these environmental problems. Reviewing some of this literature, in this chapter we evaluate this degree of anthropocentrism in management. Viewing organizational strategic thinking and behavior as the fundamental link between an organization and its environment, we present a typology of different strategic schools based on our operationalization of three criteria evaluating their degree of anthropocentrism.

THE PHILOSOPHICAL ECOLOGY LITERATURE: A BRIEF HISTORICAL BACKGROUND

To state that the end of the 1980s could be seen as a benchmark period for environmental awareness is not to say that these issues were ignored earlier. A large number of ecologists, environmental historians, ecophilosophers, and anthropologists had already debated these issues for years.

It is generally accepted that the age of ecology started with Rachel Carson's best-seller *Silent Spring* in 1962 (Cornish, 1977; Naess, 1987; Sessions, 1987).

Carson stressed the negative ecological effects of the widespread use of pesticides in agriculture, challenging the use of advanced technology in the environment. If this best-seller could be seen as a landmark in the ecology literature, it can also be seen as the influential expression of a larger philosophical movement, labeled ecophilosophy, and expressed in the writings of authors as diverse as Martin Heidegger, Aldo Leopold, John Muir, and George Santayana.

Ecophilosophy emphasizes that the roots of the environmental and ecological crisis are to be found in the human belief in anthropocentrism. Derived from the Greek *anthropos,* "man" or "mankind," and *kentron,* "center," the anthropocentric doctrine proposes that humanity perceives itself to be the center and ultimate goal of the universe, viewing the environment as a mere function existing for its sole convenience. Arguing that this anthropocentrism position is ontological, ecophilosophers have proposed that this particular view of the relationship between humanity and the environment determines specific codes of ethics toward nature, legitimizing its use for human purpose (Devall and Sessions, 1985; Heidegger, 1977; Leopold, 1949; Naess, 1987). These authors argue that this code of ethics leads to phenomena such as the view of nature as a mere storehouse of raw material for the enhancement of human power (Devall and Sessions, 1985; Zimmerman, 1987); phenomena such as "human chauvinism" and "species bias" (Passmore and Taylor, 1981); strong materialistic values and the excessive use of economic criteria in making decisions influencing the environment (Leopold, 1949; Naess, 1987); the radical objectivity advocated by the scientific community, attempting to view nature in an abstract mathematical form (Heidegger, 1977; McLaughlin, 1987); or the unquestioned faith in technology and scientific progress for controlling or transforming the environment for human use (Carson, 1962; Devall and Sessions, 1985).

For the purpose of this chapter and in an attempt to evaluate to what extent management thought and practice is representative of the anthropocentric position, we have operationalized its implications in three different ethical domains: A hierarchical, a "resourcism," and an instrumentalist ethics.

Claiming the superiority of humans over nature, the anthropocentric position leads to the establishment of a hierarchy, separating entities between "human," existing ontologically, and "nonhuman," existing only in their function for human consumption. Through this dichotomy, it becomes justified to view non-human entities as merely instrumental for human needs, consumption, or pleasure (Carson, 1962; Devall and Sessions, 1985; Leopold, 1949). We should stress that this dichotomy could also be directed toward other human beings, denying their ontological "humanness." In this case, anthropocentrism leads to ethnocentrism through processes such as racism or discrimination. We have operationalized this view in the field of management through an emphasis on fragmentation by organizational members of their stakeholders. In this view, only a small number of stakeholders and their characteristics, such as their economic value or their political influence, will be considered by organizational members. We then hypothesized that the more an organization becomes an-thropocentric, the more it will fragment the number and the characteristics of its stakeholders, ranked from their degree of perceived organizational utility.

The establishment of a resourcism ethics—the right for humans to utilize "nonhuman" entities without restriction (Passmore, 1974; Heidegger, 1977)—is associated with the previous factor. In the ecophilosophy literature, this resour-cism has been associated with two fundamental beliefs: that this resourcism can be unlimited (Carson, 1962; Devall and Sessions, 1985) and a belief in the intrinsic right to opportunism, supplanting moral values to take advantage of a perceived resource opportunity within a short-term perspective (Heidegger, 1977; Leopold, 1949). Thus, in relation to organizations, we hypothesized that a firm will be more anthropocentric if it assumes that its resourcism can be un-limited, supporting an ethics of radical opportunism.

Finally, the establishment of an instrumental ethics, based on science and technology, is viewed by ecophilosophers as the primary means for resourcism. In this view, advances in sciences and technology are considered intrinsically good, allowing for better efficiency in resourcism (Carson, 1962; Ehrenfeld, 1978; Shepard, 1982). In this case advances in science are driven by resourcism imperatives themselves (Heidegger, 1977). In the organizational domain, we hypothesized that a firm will be more anthropocentric if organizational members heavily use their technologies for resourcism, leading to a feeling of tech-nological omnipotence. In this case, we have used the word *technology* in a larger sense, considering not only mechanical devices but other techniques and methods as well, such as the use of formal processes or the use of specific theories, methods, or frameworks.

THE DEGREE OF ANTHROPOCENTRISM IN THE STRATEGIC MANAGEMENT LITERATURE

The field of strategic management is still loosely defined. While diverse authors have proposed a number of specific definitions (Andrews, 1980; Ansoff, 1965; Porter, 1980), others have presented a number of typologies, arguing that there exist different models or schools of strategic management (Bourgeois, 1980; Chaffee, 1985; Miles and Snow, 1978; Miller and Friesen, 1977; Mintzberg, 1973, 1987, 1988). However, all authors in the field agree that strategy is the fundamental link between an organization and its environment. Recently one reviewer of the literature stated that "a basic premise of thinking about strategy concerns the inseparability of organizations and environ-ments, . . . , the organization . . . [using] strategy to deal with changing en-vironments" (Chaffee, 1985, p. 89). Thus, one means for studying the degree of anthropocentrism in management theory and practice is to ask how, at the strate-gic level, an organization defines its environment and for what purpose.

In this section, we present a typology of different schools or models in strate-gic management based on the three criteria derived from the ecophilosophy

Table 19.1
Degree of Anthropocentrism in Strategic Management

	Mechanistic	Organic	Ecocentric
Fragmentation of Stakeholders	Strong emphasis on political power and economic size and strength Focus on top management, stockholders, and consumers	Decreased fragmentation considering competitive forces Traditional concept of stakeholders	No fragmentation Enlarged concept of stakeholders, communities, future generations, and nature itself
Belief in Unlimited Resourcism	Environment seen as a nuisance "out there" to be mastered or harvested Resourcism seen as an ontological right	Environment seen as turbulent, changing, and dangerous Resourcism limited by necessity of survival; concept of strategic "niche" and strategic adaptation	Resourcism seen as environmentally dangerous Limited by regulations and deep understanding of human connection with environment
Faith in Technology	Absolute. Belief in strict economic theory and unlimited progress through technological innovations	Decreased. Recognition of limited actions by individual stakeholders Great use of sociopsychological technologies for redefining reality Concept of "strategic vision"	Decreased due to ethical standards and personal "understanding" Recognition of scientific uncertainty and humility

EXTREME ← → MINIMUM

DEGREE OF ANTHROPOCENTRISM

literature. This analysis resulted in three different schools: the mechanistic, organic, and ecocentric (table 19.1).

The Mechanistic School

This first school addresses H. Mintzberg's (1973) planning mode, or regroups the design, planning, and part of the political schools as later defined by this author (Mintzberg, 1987). It also corresponds to E. Chaffee's (1985) linear model of strategy. It represents the most traditional view of strategy, based on a strong dichotomy between formulation and implementation, the use of a heavy planning structure, the belief in strict rational and sequential decision making, or the overall importance of top management assisted by a large and formal planning group. As stressed by R. E. Miles, C. C. Snow, and J. Pfeffer (1974), for example, this school tends to ignore the environment or hold it constant, searching for universal principles of structure, planning, and control, or still attempts to buffer the external environment for protecting the organization's core technology. This group seems to be the most anthropocentric of the typology. The number of stakeholders considered is greatly reduced, focusing on only a small list of characteristics dictated by strict economic theory. The degree of resourcism is extreme, considering the environment as a mere storage of resource, as well as the degree of opportunism, attempting to capitalize on favorable future trends (Glueck, 1976). The use of strategic and planning tools and processes is extensive, such as a formal planning structure or the use of heavy control mechanisms. Furthermore top management's belief in its omnipotence in strategic thinking and action is paramount. In this case, both thinking and action are claimed to be based on universal laws and principles. This school seems to have emerged from the earliest formulations of the field of strategic management in the 1960s. Thus, the characteristics of this school are found in the writing of authors such as H. I. Ansoff (1965), J. T. Cannon (1968), A. D. Chandler (1962), J. Child (1972), M. Friedman (1970), F. F. Gilmore (1970) and W. F. Glueck (1976).

The Organic School

This group regroups Mintzberg's (1987) environmental, positioning, and entrepreneurial schools, as well as his adaptative mode in strategic management (1973). It also corresponds to Chaffee's (1985) adaptative model of strategy.

This school is more recent than the previous one. Its overall purpose is to find an optimal positioning in the environment considering the strength of competitive forces (Porter, 1980; Hambrick, 1980) as well as the overall turbulence perceived in the environment (Hofer, 1973; Bourgeois, 1980). In order to adapt to these turbulences, the strategic efforts advocated by this school are more emergent, less formal and rigid, less centralized, and more incremental and flexible than in the previous school (Burns and Stalker, 1961; Lindblom, 1968; Quinn, 1980). This school emphasizes the use of different strategic analyses and actions for defining and exploiting different market niches in which the organization can survive and prosper (Rumelt, 1980; Porter, 1980; Ohmae, 1982).

Although this school still seems highly anthropocentric, it provides some important improvements to the previous school. For example, it advocates the addition of different stakeholders to be considered for strategic analysis, such as distributors, suppliers, competitors, or regulators. Also it does not assume a quasi-paramount control over the environment by the organization as in the previous school. Rather, organic strategists emphasize the need for an organization to identify rigorously its competitive strengths and weaknesses as well as identifying the diverse threats and opportunities in the environment. At first glance, it could seem that this school has diminished its degree of resourcism as compared to the previous mechanistic school.

Authors in organic strategic management stress that an organization can only adapt to and coalign itself with the environment in the light of the extent of environmental competition, turbulence, threat, and natural selection (Bourgeois, 1980; Dess and Origer, 1987; Hofer, 1973; Quinn, 1980). If the overall degree of resourcism seems to be relatively decreased, this reduction is not motivated by an attempt to reduce the potential damage that an organization can bring on its environment. Rather, this reduction is more motivated by the realization of the limited intrinsic power of an organization and its wish for personal survival. One author in this school stresses that the "organic strategist" is a person "who is wrestling bravely with a universe that he is wise enough to know is too big for him" (Lindblom, 1968, p. 27). Thus, one of the overall goals of this school is still to utilize its competencies and resources fully to take advantage of environmental opportunities, attempting to influence the environment to its advantage (Ohmae, 1982; Rumelt, 1980). In this perspective, opportunism is still seen as a paramount strategy itself. To some extent, it seems possible to characterize this school as taking a position of bounded resourcism, realizing more fully than the previous school the extent of environmental turbulences and competition and their dangers.

For the same reasons, this school can be seen as having somewhat decreased its overall belief in strategic omnipotence. However, and in the perspective of a bounded resourcism, the degree of faith of this school in strategic analyses and optimal strategic actions can still be extreme. Often the different strategies, plans, and tactics advocated by this school are presented as being based on universal laws of optimal positioning and competitive advantage (Porter, 1980).

The Ecocentric School

Although this school of strategy does not exist, we argue that it could be developed from components already presented by diverse authors in the strategic management literature. To our knowledge, no author has yet proposed a comprehensive strategic model of this type. This school draws from many different sources, including law, philosophy, religion, ethics, and social criticism, as well as deep ecology (Sessions, 1985). Here, however, we are concerned only with authors stressing an ecocentric dimension specifically related to business policy and strategic management.

While this school draws from many different domains, it emerges from two main sources: an emphasis on corporate ethics and insights derived from experiences in deep ecology.

The field of ethics applied specifically to strategic management is emerging. Currently a small number of authors have proposed different grounds on which to base their ethical standards, such as law (Andrews, 1980; Mathews, 1988; Steiner, 1979), religion (Fleming, 1987), philosophical ethics (Donaldson and Werhane, 1983), and societal morality (Carroll, 1979; Drucker, 1984; Frederick, 1986; Sehti, 1985; Sharplin, 1985; Vogel, 1986). These authors have stressed the need for a corporate ethics in social responsibility, pointing to different factors such as corporate misconduct and criminal behavior, the right of minorities and disadvantaged groups, the protection of the environment, or the need to integrate individual morality with corporate strategies. Despite these differences, these authors agree that it is not enough for an organization to analyze how environmental factors can affect its strategies, as the organic school does. The organization must also assess how corporate strategies themselves affect the environment. Therefore, a number of authors have argued that the links between corporate strategy and moral issues are paramount and need to be developed (Fleming, 1987; Steiner, 1979; Vogel, 1986).

The second source of this school seems to have emerged from experiences in deep ecology. While the previous focus in corporate ethics draws primarily from more intellectual and cognitive grounds, this focus draws primarily from an experiential and subjective origin. This difference is similar to the distinction made in the ecophilosophy literature between ecology, the scientific understanding of environmental complexity and interrelationships, and deep ecology, adding to this level of comprehension a nonlinear, individual, subjective, deeper, personal, affective, or spiritual understanding of the connection of humans with the environment (Devall and Sessions, 1985; Naess, 1987; Tobias, 1985).

In this ecocentric school, the fragmentation of the number of stakeholders is dramatically decreased. Its authors include stakeholders such as disadvantaged groups, minorities, future generations, and nature itself (animals, plants, and minerals). These authors emphasize a number of additional dimensions from which to view these stakeholders: a moral and ethical dimension (Drucker, 1984; Steiner, 1979), an affective dimension (Emery and Trist, 1973; Pauchant, 1988; Pauchant and Mitroff, 1988), an aesthetic dimension (Churchman, 1979), a spiritual or a holographic dimension (Mitroff, 1983), or a religious one (Fleming, 1987). Also the drive toward resourcism is strongly reduced. This reduction is, however, not primarily derived from a conceptual recognition of diverse environmental threats and turbulences as viewed in the previous concept of bounded resourcism in the organic school. Rather, this reduction is motivated more by ethical and moral considerations (Andrews 1980; Mathews, 1988), as well as by a subjective understanding that ecocentric relationships between an organism and its environment are more harmonious (Emery and Trist, 1973; World Commission on Environment and Development, 1987). If proponents of this school are likely to use different tools and processes present in the previous schools, they also stress the positive and negative aspects of these tools and models on the environment as a whole. Further, some authors have stressed the necessity for a multiperspective approach for viewing environments (McWhinney, 1968; Mitroff, 1983), or the necessity for scientific and personal humility in planning (Michael, 1973; Pauchant et al., 1989), while others have called for a "negotiated order" between all stakeholders (Trist, 1980; Pauchant and Mitroff, 1989; World Commission on Environment and Development, 1987).

IMPLICATIONS FOR FUTURE RESEARCH

The use of diverse ecophilosophic criteria for deriving a typology in strategic management leads to a different view of strategic schools. These schools present a decreasing emphasis in anthropocentrism following their period of introduction. As we have found, the most anthropocentric model of strategy, the mechanistic school, was introduced in the mid-1960s, the organic one in the 1970s, and the ecocentric view has mostly emerged in the 1980s, with a few exceptions. This evolution seems encouraging, indicating that some authors in the field of strategic management seem to be embracing the ecocentric paradigm. To our knowledge, however, none of these authors has specifically used the arguments developed in the field of ecophilosophy to develop their models. While this evolution is encouraging, much further research is needed in the area. First, the mechanistic school of strategy, although derived in the 1960s, is still very much present in today's organizations despite the efforts of many authors to emphasize the more realistic characteristics of the organic school (see, for example, Pascale, 1984, or Quinn, 1980). Second, it seems that the organic school will need to integrate some of the moral component of the ecocentric school. While major proponents of organic strategies have praised themselves for having removed from their models "all the material on the general manager, and on the values of society" (Porter, quoted in Kiechel, 1987), it seems, however, that a balance between these two schools is necessary considering the current state of environmental and ecological degradation. Third, the ecocentric school needs to be integrated into the mainstream of the field. Authors in this school need to integrate their diverse approaches and develop specific tools that managers in organizations can use readily.

The overall focus of research in strategic management needs to be complemented. Many authors still focus on the internal characteristics of organizations, localized on a continuum between mechanistic and organic paradigms. This focus seems to echo the trend in management theory to distinguish among organizations that are mechanistic (i.e., formal, bureaucratic, hierarchic) and those that are organic (adaptative, innovative, entrepreneurial). This particular focus in research seems to have been originated by T. Burns and G. M. Stalker, who first proposed the distinction between mechanistic and organic organizations (Burns and Stalker, 1961) and developed further by Moss Kanter who proposed a distinction between segmentalist and integrative structures and cultures (Kanter, 1983). Stressing the importance of these two paradigms in management thought and practice, a number of authors have argued that they represent 95 percent of all management theories (see, for example, Morgan, 1986).

The organic model proposes some improvement over the mechanistic model relative to the degree of anthropocentrism in organizations. If the mechanistic school considered the external environment as mostly the place in which an organization can exercise its strategic resourcism, the organic model emphasizes that this resourcism needs to be bounded, considering the presence of strong environmental turbulences and dangers. If the organic school allowed such improvement, however, it still remains highly anthropocentric as measured on the three criteria we have derived from the ecophilosophy literature.

Authors in the ecocentric school challenge this research focus on the continuum between the mechanistic and organic paradigms. Although they do not articulate specifically in these terms, it seems that they propose to move away from the internal characteristics of organizations and to focus, in addition, on their environmental and external effects. Thus, an ecocentric research focus will focus not only on where a firm needs to be located on the continuum between the mechanistic and organic paradigms if it wishes to survive and/or develop; it will add how a firm can survive and/or develop without endangering its global environment.

In table 19.2 we suggest some of the potential differences between these research questions. The ecocentric research emphasis is less directed toward the internal strategic characteristics of an organization than toward the external impact of its strategic actions on the environment. For example, while traditional research questions have been directed toward the impact of formal and informal decision making in an organization on its survival and development, an ecocentric research question will be directed toward the impact of these differences in decision making on the global environment. Similarly, while traditional research questions have been directed toward the effects of cost leadership and product differentiation (Porter, 1980) on organizational success, an ecocentric research question will be directed toward the effects that these different strategies have on the global environment.

The great philosopher Bertrand Russell argued that a vast social disaster will result from the bias that tends to "regard everything non-human as mere raw material" (Russell, 1945, quoted in Sessions, 1987, p. 110). If we take the ecophilosophic claim seriously that the root of the current environmental degradation is located in the anthropocentric bias, we need to complement our models of strategic management. In particular, we need to research the environmental and ecological impact of the diverse strategies, plans, and tactics advocated by the different strategic schools for ensuring organizational survival and develop-

Table 19.2
Characteristics of Strategic Schools

	Mechanistic	Organic	Ecocentric
Strategic Purpose	Operate and be efficient in a stable environment	Exploitation of rapid changes through innovations and explorations of new opportunities	Contribute to a better world (no separation of environment, organization, self)
Characteristics of a "Good" Product or service	Standardized and mass produced, answering stable needs	Innovative and opportunistic, answering changing needs	Standardized or innovative, but appropriateness of needs evaluated through ethical and environmental considerations
Characteristics of Decision Making	Formal, hierarchical following rules and regulations	Informal and constantly changing, based on skills and abilities	Formal and informal based on a balance between organizational ambitions and environmentally based values
Relationship with Competitors	Outpass them through cost and market leadership	Outsmart them by speed execution, strategic niches, innovations, etc.	Develop a "shared purpose" between competitors
Perception of the Environment	Seen as relatively stable, unlimited, and well understood	Seen as highly unpredictable and presenting unlimited new market opportunities	Seen as fragile and limited in resources, vulnerable to organizational actions

MECHANISTIC AND ORGANIC SCHOOLS BASED ON BURNS STALKER (1961) AND MOSSKANTER (1983) ment. We need not only to understand scientifically how an organization can survive. We also need to understand how to ensure the survival and the development of the environment.

REFERENCES

Andrews, K. R. 1980. *The Concept of Corporate Strategy*. Homewood, Ill.: Richard D. Irwin.

Ansoff, H. I. 1965. *Corporate Strategy: An Analytic Approach to Business Policy for Growth and Expansion*. New York: McGraw-Hill.

Bourgeois, L. J. III. 1980. "Strategy and Environment: A Conceptual Integration." *Academy of Management Review* 5, 25–39.

Burns, T., and Stalker, G. M. 1961. *The Management of Innovation*. London: Tavistock Institute.

Cannon, J. T. 1968. *Business Strategy and Policy*. New York: Harcourt Brace Jovanovich.

Carroll, A. B. 1979. "A Three Dimensional Conceptual Model of Corporate Social Performance." *Academy of Management Review* 4, 497–505.

Carson, R. 1962. *Silent Spring*. Boston: Houghton Mifflin.

Chaffee, E. E. 1985. "Three Models of Strategy." *Academy of Management Review* 10, no. 1, 89–98.

Chandler, A. D., Jr. 1962. *Strategy and Structure*. Cambridge: MIT Press.

Child, J. 1972. "Organizational Structure, Environment and Performance: The Role of Strategic Choice." *Sociology* 6, 1–22.

Churchman, C. W. 1979. *The Systems Approach and Its Enemies*. New York: Basic Books.

Cornish, E. 1977. *The Study of the Future*. Washington, D. C.: World Future Society.

Dess, G. G., and Origer, N. K. 1987. "Environment, Structure and Consensus in Strategy Formulation: A Conceptual Integration." *Academy of Management Review* 12, no. 2, 313–30.

Devall, B., and Sessions, G., eds. 1985. *Deep Ecology: Living as if Nature Mattered*. Salt Lake City: Gibbs Smith Publications.

Donaldson, T., and Werhane, P., eds. 1983. *Ethical Issues in Business: A Philosophical Approach*. 2d ed. Englewood Cliffs, N.J.: Prentice-Hall.

Drucker, P. F. 1984. "The New Meaning of Corporate Social Responsibility." *California Management Review* 26, 53–63.

Ehrenfeld, D. 1978. *The Arrogance of Humanism*. New York: Oxford University Press.

Emery, F. E., and Trist, E. L. 1973. *Towards a Social Ecology: Contextual Appreciations of the Future in the Present*. London: Plenum.

Fleming, J. E. 1987. "A Survey and Critique of Business Ethics Research, 1986," in W. C. Frederick, ed., *Research in Corporate Social Performance and Policy*, 9:1–24. Greenwich, Conn.: JAI.

Frederick, W. C. 1986. "Toward CSR3: Why Ethical Analysis Is Indispensable and Unavoidable in Corporate Affairs." *California Management Review* 28, no. 2, 126–41.

Friedman, M. 1970. "The Social Responsibility of Business Is to Increase Its Profits." *New York Times Magazine*, September 13.

Gilmore, F. F. 1970. "Formulating Strategy in Smaller Companies." *Harvard Business Review* 49, no. 5, 71–81.

Glueck, W. F. 1976. *Business Policy: Strategy Formation and Management Action*. New York: McGraw-Hill.

Hambrick, D. C. 1980. "Operationalizing the Concept of Business Strategy in Research." *Academy of Management Review* 5, 567–75.

Heidegger, M. 1977. *The Question Concerning Technology and Other Essays*. Translated by W. Lovitt. New York: Harper & Row.

Hofer, C. W. 1973. "Some Preliminary Research on Patterns of Strategic Behavior." *Academy of Management Proceedings*, 46–59.

Kanter, R. M. 1983. *The Change Master*. New York: Simon and Schuster.

Kiechel, W. III. 1987. "New Debate about Harvard Business School." *Fortune*, November 9, 34–48.

Leopold, A. 1949. *A Sand County Almanac*. New York: Oxford University Press.

Lindblom, C. E. 1968. *The Policy-making Process*. Englewood Cliffs, N.J.: Prentice-Hall.

McLaughin, A. 1987. "Images of Ethics and Nature." *Journal of Environmental Ethics* 7, 293–319.

McWhinney, W. H. 1968. Organizational Form, Decision Modalities, and the Environment." *Human Relations* 21, 269–81.

Mathews, M. C. 1988. *Strategic Intervention in Organizations: Resolving Ethical Dilemmas*. Beverly Hills: Sage.

Michael, D. N. 1973. *On Learning to Plan and Planning to Learn*. San Francisco: Jossey-Bass.

Miles, R. E., and Snow, C. C. 1978. *Organizational Strategy, Structure and Process*. New York: McGraw-Hill.

Miles, R. E., Snow, C. C., and Pfeffer, J. 1974. Organization-Environment: Concepts and Issues." *Industrial Relations* 13, 244–64.

Miller, D., and Friesen, P. H. 1977. "Strategy-Making in Context: Ten Empirical Archetypes." *Journal of Management Studies* 14, 259–80.

Mintzberg, H. 1973. "Strategy-Making in Three Modes." *California Management Review* 16, no. 2, 44–53.

Mintzberg, H. 1987. "Schools of Thought in Strategic Management." Paper delivered at the National Meeting of the Academy of Management, Chicago.

Mintzberg, H. 1988. "Opening Up the Definition of Strategy." In J. B. Quinn, H. Mintzberg, and R. M. James, eds., *The Strategy Process*, pp. 13–20. Englewood Cliffs, N.J.: Prentice-Hall.

Mitroff, I. I. 1983. *Stakeholders of the Organizational Mind: Toward a New View of Organizational Policy Making*. San Francisco: Jossey-Bass.

Morgan, G. (1986). *Images of Organizations*. Beverly Hills: Sage.

Naess, A. 1987. *Ecology, Community and Life-style: Outline of an Ecosophy*. Cambridge: Cambridge University Press.

Ohmae, K. 1982. *The Mind of the Strategist*. New York: McGraw-Hill.

Pascale, R. T. 1984. "Perspectives on Strategy: The Real Story behind Honda's Success." *California Management Review* (Spring): 47–72.

Passmore, J. 1974. *Man's Responsibility for Nature: Ecological Problems and Western Tradition*. New York: Macmillan.

Passmore, J., and Taylor, P. 1981. "The Ethics for Respect of Nature." *Journal of Environmental Ethics* 3, 197–218.

Pauchant, T. C. 1988. "Crisis Management and Narcissism: A Kohutian Perspective." Ph.D dissertation, University of Southern California.

Pauchant, T. C., and Mitroff, I. I. 1988. "Crisis Prone versus Crisis Avoiding Organizations." *Industrial Crisis Quarterly* 2, 53–63.

Pauchant, T. C., and Mitroff, I. I. 1989. "Crisis Management: Managing Paradox in a Chaotic World." *Technological Forecasting and Social Change.*

Pauchant, T. C., Mitroff, I. I., Welson, D. N. and Ventolo, G. F. 1989. "The Ever-Expanding Scope of Industrial Crises: A Systemic Study of the Hinsdale Telecommunication Outage." *Industrial Crisis Quarterly.*

Porter, M. E. 1980. *Competitive Strategy: Techniques for Analyzing Industries and Competitors.* New York: Free Press.

Quinn, J. B. 1980. *Strategies for Change: Logical Incrementalism.* Homewood, Ill.: Richard D. Irwin.

Rumelt, R. 1980. *Business Policy and Strategic Management.* New York: McGraw-Hill.

Sehti, S. P. 1985. "The Inhuman Error: Lessons from Bhopal." *New Management* 3(1), 40–44.

Sessions, G. 1985. *Deep Ecology.* Salt Lake City: Peregrine Smith Books. Esp. pp. 65–77.

———. 1987. "The Deep Ecology Movement: A Review." *Environmental Review* 11, no. 2, 105–25.

Sharplin, A. 1985. *Strategic Management.* New York: McGraw-Hill.

Shepard, P. 1982. *Nature and Madness.* San Francisco: Sierra Club Books.

Steiner, G. A. 1979. *Strategic Planning: What Every Manager Must Know.* New York: Free Press.

Tobias, M., ed. 1985. *Deep Ecology: An Anthology.* San Diego: Slawson Communications.

Trist, E. 1980. "The Environment and System-response Capability." *Futures* 12, no. 2, 113–27.

Vogel, D. 1986. "The Study of Social Issues in Management: A Critical Appraisal." *California Management Review* 28, no. 2, 142–51.

World Commission on Environment and Development. 1987. *Our Common Future.* New York: Oxford University Press.

Zimmerman, M. 1987. "Feminism, Deep Ecology and Environmental Ethics." *Journal of Environmental Ethics* 9, 21–44.

Explaining Corporate Responses to Environmental Crises: A Game Theoretical Approach

JOAO S. NEVES AND
RAJIB N. SANYAL

Interest, studies, and concerns about the social and ethical responsibilities of business corporations have never been greater than today (Freeman and Gilbert, 1988). For a variety of reasons, the public demand for greater social responsibility from the business sector has increased. In response, many corporations have voluntarily adopted charters delineating their social goals and embarked on a variety of behaviors ranging from offering safer products to cleaning up residues. These conducts are perceived to be indicators of socially responsible corporate citizenship (Arrow, 1979; Brown, 1979). This socioeconomic behavior is at odds with the classical economic model, whose most well-known proponent has been Milton Friedman (1962). The economic model suggests that the purpose of a business is to make profits for its owners, and anything that detracts from this goal will ultimately make the firm inefficient.

In this chapter, we present a model based on game theory to explain the dynamics behind corporate response to a social-ethical issue. The underlying assumption of this model is that while public expectations call for corporations to adopt a socially responsible posture, costs and profits, which are the determinants of the economic model, will in actuality guide corporate behavior.

GAME THEORY AND SOCIAL RESPONSIBILITY

Game theory is a branch of decision theory that deals with decision-making strategies when at least two decision makers (players) actively confront each other. The decision makers pursue different, maybe even opposite, goals, and every decision affects the payoffs of the game (von Neumann and Morgenstern, 1947). Each player anticipates the actions of the opponent while recognizing that the courses of action available to each will affect the other's responses. Depending on the characteristics of the game and the assumptions made, game theory is able to explain and predict the behavior of the players.

Game theory has been used to explain corporate behavior in a variety of areas, including strategic management (McDonald, 1975), contract negotiations (Mann and Wissinck, 1988), and ethical and social conduct. For example, Nielsen (1985) concluded that a negotiation strategy to bring about change in an ethical situation is more likely to occur in positive-sum situations. In situations in which the gains of one party are the losses of the other (zero-sum games) or when the outcomes are negative for all parties, Nielsen suggested that more radical behaviors may be necessary to deal with ethical dilemmas. Similarly Johnson (1985) uses the prisoner's dilemma situation to explain why bribery may occur in some situations when negotiating in international markets.

On an industry level, D. A. Yao (1988) explains the strategic response of the auto industry to the emissions control policies of the Environmental Protection Agency (EPA) using a game theoretical approach. R. E. Freeman and D. R. Gilbert (1988) use extensive game theory examples to analyze the Procter & Gamble and Federal Drug Administration strategies in the Rely Tampon case.

E. Gatewood and A. B. Carroll (1981) note that in many ethical or social choice situations, two players are engaged in a protracted game. The players will periodically evaluate the current payoffs and estimate future payoffs in order to choose a course of action or to defer their decision.

In the situations described in the literature, there seems to be a common denominator: a third party—the general public or specific groups of the general public—is affected by the outcomes of the game played by two principal opponents. This third party is a countervailing player who is able to influence the payoffs of the direct players. The interactive role of the third party has not been fully integrated in existing game theory models. In order to accommodate situations involving social and ethical issues, a new model, the social game model, will be described here.

THE MODEL

In the social game situation, two players are directly involved, and a payoffs matrix is defined for the beginning of the game. The payoffs matrix (table 20.1) establishes the payoffs (revenues or costs) for each player—$P_{Aij}(t)$ and $P_{Bij}(t)$—given any combination of courses of action (ij) chosen by players A and B, respectively, at a given moment in time (t). The payoffs in this dynamic game are estimated by the players, and these estimates may change over time either because initial payoff expectations were wrong or because the reaction of the third party was not fully anticipated.

The principal players of the social game could be two private organizations, two regulatory bodies, or a private organization and a governmental regulatory body. In an environmental crisis, the game is typically played by a corporation and a government agency representing the public interests. The passage of time

Table 20.1
Payoff Matrix

Period 1		Player B	
		B1 Active Course	B2 Defer Action
Player A	A1 Active Course	P A11 (t), P B11 (t)	P A12 (t), P B12 (t)
	A2 Defer Action	P A21 (t), P B21 (t)	P A22 (t), P B22 (t)

may affect the matrix of payoffs for a variety of reasons: regenerative natural factors may significantly affect the cleanup costs for either player at a later time; public outrage in the immediate aftermath of the crisis may quickly subside; public pressure may become more intense as inaction is perceived on the part of one or both players; long-term damage may be much different than was initially estimated; or government priorities may change. Throughout the crisis, the third party, the public, influences and is affected by the game. The behavior of the public is seldom uniform or predictable. The means through which the public influences the payoffs of the players are not always clear and usually difficult to organize. One or both players may try to influence or determine the reactions of the public, although total control is not possible. Despite these uncertain characteristics of the game, the principal players need to recognize the role of this third party when evaluating their alternative actions. The social game model is presented in figure 20.1.

The task of the government agency is to ensure corporate compliance with socially accepted conduct through monitoring the situation, imposing fines, and in some cases repairing damages that have occurred. The government agency is funded through tax money; it has a large territory to oversee and a wide variety of risks to monitor, and appropriated budgeted amounts impose constraints on how much it can do in a particular social or environmental crisis.

The corporate response to an environmental crisis will be guided by the desire to weather the crisis at minimum economic cost. The company is aware of the powers and budget constraints of the government agency with which it has to contend. The agency, however, is not aware of the tactics that the company may adopt, especially when it lacks expertise and information about the company's

Figure 20.1
The Social Game Model

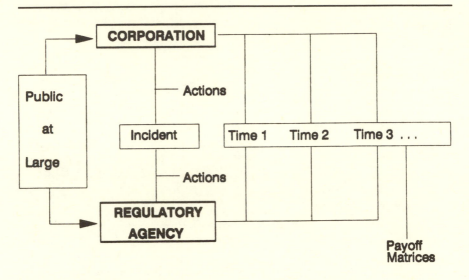

technical abilities, intentions, and costs for dealing with the crisis situation. Furthermore, if the agency is to take the responsibility for repairing the damages, often it has no independent means and has to subcontract to the industry. Hence, the government agency needs and expects cooperation from the same industry it is monitoring.

In playing the game, the company will calculate its current and future payoffs and adopt the best strategy accordingly. Its payoffs include the actual cost of the course of action, the risk of being fined by the government agency, and the impact of the third party on the current and future revenues of the company. The government agency will formulate its strategy according to the expected strategy of the company, demands of the current incident on its budgetary resources, and the costs derived from public pressure. These last costs are usually not well defined and may be reflected in the calculated risk of appointed, or even elected, officials being replaced. (Table 20.2 summarizes the game.)

DYNAMICS OF THE GAME

Game theory assumes that players are rational and motivated by self-interest. Players estimate the payoffs resulting from each combination of courses of action and display empathy to develop their strategies—that is, each player assumes that the opponent is using the same decision criterion. Given these classical assumptions, consider the environmental game whose payoff matrices over three time periods are presented in table 20.3.

Table 20.2
An Overview of the Social Issue Game: Responding to an Environmental Crisis

Players	Government agency Business corporation
Third party	Public at large (countervailing power)
Game situation	An incident has occurred that harms the public and requires large expenditures to restore. The players are expected to act but are subject to their own constraints and objectives. Costs change over time and can be influenced by the public.

Strategy sets	Corporation:
	    full restoration of situation
	    partial restoration
	    no restoration (defer action)
	Government agency:
	    fine the company/new rules
	    cooperate with the company
	    restore the situation on its own

In this hypothetical situation of an environmental accident, the cleanup costs by the company in period 1 amount to $85 million. If the company decides not to clean up, it will have to spend $10 million monitoring the situation and influencing public opinion. That decision will subject the company to a higher risk of being fined. If the regulatory agency decides to fine the company, the fine is substantially less if the cleanup efforts are in place. However, taking this active role will cost the agency substantially because it may have to fight the company in the courts. If the agency antagonizes the company and thus forfeits its cooperation in the cleanup, the costs for the agency will be much greater. Given the situation as described, both players would adopt a passive role.

As the environmental crisis persists, both players are forced to evaluate the payoff matrix later (period 2). The cleanup costs are now higher because the initial response to the environmental incident was slow. Public pressure on the agency to take action mounts, and therefore the cost of not acting rises.

Table 20.3
Payoff Matrices over Three Time Periods

Period 1		Government Agency	
		B1 Impose fine	B2 No fine
Company	A1 Clean up	95, 20	85, 5
	A2 No Cleanup	50, 35	10, 5

Period 2		Government Agency	
		B1 Impose fine	B2 No fine
Company	A1 Clean up	105, 25	95, 15
	A2 No Cleanup	60, 45	15, 30

Period 3		Government Agency	
		B1 Impose fine	B2 No fine
Company	A1 Clean up	90, 20	50, 35
	A2 No Cleanup	100, -50	20, 80

According to the new matrix, it is still preferable for both players to protract the game.

In period 3, public pressure does not subside, and the costs on the agency for not acting are unbearable. The fine to be imposed on the company will be raised to satisfy the public and to save face. This is an attractive option for the agency because the fine levied against the company exceeds the costs borne (thus the negative payoff, which represents a revenue rather than a cost). Concurrently natural regenerative forces have absorbed a great part of the most direct damages to the environment, and the cleanup is less expensive. The company will now opt for the cleanup.

According to the assumptions made, the protracted game was beneficial for both the company and the regulatory agency. Because the environmental damage and the costs to the public are not totally factored in the payoffs of the players, the environment may have suffered greater destruction than if the game had had an early conclusion. In general, it is postulated that the estimated pattern of payoffs over time for each player will determine the behavior of the players and the conclusion of the game. Table 20.4 shows alternative cost patterns and accompanying players' responses.

Table 20.4
Cost Patterns and Players' Responses to Environmental Crises

Players		Government Agency		
	Costs	Rising	Constant	Declining
Company	Rising	Early cooperative restoration	Company acts promptly	Company acts promptly
	Constant	Agency is forced to intervene	Indifferent	Company reacts; late restoration
	Declining	Agency is forced to intervene	Company protracts; late resolution	Late or no restoration

According to the cost patterns, prompt action would result if costs were expected to rise for either or both of the players. If, however, the cost patterns over an extended period of time are perceived to be declining or constant, then several alternative responses become possible. Diminishing public interest over time, as well as the possible reduction in the cost of cleaning up the environment, may explain why environmental crises are so protracted in many instances. Public officials seldom see the repercussions of such a crisis as directly increasing the costs to the agency in the future. They are likely to be bound by current budget constraints and often prefer to shift current uncertain responsibilities to future administrations.

Similar factors operate on the side of the company, with two major exceptions. First, public reaction to the company's behavior may have a much clearer and calculable impact on the company's revenues: consumer boycott of the company's products may adversely affect the company's performance and may explain the attention that companies devote to carefully staged media campaigns. Second is the risk of being fined by the regulatory agency. This risk may not be significant, however, especially if the fine is small compared to the cost of the cleanup.

CORPORATE STRATEGY

A company will estimate different levels of payoffs at succeeding time periods. The strategy to deal with the environmental crisis will then vary and may change over time. Using I. Wilson's (1975) classification, corporate social responsibility strategies may range along a continuum, with reaction and defense strategies at the low end and accommodation and proaction strategies at the high end (figure 20.2). Each of these strategies—reaction, defense, accommodation,

Figure 20.2
Wilson's Continuum of Social Responsibility Strategies

REACTION	DEFENSE	ACCOMMODATION	PROACTION
"deny responsibility"	"put up a fight"	"accept responsibility"	"take the initiative"

Low   High

Degree of Social Responsibility

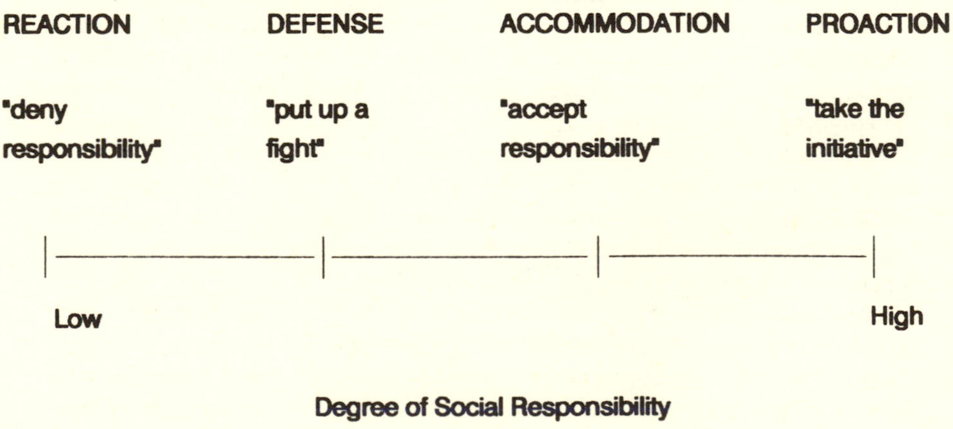

and proaction—typifies a distinctively different approach to exercising corporate responsibility:

Reaction: A company adopting a reactive strategy will deny responsibility for the crisis and strive to maintain the status quo. As part of its response, it may conduct its own evaluation of the situation and collect information.

Defense: This is a strategy of legal activism and manipulation of public opinion through a public relations program. The goal is to avoid having to undertake any additional responsibilities.

Accommodation: As part of this strategy, the company agrees to assume additional responsibilities, usually in response to threatened governmental action or adverse public opinion.

Proaction: A proactive strategy aggressively formulates a social responsibility program whose main goal is to avoid any crisis and which involves taking the initiative to resolve a problem when one occurs.

This four-strategy classification can be effectively integrated into the company's payoff calculations for different elapsed time periods. Assuming that two possible levels—low and high—of expected costs are evaluated over three sequential time periods, different corporate responses will be predicted depending on the pattern of those costs. These possible alternatives are presented in table 20.5.

PUBLIC POLICY IMPLICATIONS

As the model indicates, the ability to anticipate payoffs over a time frame significantly affects the responses of both parties in an environmental issue. Indeed, since both parties seem to have important incentives to defer costs of restoration to an undetermined future period, it is essential that deferment be made difficult and costly for both. Since both parties are playing the game keeping in mind public reaction, the formulation of appropriate public policies to deal with such issues becomes imperative.

One option that would dampen the incentive to defer is the automatic imposition of fines on the company at an increasing rate after a certain time period if an agreed-upon level of restoration has not occurred. Another option would require the company to put a certain sum of money in an escrow account immediately after the accident. This amount would be sufficiently large and forfeited by the company if restoration had not occurred as planned. Yet another alternative would be to increase the probability that future payoffs would be negative if restoration is delayed. This could be accomplished through heavier fines, stiffer regulations, or perceived greater risk of being sued.

These disincentives would have to be matched with similar measures for the government agency. Failure to take prompt and decisive action or prolonged cooperation with the industry at the expense of the environment should increase the risk of personnel and policy changes. This could be achieved by a legal

Table 20.5
Company's Expected Costs and Accompanying Strategies

Situation	Costs			Corporate Strategy
	Elapsed Time 1	Elapsed Time 2	Elapsed Time 3	
1	High	Low	Low	Reaction
2	Low	Low	High	Proaction
3	Low	High	Low	Defense
4	High	Low	High	Accommodation
5	High	High	Low	Reaction
6	Low	High	High	Proaction
7	Low	Low	Low	Reaction
8	High	High	High	Proaction

process in which the decisions of the government agency would be challenged and the actions of the agency closely scrutinized. There is also a need to strengthen the investigative and analytical capabilities of regulatory agencies to make them react effectively to environmental accidents and deal with corporate responses. This may require increased budgets and regulatory powers, including the ability to impose stiff penalties on corporations.

CONCLUSIONS

The model presented here can be used to explain corporate responses in a whole host of well-documented situations such as Union Carbide's accident in Bhopal and Procter & Gamble's Rely Tampon case. Corporations, guided by profit motive and more knowledgeable than the regulatory agencies in terms of costs and solutions, are able to estimate the payoffs of an incident over time and calculate the probability of an issue's fading from the minds of the public. If an incident's long-term damage is small, it pays to adopt a strategy of reaction or defense. If the long-term damage is perceived to be high, the corporation will adopt a strategy of proaction or accommodation.

Regulatory agencies are also influenced by public opinion, but the mechanism to translate the environmental damage to the agency's cost is often nonexistent, and so the regulatory bodies frequently lack incentives to act promptly. They also benefit from cooperative efforts with the industry. Until an organization mechanism is introduced for this type of situations that will impose on both parties greater costs if they should defer resolution of a problem, the public opinion mechanism, in its present largely imperfect role, will not be sufficient to prevent prolonged environmental crises, and considerable damage to the environment will ensue.

REFERENCES

Arrow, K. J. 1979. *The Limitations of the Profit Motive.* Chicago: University of Chicago Press.

Brown, C. C. 1979. *Beyond the Bottom Line.* New York: Macmillan.

Freeman, R. E., and Gilbert, D. R., Jr. 1988. *Corporate Strategy and the Search for Ethics.* Englewood Cliffs, N.J.: Prentice-Hall.

Friedman, M. 1962. *Capitalism and Freedom.* Chicago: University of Chicago Press.

Gatewood, E., and Carroll, A. B. 1981. "The Anatomy of Corporate Social Response: The Rely, Firestone 500 and Pinto Cases." *Business Horizons* 24, no. 5, 9–16.

Johnson, H. L. 1985. "Bribery in International Markets: Diagnosis, Clarification and Remedy." *Journal of Business Ethics* 4, 447–55.

McDonald, J. 1975. *The Game of Business.* New York: Anchor.

Mann, D. P., and Wissink, J. P. 1988. "Money-back Contracts with Double Moral Hazard." *RAND Journal of Economics* 19, no. 2, 285–92.

Nielsen, R. P. 1985. "Alternative Managerial Responses to Ethical Dilemmas." *Planning Review* (November): 24–29, 43.

von Neumann, J., and Morgenstern, O. 1947. *Theory of Games and Economic Behavior*. Princeton, N.J.: Princeton University Press.

Wilson, I. 1975. "What One Company Is Doing about Today's Demands on Business." In G. A. Steiner, ed., *Changing Business-Society Interrelationships*. Los Angeles: UCLA Graduate School of Management.

Yao, D. A. 1988. "Strategic Responses to Automobile Emissions Control: A Game-Theoretic Analysis." *Journal of Environmental Economics and Management* 15, 419–55.

IV

LOOKING TO THE FUTURE: NEW APPROACHES TO THE PROBLEMS OF BUSINESS, ETHICS, AND THE ENVIRONMENT

Economics, Ethics, and the Environment

WILLARD F. ENTEMAN

Economics and ethics do have something in common: historically, neither of them has taken environmental concerns seriously. The primary contention of this chapter is that in order for modern environmental concerns to be taken seriously, a substantial overhaul of our economic and ethical concepts is necessary.

Recently people have worried about a so-called nuclear winter. That view, which was driven by a concern with military actions, had us thinking in terms of crises. It now seems that it is possible to move gradually toward another form of environmental death. In this case, we worry about burning instead of freezing. We may be backing into an environmental death inch by inch. The crisis of nuclear war may be avoided only to find that we have created a planet that is equally uninhabitable.

It is fair to ask whether our concern for the environment is additional evidence of human arrogance. If we extend our gaze from the earth to the universe, we might conclude that life on earth is essentially inconsequential. However much we may pollute the earth, in the great scheme of things, it does not matter; we shall not pollute the universe to any significant degree. This, however, is the only life we know; this is the earth we shall leave to future generations. We seem determined to leave to those who follow us what might be called an environmental negative bequest.

In his recent book, *Day of Reckoning,* Benjamin Friedman argues that the economic courses of action that have been accepted recently in the United States will leave substantial financial indebtedness to the future.[1] With regard to the topic of concern to us, even with extraordinary efforts, we shall leave a significantly more damaged environment than the one we inherited. Such intergenerational transfers and negative bequests were not part of the conceptual structure of the past, and both our economic and ethical theories reflect that omission.

ECONOMICS

I shall start the analysis of concepts by examining some fundamental economic concepts. My emphasis will be on capitalism. I shall treat socialism only to show that it too lacks the conceptual foundations necessary to treat current environmental problems. In general, both capitalists and socialists have treated the environment as an externality.

Typically Western capitalistic economists are not comfortable dealing with issues about conceptual assumptions. In addition, to a surprisingly large extent, the same economists have accepted a distinction between normative and positive economics as valid. They have presumed that rational discourse could be held only about the latter and that the former could yield only to bias or taste.

Capitalism

Had capitalism remained as Adam Smith conceived it, there might have been little environmental problem. Smith's idea of a multitude of small firms struggling intensely to satisfy consumer demands did not necessarily carry environmental threats. Such small firms would have little impact on the environment. Smith did foresee the possibility of large corporations, and he opposed them as he did the granting of incorporation privileges, which are crucial to them. Smith's concern, however, was not environmental; it was primarily responsiveness to consumers and derivatively economic efficiency.

Capitalism and Determinism

To use the philosopher's terminology, Smith was unrelentingly a determinist. He saw firms as if they were economic atoms following the example of the dominant physics of his day. The dismal predictions of Thomas Malthus were related to environmental constraints, but Malthus shared Smith's determinism, and he assumed that one could only suffer through the environmental catastrophes.

One conceptual shift made by the environmentalists is to declare implicitly that the determinism of Malthus and Smith can be overcome. Environmentalists presume we can control our behavior and by doing so moderate our impact on the environment. With choice comes the possibility of responsibility. As long as businesspeople were presumed to be caught by deterministic economic forces, it made no sense to hold them responsible for what they did.

For better or worse, our society did not follow Smith's lead, and, as Smith feared, we now have corporate power of a high order. Richard Darman calls what we have a corpocracy, and I have argued elsewhere that nothing short of a substantial and significant ideological shift has occurred so that it is inappropriate to use the term *capitalism* to describe the economic ideology of the United States.

Capitalism, Determinism, and Instantaneous Time-Cuts

Since Smith, economists have presumed that past, present, and future are all gathered into the present and that analysis need only be of an equilibrium at that time. The presumption of the rationality of instantaneous time-cuts is deeply imbedded in economics. It is inherited directly from Smith's successful adaptation of the physics Isaac Newton invented while he also invented the infinitesimal calculus. Calculus depends on the capacity for instantaneous time-cuts and as a consequence carries with it the determinism implicit in both classical physics and classical economics. W. V. O. Quine has argued, persuasively, I think, that mathematics is not ontologically neutral. From the perspective of economics, all was well as long as the values for the equations were currently existing values or future values that can be discounted into the present.

The system, however, is conceptually unable to account for intergenerational transfers because the economic interests of future generations are not in the present moment to establish the equilibrium. Unless nature is inexhaustible, the negative bequest of one generation to another cannot be ignored. The assumption of the infinite exploitability of nature should be examined, and, in doing so, we can examine briefly the economic expression of nature in the concept of property.

Capitalism, Property, and Zero-Cost

Christianity and Judaism, the two religious traditions in which capitalism grew, did not make constraining demands in regard to nature and the environment. The Bible instructs us to "have dominion over the fish of the sea, and over the fowl of the air, and over all the cattle, and over all the earth, and over every creeping thing that creepeth upon the earth" (Genesis 1: 26). The presumption was that humans could not have any substantial long-term impact on the environment. It is not surprising, therefore, that private property interests were readily accepted into Christian and Judaic schema.

The concept of private property is tied up intimately with the concept of environment. John Locke, to whom we naturally turn for an articulation of the original concept, had in mind tangible property first in one's own body and second in nature ("Tho' the Water running in the Fountain be everyones, yet who can doubt, but that the Pitcher is his only who drew it out?").[2] The labor theory of value is joined with a zero-cost assumption in regard to the environment. Water running free and clean is without value until put in the pitcher and given value. Water as such has no economic value (and no cost).

The assumption of the environment as of zero cost is as deeply imbedded within capitalistic economics as is the deterministic assumption. They cannot be exorcised without abandoning the ideology itself. Nevertheless, environmentalists argue that the environment does not have a zero cost, that we do have the capacity for permanently destroying the environment, and that we have the ability to create our own environmental winter.

Capitalism and Intergenerational Transfers

We might look to Smith to attempt to find some treatment of intergenerational transfers in general. There are two areas, education and public debt, in which we see hints from Smith about such issues.

In the later books of the *Wealth of Nations,* Smith acknowledges that an educated populace is important for the society. He argues that the wealthy can be depended on to educate their children out of parental self-interest; however, there could be no similar expectations for the "common" people, and, given the state's legitimate interest in an educated populace, it would have to provide public education. It is tempting to think of this as a case of intergenerational transfer (of a positive sort), but a closer reading of Smith does not warrant this conclusion. Rather, Smith discussed children merely as a profitable commodity.

In the area of public debt, we may hope for an example of negative intergenerational transfer—the transfer of profligate spending on the part of one generation to future generations. It comes as no surprise that Smith is opposed to public indebtedness. He acknowledges that the need may arise in times of war, but he suspects the motives of government officials in allowing indebtedness to grow in peaceful times. As far as Smith is concerned, the problem with public indebtedness is not that it leads to negative intergenerational transfer but that it leads to public slothfulness and to increased governmental power, which, Smith believed, meant necessarily a diminution in the responsiveness of the economy to current consumer needs.

The fundamentals Smith laid down in this regard have not changed over the years. We are reminded in this context of Fritz Machlup's wry observation that Smith was both the Adam and the Smith of the modern science of economics. It is not surprising that some economists have simply dismissed the issue of intergenerational transfers by attacking what they take to be its underlying premise. Wilfred Beckerman, for example, leads us down a logical slippery slope saying we have no moral duty to prevent copper from becoming extinct to saying that we have no moral duty to prevent any particular animal species from becoming extinct to saying that we have no moral duty to prevent the extinction of the human race. It can be argued, he says, "since, by and large (and present company excepted, of course), the human race stinks, the sooner it is extinct the better."[3] One is tempted to dismiss this as another example of Beckerman's well-known pedagogical humor; however, it would be mistaken to dismiss this—or other Beckerman jests—as merely humor. The lesson is there to be learned, and what we learn is deeper than Beckerman intended: that after over two hundred years, there is some reason to question the economic concepts themselves.

Socialism

Socialism has not been noticeably more sensitive to environmental issues than capitalism. In the socialist state, the society is free to use the natural environment in whatever ways advance the cause of the society. Capitalism is an economic ideology oriented to the consumer; socialism is an economic ideology oriented to the worker. For both, the concern is with existing people, not a trade-off between current and future generations.

Socialism and Determinism

Socialism is no less a deterministic economic ideology than capitalism. Instead of a microdeterminism of firms acting in accordance with economic laws, socialism presents a macrodeterminism driven by the organic destiny of the society. Individuals have no more choice in the socialist ideology than individual cells have choice as part of the body. We capture here just the meaning Jean-Jacques Rousseau had in mind when he made the distinction between the "will of all" and the "General Will".

Socialism, Instantaneous Time-Cuts, and Teleology

Given the organic nature of socialism, it has not been responsive to the mathematics of the calculus and instantaneous time-cuts. Socialism is a teleological ideology, not one confined to mechanical causation. Where capitalism abandoned teleology while adopting instantaneous time-cuts, socialism eschewed instantaneous time-cuts while adopting teleological causation. Both are fully deterministic.

Socialism and Property

Socialists are opposed to private property; however, they are insistent that property remain because it will belong to "the people." The labor theory of value, still central to socialism, retains the elementary concept of property. Socialists presume the environment is for the use and exploitation of the current generation.

Socialism and Intergenerational Transfer

The organic destiny of society gives the socialist a structure within which intergenerational considerations might be made; however, it is no simple matter to take future needs into account. It is difficult to know to what extent a current generation should sacrifice for future generations, and in pursuing this approach, we run directly into the Achilles' heel of socialism: the determination of the overarching organic nature of the society. Totalitarianism has come about in many cases just because someone claimed he knew what the General Will demanded.

ETHICS

If the conventional economic concepts have not given attention to environmental issues, it seems natural to turn to ethical concepts because environmental concerns involve both economics and ethics.

Determinism

We have already seen that the prevailing economic approaches share determinism in common. William James drew a distinction between what he called hard determinists and soft determinists. For the hard determinists, it followed that since people have no real choice in what they do, they should not be held morally responsible. By contrast, the soft determinist asserts that ascription of moral responsibility is independent of whether the agent has choice. Soft determinists have been correct in insisting that jumping from the observation that there is moral language to the conclusion that people have free will is a non sequitur. It still seems difficult, however, to understand how responsibility can be assigned where there is no choice. Although a tidal wave can cause environmental disaster, we do not hold the wave morally responsible for those disasters. We do, however, hold management of the Exxon Corporation responsible, at least in part, for the Prince William Bay disaster. Determinism runs counter to an insistence on environmental responsibility, and it must be abandoned if such responsibilities are to be taken seriously.

Ethical Teleology (Utilitarianism)

For utilitarians, an act is right just insofar as it maximizes community happiness. The utilitarians, however, leave us without specification as to how the community is to be defined over time. The most reasonable interpretation of "community" is that it includes all relevant people. If we are to include future generations, however, it would seem that the magnitude of their happiness will always overwhelm the magnitude of the happiness of people alive currently.

The moral philosopher Richard T. De George, in what seems to be a philosophic reprise of the position taken by the economist Beckerman, asked what our moral obligations are to future generations. His answer is that we have none: "presently existing human beings have no obligation to future-and-not-yet existing set or class of human beings."[4] De George's analysis gets us around the issue, but it is difficult to imagine a utilitarian moral rule to support the view that the current generation is morally permitted to take away from the quality of life of future generations without even considering those generations.

William T. Blackstone, who identifies himself as a rule utilitarian, has tried in recent times to turn utilitarianism to the task of the environment. He argues that there is a fundamental human right for a "livable" environment. The problem is that our current "livable" environment is bought at the expense of the environmental quality of future generations.

If the current generation is required to maximize the potential quality of life of generations (including future ones), the current generation will be required (morally) to live at subsistence level. The current generation plus one will also be so required. That generation plus one more will also be so required, and so on. By mathematical induction, all actual generations will be so required. Consequently all people for all futures will be morally required to live at subsistence level—a curious conclusion for utilitarianism. The attempt to achieve maximum happiness actually ends in producing minimum happiness.

Deontology (Kantianism)

The problems of deontology are not those of utilitarianism, but they are no less fatal in facing the environmental issues. At the base, the solution to environmental issues will involve us in marginal trade-offs. Telling the modern executive to act always such that he or she could will the personal principle of the act to be applied universally does not help the executive in the decision-making process when the issue is environmental. The modern executive faces a multitude of stakeholders, all with competing interests. The interests of the stockholders are not the same as the interests of the customers, the employees, or the local community residents. The modern executive must balance all those interests, and the society is set up so that no one of those interests can become universal. Kant's categorical imperative is irrelevant in such a context.

John Rawls has taken up the case for social contract theory in the tradition of Kant. He has suggested ways of treating such trade-off issues as presented by environmental concerns and has even given a brief treatment of intergenerational transfers. While his approach is promising, its fundamental direction has problems analogous to those faced by the utilitarians. If we are to place ourselves behind the veil of ignorance, we shall be ignorant of what generation we shall belong to when the veil is lifted. Purely logical and mathematical analysis behind the veil, however, will tell us that the probability that we shall be part of future generations is higher than that we shall be part of near-term generations. Consequently, behind the veil, we would want to make sure that the future environment is as beneficial as possible. We would not want to inherit the environment that we of this generation will leave to our successors. We come, then, to as good an approximation as we can to Kant's admonition not to manipulate others. In order to carry that out, however, we shall have to be, in essence, manipulated by future generations (or the abstraction of them). That will always be true of any given generation, and thus each generation will be effectively manipulated by future generations. We shall all be used as means only ad infinitum.

FROM OLD CONCEPTS TO NEW CONCEPTS

We should not be surprised that the economic and ethical conceptual structures of the nineteenth century will not endure for the realities of the twenty-first century. The environment forces us to reexamine our capitalistic, socialistic, teleological, and deontological assumptions. We have not done so systematically yet, but the first step will be to recognize that the old ways will not do. Here I examine briefly some alternative concepts. I cannot present a completed alternative because I have not been able to think through all the implications. Nevertheless, I believe that as intellectuals, we have an obligation to bend our efforts to such a task. It must be with some sense of irony that we listen to self-righteous academics reproach businesspeople for moral failures in environmental areas while the academics have not done their job: keeping intellectual concepts straight, clear, and relevant.

Managerialism

I have suggested using the term *managerialism* to describe a new ideology that asserts that social decisions are the result of neither atomistic firms engaged in competition to maximize their own self-interest nor an overarching collective social consciousness driving the society. Managerialism declares, rather, that social directions result from the multitude of transactions that happen regularly among the managements of the organizations of society. Some of those organizations are corporations; some are labor unions; some are trade associations; some are government agencies; some are charities; and so forth. The managements of these organizations engage in numerous transactions that run a gamut from the routine to the dramatic. With no overarching collective purpose, they set the social direction by virtue of their decisions. It is important to point out that I am not an apologist for this ideology. I do not identify it because I admire it; I identify it because it is operative.

The Environment as Zero Cost

In capitalism, zero cost is to the environment as employment at will is to employees. Both had their place; both are outdated. These concepts are changed only at the ultimate cost of capitalism itself, but in the case of employment at will, the change is almost complete, and with regard to zero cost, the change must be made while there still is enough environment to protect.

"At the Table"—Not Just a Government Assignment

In the transaction process, the only interests addressed are those that are represented and part of the process. To simplify this last point, consider a standard labor-management negotiation. Typically the only parties to such negotiations are representatives of labor on the one side and representatives of management on the other side. Consumers may well have an interest in the negotiations, but unless they are represented, their interests will be ignored.

Just as consumers will be ignored unless they are effective in the transaction process, so the environment will be ignored unless it is effective in the transaction process. In contrast with other stakeholders, however, the environment cannot negotiate for itself. Understandably it has taken longer for environmental concerns to be represented. Some people have taken an interest in the environment, and they have created various groups to represent environmental concerns.

In some cases, the managers of other organizations have been forced to engage in transactions with managers (representatives) of the environmentally based groups. In essence, those groups are forcing the other organizations to recognize that the environment is not a zero-cost alternative. Managers of the environmental organizations have also transacted with governmental units to gain power.

Following the lead of the union movement, however, it should be clear that involving the government is neither a necessary nor a sufficient condition for solution of the issues. The government itself is an actor in the transactional managerialist drama. Contrary to socialist assumptions of the beneficence of government, in managerialism, we have learned the government can be as much part of the problem as part of the solution.

Anti-Determinism

Managerialism declares that managers have some limited discretion. Not all managers have discretion, however. Some are effectively constrained by external forces over which they have no substantial control. That is not true for all, however, and most managers find that they have some discretion over decisions. It is precisely in the area of discretion that we may be justified in holding them responsible for decisions. We must move our concepts away from the deterministic scheme implicit in capitalism and socialism to an approach in which managers do make discretionary choices and can be held responsible for those choices.

New Economics and New Accounting

To say that economists have ignored the environment is not to warrant the conclusion that environmentalists should ignore economics. If neither standard ethics nor standard economics are conceptually empowered to deal with environment and yet if the environmental issues are important, we should begin to speculate on the conceptual changes necessary to deal with those issues.

In the past thirty years, a literature has developed in environmental economics. The problem does not lie with the ingenuity of the economists; it lies with the basic assumptions of economics. For example, there is a presumption that the only alternative to a free marketplace is government intervention. Thus, economists, in attempting to get the environmental issues dealt with, turn to the government.[5]

Other approaches, however, have developed for the allocation of scarce environmental resources. Environmental interest group organizations have had a major impact on environmental policy formulation. They cannot be ignored in a successful economic analysis. The concepts of economics need to be changed to accommodate such developments. An economics of managerialism that reaches beyond determinism and instantaneous time-cuts without including such elusive concepts as General Will should be developed.

The presumption of zero-cost environmental impact needs to be revised so that environmental impact will be part of managerial analyses. Recognition of this may suggest changes in accounting systems. Accounting and economics need to carry similar conceptual assumptions, or they will not support each other. Currently deterioration of the environment is not accounted for as an expense, nor is accumulated deterioration considered a liability. That lack is, in one sense, merely a convention. In another sense, it is a deep conceptual issue that accountants have inherited from economists.

Actually the conceptual barrier was broken some years ago when Congress established the depletion allowance for extractive industries. The theory was that as a corporation used its mineral resources, it depleted its assets and should be allowed a (noncash) depletion allowance as an expense, which then translated into a decreased tax bill and, thus, greater cash profits. The arithmetic sign for depletion is not what should be at stake. It could be as easily negative as positive. Thus, we could reestablish depletion, and we could increase the tax bill in accordance with environmental cost. The money so collected could be kept in a privately administered fund, which might be used to support efforts to improve the environment.

Normative versus Positive Economics Redux

The economists' radical distinction between normative and positive economics will have to be revised. Curiously that distinction is not inherited from either Smith or Marx. The notion of value-free science is an early twentieth-century positivist view that the social scientists adopted. It was convenient because it enabled economists to sidestep ideological issues that threatened to undermine the capacity for economics to make any scientific progress. We must conclude by now that any economics carries with it ideological, moral, and value-laden assumptions. The assumptions of determinism, the calculus, and zero cost of environmental use are all value laden and antienvironmental. Once determinism is abandoned, discretion is possible, and ethical judgments make a difference. Under those conditions, the economists and the philosophers can join in an effort to bring rigorous understanding to these problems in the context of an ideology relevant to us as we enter the twenty-first century.

NOTES

1. Benjamin M. Friedman, *Day of Reckoning* (New York: Random House, 1988).

2. John Locke, *Of Civil Government*, bk. V.

3. Wilfred Beckerman, "The Case for Economic Growth," *Public Utilities Fortnightly,* September 26, 1972.

4. Richard T. De George, "Do We Owe the Future Anything?" in *Law and the Ecological Challenge* (Buffalo, N.Y.: Wm. S. Hein & Co., 1978).

5. See William J. Baumol and Wallace E. Oates, *The Theory of Environmental Policy* (Englewood Cliffs, N.J.: Prentice-Hall), and A. Myrick Freeman III, *The Benefits of Environmental Improvement* (Baltimore: Johns Hopkins University Press, 1979).

The Principle of Integrity and
The Economy of the Earth

LAURA S. WESTRA

Henry Regier, director of the Institute for Environmental Studies, University of Toronto, recently wrote:

> The Ecological Committee of the International Joint Commission's [IJC] Science Advisory Board and the Board of Technical Experts of the Great Lakes Fishery Commission convened a workshop on "Ecosystem Integrity in the Context of Surprise," at Burlington, Ontario on June 14–16, 1988. The intent was to discover conceptual and practical meaning in the language of the U.S./Canada Water Quality Agreement of 1978, as revised in 1987, and specifically in the statement: "The purpose of the Parties is to restore and maintain the chemical, physical and biological integrity of the waters of the Great Lakes Basin Ecosystem . . . ;" where the latter is defined as: " . . . the interacting components of air, land, water and living organisms, including humans within the drainage basin of the St. Lawrence River."

The concept of integrity demands analysis because it is used in both its environmental (descriptive) sense and its moral (prescriptive) one. It is worth noting that integrity has such favorable connotations in purely interhuman context that it almost begs the question to propose to use it in a purely descriptive manner. Some have suggested as an alternative *integrality,* and perhaps that is a good choice if the context is purely scientific.

On the other hand, in Aldo Leopold's famous statement, the expression is somewhat equivocal, as it appears to have both senses—that is, it is both descriptive and requiring approbation at one end and the same time.[1] Biologist Henry Regier says: "Like the terms *health* and *wholeness, integrity* has been applied to a broad spectrum of phenomena. At least implicitly, the underlying paradigm is usually that of a living system, either in a natural biotic sense, or in a cultural noetic sense, or both."[2] I agree in viewing integrity primarily in the sense of wholeness of a living system. It is, first, desirable state of affairs. Our use of the term in human context suggests a person of character, not easily swayed, ethically unassailable, as well as basically honest. In the biological sense the claim is made that that which is naturally one should not be interfered with or torn asunder.

If it is prima facie such that it should not be interfered with, then some sense of value or appropriateness needs to be interjected in its cultural counterpart, as only the natural version (i.e., ecosystems) appears to be strong and valid enough to stand as it is, thus possessing inherent worth and value. For instance, I believe the "vigor" and "health" of the South African system do not amount at this time to an integrity that should not be disturbed or dissected.

Regier speaks of "two polarities or subsystems within the Great Lakes Basin ecosystem: the natural and the cultural." He adds that "these can only be distinguished in a general way—we see no clear boundary between them."[3] I think he is correct insofar as the difficulty of clearly separating natural from cultural integrity is concerned. I understand culture to mean the specific activities of one member of the biota, that is, human beings, and thus as a (partially) natural activity. Integrity, naturally present in undisturbed natural ecosystems, requires a constant, or at least a deliberate, effort on the part of humans so that "these two subsystems [which] are now interacting adversarially" would complement one another through natural interaction instead.[4] Therefore, integrity slips almost imperceptibly here from being merely descriptive of a state of affairs to being prescriptive, in the sense of manifesting a state of affairs that should be brought about.

If I understand him correctly, it is in this way that true integrity can be brought about. Regier further cites Thomas Jorling (1972 U.S. P.L. 92–500), as the latter uses the concept of harmony to describe this desirable state of affairs.[5]

I will return to the concept of integrity after presenting some specific aspects of the problems concerning the Great Lakes Basin, primarily the presence and the effects of toxics in the region. In mid-April 1989, an intensive workshop was convened at Niagara-on-the-Lake, Ontario, by the Great Lakes Institute (State University of New York at Buffalo), comprising lawyers, epidemiologists, toxicologists, and public health professionals from both Canada and the United States to discuss the need for new public policy based on findings about toxics in the Great Lakes. The main basis of information for the latter is to be found in the states of health in the ecosystem, nonhuman and human both. Pesticides, heavy metals, PCBs (polychlorinated biphenyl), dioxins all have documented effects on fish, birds, and mammals in the area: fragile eggshells (leading to 80–100 percent loss of some bird species), reproductive impairments, cancers, and tumors in fish and mammals are some of the effects, as well as a wide range of deformities in insect larvae. Abnormal parental behavior is another contributing factor to species loss, and so is neurological dysfunction in many species from birds to whales. Many of these abnormalities remain to affect several generations.[6]

Against this background, "It should not be surprising that human tissues also reflect the trend and state of ecosystem contamination."[7] PCBs show up in mother's milk, for instance, and congenital deformities, adverse reproductive outcomes in females (including significantly decreased sperm count in males), decreased birth weight and head circumference, and increased rates of cancer of all types, as well as circulatory and immune system diseases, are some of the results documented.[8] Further, psychosocial conditions arising from exposure to high levels of hazardous substances are also to be expected. The impact of feelings of fear, anger at having no control over one's circumstances, trapped in homes and communities from which no escape might be financially possible, and within which, paradoxically, victims find the only appropriate group support has been documented from New York (Lewiston and Love Canal) to Three Mile Island and to South Carolina.[9]

An aggravating factor in such cases has been that "a high level of distress was shown to be associated with significantly poorer DNA repair in lymphocytes, as compared to low-distress subjects," increasing the likelihood of cancer, infectious disease, and the like.[10] Technological and scientific advances have significantly extended our life span, but, even in that context, "the public rightly perceives the risks around them to have become more severe."[11] In Canada, against this somewhat terrifying background, we are euphemistically (or optimistically) assured "the right to life" within the Charter of Rights and Freedoms (section 7 guarantees the "right to life, liberty and the security of persons"), "which does not now include but someday may be interpreted by the courts to include the right to quality of life or a right to health."[12]

For the time being, the enactment of an environmental bill of rights by the federal Parliament and the provincial legislatures would be the next best solution, according to environmental lawyer Paul Muldoon. Yet for now only Quebec has an Environment Quality Act (EQA), where section 19.1 provides for a qualified right, meaning that the standing rule is relaxed only when there are regulatory provisions governing the polluting activity complained of, and those provisions are being violated.[13] In essence, the meaning is that class action generally is not allowed for environmental damage; rather only specific citizens may sue. This clearly discourages anyone whose responsibility would be to prove harm, at great expense and—possibly—only after the harm (such as serious or fatal disease) had in fact occurred. To all intents and purposes, this leaves citizens largely unprotected, given the time span required for diseases to develop and the prohibitive legal and court costs.

This is why, in spite of its limitations, the EQA provides "an expedited way for groups and individuals to go to court and enforce the existing environmental laws." For Ontario, Ruth Grier, of the New Democratic Party (NDP), introduced bill 13 (which has now had two readings in the legislature but is likely to be replaced by a similar bill, put forth by the Liberals instead, as they have become aware of the viability of such a bill). Once again, such bills would enable citizens to sue through class action, they would protect whistleblowers, and they would flesh out the meaning of "life and security of persons" in the Charter of Rights. Similar environmental protection acts exist in Minnesota and Michigan, and Wisconsin possesses excellent environmental laws, as well as legal precedent ensuring, for instance, the protection of lakes and wetlands even to the extent of effecting legal takings in cases of actions with consequences that might entail environmental degradation. There is no need to prove specific harm; rather the appeal is to the need to leave environments undisturbed, where harm might be envisioned in the environment itself, in order to protect the heritage and rights of future generations.[14]

THE ROLE OF THE PHILOSOPHER AND SAGOFF'S PROPOSAL

Against this background, two questions need to be raised: (1) Is there anything that a philosopher can contribute to the solution of these problems? And, if the answer is affirmative, (2) does the concept of integrity help to develop an understanding of the goals and aims we need to espouse, as well as the best means to their implementation? I propose an affirmative answer to both questions. There is an abundance of literature attesting to the fact that questions such as those I have already discussed are not exclusively or even primarily technological or scientific questions, and it will not be necessary to repeat the insights of such thinkers as K. Shrader-Frechette or A. MacIntyre, to mention but two of the most prominent ones.[15] On the other hand, the recent work by Mark Sagoff, *The Economy of the Earth,* needs special mention. While most others argue that the citizen and the ethician ought to have a place in policy making when the questions raised affect the public interest, Sagoff adds that a special role is to be played by the economist, unlike the dominant role he or she normally plays. Beyond the existence of rules of morality and logical consistency, which are often disregarded in risk-cost benefit analysis (RCBA)s, Sagoff suggests the existence of a national idea, a vision, one might say, that goes beyond the satisfaction of preferences in the marketplace but that cashes out to some values, the implementation of which is the goal of the government, as representative of the public.

He argues convincingly that there is a strong difference between individual preferences and desirable social values and that, since the latter cannot be collapsed within the ambit of the former, a tally of preferences as indicated by market trends and results will not necessarily yield desirable policy options.[16] It is noteworthy that these theories are unfolded against the background of problems of toxics and radioactive wastes buried (but not forgotten) in a disposal site in Lewiston, New York (near the site of the Lake Ontario Ordinance Works).[17] The experience of the area citizens, their terror in the face of the mounting number of leukemia cases in children, and their demand for explanations and solutions are all briefly detailed and discussed. Sagoff concludes "The residents of Lewiston asked for an explanation, justice and truth, and they were told their wants would be taken care of. They demanded to know the reasons for what was continually happening to them. They were offered a personalized response instead."[18] When officials offered estimates of their willingness to pay for safety and cost-benefit analyses coupled with talk of trade-offs, they were angry, not impressed, just as they had been when their legitimate anxiety for their lives and those of their children was deemed "irrational."[19] What was, and always is, at stake in this case and those like it is the unrecognized difference between consumer and citizen, between market preferences and values, to which economic considerations do not apply.

The function of social policy makers, Sagoff argues, is to conform to what we are, the values that represent "our [U.S.] national goals and aspirations." In fact, the government, through the requirements of the Clean Water Act and the Clean Air Act (or of any environmental protection act in Canada), does not suggest or even permit a rebalancing of its goals by the criteria of economic theory; therefore the role of administration is not to translate value-affirming policy into market values: "The principal purposes of legislative action are to weigh and affirm social values and to define and enforce the right and duties of the member of the society through representative democracy."[20] For instance, "this is right" or "I believe this because . . . " is not equivalent to "I want this . . . " and "This is what I prefer . . . ," as the analyst supposes, Sagoff argues. Thus, "segregation is a national curse, and if we are willing to pay for it, that does not make it better, but only makes us worse. Similarly the case for or against abortion rights must stand on its merits; it cannot be priced at the margin."[21] In the same manner, environmental values embodying safety and justice for all citizens are not negotiable or amenable to economic calculation. It is for that reason that we must regain a deontological perspective in which a claim that something is right is an objective one and not to be sought in and through market preferences; like love and other deeply meaningful things, environmental values are moral and aesthetic. "These things," Sagoff says, "have a *dignity*, rather than a price."[22] Citizens of the United States (and no doubt Canadians) have deeply held and cherished values and beliefs. Their demands in regard to ecology provide an "independent obligation [to] government(s) to preserve individuals share and to protect public safety and health."[23]

If we find Sagoff's argument convincing, we, as philosophers, need to reenter the field of policy making, perhaps not as Platonic philosopher-kings or -queens but at the very least as part of a team composed of scientists and policy makers. Both conceptual analysis and ethical discussion are within our province, and both can only benefit from dialogue cooperation that is interdisciplinary.

The complex concept of integrity lends itself well to embodying the values referred to, as well as the advocated philosophical discussion, as it is introduced, right at the outset, as a philosophical rather than a scientific term. I will use it to suggest a principle on which to base the values we want to see implemented. I will show how it can ground a categorical imperative that goes beyond the Kantian deontology Sagoff suggests without, however, conflicting with it.

A PROPOSAL FOR AN ETHIC OF RESPECT
AND A NEW CATEGORICAL IMPERATIVE

A different perspective and a much broader understanding of rationality and justice are elicited by today's environmental concern; stoicism suggests a worthwhile starting point for these positions. To my knowledge, the only reference to a somewhat Stoic ethic in this context (termed an ethic of *naturam sequere*) is to be found in W. K. Frankena, who apparently deems it unworthy of detailed attention.[24] Elsewhere, however, he raises another pertinent question: do we need to have recourse to the realm of morality at all, or can rationality of means (for survival, for instance) be judged sufficient to motivate us to deal appropriately with the environment?[25] It might seem as though ecological concern would be one of the easiest motives to pursue, aside from morality, once the facts are understood. Unfortunately recent history disproves this. The tragedy that may well befall the human race is seen as either too far into the future to matter or at least as far enough to persuade many to see immediate gain as greatly preferable to the restrictions of environmental concerns. Most of us have learned the lesson of consumerism too well. An Arab proverb says, "Before the palm tree can be beautiful, our belly must be full of dates." It is a truism, as indeed survival comes before aesthetic enjoyment. Unfortunately environmental concern is seen as aesthetic preference rather than urgently needed for survival, whereas survival and even nourishment have taken on an unprecedented coloration of unrestricted choices, preferences, and actions, now viewed, at least in the Western world, as our deepest right. Economic interests and scientism have succeeded in typecasting environmental concern as a marginal worry, a luxury most of us (we are told) cannot really afford, in the face of the hard facts of economic need, unemployment, the necessity for profits, and so on. This line of argument shows only why we need to seek seriously an environmental ethic for prudential reasons; it does not show that nonhuman entities or the wholer world should be morally considerable and even less why this should be so.

The position I propose suggests a radically new starting point. It is not one that starts from the consideration of our own humanity—the capacities and achievements that represent our standards of value—and then attempts to locate some of these outside the human community. Many argue that that enterprise has gone as far as it can, and that is not far enough.[26] My position is one of two-level monism. Our first step is to acknowledge that about which no choice is possible, that is, our inescapable membership in our ecosystem. That is something we cannot ignore or bypass in any of our actions; therefore it ought to have primacy in moral consideration as well as moral theory directed at action. Thus, whatever else we need in a moral theory (and in its definition of both rationality and justice), we cannot consistently design or discover one that is totally divorced from the most basic realities of our existence.

Just like science needs to return from abstract models to reality in order to prove its hypotheses valid, so too ethics cannot counsel, and even less command, something that does not fit the reality of our physical existence. Even the most Platonic and irreducibly dualistic theory of morality requires that the theory should not fit angels only, or disembodied spirits, but human beings. This ought to be our first step, even before reading other decisions on utilitarianism versus Kantianism, virtue ethics versus contractarian justice, and so on. It can easily be objected that such a principle is just a truism, is too general, and does not offer guidance in dealing with either humans or nature. I think it is very helpful in limiting the parameter of our ethical argument by presenting a solid and uncontrovertible starting point. At any rate, let us start with it and see where we may go from here:

1. The first moral principle is that nothing can be moral that contradicts the physical realities of our existence or cannot be seen to fit within the natural laws of our environment.[27]

This appears to be paradoxical; how can we act or design policies that "contradict" or "fail to fit within natural laws" when all our acts are as much part of nature as we are? I have argued that while animals' actions and reactions cannot fail to fit, human agency indeed can fail (witness our interference with laws that will eventually affect the survival of our species). We cannot act outside natural laws in the sense that whatever we affect will deteriorate according to these laws. But our freedom to choose and implement ends independently of natural goals (always specific or holistic, rather than purely individual) allows us to choose not only to make ourselves unfit but also to curtail our species' own fitness for survival. It also permits us to affect adversely the whole environment, that is, to interfere with the persistence of all life. Further, it is worth noting that even to say that our "ought" cannot and must not contradict nature's "is" is not to claim that all and any natural "is" translates into a human "ought."

Our next step should be to unpack that "is." This task has been pursued elsewhere,[28] and those arguments cannot be duplicated here. The Stoic component can be seen in the argument that nature needs to be understood and that it is an arena wherein the basic principles are respect coupled with indifference and hostility.[29] Respect is found in the limited, selective, unavoidable killing that animals practice purely for survival (not for sport, trivialities, or curiosity-science). It has been argued that ecosystems are meant to function that way; all entities within the biota will use everything else that serves to facilitate their own survival.[30] Thus "hostility" and "respect/indifference" (the latter applicable by animals to those species which are not vital to their survival) also serve to help reconcile an environmental and animal ethic, saving some aspects of both Albert Schweitzer's respect-for-life doctrine and Paul Taylor's respect for nature yet differing from both.[31]

The first principle for which I have argued generates a categorical imperative in two basic formulations. The first is:

1a. Act so that your action will fit first (and minimally) within universal natural laws.

The reference to the primacy of natural laws not only prohibits environmental abuse but solves the difficulties of joining animal and environmental ethics without forcing us to complete vegetarianism, or, worse, to guilt and outrage at the use of anything we might need to survive, which is the major problem of Schweitzer's ethic. His reverence stops at individual lives rather than extend to all nature and in that sense is against the natural functioning of the world; thus it manifests a lack of respect to life's laws as they truly exist in nature. In this sense, the principle and the ethic I propose eliminate the dichotomy and reconcile systemic with individual concern by extending respect and reverence to the ways of the environment as well as to the specifics and the wholes within it.[32]

The second way in which my first principle and categorical imperative may be used is to permit a hierarchical ranking of approaches and to sanction as permissible, rather than contradictory to fairness and justice, an interhuman ethic that is not exhausted by our environmental ethic stance. In other words, just like the wolf will act in certain ways within its pack, giving primacy to its own survival, followed by that of spouse and offspring perhaps, and then exhibit certain appropriate behavior in regard to others within the pack but in a very different manner with prey, on one hand, and with other entities to which it is indifferent, on the other, some form of this sort of behavior is appropriate to humans as well. We need not extend to animals and others within the environment, species, and ecosystems human fairness, justice, and so on. In fact to do so manifests a disrespect for the ways of natural entities themselves, to whom we see ourselves as imposing benevolently our standards. It is rational and appropriate for a wolf to treat other wolves in a way quite different from the way in which it treats us. Indifference, noninterference, and—in the case of special need—predation are the hallmarks of the wolf's possible treatment of humans. The same should obtain interspecies, that is, between us and others that do not belong to our species. Of course, if we have interfered previously, then it is fair to use interhuman (or intraspecific) ethics as our guide and apply retributive justice.

This suggests a second formulation of the categorical imperative suggested in 1a. This should read:

1b. Act so that you manifest respect and understanding acceptance of all natural process and laws.

When restated in this form, it clearly requires that everything about ecosystems that is possible to learn should be learned. A hierarchical pluralism reigns; for instance, nothing that happens spontaneously (that is, without our interference) is not in some way or time life enhancing for individuals, species, or ecosystems, and conflicts arise but rarely. When they do, they are usually resolved within the larger picture, that is, in favor of ecosystemic integrity even at the expense of some individuals or species. Our lesson from nature here is that as long as we do not allow this to interfere with the ecosystemic laws that sustain survival, it is appropriate and fitting that each species should have its specific ethics and that that intraspecific and interspecific ethics should differ.[33] The direction of our moral discourse is altered; in fact, it is reversed. We have an all-encompassing monism as the ground of our moral reasoning. Within it we can fit various fitting ethics, somewhat like a set of nesting wooden Russian dolls, one inside the other.[34]

The position I suggest does not attempt to stretch and extend interhuman ethics to cover other entities and wholes in response to a perceived, overwhelming need; rather it is a position that draws its inspiration from the original insights of Stoic thinkers and Plotinus. The whole cosmos is viewed as governed by a logos that is essentially divine, or a first principle that is the source of the rational laws and justice of the universe, as well as the actual source of all that exists within it. These laws and that justice are not viewed (as they are in all other traditions, and particularly in modern ethical doctrine) as something we need to understand in order to control; rather, they are viewed as in the universe as a whole, as a manifestation of the divine, something that still demands study and understanding but only if interwoven with awe, respect, and humility. The switch required is that between a user stance and that of a respectful disciple perhaps (though not a mindless follower). The difference in attitude is, to some extent, that advocated by Schweitzer, and it is a crucial one.[35] There are obvious objections that can be made to my position: that it is a fallacy to move from an "is" to an "ought" and the position for which I argue is a defensible one within a Stoic or Plotinian context or within a "religious" one of some sort but has no philosophical value as such outside these traditions. Of course, this is not a critique MacIntyre could offer; given the thrust of his own argument,[36] he could only require that I engage convincingly for what is better or even right, but I provide no strong obligation to follow my imperatives other than prudential considerations.

I will briefly address these objections. First, it is not necessary for my argument to move from an "is" to an "ought"; it is sufficient that the "is" should be seen as a limit to whatever "ought" we might be able to defend. This is a broadening of a purely environmental ethics,[37] but it is also an implicit premise in all ethical doctrines. For instance, one could not prescribe the use of a utilitarian calculus unless we possessed the ability to calculate and unless pleasure and pain were facts of our existence. Although the obligation does not stem from that capacity, it could not be there unless the capacity was there as well; thus that capacity provides the factual limit to our prescriptions. Second, the respect I advocate as foundational for a principle that is both transcendent and immanent does not require a commitment to an act of faith (this is the objection, I take it, that would make my position "unphilosophical") and to an exclusive religious belief, even less to a personal deity; however, it might be viewed as a first step in a direction that might ultimately permit either of these positions; but precisely as a first step, it also stands alone, and as such it is defensible as a separate position.

Finally, on the question of obligation, it may be the case that—following Kant—too much emphasis has been placed on the absolute division between obligation and prudence. For instance, neither virtue ethics, such as the Aristotelian concern with isolating the "truly human" activity while tracing the link between contemplation and happiness (as "living well"), nor Plato's quest for the "good" and the Socratic appeal on behalf of the "philosophic" life, with its concern for goodness and harmony and the health of one's soul, excludes a somewhat prudential component. Nor is it possible or necessary to exclude enlightened, universalized prudence from ethical doctrines that consider happiness or rationality as an ultimate value.

In this case, it is even less obvious why a prudential component should render an approach to morality less credible if it is extended to the human race as a whole, particularly when the latter is not even singled out by the imperatives I suggest.

CONCLUSION

I began by touching on the acute problems encountered in the Great Lakes Basin and the ideal of integrity, suggested as the desirable goal of policy and legislation by the IJC and the environmental regulatory agencies of both Canada and the United States. The notion was clearly deemed to be a philosophical rather than a scientific one, thus one to the understanding of which philosophers can indeed contribute significantly. Then we saw that Sagoff's argument in the *Economy of the Earth* defends the position that preservation and environmental concern must be seen not as market preferences of consumers but as a national and, given the connotations of pollution as a phenomenon not limited by boundaries, an international global ideal to which all countries' citizens qua human beings aspire to. A picture of integrity has emerged as a goal designed against the background of scientific information but not scientific in and of itself; it is an ideal that can be implemented only in and through a society that cannot ignore economic realities yet has "an ethical, not an economic justification."[38]

General policy statements in both countries appear to demand that we proceed (albeit gradually) toward a zero-risk state. Sagoff cites the U.S. Clean Air and Clean Water acts; neither suggests or even permits economically adjusted trade-offs—and this is as it should be. In that case, it is eminently appropriate that philosophers should have a strong voice in their formulation, in the analysis of their meaning and explication, thus ultimately the definition of appropriate policy to implement them.

Although Sagoff does not confront explicitly the question of integrity, he does say that the "absolute purity" suggested by the environmental protection acts is not a feasible ideal.[39] Even in scientific terms, it seems as though pristineness (like virginity) cannot be regained once lost. The meaning of the goal of integrity in that case might be viewed as restoring harmony, whereby the human component of the biota is not setting itself over and against other components but exists in accordance with the requirements of natural laws, occupying its rightful niche and affirming its own identity and difference from other components without however endangering the biota wherein people dwell.[40]

The harmony indicated is almost like the Platonic harmony in the soul, writ large. Justice, for Plato, the ultimate virtue and aim of the philosophical life, was no other than a harmony of parts of the soul, each performing the function it was meant to do. While we can argue about the possible arbitrariness of imposing certain specific roles on parts of the soul, the scientific, factual reality of roles appropriate to all parts of the biota is indisputable. We know, minimally, what is capable of affecting the ecosystem, what interferes with its stability, integrity, and beauty, and what disrupts its functioning and degrades it thus interfering ultimately not only with its continued existence in a healthy, harmonious state but with ours as well.

The internal harmony Plato advocated can now be integrated within an external harmony of Stoic origin: no longer are extrinsic and intrinsic irretrievably opposed; rather, their harmonious reconciliation enhances both forms of harmony. The ideal I propose is both moral and factual, prescriptive and descriptive. The integrity of human activity is restored in a sense that is intensely personal as well as objectively and demonstrably communitarian, where the community is understood as ecosystemic and global rather than urban, regional, or otherwise divisive. If this approach is found to be persuasive and the corresponding obligation is accepted, then we need not face the dichotomy Sagoff envisions. On one hand, for instance, he says "There are some duties that are absolute: for example the duty not to murder or enslave others." However, he asks, "The question arises whether the duties expressed in environmental and social legislation involve perfect or imperfect obligations. Do they state goals we must achieve regardless of costs? Do they also involve some imperfect duties?"[41] He then goes on to suggest that if environmental infractions lead to "identifiable deaths" that can be attributed to particular exposures, then the government's obligation is "to prohibit this sort of serious accident through statutory and tort law."[42]

The admission of a first principle such as the one I recommend would provide an obligation without the need to have, as one public health official recently said, "bodies lined up," before the fatal danger can be stopped.[43] His point was that just as in the case of altered Tylenol bottles, when decisive, immediate action could be legally taken on risk possibility, rather than on "proved deaths," so too environmental dangers should be judged on similar fashion—on the possibility of danger, not on required visible proof.

As Sagoff's own analysis of the case in Lewiston, New York, shows,[44] the legal and political processes requiring proof of harm, as in tort law, are lengthy, uncertain, and open to manipulation by economic interests. In that case, the very recognition of the strong position of values and a moral vision should exclude such impediments to a truly just and moral solution.

NOTES

1. Aldo Leopold, *A Sand County Almanac* (New York: Oxford University Press, 1968), p. 224.

2. Henry Regier, "Integrity and Surprise in the Great Lakes Basin Ecosystem," unpublished paper, September 2, 1988.

3. Ibid., p. 3. See George M. Woodwell, "The Challenge of Endangered Species," in *Extinction is Forever*, ed. Ghillian Prance and Thomas Elias (New York: New York Botanical Gardens, 1977).

4. Regier, "Integrity," p. 3.

5. Ibid., p. 6.

6. Thomas Muir and Anne Sudar, "Toxic Chemicals in the Great Lakes Basin Ecosystem," pp. 44ff., unpublished paper (1987).

7. Ibid., p. 31.

8. Ibid., pp. 44ff.

9. M. R. Edelstein and A. Wandersman, "Community Dynamics in Coping with Toxic Contaminants" (October, 1989).

10. Muir and Sudar, "Toxic Chemicals," p. 82.

11. William Frendenburg, "Perceived Risk, Real Risk: Social Science and the Art of Probabilistic Risk Assessment," *Science* 242, p. 44.

12. Paul Muldoon, "The Fight for an Environmental Bill of Rights," *Alternatives* 15, no. 2 (1988): 35.

13. Ibid.

14. Chief Justice Hallows, "Just vs. Marinette County, Supreme Court of Wisconsin, 1972, 56 Wis. 2d 7, 201 N.W. 2d 761," in *Ethics and the Environment*, ed. D. Scherer and Th. Attig (Englewood Cliffs, N.J.: Prentice-Hall, 1983), p. 132.

15. See, for instance, S. Shrader-Frechette, "Science Policy," in *Ethics and Economic Methodology* (Dordrecht: D. Reidel Publishing, 1985), pp. 32–64; cf. A. MacIntyre, "Utilitarianism and Cost-Benefit Analysis: An Essay on the Relevance of Moral Philosophy to Bureaucratic Theory," in *Ethics and the Environment*, pp. 139–51.

16. M. Sagoff, *The Economy of the Earth* (Cambridge: Cambridge University Press, 1989), pp. 24ff.

17. Ibid.

18. Ibid., p. 47.

19. Ibid.; cf. Edelstein and Wandersman, "Community Dynamics."

20. Ibid., p. 9; cf. also n. 15 in chap. 2.

21. Ibid., p. 45.

22. Ibid., p. 69.

23. Ibid., p. 115.

24. W. K. Frankena, "Ethics and the Environment," in *Ethics and Problems of the 21st Century*, ed. K. E. Goodpaster and K. M. Sayre (Notre Dame, Ind.: Notre Dame Press, 1979), pp. 3–20.

25. W. K. Frankena, "Obligation and Motivation in Recent Moral Philosophy," in *Perspectives on Morality (Collected Essays)*, ed. K. E. Goodpaster (Notre Dame, Ind.: University of Notre Dame Press, 1976), p. 51.

26. Christopher Stone, "Moral Pluralism and the Course of Environmental Ethics," *Environmental Ethics* 10, no. 2 (Summer 1988): 139–54.

27. Holmes Rolston III, *Environmental Ethics* (Philadelphia: Temple Press, 1988), p. 79.

28. Holmes Rolston III, "Is There an Ecological Ethics?" in *Ethics and the Environment*, p. 48. Cf. L. Westra, "Technology Risk Assessment and the Is-Ought Fallacy: A Critique of Shrader Frechette," in *The Agrarian* (Clemson, S.C.: Clemson University, 1987).

29. Laura Westra, "Ecology and Animals: Is There a Joint Ethic of Respect?" *Environmental Ethics* (forthcoming).

30. This does not negate the existence of some symbiotic relations between animals and plants, bacteria and animals, and bacteria and humans. It does prove that a "user" stance is a fact of natural life, although in some instances hostility is not a factor.

31. In an earlier, much longer, and detailed version of this chapter, I take up the challenge of two other ethics, based respectively on reverence for life and respect for nature, the former by Albert Schweitzer and, the latter by Paul Taylor, both of which bear a certain similarity to my own position.

I find the former inspiring, but not only insufficient as a guiding principle (a problem already noted by both Callicott and Goodpaster) but also self-contradictory; it demands reverence for individual lives yet manifests a clear distaste for the very laws according to which those lives unfold and sustain themselves. (See A. Schweitzer, *Civilization and Ethics*, 3d ed., (London: Adam and Charles Black, 1946); J. Baird Callicott, "Intrinsic Value of Nonhuman Species," in *The Preservation of Species*, ed. Bryan Norton (Princeton: Princeton University Press, 1986); K. Goodpaster, "From Egoism to Environmentalism" in *Ethics and Problems of the 21st Century*, p. 32.

As far as the latter is concerned, I feel it does not help to maintain the coincidence of intraspecies (i.e., interhuman) ethics and interspecies ethics, for reasons that will become clear in the rest of this chapter. Taylor's concept of "inherent worth" for nonhuman entities centers on the disproof of human superiority. This negative approach is not sufficient to provide a determinate content for the concept on which Taylor's ethic is based. Further, his exclusion of all animals beyond the wild renders his ethic incomplete, to my mind. See Paul Taylor, *Respect for Nature* (Princeton: Princeton University Press, 1986), pp. 44–45, and for an excellent discussion of Taylor's holism, see Bryan G. Norton, *Why Preserve Natural Variety?* (Princeton: Princeton University Press, 1987), esp. pp. 178–79.

32. Westra, "Ecology and Animals."

33. The result of this position is that no action of any individual within a species should conflict with the life enhancement of the whole ecosystem except for survival (immediate) or survival-related activities (future), and the latter must not be wasteful or proceed through disrespectful means but need not be minimal to be appropriate morally. For instance, just as bees can store honey and squirrels nuts, so too we can cultivate and perhaps eat both a carrot and a fish without guilt.

34. Stone, "Moral Pluralism," pp. 140–46 where, by contrast, a pluralist position is advocated.

35. Schweitzer, *Civilization*, p. 241.

36. Alasdair MacIntyre, *Whose Justice? Which Rationality?* (South Bend, Ind.: University of Notre Dame Press, 1988), p. 394.

37. Holmes Rolston III, *Environmental Ethics*, p. 79. For both objections and the discussion that generated my responses, I am indebted to Evandro Agazzi, Kenneth Schmitz, Thomas Hill, Jr., and T. Mayberry.

38. Sagoff, *Economy of the Earth*, p. 199.

39. Ibid., p. 212.

40. M. Heidegger, "Building, Dwelling, Thinking," in *Basic Writings,* ed. D. F. Krell (New York: Harper & Row, 1977), pp. 319–40. Heidegger's discussion centers on man's "dwelling" on earth, as an aware, saving, concerned living, contrasted with an exploitative stand.

41. Sagoff, *Economy of the Earth,* pp. 218–19.

42. Ibid.

43. Dr. Henry Anderson, section chief of the Environmental and Chronic Disease Epidemiology Section, Wisconsin Division of Health, participated in the Public Health Policy Group discussion that took place in a workshop at Niagara-on-the-Lake, April 17, 1989.

44. Sagoff, *Economy of the Earth,* esp. chap. 2.

From Environment to Biosphere: The Necessary Reanimation of Ethical Discourse

BRIAN EDWARD BROWN

A sustained reflection on the relationship between business and the environment, capable of delineating the specific responsibilities of business, must be grounded on an adequate conception of environment. Originally environment connotes the mere aggregate of things, conditions, or influences that surround one; it is the locale or general background for one's activity. Applied to the physical world, one's environment generally refers to the atmosphere, waters, and terrain that together constitute one's immediate and proximate surroundings. In such a conception, the environment of atmosphere, water, and terrain assumes the notion of background entities over and against which human activity runs it course. However much endowed with vitality, the environment is the passive context of variously constituted matter, a framework for human self-expression. This mode of thinking in which environment is largely a particular locale of natural objects fosters a conception of discrete, independent air-water-landscapes whose value is determined by their usefulness to human pursuit. Thus, damage or threat to the environment is evaluated in terms of the interference with the human use or enjoyment of a particular locale through pollution or depletion of the air-water and/or land within that locale.

The inadequacy of this anthropocentric notion of environment as mere surrounding is the reification, fragmentation, and stagnation with which it obscures the vital, comprehensive, interconnected, and dynamic nature of planetary life. If the human community and its commercial enterprises are to assess their responsibilities to the environment, a more biologically informed definition of that reality is needed.

Stretching around the earth in a relatively thin layer is the living world or biosphere within which every organism is linked, however tenuously, to every other. Microbes, plants and mammals, soil dwellers, and ocean inhabitants form an integral community, each drawing and cycling energy and nutrients from the sun, water, air, and earth.[1] The science of ecology continues to discover the intricacies of interdependence that link the different species to each other and that interconnect the distinctive habitats to the whole. It is this image of a planetary community of life-forms where each contributes to and interdepends with the whole that must inform all discussions of environment.

To know that every act of pollution and resource depletion is no isolated event but contributes to a collective impact of increasingly accelerating global proportions is to move more closely to an understanding of environment not merely as regional or local surroundings but as planetary biosphere. The harm to the quality and integrity of an immediate locale is not confined but, given the organic interrelatedness of the biosphere, persists. The notion of destructive duration is complemented by the expansive scope implicit in any act of pollution to the biosphere. These more organic conceptions of space and time are necessary to any evaluation of responsible human activity within the community of life. There can be no adequate assessment of potential risk and harm of an activity without a correct perception of the extent and persistence of the damage that may ensue. The change of designation from environment to biosphere identifies the integrity of planetary life as the appropriate paradigm for all determinations of risk and consequent responsibility.

All too often, however, environmental issues are discussed in a context devoid of all reference to the myriad biotic communities and their complex and pervasive interdependencies that together sustain the vitality of the air-water-landscapes. Economic valuations are made, and competing interests are raised with regard to private and public property interests, development and preservation, recreation and wilderness. What largely animates concern in a determination of any of these issues, however, is the human good to be derived from the use of the environment. Absent from the analysis is an awareness of the intrinsic value of the nonhuman members of the biotic community. Failure to regard their role is to impoverish the long-range vitality and health of the area in question. The irony is that those life-forms that are routinely disregarded as insignificant and the most vulnerable to environmental changes are nevertheless crucial to the sustenance of the more complex organisms. The biosphere, as a whole or regionally, is an integral community of so effective an interdependency that each life-form is inherent to the whole. Absent this attention to the whole and the value of each that sustains it, determinations about ethical activity are incomplete and superficial. Some examples follow of shortsighted ethical valuations that neglect consideration of the health and integrity of the nonhuman members of the life community and restrict ethical decision making about an environment to human concerns.

The illegal dumping of toxic materials in ground or water has been described as an injustice. Unfortunately the notion of justice applied is narrowly circumscribed to fairness in market competition. The costs of safe disposal of toxics, the argument runs, must be borne equally by all competitors. Otherwise the unscrupulous business that disposes of pollutants irresponsibly would gain a cost advantage over more honest businesses. The polluting firm is unethical in its nonpayment of the full cost of its operations, displacing those disposal costs on an innocent public who may be affected by the contaminated water and soil.

The moral analysis proceeds no further than the disapproval of a dishonest competitive edge through a harmful cost displacement onto third parties. In such a scenario the environment involved figures as no more than the instrumentality of the offending competitor's gain. The dumping is condemned primarily for the unfair market advantage it provides and the human health endangered. Clearly the environment here functions as mere surroundings, as the background condition for the resolution of competing human values. No consideration is taken of the immediate and long-term effects that dumping has on the health and integrity of the aquatic and land biota. Whether the notion of justice can be extended to these life-forms will be determined only if their presence and role are acknowledged. To address the injustice of dumping without heeding those organisms whose habitat may be contaminated is to trivialize the ethical discussion and to misperceive the scope of the risk. Harm to the least visible members of a bioregion may well threaten the delicate balance of the whole and in the end may threaten a more serious human harm. The ethics of dumping can be adequately engaged only when the environment affected is correctly perceived as an integrated life community, a particular region of the planetary biosphere.

An example of truncated ethical discourse for failure to conceive of the environment as biosphere is the economic analysis of utilitarianism. Once again, environmental harms are interpreted as failures of the market mechanism. The evils of pollution lie not with its destruction of the planetary life community but with its economic inefficiency. It is said that the market price for the commodities of a business that pollutes often does not reflect the true cost of production. The internal or private costs of the polluter do not include the external costs of the pollution itself, which is imposed on some immediate segment of society. The resulting disparity between the lesser private costs of the polluter and the higher external costs to society indicates a failure of the market to price commodities accurately. From this results a misallocation of resources since more of the commodity is being produced than society would demand if it had an accurate measure of what it is actually paying to produce the commodity. The resources being consumed by overproduction of the commodities are resources to be used to produce other commodities—thus, the misallocation of resources. At the same time, resources are being wasted because the polluter, not taking into account the external or social cost of the pollution, has no incentive to decrease or eliminate them and thus continues the pollution. Those most immediately affected by the pollution must spend more to counter the effects of the pollution than other consumers, and thus they have less to spend on their share of market commodities. Consequently their share of goods is not proportioned to their desires and needs as compared to other buyers not so immediately burdened by the costs of the pollution. Pollution is wrong, finally, because it imposes price differentials into the market where everyone does not pay equal prices for the same commodities.[2]

In the utilitarian conception, then, harm to the environment is primarily a breakdown of the market mechanism, leading to the misallocation and waste of resources and an inefficient distribution of commodities. The remedy for these wrongs is merely to ensure that the costs of pollution are properly absorbed by the producer.[3] So long as the producer pays for the harms imposed on others by the polluting activity, the equity of this environmental ethic is satisfied. Since the environment is essentially a series of commodities, each with a quantifiable value, there is no notion of irreparable damage. Yet how can the biosphere be priced?

In contrast to such ethical valuations that fail to conceive of the environment adequately as a planetary community of interdependent life, or biosphere, the UN *World Charter for Nature* represents the desired paradigm.[4] In October 1982, the thirty-seventh session of the General Assembly adopted the *World Charter* as a formal resolution by a vote of 111 to 1 (the United States voting against the resolution). While its implementation remains still to be translated into specific codes with national and international enforcement procedures, the charter is a significant statement of ethical principles governing human activities within the biosphere.

The charter opens with the recognition of nature as a living reality whose diversity of life-forms makes possible the benefits derived by humanity. The interdependence between the human and all other species is apparent in the charter's notice that excessive exploitation and destruction of species' habitats ultimately jeopardize their beneficence to the human.[5] The charter proceeds to reaffirm that humanity is but "a part of nature" and that human civilization "is rooted in nature."[6] The artistic and scientific achievements of human culture, as well as the creativity of the human mind, are derivatives of nature.

The charter's insistence on human contingency reverses the persistent notion of human nature as a thing removed from, superior to, and without responsibility for other organisms. The charter strikingly repudiates the anthropocentrism of according value to other life-forms merely in terms of their utility to human purposes. Instead, "every form of life is unique, warranting respect regardless of its worth to man, and, to accord other organisms such recognition, man must be guided by a moral code of action."[7] The charter thus identifies and grounds human ethical responsibility toward nature on the inherent value of organic individuality and diversity: nature as a community of beings of intrinsic worth.

What are the delineations of the moral code of action that the charter claims must guide human behavior? Fundamental to the ecological ethics of the charter is the necessity for human self-awareness of its capacity to destroy the natural world through excessive consumption, misuse, and habitat destruction.[8] Without the conviction of its destructive impact within the biosphere, the human species will experience no moral commitment to integrate its civilizational processes within the larger life-support systems of the planet. To remain ignorant of its ongoing disruption of the delicate organic interdependencies that sustain planetary life is to dull human sensitivity to a more expansive ethical concern. Without critical self-evaluation of its often destructive presence within the biosphere, the human species will be unable to recognize the ethical challenge of using planetary resources "in a manner which ensures the preservation of species and ecosystems."[9]

The charter next identifies five general principles "by which all human conduct affecting nature is to be guided and judged":[10]

1. Nature shall be respected and its essential processes shall not be impaired.

2. The genetic viability on the earth shall not be compromised; the population levels of all life forms, wild and domesticated, must be at least sufficient for their survival, and to this end necessary habitats shall be safeguarded.

3. All areas of the earth, both land and sea, shall be subject to these principles of conservation; special protection shall be given to unique areas, to representative samples of all the different types of ecosystems and to the habitats of rare or endangered species.

4. Ecosystems and organisms, as well as the land, marine and atmospheric resources that are utilized by man, shall be managed to achieve and maintain optimum substantial productivity, but not in such a way as to endanger the integrity of those other ecosystems or species with which they coexist.

5. Nature shall be secured against degradation caused by warfare or other hostile activities.[11]

Fundamental to the first two principles is the charter's insistence on a thorough reformation in the human understanding of and attitude toward the concept of environment. The popular notion of discrete, inert physical surroundings must give way to a conception of nature as a living reality, an integral community of diverse life-forms where each contributes its unique genetic heritage to the viability of the whole. Only with such a conception will human arrogance, initially unconscious of its own status as derivative from the life-giving whole, mature to a necessary respect and responsibility for the multiplicity of organisms, their diverse habitats, and their larger ecosystemic interdependencies.

The charter proceeds to specify how this more biologically informed concept of nature needs to be translated into political, social, economic, and managerial processes. Thus, within the broad and varied arenas of political decision making, all attempts to address human needs must be firmly grounded in the recognition that satisfaction of those needs can be met only by ensuring the integrity of the entire biosphere.[12]

To advance a political agenda on the priority of human needs without an assessment of the collective and long-term impact that the satisfaction of those needs may exact on planetary life is irresponsible. While the charter does not so elaborate, its logic would support the necessity of evaluating the meaning of "human needs" as opposed to "human desires." Without determining the specifics of that distinction, the charter clearly suggests that ethical political discourse must engage the issue that the integrity of the biosphere, in the complex diversity of organisms that together sustain it, must define the context within which political decisions are made, respecting the satisfaction of human needs, however they may be defined.[13]

Similarly the planning and implementation of social and economic development activities must recognize the parameters of the biosphere. The long-term capacity of the planet's living systems to maintain their natural stability, regenerating themselves within their respective habitats and contributing to the vitality of the whole, is the limit against which ethical planning for human population growth and improved standards of living must conform. Implicit in the charter is a condemnation of a heedless human expansion linked with a short-term design for increased economic development. The charter is aware of the very real dangers of international conflicts over increasingly scarce resources, which such expansion and expectation would bring.[14] But the charter is fundamentally concerned to protect the earth as a biologically diverse and productive entity against the physical constraints that such ill-conceived human activity would threaten it.

The charter's standards for the ethical management of the earth's resources are again animated by the awareness of the planet as a living reality, to be used with respect.[15] Human use of the biosphere must not exceed its natural capacity for regeneration. Agriculture, grazing, forestry, and fishing practices and techniques must be adapted to the natural rhythms of the earth's soils and waters as organic communities of fertility and decomposition. Science and technology may be used to enhance the productivity of the planet's living resources only if they simultaneously maintain and safeguard their long-term vitality and stability. Even in its consumption and exploitation of the earth's nonrenewable inorganic resources, the human species must weigh the compatibility of the uses it makes of them and the consequences of their depletion on the well-being and functioning of the biosphere's multiple and diverse communities of life.

Finally, the charter specifies that humanity must evaluate its activities in the light of the impact they will have on the biosphere. Activities that are "likely to cause irreversible damage to nature" must be avoided.[16] Activities that are "likely to pose a significant risk to nature" must be exhaustively examined to show that their expected benefits would outweigh the potential damage to nature.[17] If in the course of the review potential adverse effects could be anticipated but their consequences not fully understood, the proposed activity should not proceed. Similarly activities "which may disturb nature" must be preceded by an assessment of their consequences.[18]

The charter's use of the general term *activities* without further specification signifies its intent that humanity's obligation to evaluate its presence carefully within and as part of the biosphere is comprehensive and inclusive. Whether the activity is local or regional, national or international in scope, whether the process involves commerce, manufacture, land development, technological innovation, scientific exploration, or investigation, no human enterprise is exempt from the ethical review of the impact the respective activity will have on the organic processes of the planet.

The significance of the *World Charter for Nature* cannot be overestimated. As a formal resolution of the General Assembly, it represents a striking consensus of the international community on the necessity of protecting the planetary biosphere. Its mandates and strictures are not yet self-implementing international law, since they await legislation from the various national jurisdictions, which thus far have only resolved on their desirability and importance. Nevertheless, the charter is singular as an international document that advocates human ethical behavior toward nature. More, it identifies nature not merely as an object of anthropocentric concern, an environment that, if contaminated or otherwise damaged, interferes with human use and enjoyment. For the charter, nature is a subject in its own right, a totality of diverse, unique, interdependent life-forms, of which the human is but one and without which the human would not be possible.

To engage in reflection and discourse on ethics and the environment is the compelling intellectual and moral exigency of the present. Habitat destruction, massive species extinctions, depletion of genetic diversity, increased desertification, ozone destruction and planetary warming, acidification of rain, and toxic and nuclear waste urge sustained attention from every component of human cultural process. Commerce, law, medicine, education, and religion must direct themselves not merely to solve these global degradations but to reflect deeply on what they signify.

At the heart of the multiple crises that threaten lies a severe disjuncture between the human species and the larger dynamics of planetary life. The human has lost the vital sense of its connection to and participation with the community of organic life from which it has emerged and by which it has been sustained. Symptomatic of the cleavage is the connotation regularly implied in the use of the word *environment*. Often the sense is that of mere surroundings and the physical things of air, water, and land that define a particular locale or region. Reference to environment is routinely spatial and insufficiently vital, dynamic, and interrelated. Thus, to speak of ethics and the environment may often go no further than to suggest the impermissible uses of air, water, and land by one person or group that would damage or interfere with the consequent use or enjoyment of those same things by others.

An exercise in that form of environmental ethics runs the risk of perpetuating the radical ignorance and consequent alienation that is the source of the dangers confronting the planet. Of the greatest importance and the first step of any ethical reflection and discourse is to reanimate and expand the concept of environment and abandon its tendency to reify and objectify the living planet. The substitution of *biosphere* for *environment* will achieve that purpose. Without more, it is incapable of solving the degradations that currently threaten global life. But to the extent that it conveys within the ongoing ethical concern the primary subjectivity of the planetary community of life-forms where each contributes to and interdepends with the whole, *biosphere* is the more appropriate designation. To ponder the specific ethical responsibilities of the human species to the other members of the biosphere is to engage in reeducation toward reintegration, without which all other discussion will be superficial and all other solutions to the present crises unavailing.

NOTES

1. See Norman Myers, ed., *Gaia: An Atlas of Planet Management* (Garden City, N.Y.: Anchor Press of Doubleday, 1984), p. 12.

2. For the more detailed explanation of this utilitarian assessment, see Manuel G. Velasquez, *Business Ethics: Concepts and Cases,* 2d ed. (Englewood Cliffs, N.J.: Prentice-Hall, 1988), pp. 240–46.

3. See ibid., pp. 246–51.

4. *World Charter for Nature,* G.A. Res. 37/7, 37 U.N. GAOR (48th plen. mtg.), U.N. Doc. A/37/L.4 and Add. 1 (1982).

5. Referring to a previous related resolution of October 30, 1980, the General Assembly reiterated "its conviction that the benefits which could be obtained from nature depended on the maintenance of natural processes and on the diversity of life forms and that those benefits were jeopardized by the excessive exploitation and the destruction of natural habitats." Ibid., p. 1.

6. Ibid., p. 3.

7. Ibid.

8. "Man can alter nature and exhaust natural resources by his action or its consequences and, therefore, must fully recognize the urgency of maintaining the stability and quality of nature and of conserving natural resources." Ibid.

9. Ibid., p. 4.

10. Ibid.

11. Ibid., sec. I: General Principles, p. 4.

12. "In the decision-making process it shall be recognized that man's needs can be met only by ensuring the proper functioning of natural systems and by respecting the principles set forth in the present Charter. In the planning and implementation of social and economic development activities, due account shall be taken of the fact that the conservation of nature is an integral part of those activities." Ibid., sec. II: Functions, paras. 6–7, p. 4.

13. See ibid., sec. II: Functions, para. 8, p. 4.

14. "The degradation of natural systems owing to excessive consumption and misuse of natural resources, as well as to failure to establish an appropriate economic order among peoples and among States, leads to the breakdown of the economic, social and political framework of civilization. Competition for scarce resources creates conflicts, whereas the conservation of nature and natural resources contributes to justice and the maintenance of peace." Ibid., p. 3.

15. See ibid., sec. II: Functions, para 10(a)–(d), p. 5.

16. Ibid., para. 11(a).

17. Ibid., para. 11(b).

18. Ibid., para. 11(c).

Ecological Sabotage and the Ethics of Radical Environmentalism

EDWIN C. HETTINGER

A Charleston developer petitions the South Carolina Coastal Council to fill one hundred acres of marsh in order to build three-story condominiums. At the hearings, the vast majority of citizens oppose the plan, arguing that the development will scar the marsh with another human intrusion and further threaten local animal and plant species. In a closed meeting, the council approves the plan. Publicly it argues that the development's economic benefits far outweigh its environmental costs.

The *Charleston News and Courier* publishes an editorial opposing the plan and questioning the legality of the decision. It notes that the requirement for an environmental impact statement has been waived and that personal and financial connections between council members and the developers suggest a conflict of interest. Opponents of the plan take the council to court, but the developer moves forward.

On the morning the bulldozers are scheduled to fill the marsh, a group of fifty protesters form a human chain between the machines and the marsh. Angry shouts are exchanged, and the drivers threaten the protesters. Police arrive and begin carrying them away. More people join the protest. As a television news team arrives and begins to broadcast reports from the scene, a bulldozer strikes a protester, knocking her unconscious. The developer sends the operators home, vowing to fill the marsh the next day and demanding police protection.

During the night, a group of ecological saboteurs slip into the development compound and pour sand into the crankcases of the bulldozers. The next morning, despite 150 protesters, the earthmovers begin their work under police protection. Several minutes later the machines grind to a halt one by one. Over the weekend, the local chapter of the Sierra Club gets a temporary court injunction stopping the project. New hearings on the development are held. Eventually the earlier council decision is overruled by a court on the grounds that it violates South Carolina's Wetlands Protection Act. The marsh has been saved.

A crucial element in the defense of the marsh was an act of ecological sabotage. The use of such tactics in similar circumstances is becoming increasingly widespread in the environmental movement. Members of Earth First!—a radical environmental group committed to direct action—spike trees to prevent the lumber industry from turning 2,000-year-old redwoods into picnic tables; they sabotage earthmovers and pull up survey stakes to hinder the Forest Service's attempt to build thousands of miles of new roads into de facto wilderness areas.[1] The Sea Shepherds, another direct action group, have claimed responsibility for sinking five whaling vessels of nations they claim are violating the international moratorium on whaling. These tactics are called "ecotage" or "monkeywrenching,"[2] which involves putting "a monkeywrench into the gears of the machine destroying natural diversity."[3]

Mainstream environmental groups have publicly criticized ecotage as being detrimental to the environmental cause. They claim that it gives environmentalists a bad name and could result in a backlash that would severely set back the environmental movement. The editor of *Environmental Ethics* has likened ecotage with terrorism and claims that ecological saboteurs are nature chauvinists and are antihumanistic.[4] Even Greenpeace, once the most militant environmental group, has criticized monkeywrenching because it involves the destruction of property, a tactic it forswears.

THE ECOTEUR'S JUSTIFICATIONS

The ecological saboteurs (or "ecoteurs") consider themselves to be earth warriors engaged in a struggle to defend the few remaining wild areas of the planet from the onslaught of industrial civilization. They see their acts as a public articulation of the view that wildernesses and species in addition to human beings have a right to exist. From their perspective, "sabotage of inanimate machines for ecological purposes" is a fitting and effective response to the immoral and sometimes illegal poisoning of air, water, land, and food. It is a desperate but necessary tool to stop the eradication of species, the destruction of wild ecosystems, and human tampering with the global equilibrium. They conceive of their movement as part of a natural process by which the earth combats the cancerous growth in human population and development.

Destroying property is a tremendously controversial tactic, and thus the ecoteurs face a major burden of justification. Law breaking is potentially legitimate only as a last resort, when all political means to bring about change have failed. But the environmental movement has been immensely successful. From its beginning with the creation of the national parks and wilderness areas, to the recent passage of the endangered species, clean air, and clean water acts, the movement has made great strides working within the democratic process. Millions of people worldwide belong to environmental groups. The development of the green political parties in Europe and the beginning of such movements in the United States portend bright prospects for environmentalism.[5] Given its major successes and the promise for continued change, what room is there in the environmental movement for undemocratic, illegal, and violent acts of property destruction?

The Failure of the Environmental Movement

The ecoteurs respond that the achievements of the environmental movement are superficial. Only by abandoning the original goals of the movement can one see it as a success story. Dave Foreman of Earth First! says in response to such an objection:

You say the environmental movement has been immensely successful. Only on the surface, I think. It appears to be successful because it asks for so little and actually threatens the corporate state to such a minor extent. The great ecologist Paul Sears suggested preserving twenty-five percent of our land in a wilderness condition. We've protected only one and one-half percent. The Sierra Club has asked for only three percent. That's success? The California condor faces imminent extinction. The grizzly may soon be eliminated from the lower forty-eight states. That's success? Thousands die each year because of toxic substances in our air, our water, our soil, our food, our mother's milk—that's success?[6]

Given the severity of the environmental crisis, including the unparalleled pace at which wild species and ecosystems are being wiped off the face of the earth, the suggestion that the traditional environmental movement has been successful is unconvincing. From the ecoteur's perspective, traditional environmentalism is failing, and there is a need for other approaches to the problem.

The Failure of Democracy in Environmental Affairs

Ecoteurs defend their tactics not simply by noting the dubious results of the environmental movement but also by focusing on the recent thwarting of democracy in environmental affairs. They often claim that their illegal tactics are in response to illegal acts on the part of business, industry, and government and that ecotage is in support of existing laws that are not being enforced.

Since the early 1980s, the environmental movement has been engaged in one legal fight after another, with environmental groups suing federal agencies for failing to uphold congressionally mandated environmental goals and taking businesses to court for flaunting environmental laws. Cases of official lawbreaking abound. For example, the Forest Service subverts the law when it treats national forests as tree farms to be developed for the wood products industry. The Environmental Protection Agency breaks the law when it fails to institute congressionally mandated regulations prohibiting the poisoning of the environment. The

Food and Drug Administration breaks the law when it refuses to carry out its congressional mandate to determine if the chemicals put on and in foods are safe. The Fish and Wildlife Service breaks the law when, in opposition to scientific opinion, it refuses to list the spotted owl as an endangered species and thus allows the remaining old-growth forests to be logged. The industries and businesses that support and encourage this regulatory undermining of the nation's environmental protection legislation are culprits as well.

Reagan's Rogues

The breakdown of democratic procedures in the environmental arena becomes even clearer when one notices who has been running the federal agencies charged with environmental protection. It is probably not coincidental that the rise of ecotage occurred during the Reagan administration, headed by a president who believed that trees cause the majority of air pollution.

Who was in charge of the U.S. Forest Service when ecotage in the form of tree spiking became popular? It was John Crowell, whose previous position was vice-president and general counsel for the Louisiana Pacific Corporation, one of the largest purchasers of timber from national forest lands.[7] Robert Burford, a life-long rancher who held grazing permits for thousands of acres, was put in charge of the Bureau of Land Management's 250 million acres of public land. Before his federal appointment, he had been in several confrontations with the bureau over unauthorized grazing and deteriorating rangeland. At the Department of Interior, we first had James Watt, whose antienvironmental policies were well known. Besides trying to open established wilderness areas to mining and oil and gas leasing, selling federal coal at well below market value, and advocating a halt to the purchase of national parklands, Watt believed that the nation's public lands would best be protected if they were privately owned. Next came Donald Hodel, whose environmental views are suggested by his notorious remark that if the ozone layer really is disappearing, we can best protect ourselves by buying hats and sunglasses. Finally, consider Anne Gorsuch Burford at the Environmental Protection Agency. Before she resigned under congressional pressure after refusing to turn over documents concerning the cleanup of hazardous waste dumps under Superfund, she diminished the agency's budget, staff, and law enforcement activities and turned it away from its traditional role as the nation's protector of environmental health.

In essence, individuals representing the interests of the regulated industries were put in charge of the federal programs designed to carry out the nation's environmental policy. The ecoteurs argue that given the overwhelming support of Americans for strong environmental policies, the democratic system of government has clearly broken down on environmental protection and preservation. The ecoteurs thus reject as inadequate and unfair the current rules and procedures for settling environmental disputes.[8]

EARTH-CENTERED ENVIRONMENTAL ETHICS AS
JUSTIFYING ECOTAGE

The most forceful justification for ecotage, however, is not based on illegal thwarting of the will of the Americans by government and industry, nor does it appeal to human interests more generally.[9] Rather, it is the noninstrumental value of the earth's natural objects and ecosystems and the well-being of the planet's wild living things that provide the strongest reasons for ecotage. This defense is earth centered rather than human centered. It arises out of respect for the earth and its wild communities of life. It is based on a duty to defend others when their existence is threatened and their well-being is systematically ignored.

Showing that an earth-centered environmental ethic is preferable to traditional normative ethics is no easy task. In the last decade, however, philosophical writing on the ethical treatment of animals has undermined the anthropocentric biases of traditional Kantian and natural law ethical theory and has shattered the established boundaries of the moral club. Peter Singer and Tom Regan have been most persuasive in rejecting human speciesism. Lacking the human genetic structure is not, they argue, a morally legitimate reason to ignore a creature's well-being or rights.[10] Recent work in environmental ethics has carried this criticism of traditional normative ethics further by attacking both the sentience chauvinism of utilitarianism (which unjustifiably ignores the well-being of non-sentient creatures)[11] and by demonstrating the importance of a holistic earth-centered perspective.[12] An ethic that addresses the question of the proper role of human beings on the planet, instead of simply focusing on how humans should treat each other and ignoring everything else, is indispensable to an adequate normative moral theory. Understanding such an ethic is essential if ecotage is to be evaluated fairly.

Biocentric Ethics: Not for Sentient Creatures Only

In what may well be the most carefully argued and theoretically well-grounded environmental ethic to date, Paul Taylor argues for a life-centered (or biocentric) environmental ethic.[13] Wild living plants and animals, he argues, have a good of their own.[14] Unlike inanimate objects, including artifacts such as lawn mowers, they can be benefited or harmed without reference to other beings. For example, acid rain is bad for trees themselves and not simply bad for the timber companies that plan to make a profit from them. Wild living things have innate proclivities and natural tendencies toward growth and survival that give them a well-being specifiable independently of the purposes of human beings. Biocentric ethics requires us to see such beings as worthy of respect in the sense that they should not be treated merely as a resource for our ends. Their good is deserving of promotion for its own sake, just as is the good of sentient creatures.

Embracing such an attitude of respect for all natural living things becomes rational once one takes an unbiased and ecologically informed philosophical worldview toward the nature of human beings and their proper place on the planet.[15] Instead of focusing on the differences between humans and other species—the dominant approach in the history of Western philosophy—an adequate understanding of human life requires a rediscovery of the similarity between us and other creatures.[16] We are, after all, fundamentally animals, and this is something culture cannot expunge despite constant downgrading of our biological nature. We are akin to other creatures in that we arose from the same evolutionary processes they did and are subject to the same laws of genetics, natural selection, and adaptation. We face similar environmental challenges as other species; we can no more realize our good without satisfying our biological necessities than they can realize theirs without doing the same.

Human beings are nonprivileged members of the earth's community of life. We are not here to subdue, dominate, and control nature but to fit in and to live in harmony with our fellow creatures. Humans are, after all, recent arrivals on the planet; "the earth was teeming with life" long before we came, and our original emergence as a species was of no particular importance.[17] There was no round of applause from the community when chance mutations brought homo sapiens on the scene. We are relative newcomers on a planet that has been the home of other species for hundreds of millions of years.

There is no guarantee that our species will survive. Given the damage we have caused to the ecological balance on the earth, the possibility of human extinction is real. It is humbling to realize that if the human epoch were to end, this would greatly benefit the millions of other species on the planet for which the human race is a serious threat. Instead of viewing human life as the final crowning achievement of the evolutionary process, it makes more sense to see us as possibly nature's most terrible and dangerous mistake.

Once we give up the dogma that the earth and its living creatures were made for human beings and reject the self-centeredness and speciesism on which it is based and then focus on the similarities between humans and other creatures, we will see ourselves as only one member of the earth's delicate web of life. From such a worldview, a biocentric environmental ethic that requires us to take seriously the well-being of other creatures and to share the planet with them becomes a rationally enlightened possibility.

Evaluating Human Behavior from an Earth-Centered Worldview

Let us assume that one accepts an earth-centered ethic of this sort.[18] One would then view the recent behavior of the human species toward other members of earth's community of life as criminal at best and ecocidal at worst. Humans are paving and polluting the planet—turning natural living ecosystems into artificial dead environments of plastic, neon, steel, and asphalt. In the process, we poison what remains of the wild with acid rain, toxic chemicals, pesticides, agricultural runoff, and industrial wastes. In America, we have turned the great plains from a waving sea of 10-feet-tall wild grasses—once an incredibly rich and diverse ecosystem that was a home for buffalo, elk, wolves, and bear—into thousands of square miles of manure-filled and pesticide-laced agricultural monoculture. The small percentage of the lower forty-eight states that remains quasi-wilderness is constantly under assault from new plans to develop, mine, graze, drill, or clear-cut. Rain forests, comprising 7 percent of the earth's surface and containing over half the remaining species of life on the planet, are being destroyed at a yearly rate equal in size to the state of West Virginia. Wilderness as something relatively untouched by human hands is soon to be gone forever.

Humans spreading over the face of the earth, destroying other life-forms in the process, and threatening the planet itself is not unlike a cancerous growth in a human body that infects other organs and eventually threatens the well-being of the whole. In recent years, humans have been engaged in systematic species-cide.[19] Before the end of the century, we will wipe out more species than "all the mass extinctions of the geological past put together."[20] One wildlife biologist has called it a "holocaust."[21] Others have suggested that vertebrate evolution may itself be coming to an end.[22] Additionally, by warming the planet and destroying its protective ozone shield, human industrial civilization is tampering with the global equilibrium in dramatic ways not fully known or understood.

In short, humans are engaged in an all-out war on other forms of life and in the process are threatening themselves. John Muir, naturalist and founder of the Sierra Club, is often quoted as saying that if there were a war between humans and bears, he would be on the side of the bears. In fact, there is such a war, and the ecoteurs have chosen the side of the bears. They ask the rest of us: Which side are you on?

The Failure of Democracy from an Earth-Centered Perspective

From the perspective of an earth-centered ethic, conflicts between human well-being and the well-being of the planet's wild living things pose terrible dilemmas, which we are morally required not to ignore. Clearing land for development, for example, ceases to be purely a matter of human economics and becomes a question of weighing the existence and well-being of the wild plants and animals that make their home on this land against the human desires for yet another shopping mall, condominium complex, or parking lot. Once we have acknowledged that the well-being of other living creatures is morally considerable in its own right and have refused to subordinate their well-being to ours, then questions of distributive justice between human civilization and the natural world become real and compelling. To resolve such conflicts fairly, we need a set of principles of interspecies distributive justice that are guided by an earth-centered vision of the place of human civilization in the natural world.

While I provide no elaboration of such principles here, I suggest it is clear that humans have not fairly resolved these conflicts in the past and will not do so in the near future.[23] The reasonable needs of a reasonable number of people on the planet provide good reasons to sacrifice the well-being and existence of other living things, for all life depends on other life. But the artificially created and insatiable desires of an intemperate species whose population growth and rate of resource consumption are utterly out of control will not, under any fair and reasonable set of principles, justify sacrificing the planet's remaining wild living creatures and ecosystems.

The failure of the environmental movement and the inadequacy of current democratic procedures in environmental affairs take on a profound new meaning when seen from this perspective. An earth-centered ethic demands that the well-being and value of the nonhuman world carry significant weight in moral, political, and legal institutions. But these ideas are not even treated seriously by most people (including many environmentalists); much less are they embodied in our institutions. The well-being of nonhuman entities is rarely considered for its own sake in the supposedly democratic procedures by which we carry out environmental policy. Only if human beings are affected do we take an environmental problem seriously.

Legislation such as the Wilderness Act, the Marine Mammal Protection Act, and the Endangered Species Act may seem to embody legally the values of an earth-centered ethic. There have, for example, been court cases in which a nonhuman species was plaintiff and won a judgment against a human defendant.[24] But these acts are anthropocentrically motivated and discriminatory in their scope. They protect only endangered species and not individual animals and plants. Even endangered species are given protection only if there is no significant economic impact. When the Supreme Court ruled in favor of the snail darter against the Tennessee Valley Authority, Congress quickly passed legislation exempting the Tellico Dam from the requirements of the Endangered Species Act.[25]

Since nonhuman members of the earth's community of life cannot represent themselves, someone must hold their proxies, and environmental groups are the most obvious candidates. But instead of being treated as representatives of the interests of wild living things and spokespeople for the noninstrumental values of natural ecosystems, environmental organizations are increasingly seen as merely another special interest group on a moral par with lobbyists for developers and industry. In fact, all too often environmental groups do represent the elitist interests of backpackers and sports enthusiasts instead of the good of wild plants and animals.

Thus the well-being and value of the majority of the creatures on the planet are systematically and institutionally ignored. If nature were an intentional agent, it would be justifiable for it to whip up storms, floods, and other devices to protect itself against the powerful and blindly self-interested human species. Ecotage becomes a justifiable possibility once one sees the ecoteurs as surrogates who protect the well-being of entities and ecosystems ignored by our anthropocentric moral, legal, and political institutions. Violence against property that protects wild living things is a violation of democratic institutions in the spirit of a more inclusive vision of democracy.

It may well be that under certain circumstances ecotage is not merely excusable or morally permissible but is required by duty. Ecotage is a natural and practical result of taking an earth-centered ethic seriously. Many of us would protect human life and well-being with these methods. Why shouldn't these methods be used to protect the existence and well-being of the planet's wild communities of life?

NOTES

I thank the Faculty Research and Development Committee of the College of Charleston for a grant that supported this project. I also thank Beverly Diamond, Tom Digby, Dave Foreman, Margaret Holmgren, Jasper Hunt, Martin Perlmutter, and Bill Throop. The views expressed here are my own and are not to be attributed to any of those who helped me in writing this chapter.

1. Spiking involves hammering nails into trees. The nails, which are harmless to the trees, destroy expensive saw mill blades, and this makes harvesting the trees uneconomical. This protects the trees from being cut, thereby saving the wild and endangered communities of which they are part.

2. This term comes from Edward Abbey's novel *The Monkey Wrench Gang* (New York: Avon Books, 1975), the inspiration for the Earth First! movement. The story is about a roving band of environmental warriors engaged in illegal activities (such as sabotaging construction equipment and chopping down billboards) in order to protect the Southwest from mining and development. Their ultimate goal is to blow up the Glen Canyon Dam in order to "free" the Colorado River.

3. Dave Foreman, *Ecodefense: A Field Guide to Monkeywrenching,* 2d ed. (Tucson, Ariz.: Ned Ludd Books, 1987), p. 14.

4. Eugene Hargrove, "Ecological Sabotage: Pranks or Terrorism?" *Environmental Ethics* 4, no. 4 (Winter 1982): 291–92.

5. This argument is forcefully made in ibid.

6. Dave Foreman, "More on Earth First! and the Monkey Wrench Gang," *Environmental Ethics* 5, no. 1 (Spring 1983): 95–96.

7. The information in this paragraph comes from "Reagan's Rogues," *Sierra* 73, no. 6 (November-December 1988): 20–21.

8. With a new administration that appears to be more committed to environmental protection and thus is more in tune with the environmental desires of Americans, the force of this dimension of the argument is considerably diminished. For example, William Reilly, the new administrator of the Environmental Protection Agency, is a former director of the World Wildlife Federation.

9. Given the severity of the environmental crisis, even purely anthropocentric considerations may well have sufficient weight to justify certain acts of ecotage.

10. See, for example, Peter Singer, *Animal Liberation* (New York: Avon Books, 1975), and Tom Regan *The Case for Animal Rights* (Berkeley: University of California Press, 1983). For an analysis of the concept of speciesism, see Edwin C. Hettinger, "The

Responsible Use of Animals in Biomedical Research," *Between the Species* 5, no. 3 (Summer 1989): 125–27.

11. For example, see John Rodman, "The Liberation of Nature?" *Inquiry* 20 (Spring 1977): 91.

12. See, for example, J. Baird Callicott's work, including, perhaps most importantly, "Animal Liberation: A Triangular Affair," *Environmental Ethics* 2, no. 4 (Winter 1980).

13. Paul Taylor, *Respect for Nature* (Princeton: Princeton University Press, 1986).

14. Taylor, along with many others, rejects Joel Feinberg's claim that talking of the well-being of nonsentient living things (such as plants) is metaphorical only. See Feinberg, "The Rights of Animals and Unborn Generations," in *Philosophy and the Environmental Crisis*, ed. William T. Blackstone (Athens: University of Georgia Press, 1974), pp. 51–55. Plants can flourish and have their well-being diminished. For a persuasive response to Feinberg's position that parallels the one I develop here, see Robin Attfield, "The Good of Trees," *Journal of Value Inquiry* 15 (1981): 35–54.

15. The ideas in the next three paragraphs are based on Paul Taylor's powerful defense of the "Biocentric Outlook on Nature." See *Respect for Nature*, pp. 99–168.

16. Aristotle, for example, is frequently interpreted as claiming that the essence of a species is determined by the way in which it is different from everything else.

17. This is Taylor's phrase. See *Respect for Nature*, chap. 3.

18. A biocentric ethic is not identical with an earth-centered ethic. The type of earth-centered ethic I embrace adds an additional component to biocentrism's respect for all wild living things. It acknowledges the noninstrumental value of those natural beings that do not have a well-being of their own (e.g., ecosystems such as rivers and inanimate objects such as glaciers). Furthermore, it differs from Taylor's biocentrism in its insistence on the importance of a holistic perspective in resolving questions of interspecies distributive justice.

19. Farley Mowat's *Sea of Slaughter* (New York: Bantam Books, 1984) is a powerful documentation of part of this eradication of other forms of life.

20. Norman Myers, *The Sinking Ark* (Oxford: Pergamon Press, 1980). The quoted phrase is from selections reprinted in *People, Penguins, and Plastic Trees*, ed. Donald VanDeVeer and Christine Pierce (Belmont, Calif.: Wadsworth, 1986), p. 112.

21. Jack Randolph, assistant director for the Virginia Department of Game and Inland Fisheries, as quoted in the *Charleston News and Courier*, October 1, 1989, p. 2.

22. Dave Foreman attributes this remark to Michael Soule, the founder of the Society for Conservation Biology.

23. See Taylor's *Respect for Nature*, chap. 6, for an insightful and detailed elaboration of such principles.

24. See Roderick Nash, *The Rights of Nature* (Madison: University of Wisconsin Press, 1989), p. 177.

25. Ibid., pp. 177–79.

Getting the Environment into the Business School

JAMES E. POST

The relationship between myth and fact can be striking. For example:

Myth: American corporations are guilty of negligence on environmental matters.

Fact: A great many U.S. companies are showing a strong environmental conscience.

Myth: American business schools are at the cutting edge of emerging issues.

Fact: Little or nothing is being done by business schools to understand the implications and impact of environmental problems such as global warming. Business schools are years behind corporate practices.

The 1990s is certain to be the decade of the environment. The G-7 communiqué (United States, Japan, West Germany, France, Britain, Italy, and Canada) in the summer of 1989 put the political spotlight on building broad public support in all nations for environmental action. And events such as the wreck of the *Exxon Valdez* in Prince William Sound, Alaska, demonstrate the central role of management systems and corporate policies in dealing with environmental issues.

The 1990s is certain to be the decade of the environment. The G-7 communiqu/ae (United States, Japan, West Germany, France, Britain, Italy, and Canada) in the summer of 1989 put the political spotlight on building broad public support in all nations for environmental action. And events such as the wreck of the *Exxon Valdez* in Prince William Sound, Alaska, demonstrate the central role of management systems and corporate policies in dealing with environmental issues.

Trash, toxic waste, global warming, the greenhouse effect, and acid rain are but a few of the many examples of environmental issues challenging managers in the public and private sectors as we enter the 1990s. The Environmental Protection Agency estimates that between $80 billion and $90 billion is being spent each year on environmental responses by business. Trash cleanup is a $150 billion business. Environmental issues are now among the most powerful influences on business profitability and performance. Corporate America is waging a vigorous battle to get environmental expenses under control, avoid environmental catastrophes, and maintain credibility with the public. Much remains to be done, but much has already been accomplished.

By comparison, American business schools have done relatively little to respond to those issues. Students in engineering, law, and public administration are all far better informed than business students. Business education has, however, passed through fifteen years of academic turbulence. First, the curriculum was computerized, then internationalized, and then submitted to the ethics revolution. Now, having barely digested those changes, we are beginning to wrestle with transforming a curriculum that ignores natural resource and environmental consequences to one that acknowledges that nothing else much matters if the planet is destroyed by human folly.

Corporate executives are in the vanguard of leaders urging business schools to take the issues seriously. Beginning in 1985, the National Wildlife Federation's Corporate Conservation Council (NWF/CCC), of which such companies as Dow Chemical, Du Pont, 3M, General Motors, and Browning Ferris are active members, has sought to promote the teaching of environmental issues in business schools. The council supported environmental education long before recent oil spills made front-page news and rock stars discussed their new-found concerns for rain forests. It believes that students must recognize business operations as being inherently linked to environmental issues. To promote this understanding, the council has supported efforts that sensitize tomorrow's managers to the critical importance of environmental sustainability.

The concern and commitment of the members of the council have been an important stimulus in developing a new approach toward environmental education. In this chapter I will provide an overview of the approach that the faculty consortium has followed in responding to the council's concerns. The curriculum project is discussed in detail in its first report.[1] Interested readers can also expect a second report that expands on the phase I developments.

THE CURRICULUM DEVELOPMENT PROJECT

The NWF/CCC curriculum development project is a three-year multiphase program. The program includes the development of one or more curriculum approaches, specific course outlines, and appropriate teaching materials. Figure 25.1 summarizes the key activities in each of the three phases.

During phase 1, background research has led the consortium members to review the large and multifaceted literature on environmental matters. Business schools remain well behind their professional colleagues in schools of law, engineering, public health, and public administration in addressing the environ-

Figure 25.1
NWF/CCC Curriculum Project

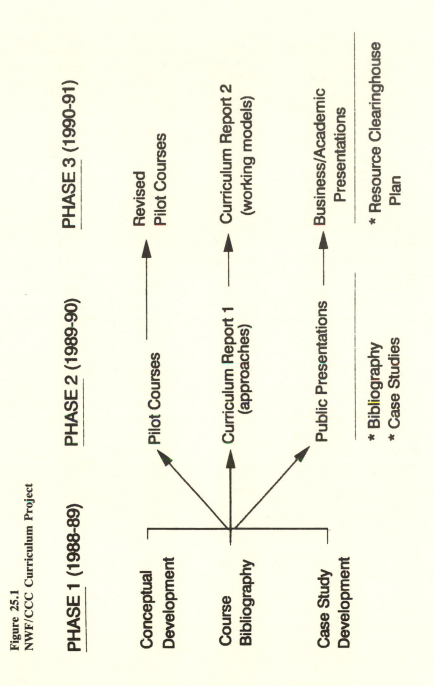

mental agenda. To the extent that business schools do address issues of natural resources and environmental risks, these questions are posed primarily in business and society courses. That is appropriate, but we are increasingly convinced that it is inadequate to comprehend and focus faculty and student attention on the large agenda of pressing issues.

The basic questions that management faculty need to ask with respect to the environment are not well understood. Certainly there are basic issues of corporate responsibility. There are issues in conducting all phases of an organization's activities with an eye toward environmental impact. But there seem to be many more questions; crisis and tragedy propel many to the forefront. For example, when the *Exxon Valdez* catastrophe occurred in Alaska, the spotlight shifted from human error to systemic breakdowns. Exxon's management system was, in large measure, the culprit. It created the conditions that led to the human failures that precipitated the accident; it also led to the slow and oft-perceived cavalier fashion in which Exxon's senior management responded to the public concern and outrage. Thus, both normal and crisis management need to be studied.

There are two basic views of how business schools might proceed to address environmental matters more effectively. One approach is to develop a specialized course that looks at the full range of environmental policy issues and relates them to other areas of management activity. A second approach is to integrate the environmental issues into other core courses in the curriculum. This pattern of choice is similar to that which business educators have faced in considering how to introduce ethics into the curriculum and how best to address international and globalization themes.

The consortium members decided that a reasonable approach would be to develop pilot courses to serve as incubators for curriculum development. A pilot course can serve as a vehicle for both developing a conceptual and theoretical approach to the issues and for focusing efforts to develop pedagogical techniques and teaching materials. During the 1989–1990 academic year, pilot courses are being offered at the three universities with which the faculty are associated.

Conceptual Approaches to Course Development

A broad literature permits faculty members to start from a wide variety of approaches in building an environmental course. Seven approaches are expanded on in the curriculum report:

1. Environmental problems approach
2. Public policy approach
3. Corporate policy approach
4. Environmental ethics approach
5. Industry life cycle approach
6. Economics approach
7. Ecological principles approach

Each approach has a literature to which the faculty member might be drawn, and each suggests a conceptual flow that might occur over an entire semester or some segment of it. As a practical matter, faculty members are likely to integrate and synthesize ideas from various approaches. That has certainly been the case in the development of the pilot courses, including the one I have been teaching at Boston University.

BOSTON UNIVERSITY EXPERIENCE

During the fall 1989 semester, I taught a graduate-level elective course entitled "Managing Environmental Issues." This course is an elective in the MBA program at Boston University and was sponsored by the Management Policy Department, of which I have been chairman for the past three years. The department's general responsibilities are to teach courses in the areas of strategic management, business-government-society, external relations, business ethics, and the legal-political environment. The Management Policy Department is also the administrative home for coursework in international management. All of these courses have a concern for the manager who must understand and respond to both the internal and external dynamics of the organization and the environment.

A prominent theme in our teaching and research has been the integration of traditional strategic management concerns with an appreciation and understanding of the manner in which the social, political, and regulatory environment shapes and influences industry fortunes. Given this tradition and perspective, the "Managing Environmental Issues" course was designed to have the perspective of general managers in the private and public sectors facing the challenges of dealing with environmental and natural resource issues.

Several key assumptions influenced the design of the pilot course. First, most management students are relatively unfamiliar with the factual dimensions of major environmental problems. It was assumed that communication of factual knowledge would be one important facet of the course. This has proved true. As each of the modules has evolved, students have commented on the extent to which their eyes have been opened to the scope and complexity of the environmental issues discussed. A second assumption was that this information would build a student awareness that the complexity and difficulty of environmental issues require public and private sector cooperation and that these issues present important challenges to managers in both the public and private sectors.

A third assumption was that class discussion would have to touch at least three levels of management action. In some respect, the easiest level is the broad strategic level. It is somewhat easier to see the broad and longer-term directions in which a society must move to resolve these issues than it is to see the near-term steps that can actually be taken. To prevent overgeneralization, we have also focused on the operational level of managerial actions. At each point in the course, we have posed the question (which has not always been adequately answered) of what individual managers and individual organizations can do to address this problem. This management action has been viewed in the context of routine, or normal, operations and in crisis situations.

The early planning for the course involved an inventory of key concepts that might be introduced in looking at environmental issues. A grid was created that related some fundamental general management concepts to pressing current issues in a group of environmental policy areas (figure 25.2). The list of environmental policy issues numbered fourteen at one stage, and the number of concepts also exceeded a dozen. The number of issues and concepts is somewhat arbitrary, depending on how one defines them. The important point is that such a planning grid facilitated a first cut at thinking through the environmental issues that might best be addressed or understood through various concepts.

A second step was to look systematically at how each of the policy areas related to the interdependence between corporate policy and public policy. This common stake is as great in the environmental area as perhaps any other area of economic and social activity and poses questions to leaders in both sectors as to what constitutes sensible policy action and how can that action be implemented. A simple matrix illustrates the conceptual relationship among these questions (figure 25.3). In each of the environmental policy areas, an exercise was undertaken to fill in the cells in the matrix with appropriate information or case examples that could illustrate the issues. A number of case studies were initiated on this basis.

Following nine months of planning and materials development, a final course syllabus emerged; it is organized around five basic modules.

Module 1, "The Evolution of Environmental Thinking," deals with the evolution of environmental philosophy in the United States and, to a lesser extent, in other nations. The evolution of public policy from the conservation era of the early twentieth century to the modern regulatory and policy framework of the 1970s and 1980s is reviewed. Given the timing of the course, the transition from the Reagan to Bush administration provided an excellent opportunity to utilize current policy documents as an illustration of the prominence of the issues and the innovative thinking being brought to bear on the environmental agenda. Existing case studies focusing on the Environmental Protection Agency during the 1970s and 1980s were utilized along with the current policy documents.

Module 2, "Dealing with Waste," recognizes that the manner in which people deal with waste is a fundamental decision that shapes our entire perspective and approach toward the environment. If a society places no value on air and water and views the by-products of industrial and commercial processes as nuisances to be disposed of, it is inevitable that waste will accumulate in all forms and in all places. This module also looks at the earliest public concerns for waste as a public health issue. A number of case studies have been developed to look at current concerns surrounding the variety of waste problems. A case study on the first state-level mandatory recycling law has been developed, and the economics and politics of landfills as a solid waste management alternative were discussed. The importance of toxic waste as a public issue and as a burgeoning industry was

Figure 25.2
Environmental Policy Areas and Concepts

Concepts

Environmental Policy Areas	Cost Benefits	Stakeholders	Values/ Ethical Views	Policy Formation	Implementation
Solid Waste					
Toxics					
Groundwater					
Wetlands					
Global Warming					
Rainforest					

Figure 25.3
Private Sector/Public Sector

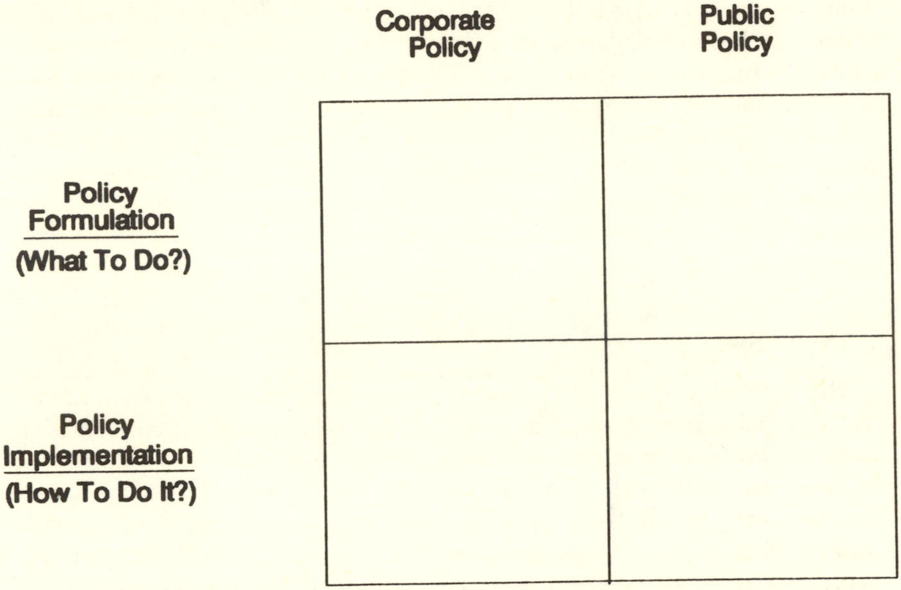

	Corporate Policy	Public Policy
Policy Formulation (What To Do?)		
Policy Implementation (How To Do It?)		

developed over several classes. Finally, corporate responses to pollution prevention through waste reduction and waste minimization were examined through a series of case studies. In these studies, both the formulation of corporate policy and the implementation of programs of action were analyzed in detail.

Module 3, "Externalities of Industrial Activity," provided a focused opportunity for examining historic and current commitments to dealing with three major areas of externalities: air pollution, water pollution, and normal accidents (including oil spills).

"Global Environmental Concerns" is module 4. The great attention being given in the media to such global matters as the greenhouse effect and global warming has created a substantial base of material and facilitated the discussion of global environmental matters. The existence of chlorofluorocarbons (CFCs) in the ozone layer and the decision of Du Pont to phase out CFC production provided a foundation for discussion of the managerial decision problems. Other topics covered included the destruction of (and efforts to preserve) the Amazon rain forest, the evolution of such new devices as debt for nature swaps, and creative use of markets to redress imbalances in the valuation of natural resources.

Module 5, "Setting Management Priorities," the final module, used several classes to deal with the key questions of how to set priorities and build organizational cultures that support responsible environmental action. Prominence was given to risk assessment and risk communication, including community right-to-know requirements. The problems of establishing and maintaining priorities within government were discussed through materials dealing with trade-offs that states have had to make between committing scarce resources to highly visible problems, such as toxic dumpsites, and broader, less crisis-driven problems such as radon exposure. Private sector priority-setting was examined by looking at the influence of institutional investors to promote good practice through such statements as the Valdez Principles, codes of conduct, and seals of approval. A final session on building an environmentally responsible corporate culture studied in detail a leading company that has made environmental responsibility one of its core values.

CONCLUSION

The NWF/CCC curriculum project will make available to interested academic and nonacademic audiences the results of the pilot course efforts. Teaching materials will also be made available as they are completed. The necessity for building environmental policy courses seems considerable. The efforts I have described are the beginning of what I believe will be a continuing effort to understand and communicate about these vital issues. There is abundant evidence that this planet cannot survive without responsible environmental policies and responsible environmental stewards. As educators, we have a responsibility to become informed about these matters and to respond by educating others to comprehend the significance and importance of the problems and to build the intellectual skills and understanding to be able to act.

NOTE

1. National Wildlife Federation Corporation Conservation Council, *The Natural Environment: Issues for Management, Curriculum Planning Report I* (Fall 1989).

26

Environmental Attitudes, Behaviors, and Decision Making: Implications for Management Education and Development

GORDON P. RANDS

Growing recognition exists among corporate leaders that environmental issues are here to stay and that environmental protection must be considered a normal part of doing business. It will become increasingly clear that positive corporate environmental performance cannot be adequately addressed through either management policies or the efforts of environmental staff specialists; it must be institutionalized by being incorporated into the fundamental responsibilities of line management.[1] This will require increased environmental awareness, sophistication, and skills on the part of managers. Where and how will managers develop such attributes so as to be able to address environmental issues to the benefit of both the firm and society?

ENVIRONMENTAL EDUCATION

Environmental educators have identified five major categories of objectives for environmental education.[2] Individuals and social groups should, as a result of environmental education, acquire or gain *awareness* of and sensitivity to the environment; a basic *understanding* of the environment and its problems, values, and feelings of *concern* for the environment along with a desire to contribute to environmental protection; *skills* useful in identifying and solving environmental problems; and opportunities for *participation* in working toward resolution of environmental problems.

An ideal system of environmental education for managers would involve general education, the business school, and the corporation. The development of environmental awareness, understanding, and concern would be the focus at the elementary, secondary, and general undergraduate levels. Management school education would emphasize understanding the specific roles of business firms and managers in environmental protection, as well as the challenges that the organizational context of business provides, and developing the skills and insights that will enhance individuals' abilities to overcome these challenges and participate in the achievement of both business and environmental goals. Corporate environmental education would emphasize the corporation's commitment to environmentally sound operation, identify the areas of environmental impact associated with company operations, help managers understand the organizational culture and the implications it poses for managerial environmental action, and refine the skills required for effective environmental performance.

Unfortunately environmental education has not yet been sufficiently incorporated into the elementary, secondary, and general university curriculum to develop an environmentally knowledgeable and concerned citizenry. Even when such widespread environmental education does occur, it will not be entirely sufficient to prepare individuals to deal with environmental issues as managers. Until it is achieved, however, the challenge to management education is even greater.

The inadequacy of management schools in preparing managers to address environmental issues was noted by every speaker at a symposium on "The Environmental Consequences of Management" at the 1989 annual meetings of the Academy of Management. A similar message subsequently appeared in the *Wall Street Journal* from a free enterprise–oriented resource economist:

Managers must begin to develop their own [environmental] expertise. Unfortunately, no executive business or MBA program effectively prepares management to make discriminating choices on environmental matters. Perhaps a "Business and Environment Program" could be offered to executives or developed as an option for MBA programs.[3]

CCC CURRICULUM DEVELOPMENT PROGRAM THEORY OF ACTION

The Curriculum Development Program of the National Wildlife Federation's Corporate Conservation Council is a major effort to address the current and future state of management school attention to environmental issues. The underlying logic, or theory of action,[4] of the program (figure 26.1) suggests some fundamental questions regarding how the environmental education of managers should be conducted and what the goals of such efforts should be.

The immediate objectives of the program are noted at the bottom of the diagram (2 and 3). It is believed that these outputs, accompanied by other program activities, will result in the achievement of midrange objectives (4–8). I believe that the ultimate goals (9–11) are also implicit in the program. This logic is based on certain assumptions at each stage, which are clearly open to question. These assumptions, particularly those at higher levels, raise questions that should be of concern to all those interested in improving corporate environmental performance.

Will simple exposure to issues lead to greater understanding of environmental

Figure 26.1
Curriculum Development Program Theory of Action

---

11. Improved environmental quality

10. Less environmentally damaging firm actions

9. More environmentally sensitive corporate decisions

8. More individual concern for the environment by managers	Better problem-solving skills with respect to environmental issues
7. Greater understanding of and sensitivity to environmental issues	Better understanding of the essential interconnectedness of business issues and environmental issues

6. Improved business student exposure to business-environment issues

5. Increased design and offering of business-environment courses and units

4. Increased ease for faculty of designing and offering a course

3. Greater availability of cases, readings, syllabi, and other materials

2. Materials inventory and development, course design, pilot courses, and program evaluation and dissemination activities

1. Funding business school faculty

---

issues and their interweaving with business activities? Clearly this would depend on the instructor's understanding, choice of materials, and teaching skills.

Will increased knowledge and understanding be reflected in environmental problem-solving skills or in increased student concern for environmental quality? Such results are unlikely unless they are the goals of the instructor and are reflected in course design and instruction.

Are increased skills and concern a prerequisite for more environmentally responsible corporate decisions? If so, can these be expressed effectively given the realities of corporate life? While these issues are out of the instructor's control, attention to organizational dynamics such as power, decision making, and socialization may increase the chances that students will retain their values and utilize their skills effectively.

Does the formulation of environmentally sound policy automatically translate to environmentally sound corporate action? The organizational change and strategy implementation literature make it exceedingly clear that it will not. Issues surrounding environmental policy implementation may well be deserving of special attention in business and environment courses.

Finally, it is obvious that we cannot place all the burden for environmental improvement on corporate shoulders. Neither should we imply that the hopes for improved corporate environmental performance are solely dependent on management education in the business school or the corporation. But the environmental challenges we face are so wide-ranging, so intrinsic to the nature of productive activity, and of such vital importance that those of us in management education must begin to address them and contribute our fair share to their resolution.

EDUCATING MANAGERS ABOUT THE ENVIRONMENT: FUNDAMENTAL QUESTIONS

We must consider some fundamental questions that relate to how we educate managers about business-environment relationships, focusing on the nature and importance of individuals' environmental attitudes:

1. What is the relationship of knowledge, attitudes, decisions, and behaviors involving the environment?
2. What implications does the study of environmental ethics have for individuals' environmental attitudes and behaviors?
3. What implications does the organizational context pose for individual environmental concern, individual decisions and actions, and corporate environmental performance?
4. What managerial skills, abilities, and orientations are required by the firm? by society?
5. What are the necessary goals of management environmental education? Are these educationally appropriate?

ENVIRONMENTAL ATTITUDES AND BEHAVIORS

A Model of Environmental Concern

The dominant model in attitude theory suggests that one's attitudes provide the basis for one's subsequent behaviors and decisions.[5] An application of this model to environmental beliefs and actions, extended to include both educational inputs and environmental outcomes, is shown in figure 26.2.

The concepts presented in figures 26.1 and 26.2 require us to consider the basic goals of educating managers about the environment. If business-environment courses provide managers with a better understanding of environmental problems but do not foster greater environmental concern, will these individuals be likely to contribute to improved corporate environmental performance? Does consistently sound environmental performance require that employees be en-

Figure 26.2
A Model of Environmental Attitudes and Behavior

Information ▶ Understanding ▶ Concern ▶ Behavioral ▶ Individual ▶ Environmental
                                    Intention   Behavior   Outcomes

vironmentalists? Can the corporation have an environmental conscience if its employees, particularly its managers, do not?

The research literature on environmental concern found in the fields of environmental education, environmental psychology, and environmental sociology offers insights regarding the questions posed thus far. Studies of environmental concern are of four basic types: studies of attitudes toward a specific issue or set of issues, studies of environmental behaviors, studies of the relationship between environmental attitudes and behaviors, and studies of the underlying determinants of environmental concern.

Attitudes toward a Particular Issue

Studies of this type have utilized a wide variety of measurement instruments and have been criticized as describing rather than explaining environmental concern.[6] One research study that used a number of different subscales found that the scales were not highly intercorrelated, suggesting that environmental concern is not unidimensional.[7] Individuals are likely to have varying levels of concern about different types of environmental problems. Thus the issues that generate the most public concern are not necessarily those that are most important to overall environmental quality.

Performance Implications

Strategic response based on public concern may not produce the most important environmental results.

Public affairs, issues management, and other activities feeding into the strategy formulation process should not emphasize trendy environmental issues at the expense of less salient but more ecologically important issues and corporate actions.

Educational Implications

Address a variety of issues (in introductory courses) so as to increase the likelihood of touching on some issues of interest to everyone.

Help instill an understanding of the interconnectedness of environmental issues.

Help students begin to appreciate the cumulative environmental impact of even small actions.

Help students develop an appreciation of the need for, and skills in, prioritizing issues on the basis of environmental impact more than on the basis of public relations. The latter is important but not paramount.

Environmental Behavior

Most of the research on environmental behaviors has focused on energy conservation in the residential-consumer sector and on repetitive rather than one-time behaviors, although one-time behaviors may well make a greater contribution to energy conservation, and the industrial-commercial sector consumes roughly 50 percent of the energy used in the United States.[8] More attention should be given in future research to environmental behavior at the organizational level because of the impact of company behaviors.

The increasing importance of work organizations in the face of the declining influence of traditional socializing institutions suggests that serious consideration be given to the potential for business firms and other work organizations to participate in shaping pro-environmental behavior of employees, in both the workplace and beyond. Corporate environmental programs such as vanpooling, recycling, office energy conservation, and volunteer involvement in community environmental activities can have not only direct environmental impacts but indirect impacts as employees engage in similar actions in home and recreational settings. Such a multiplier effect could likely be enhanced by employee education regarding pro-environmental corporate practices in such areas as manufacturing, transportation, philanthropy, and site management, as well as by promotion of similar employee activities away from the workplace.

Several general findings have emerged from research on energy conservation, which likely apply to other environmental behaviors.[9] First, monetary rebates and incentives appear to be highly effective means of encouraging energy conservation. Reliance on education, persuasive communication, and moral appeal alone has generally been insufficient at promoting widespread conservation.[10] Second, feedback regarding the actual amount of energy saved by conservation efforts appears to be important because individuals seem to be poor self-monitors of their level of consumption. Third, acceptance of personal responsibility for energy conservation appears to enhance efforts to promote conservation. This finding should be of particular interest to philosophers and management educators.

S. H. Schwartz theorizes that moral norms against harming others are activated only when individuals are aware that their actions will cause harm and accept some responsibility for these actions and their consequences.[11] Research pertaining to environmental behavior has been somewhat supportive of the theory, particularly the aspect of acceptance of personal responsibility, although there has been some disagreement over whether the norms involved are moral (against harming other humans) or environmental (against harming the environment), as well as whether environmental norms should be considered to be moral norms.[12] One researcher suggests that as institutional mechanisms have been developed to address the environmental crisis, feelings of personal responsibility for the negative consequences of actions may have declined, despite an increase in environmental concern.[13]

These three general findings have a number of implications for corporate environmental performance and management environmental education:

Performance Implications

Reward systems are important in promoting pro-environmental behavior and implementing corporate environmental policies.

A variety of motivational and control approaches are required, because of the diverse nature of individual environmental motivations.

Effective environmental evaluation systems are critical.

Organizational structures and systems should simultaneously fix specific environmental responsibility with roles and job descriptions and promote and encourage acceptance of personal responsibility for company environmental performance in areas beyond one's job.

The relationship of these points to concepts of organizational behavior and theory is readily apparent.

Educational Implications

Help students recognize the environmental importance of individual behavior within the corporation.

Emphasize not only environmental policy formulation but policy implementation and evaluation.

Help students recognize the contribution of organizational reward and incentive systems to corporate environmental performance (but do not focus exclusively on economically rational models of environmental behavior).

Help students recognize the need for diverse motivational approaches.

As educators, recognize that students are differentially described by the five models mentioned in note 10. Different educational strategies and rationales for corporate environmental performance will be of varying appeal to different individuals.

Give attention to the problems of designing and implementing effective environmental evaluation systems in organizations.

Help students understand the importance of acceptance of personal responsibility to environmental performance.

Help students understand the organizational implications and the difficulty of such efforts.

Promote personal acceptance of responsibility.

Identify and promote a role for managers in helping other employees develop a sense of personal environmental responsibility.

The last two points clearly reflect a normative bias. The appropriateness of such a position will be discussed later.

It is not clear whether environmental behavior is the same as environmental decision making. One of the reasons for focusing on managers as a class of individuals is that their decisions, when implemented, have an impact much broader than their own individual behavior. Research suggests that there are many problems of bias that affect perception and decision making.[14] No research appears to have been conducted, however, that examines the relationship of managers' personal environmental behavior and managerial decisions or the role of biases in such decisions.

These questions relate to the third body of studies—those exploring the relationships between the different components of environmental concern.

Environmental Attitudes and Behavior

While many studies of environmental attitudes and behaviors have found only weak attitude-behavior relationships, research suggests that this may be largely the result of methodological weaknesses that can be overcome through better instrument design[15] and through research designs that pay close attention to the role of situational factors that can either inhibit or facilitate acting on behavioral intentions.[16]

Several factors have been identified that play such a role—one similar to that played by organizational factors that can pose barriers to the implementation of corporate policy. These factors include lack of knowledge or skill in carrying out intended behaviors, costs of carrying through with intentions, the relative salience of competing demands for attention, and lack of social support from family members, neighbors, local opinion leaders, and the like. The existence of such factors that weaken the attitude-behavior relationship has a number of performance and educational implications:

Performance Implications

Employee knowledge of corporate environmental policies or the specific actions they require cannot be assumed by managers.

Managers must attend to the development of needed employee understanding and skills in the environmental area.

Because not all costs and benefits of actions are always apparent and environmental protection has traditionally been seen as a drain on profits, costs of such activities may tend to be overestimated and opportunities for environmental improvement forgone unnecessarily.

A demand's salience reflects its immediacy and perceived significance, and managers encounter many highly salient demands.

Clear corporate environmental performance goals, with timetables and consequences for achievement and nonachievement being reflected in the reward system, are very important.

The support of the chief executive officer (CEO) for environmental protection is critical.

Support at all managerial hierarchical levels is needed, and thus corporate environmental policies are potentially very fragile.

Educational Implications

Provide not only examples of problems but of environmentally sound behavior by corporations and their employees.

Help students learn and gain experience in applying environmental problem-solving skills.

Help students recognize the role managers have in assisting subordinates in the development and use of such skills.

Help students appreciate the full range of costs and benefits associated with various aspects of environmental performance.

Provide examples of direct cost savings that have accompanied environmentally sound corporate behavior.

Help students understand (through case illustrations) how environmental problems that are insufficiently attended to can result in corporate crises and other negative impacts for a company or manager.

Help students understand how managers affect (both intentionally and unintentionally) the salience of demands their subordinates encounter.

Illustrate the genuine interest of business in positive environmental performance by inviting corporate executives, especially CEOs, to speak on the topic.

As corporate recruiters do much to focus the attention and course of study of business students, widespread student acceptance of the need for developing environmental awareness, understanding, and skill would be greatly fostered by executives directing recruiters to pay special attention to these areas.

Determinants of Environmental Concern

The role of three classes of potential determinants of environmental concern has been examined: personality factors, demographic variables, and value systems.

Personality Factors

Relatively few studies have examined the role of personality factors in environmental concern. Among the factors that appear to contribute to environmental concern are an internal locus of control (being self- rather than other-directed), high cognitive consistency (therefore tending to strive to minimize incongruence among one's values, attitudes, and behaviors), and high cognitive complexity and the related ability to engage in integrative thinking.[17]

Due to the tentative nature of this limited research and the difficulties of affecting personality factors, few clear implications for corporate performance or educational practice are apparent. Perhaps the most likely targets are educational, selection, and appraisal procedures that encourage and reward integrative thinking.

Demographic Variables

Research on demographic factors has indicated that the well educated, the young (or more accurately, baby boomers), urban residents, and liberals express considerably more environmental concern than their counterparts, but the amount of variance explained by these variables is not very great.[18] Few, if any, useful implications seem to flow from these findings.

Value Systems

Finally, a fair amount of research has appeared that suggests that a much greater explanator of variance in environmental concern is the nature of one's value system or worldview. Several researchers suggest that an important distinction exists between what is labeled the dominant social paradigm or cornucopian worldview and the new environmental paradigm or catastrophic worldview[19] (table 26.1).

The dominant social paradigm (DSP) is hypothesized to consist of a number of factors, of which the four primary ones are support for private property rights, support for economic growth, faith in material abundance, and support for laissez-faire government. Business executives as a group scored quite high on the DSP and low on environmental concern, while environmentalists' scores were the reverse, thus suggesting the existence of a very different view of the world, the new environmental paradigm (NEP). The general public was in the middle, scoring fairly high on both measures. Lester Milbrath suggests that business leaders and environmentalists are the leading proponents of these different worldviews and that they are in essence competing for the allegiance of the uncommitted middle (comprising approximately 60–70 percent of the population), who want many elements of both visions of society.[20] These researchers suggest that the paradigms are so fundamentally different that holding elements of both will eventually result in substantial dissonance on the individual and societal levels. How will the conflict between these two worldviews be resolved by individuals and society? At least four scenarios come to mind:

1. Rejection of the NEP, resulting in accelerated environmental decline.
2. Rejection of the DSP, resulting in the ushering in of Ecotopia.[21]
3. Continued "blissful ignorance" of the tensions, expressed in contradictory efforts and a failure to take innovative action.
4. Recognition of the tensions accompanied by a commitment to work to achieve a middle ground—albeit a fragile one—that enables some of the important tenets of each paradigm to coexist.

The first two scenarios are unlikely, and each would be accompanied by a tremendous amount of social disruption in either the long or short term. It is, I suggest, the responsibility and challenge of those involved in management education to help bring the fourth scenario about, rather than to allow the third scenario to occur, which is probably more likely.

Several important performance and educational implications emerge from the apparent adherence to extremely different value systems by business executives and environmentalists:

Performance Implications

Value differences contribute to difficulties in communication between the two groups, both as they are sensed (increasing mistrust) and overlooked (decreasing understanding of the others' arguments and proposals).

Difficulties in communication discourage engaging in further attempts to do so. This tends to impede the flow of vital information to business, increase the polarization between the two parties, and increase the role of government in dealing with environmental issues.

Educational Implications

Help students explore and understand the nature and logic of the values of environmentalists.

Help students understand the differences between value systems of the two groups, recognize the difficulties this can pose for communication, and appreciate the need for and possible means of improving communication.

Encourage students to search for ways to integrate elements of the value systems and to reflect on their personal values in the light of the contrasting values identified.

ENGAGING IN MANAGEMENT ENVIRONMENTAL EDUCATION

The review of the research literature on environmental attitudes, behaviors, and their determinants has illustrated that the model of environmental behavior and outcomes presented initially is far too simple. A more realistic, yet still oversimplified, model is presented in figure 26.3. This model is different from that in figure 26.2 in two fundamental respects. First, it identifies various factors external to the educational setting (provision of information) that affect understanding, concern, and individual behavior. Second, it recognizes the degree to which the environmental outcomes of corporate actions depend on a series of decisions by different individuals to make policy recommendations, formulate, and implement policies rather than just on the direct individual behaviors that have been the focus of past research. Each of these decisions is subject to many, if not all, of the same influences as individual behaviors.

The model would seem to have three basic messages for those engaging in educating current and future managers about the environment. It suggests important information that should be communicated to managers to assist them in their efforts to improve corporate environmental performance. It illustrates why providing factual information may have relatively little discernible impact on behavior. Perhaps most important, it requires us to ask what responsibilities we

Table 26.1
Comparison Paradigms

New Environmental Paradigm	Dominant Social Paradigm

1) High valuation on nature
  a) Nature for its own sake (worshipful love of nature)
  b) Holistic—humans interrelated with nature
  c) Environmental protection over economic growth
	1) Lower valuation on nature
	  a) Use nature to produce goods
	  b) Human domination of nature
	  c) Economic growth over environmental protection

2) Generalized compassion
  a) Toward other species
  b) Toward other peoples
  c) Toward other generations
	2) Compassion only for those near and dear
	  a) Exploit other species for human needs
	  b) Unconcerned for other people
	  c) Concern for this generation

3) Carefully plan and act to avoid risk
  a) Science and technology not always good
  b) Stop further development of nuclear power
  c) Develop and use soft technology
  d) Use regulation to protect nature and humans (government responsibility to protect people from risk)
	3) Accept risk to maximize wealth
	  a) Science and technology great boon to humans
	  b) Proceed swiftly to develop nuclear power
	  c) Emphasize hard technology
	  d) Deemphasize regulation—use market (individual responsibility for risk)

<table>
</table>

4) Limits to growth
   a) Resource shortages
   b) Population explosion—limits needed
   c) Conservation

5) Completely new society (new paradigm)
   a) Humans seriously damaging nature and themselves
   b) Openness and participation
   c) Emphasis on public goods
   d) Cooperation
   e) Postmaterialism
   f) Simple lifestyles
   g) Emphasis on worker satisfaction in jobs

6) New politics
   a) Consultative and participatory
   b) Focusing of partisan dispute on human relationship to nature
   c) Willingness to use direct action
   d) Emphasis on foresight and planning

4) No limits to growth
   a) No resource shortages
   b) No problem with population
   c) Production and consumption

5) Present society all right (keep DSP)
   a) Humans not seriously damaging planet
   b) Hierarchy and efficiency
   c) Emphasis on market
   d) Competition
   e) Materialism
   f) Complex and fast lifestyles
   g) Emphasis on jobs for economic needs

6) Old politics
   a) Determination by experts
   b) Focusing of partisan dispute on management of the economy
   c) Oppose direct action—use normal channels
   d) Emphasis on market control

Source: Lester W. Milbrath, "Culture and the Environment in the United States." *Environmental Management,* 9, no.2 (1980): 167. Used by permission of Springer-Verlag.

Figure 26.3
Model of Corporate Environmental Action

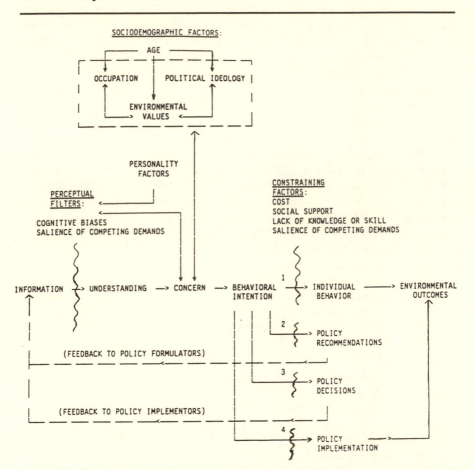

have and tactics we should use as formal or informal educators of managers. Given the huge impacts of business activities on the environment and the relatively small impact that simply providing factual information in a value-free manner is likely to have, should management educators become advocates for the environment? What should the goal of management environmental education be?

Extremely insightful, carefully fashioned governmental policies accompanied by managerial willingness to comply with regulations and a reasonable degree of managerial environmental awareness and understanding could likely prompt the requisite amount of environmentally sensitive corporate action needed to achieve environmentally sustainable economic activity. We might envision the necessary goal of management environmental education to be the development of managerial environmental understanding.

It is highly questionable whether our government leaders have the wisdom or political will to enact the necessary policies, much less implement them effectively. Norman Bowie has suggested that corporate obedience to the law does not necessarily imply refraining from efforts to weaken the nature of newly proposed laws and regulations.[21] The history of the movement from the concept of corporate social responsiveness to the practice of social issues management should provide adequate demonstration that an understanding of issues and public concern regarding them is not sufficient to promote exemplary social performance. In the likely absence of excellent government policies, managerial understanding may be inadequate. Managerial environmental concern will probably be required.

Personal acceptance of responsibility for harm caused by an action may be a critical factor in encouraging pro-environmental behavior. Thus in addition to managerial understanding and managerial concern, managerial responsibility appears to be a necessary quality if corporate environmental performance is to improve to the degree needed. This requires not only an understanding of the relationship that all the corporate functions have to environmental performance but also a consideration and acceptance of individual responsibility for environmental performance. This latter area is one in which the study of ethics can make an important contribution. There is a general tendency in business and society texts to focus on corporate responsibility to the exclusion of personal responsibility, even in their discussions of ethics. While this is understandable, it clearly can be dangerous in that it tends to suggest that corporate social responsibility rests primarily with top managers rather than extending throughout the corporation. Attention must be given to the personal responsibility all individuals have for the environmental consequences of their actions, as well as to the nature of the harms associated with various actions. This suggests the importance of education in both ethics and ecological principles.

Finally, understanding, concern, and acceptance of responsibility may count for naught if managers lack the skills in analyzing organizational conditions, advancing recommendations, formulating and communicating policies, and designing structures and systems so as to facilitate the implementation of policy. Training in such skills is beyond the scope of management environmental education alone but is, or should be, a major focus of management education in organizational behavior and development. The importance of managerial skill application to issues of corporate environmental performance must not be underestimated.

CONCLUSION

Environmental protection is perhaps the most critical issue facing humanity. Accordingly, those involved in management education must be willing to consider and grapple with the questions I have raised. We may have to put aside our presumed value neutrality, which in fact does not exist. Norman Bowie has pointed out elsewhere that one of the dangers of the typical treatment of the egoistic paradigm of human nature in the fields of finance and economics is that individuals may tend to act as if the paradigm is desirable or true, with many resulting dysfunctional consequences for society.[23] The same point can be made regarding the treatment of the dominant social paradigm in business schools.

It may be asking a great deal of management education to become a proponent of a version of the new environmental paradigm, but this may in fact be vitally needed. If managerial understanding is insufficient to produce environmentally sustainable business activity, schools of management must become willing to promote managerial concern and managerial responsibility. Given the impact business activity has on the quality of the global environment, I believe that the fate of many species, of future generations' quality of life, of the business system, and perhaps of humanity itself may be dependent, to a modest but meaningful degree, on the willingness and ability of management education to shoulder such a responsibility.

NOTES

1. Robert W. Ackerman, "How Companies Respond to Social Demands," *Harvard Business Review* (July-August 1973): 88–98. Ackerman describes a common three-phase pattern of corporate social response: (1) increased executive attention to the issue leads to formulation and announcement of corporate policy regarding the issue; (2) when the policy is not sufficiently implemented, responsibility for the issue is given to an individual or staff department, resulting in organizational learning about the issue and company practices in the area, but little real action; (3) line management is forced by the chief executive officer to accept responsibility for policy implementation, generally by incorporation of social policy performance into performance appraisal and reward systems.

2. Alan M. Schwartz and John Miles, "The Status of Post-Secondary Environmental Education in North America," *Environmental Professional* 9 (1987): 352–56. The five categories of objectives cited were identified by participants in an international conference on environmental education held in 1977 in Tbilisi, USSR. Other observers have enumerated more or fewer categories but basically addressed the same basic ideas.

3. John Baden, "Save the Environment without Destroying Your Profits," *Wall Street Journal,* August 21, 1989.

4. Michael Quinn Patton, *Utilization-Focused Evaluation* (Beverly Hills: Sage Publications, 1986).

5. The dominant attitude model holds that attitudes consist of three components: a cognitive or knowledge component, an affective or emotional component, and a conative or intentional component. These are reflected in figure 26.2 by understanding, concern, and behavioral intention, respectively. For a review of this and other models in attitude theory, see Robyn M. Dawes and Tom L. Smith, "Attitude and Opinion Measurement," in Gardner Lindzey and Elliot Aronson, eds., *Handbook of Social Psychology,* 3d ed. (New York: Random House, 1985), pp. 509–66, and William J. McGuire, "Attitudes and Attitude Change," in Lindzey and Aronson, *Handbook,* pp. 233–345.

6. Riley E. Dunlap and Kent D. Van Liere, *Environmental Concern: A Bibliography of Empirical Studies and Brief Appraisal of the Literature,"* Public Administration Series Bibliography 44 (Monticello, Ill.: Vance Bibliographies, 1978).

7. Kent D. Van Liere and Riley E. Dunlap, "Environmental Concern: Does It Make a Difference How It's Measured?" *Environment and Behavior* 13, no. 6(1981): 651–76.

8. Paul C. Stern and Gerald T. Gardner, "Psychological Research and Energy Policy," *American Psychologist* 36, no. 4(1981): 329–42.

9. Glenn Shippee, "Energy Consumption and Conservation Psychology: A Review and Conceptual Analysis," *Environmental Management* 4 (1980): 297–314.

10. Paul C. Stern and Elliot Aronson, *Energy Use: The Human Dimension* (New York: W. H. Freeman, 1984). Stern and Aronson offer five models of individuals as energy users: the economically rational investor who utilizes cost-benefit analysis; the consumer who focuses primarily on the egoistic benefits of energy use; the social group member whose behavior is influenced significantly by peers and other important sources of social cues; the personal values holder who strives to behave in congruence with them; and the problem avoider who has so many demands on his or her attention that the need for conservation behavior fails to become salient until it reaches a fairly high threshold level. While the finding reported in the text seems to provide the most support for the first model, Stern and Aronson suggest that none of these ideal types is correct to the exclusion of the others; rather, different individuals are likely better described by different combinations of the various models.

11. S. H. Schwartz, "Moral Decision Making and Behavior," in Jacqueline Macaulay and Leonard Berkowitz, eds., *Altruism and Helping Behavior: Social Psychological Studies of Some Antecedents and Consequences* (New York: Academic Press, 1970).

12. Frederick H. Buttel, "New Directions in Environmental Sociology," *Annual Review of Sociology* 13 (1987): 465–88.

13. Thomas A. Heberlein, "Norm Activation and Environmental Action: A Rejoinder," *Journal of Social Issues* 33, no. 3(1977): 207–11.

14. Alan Miller, "The Influence of Personal Biases on Environmental Problem-solving," *Journal of Environmental Management* 17 (1983): 133–42. See also chap. 3 by Kenneth Goodpaster in this book.

15. Russell H. Weigel, David T. A. Vernon, and Louis N. Tognacci, "Specificity of the Attitude as Determinant of Attitude-Behavior Congruence," *Journal of Personality and Social Psychology* 30, no. 6(1974): 724–28; Russell H. Weigel and Lee S. Newman, "Increasing Attitude-Behavior Correspondence by Broadening the Scope of the Behavioral Measure," *Journal of Personality and Social Psychology* 33, no. 6(1976): 793–802.

16. J. Stanley Black, Paul C. Stern, and Julie T. Elworth, "Personal and Contextual Influences on Household Energy Adaptations," *Journal of Applied Psychology* 70, no. 1(1985): 3–21.

17. Thomas A. Heberlein and J. Stanley Black, "Cognitive Consistency and Environmental Action," *Environment and Behavior* 13, no. 6(1981): 717–34; Miller, "Influences of Personal Biases"; Linda J. Trigg, Daniel Perlman, Raymond P. Perry, and Michel Pierre Janisse, "Anti-pollution Behavior: A Function of Perceived Outcome and Locus of Control," *Environment and Behavior* 8, no. 2(1976): 307–13.

18. Buttel, "New Directions"; Diane M. Samdahl and Robert Robertson, "Social Determinants of Environmental Concern: Specification and Test of the Model," *Environment and Behavior* 21, no. 1(1981): 57–81. These researchers note that the aspect of liberal ideology that appears to be important is not so much "welfare state liberalism" as "anti-laissez-faire" liberalism.

19. Stephen Cotgrove, *Catastrophe or Cornucopia: The Environment, Politics and the Future* (New York: John Wiley & Sons, 1982); Riley E. Dunlap and Kent D. Van Liere,

"The New Environmental Paradigm," *Journal of Environmental Education* 9, no. 4(1978): 10–19; Riley E. Dunlap and Kent D. Van Liere, "Commitment to the Dominant Social Paradigm and Concern for Environmental Quality," *Social Science Quarterly* 65 (1984): 1013–28; Lester W. Milbrath, *Environmentalists: Vanguard for a New Society* (Albany: NY: SUNY Press, 1984).

20. Milbrath, *Environmentalists*.

21. Norman Bowie, "Morality, Money, and Motor Cars," in *Business, Ethics, and the Environment* (Westport, Conn.: Quorum Books, 1990).

22. Ernest Callenbach, *Ecotopia* (Berkeley, Calif.: Banyan Tree Books, 1975).

23. Norman Bowie, "Challenging the Egoistic Paradigm" (paper presented at the Strategic Management Research Center Colloquium, University of Minnesota, Minneapolis, October 13, 1989).

27

From Environmentalism to Ecophilosophy: Retooling Cultures for the Twenty-First Century

HAZEL HENDERSON

Environmentalism heretofore has been generally known as a safe, middle-class issue. Who could be against clean air and water, tidying up the neighborhood, recycling and preserving species and wilderness? This was the kind of platform on which George Bush felt comfortable and even espoused recently by Britain's Margaret Thatcher.[1] However, the further one is drawn into environmental issues, the more the truth—long recognized by environmentalists—emerges. Environmentalism implies nothing less than a major emergent philosophy, global in scope, that challenges virtually every prior Western philosophical system. Just as new voices, such as that of the U.S. State Department's Francis Fukuyama, announce anew the end of history and human ideological evolution, the entry into the world scene of environmentalism portends the newest major contender.[2] This emerging ecophilosophy, in whatever culture it has arisen (and there are green parties now in more than a dozen countries) shifts our focus from anthropocentrism to biocentrism—from attention on human and cultural affairs to the affairs of planet earth as a living system of interdependent species. This Gaia hypothesis of two bioscientists, James Lovelock and Lynn Margulies, first proposed two decades ago, has penetrated Western culture and is helping to drive the new ecophilosophy.[3]

With this new ecological perspective, most of the proud saga of human history is telescoped into a brief account of a recently arrived two-legged species currently experiencing a classical, unremarkable "breeding storm," as biologists would say, exhibiting similar behavioral patterns to other species, such as deer, rodents, and marsupials. When a species overruns its ecological niche, behavior of phenotypes (individual members of the species) changes. They may become aggressive or apathetic, for example, or begin to ignore their young or show signs of cannibalism, until their diminishing habitat causes starvation and disease, and the changing ecology reduces their numbers to fit the limited carrying capacity. Ethical conclusions drawn from such biological views of humanity range from callous calls for "triage"[4] to propositions that we are instinctively altruistic.[5]

Most of the edifice of knowledge and culture in industrial societies is shockingly belittled by such new worldviews growing out of our rising awareness of our dependence on the planetary biosphere. Particularly violated is our Western cultural heritage: the Enlightenment as progress, scientific rationality, and the march of positivism, not to mention our Judeo-Christian traditions, which see humans (or at least men) at the apex of the pecking order of creation, with dominion over all other species and the earth.[6] Yet even here, ecophilosophy has created a ferment, and many of these religious orders have held soul-searching conferences over the past decade and have retooled the notion of dominance to the more species-ecumenical (but no less arrogant) idea of stewardship.[7] Humanism too has been accused of vulgar anthropocentrism—a change it has found unavoidable.[8]

It is not surprising that the new generation of environmentalists began during the 1960s to roam the world in search of other cultural and religious traditions that held the earth and other life-forms in higher regard.[9] Thus, elements of Buddhism, Taoism, Hinduism, and Islamic traditions were combined with ecological wisdom from many ancient, indigenous cultures, from Australia's Aboriginals to native Americans. These were in turn interwoven with insights glimpsed from the prehistory of Neolithic, matrilineal worshippers of the Great Mother Earth in all her iconic forms, by Erich Neumann, Marija Gimbutas, Joseph Campbell, and Riane Eisler.[10]

The overarching search was for value systems with radically expanded spatial sand time horizons. Environmentalists believed that only by thus reconceptualizing the brief history of the human species and its place on this ancient, living planet could deeper ethical principles be found.[11] These longer time frames might engender greater concern for future generations and promote human survival as our numbers continued to explode. It also seemed necessary to many environmentalists, including me, that the earth itself would need to be "resacralized," as in earlier times, as embodying the spirit and wonder of the creation.[12] We hoped that this might become an antidote to the array of anthropocentric philosophies of human superiority and domination of nature that had helped fuel the spectacular, if ambivalent, successes of the Industrial Revolution.

All of this seeding of new perceptions, values, and paradigms continued throughout the 1970s and into the 1980s, when environmentalism was thought to be in decline. It was indeed eclipsed in the United States by Reaganism and in Britain by Thatcherism and the peaking of the dominant paradigms of industrialism: materialism, technological optimism, and general obliviousness to the natural resources on which it was based, which some now refer to as "economism."[13] However, environmentalism continued to flourish in other countries, particularly in Germany with the rise of the first green party.[14] In the United

States after eight years of Ronald Reagan's politics of denial, there is today a resurgence of interest the problems that were left festering during this last great materialist spree: poverty, homelessness, illiteracy, a gamut of global restructuring issues, and the worsening state of the planet itself. Indeed, in the late 1980s, the planet took over as the great teacher of humanity: a vast, programmed learning environment with all the necessary positive and negative reinforcers to nudge us toward greater wisdom and maturity. As nature's feedback turned negative—acid rain, ozone depletion, dying lakes and growing deserts—all plainly visible from satellite photographs—human attention at last began to focus on the disastrous, irreversible effects we had wrought on our life-support system.

As politicians and corporate executives rush to jump on the environmental bandwagon, they too are unraveling the deeper message: our entire industrial value system, which the technologically advanced nations of the Northern hemisphere have been busy prescribing and promoting to the nations of the Southern hemisphere in the name of economic development and progress, has come unstuck. Indeed, as many desperate, indebted, ecologically ravaged, and starving countries have pointed out, after three decades of development, the process has gone into reverse, and it is clear to many of them that the European model of industrialization is not repeatable.[15]

The irony is that the challenge of ecophilosophy and the challenge from the so-called Third World are equally aimed at both major methods of macroeconomic managing industrialism: both centrally planned, socialist societies and free-market, mixed models of capitalistic industrialism.[16] Indeed, both shared the same underlying goals of industrialism, and most of the economist followers of both Adam Smith and Karl Marx, from left to right, share their enthusiasm for industrialism as the best answer to human aspirations. From Walt W. Rostow's *Stages of Economic Growth* treatise in the 1960s to Fukuyama's much-quoted "The End of History" in 1989, to Deng Xiaoping in China and many in the restructuring communist world, the goal of industrial economic development is still dominant. The notion has barely dawned among them that global environmentalism and its underlying ecophilosophy constitute a major overarching paradigm that will from now on compete with economism and industrialism in both East and West, as well as North and South, in the twenty-first century.

Increasingly political parties, corporate ethics statements, major magazines, and new journals[17] are espousing environmentalism—only to learn that its inescapable conclusions challenge almost everything they have been taught to believe in: economic growth, technological progress, the Protestant ethic, materialism, individualistic market competition, even scientific theories based in the mechanistic worldviews of Isaac Newton and René Descartes.[18] A case in point is a recent survey of the environment, "Costing the Earth," published by the London-based *Economist*.[19] The intellectual contortions of the editors were evident in the title, as well as in an editorial, "Growth Can Be Green," which made heroic efforts to salvage the now-dysfunctional discipline of economics, whose narrow, shortsighted accounting systems have proved clearly culpable in causing many environmental problems. Economic growth could be reformed and "green growth will indeed be somewhat slower than a dash for the dirty variety," the *Economist* admitted, adding that "at present, most economic activity takes little account of the costs it imposes on its surroundings. Factories pollute rivers as if the rinsing waters flowed past them for free, power stations burn coal without charging customers for the effects of carbon dioxide belched into the atmosphere, loggers destroy forests without a care for the impact on wildlife or climate. These bills are left for others to pick up—neighbors, citizens of other countries and future generations."[20] It is worth quoting the *Economist*'s change of heart further:

Conventional statistics of economic growth are . . . particularly blind to the environment, national income accounts (Gross National Product) take no notice of the value of natural resources: a country that cut down all its trees, sold them as wood chips and gambled away the money . . . would appear from its national accounts to have got richer in terms of GNP per person. Equally, they show measures to tackle pollution as bonuses, not burdens. . . . It would be easier for politicians to talk rationally about effects of sensible environmental policies on growth if governments agreed to remove some of these oddities from the way they keep their economic books.

This rapid rethinking and exposing of errors in economic theory and practice that they have not noticed for fifty years is to the *Economist*'s credit. At least environmentalists can be grateful that their unheeded and identical critiques of the past twenty years are at last being heard. Yet kissing such a massive turn-around off as a new verity that economic theory has already embraced is little more than barefaced intellectual sleight-of-hand, to which many others in the profession are also resorting. Rather, summed up in these short paragraphs is nothing less than a social, economic, and philosophical revolution that has already begun. Implementation of these new environmental insights and goals will require a greater restructuring of today's industrial societies than even the extraordinary restructuring we witnessed in the late 1980s.

Meanwhile, this kind of intellectual glibness of our overcrowded, competitive economics profession seeks to gloss over their centuries of erroneous theorizing. Economists are embracing environmental values without even pausing their pontificating long enough to reflect on the implicit ethics of ecophilosophy. When they do, they will find values far too long term and intergenerational ever to fit into any purely economic formula.[21] It is for this reason that I have spent the past fifteen years lecturing and writing about the end of economics as a generalized theoretical approach to public policy. Instead I have pointed to the many posteconomic policy tools and interdisciplinary models readily available for mapping longer-range issues and the dynamic behavior of rapidly restructuring complex societies.[22]

Today even the business press is replete with jokes about economists and their forecasting failures, and *Business Week* pronounced recently, "Clearly, the major economic problems don't lend themselves to macro-economic solutions."[23] Many honest economists who have transcended their discipline are beginning to admit publicly that they too are shifting to newer, sharper policy tools. For example, Herbert Simon, when accepting his Nobel Memorial Prize in Economics, stated that he had not used economic methods for a decade, and had switched to game theory and other decision sciences.[24] Figure 27.1 summarizes the different approaches economists, futurists, and systems theorists use, showing clearly the new focus on longer time horizons and broader social factors. In figure 27.2 the major new change models now being used to map dynamic systems are outlined.

Today social change and the general restructuring of nations and their institutions are being driven by at least six massive globalization processes, which I have explored elsewhere:[25] the globalization of technology and production; work, employment, and migration; finance, information, and debt and the new factor that money and information have now become interchangeable; the global scope of military weapons and the arms race; the human impacts on the planetary biosphere; and the emergence of a global culture and consumption patterns. The seventh great globalization process involves reactions to the prior six; these new interdependencies are driving the current restructurings and realignments between nations. The most striking effect of all this interactivity is the loss of sovereignty for every nation, with national leaders no longer able to deliver on their customary promises to protect their citizens in time of war, to shield them from pollution and environmental hazards, to maintain full employment, or to manage their domestic economies. The variables needed to control these conditions have now migrated beyond domestic reach into the global arena (figure 27.3). Furthermore, all this interactivity accelerates change, and it is clearly irreversible; this requires a shift in our knowledge structures, curriculum, and research methods, which is now underway.

Today the lag is evident not only in the social and policy sciences but also in academia, with its narrow focus on fragmented disciplines and tenure reward systems. Similar lags in our institutions, including government, business, labor, and religious denominations, create frustrations, since individuals learn much faster than institutions. As these great global changes roll onward, we see three zones of this great transition (figure 27.4: (1) the breakdown zone, where old institutions and forms are destructuring; (2) the bifurcation zone, of greatest uncertainty, as people move to reposition themselves as old ground becomes shaky; and (3) the breakthrough zone, where we see new forms emerging and new structures, knowledge, values, and goals. We also see in the most mature industrial societies, such as the United States and Britain, a classic bifurcation of industrial values occurring (figure 27.5), with the peaking of the short-term, expansionist values that were so successful in the past: competition, greed, material consumption, and individualism, leading to massive debt, the twin deficits, addiction, and other social problems we are now facing. On the other hand, we see the emerging of new values more suited to the next, postindustrial

Figure 27.1
Differing Perceptions, Assumptions, and Forecasting Styles between Economists and Futurists

ECONOMISTS	FUTURISTS
Forecasts from past data, extrapolating trends	Construct "What if?' scenarios; trends are not destiny
Now also use optimistic, pessimistic forecasts	Identify "Preferred Futures" plot trends for cross-impacts
Change seen as disequilibrium (i.e. equilibrium assumed) all other things equal "normal" conditions will return	Fundamental change assumed (transformation assumed) -- no such thing as "normal" conditions in complex systems
Reactive (invisible hand assumed to control)	Pro-active (focus on human choices and responsibilities)
Linear reasoning; reversible models	Nonlinear reasoning; irreversible models, evolutionary
Inorganic system models	Living system, organic models
Focus on "hard" sciences and data	Focus on life sciences, social sciences, "soft," fuzzy data, indeterminacy
Deterministic, reductionist, analytical	Holistic, synthesis, seeks synergy
Short-term focus (e.g. discount rates in cost/benefit analysis)	Long-term focus, intergenerational costs, benefits, and trade-offs
Data on noneconomic, nonmonetarized sectors seen as "externalities" (e.g. voluntary, community sectors, unpaid production, environmental resources)	Includes data on social, voluntary unpaid productivity, changing values, life-styles, environmental conditions; maps contexts, external variables (use posteconomic models: technology assessment, environmental impact, social impact studies)
Methods tend to amplify existing trends (e.g., Wall Street psychology)	Methods "contrarian" (e.g.. look for anomalies, check biases in perceptions, cultural norms)
"Herd instinct" in investing, technologies, economic development	Identify potentialities that are latent
Entrepreneurial when "market" is identified	Socially entrepreneurial (Schwartz) (e.g., envision future needs. create markets)
Precise, quantitative forecasts (e.g. gross national product for next quarter of year;annual focus)	Qualitative focus (e.g., year 2000 studies, anticipatory democracy). data from multiple sources. plot interacting variables. trends in long-term global contexts

Figure 27.2
Emerging Change Models

Earth System Science

(N.A.S.A. Program on Global Change
International Division, Washington, D.C.)
(interdisciplinary: plate tectonics, biogeochemical
and solar-driven processes, strato and
meso-sphere)

Catastrophe Mathematics

(Rene Thom, Structural Stability and
Morphogenesis [Paris, 1972])
Models at least seven modes in which
systems change their states

Cybernetic Models

Homeostasis and metamorphosis
governed by feedbacks, negative and positive
(Magoroh Maruyama, "Paradigmatology" in
H. Henderson, Politics of Solar Age [1981])

Order through Fluctuation Models

(Ilya Prigogine, From Being to Becoming
[San Francisco, 1980])

Chaos Theory Based on Attractors

(Ralph Abraham, Dynamics: The Geometry
of Behavior [Santa Cruz, 1984]).
Point, periodic, and chaotic attractors can
"magnetize" systems into new states

293

Figure 27.3
Emerging Era of Global Interdependence

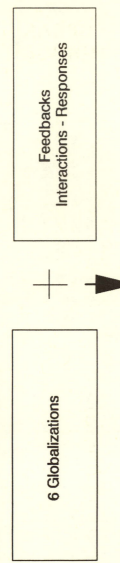

Feedbacks
Interactions - Responses

6 Globalizations

+

- Loss of National Sovereignty
- Acceleration and
- Irreversibility of Changes

Requiring a paradigm shift in knowledge/research methods

From focus on exactitude, static equilibrium, classical reductionism

Toward focus on research methods/policy tools based on systems view: Dynamic, nonlinear, probabilistic, feedback driven models of disequilibrium (e.g., chaos theories)

Figure 27.4
Three Zones of Transition

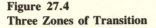

Zone
1

Zone
2

Zone
3

BREAK DOWN

FIBRILLATION BIFURCATION

FLIP-FLOP
MAX. UNCERTAINTY-OPPORTUNITY
'UPPING THE ANTE'

BREAK THROUGH

DESTRUCTURING
POLLUTION
CULTURAL CONFUSION
WARS-CONFLICT
SLOW MOTION CRISIS
ERRATIC GOVERNMENTS
INCOHERENT MEDIA
POLITICS
SCIENCE
ECONOMIC
DESTABILISATION
DIS-INFORMATION
ANARCHY
TOTALITARIAN DECAY
PAEDOMORPHOSIS
EXTINCTION

MORE/WORSE MORE/BETTER
BAD NEWS   GOOD NEWS
&
AMBIVALENCE

CHOICES   ACTION
REORDER   PRIORITIES

CLARIFY VALUES-GOALS

ADAPTATION ADAPTABILITY

'THIRD WAY'
NEW STRUCTURE
NEW FORMS
RE-CONCEPTUALISE
NEW MAPS
NEW CRITERIA
FOR SUCCESS
NEW INDICATORS
NEW GOALS-VALUES
GLOBAL WIN-WIN
PLANETARY CULTURE
SUSTAINABLE SOCIETIES
APPROPRIATE TECHNOLOGY

METAMORPHOSIS

ACCELERATION

stage, in a globally interdependent twenty-first century: greater emphasis on cooperation, savings, longer-term investment and management strategies, and environmental conservation and sustainable forms of development (defined as meeting the needs of current populations without foreclosing options for meeting those same needs of future generations).

The year 1988 saw the end of the cold war era. The United States and the Soviet Union saw that their arms race had led only to the slow, mutual destruction of their own economies—and that Japan had won the cold war. The new era, as we move into the twenty-first century, is that of global interdependence and mutually assured development, since no nation still thinks it can achieve world

Figure 27.5
Values Bifurcating in Postindustrial Societies

SHORT VIEW (Peeking of Old Values)	LONG VIEW (Emerging Values)
Reductionist, Focus on "Micro Rigorous" Research Quantitative, Hierarchical, Dominator	Integrative, Larger Contexts, Qualitative Participatory, Partnership
Greed, Individualistic, Competitive	Concern for Community, Cooperation
Speculation, Paper Asset Shuffling	Socially Responsible Investing
Borrowing, Leveraged Buyouts, etc. Debt Financing, Credit Cards	"Valdez" Principles, Sullivan And Other Investing Criteria, Investing in People
Budget and Trade Deficits, International Debt	Increase Savings Rates, Balance Budget
Consumption Values and Addictions (Drugs, Food, Shopping, Sex, Money)	Frugality, Search for "Inner" Satisfactions and Personal Growth
"Lifestyles of the Rich and Famous" Advertising Geared to Infantile Desire	Shopping Guides for a Better World "Eco Labeled" Products
Crisis Model of Problem Solving	Proactive Preventive Problem Identification, Early Warning
"Band-Aid" Remedies, Technological "Fixes"	Proliferation of New Indicators of Major Social Trends, Geared to Provide Feedback to Specific Social Goals
Gross National Product, and Macro Economics Aggregates are Sufficient to Measure Progress as Increase in Per Capita Income	Rise of Green Parties and Movements, Treaty of Montreal, etc.
Little Environmental Concern	Interest in Negotiations, Conflict Resolution, Diplomacy, Citizen Diplomats
Non Ratification of Law of the Sea Treaty Government Investment in Armaments, Hardware	Concern and Debate Over Ethics, Values
Tax Code Subsidizes Resource Depletion "Business as Usual", "Economism" has Won	

hegemony. Most see that our entire planet is becoming a single global commons; we all must share its atmosphere, oceans, and electromagnetic spectrum. Even the global financial system that grew out of conditions of a competitive world marketplace has emerged as a seamless commons of currency traders and twenty-four-hour asset managers, stock markets, and debtor and creditor nations—all in the same boat. When a former marketplace's niche is all used up and it becomes massively interlinked, its condition changes to that of a commons (any shared resource), and win-win (cooperative) rules apply. If win-lose rules are still applied, as if it were a market, then the result is lose-lose as I have detailed elsewhere.[26] Economic theory is now trying hard to catch up with research on how to manage these common resources, since these are the issues of the future. In most economics textbooks, however, theories of these commons are usually relegated to a mention or footnoted under the more familiar term *market failures*. Systems theorists reframe these issues as those of open systems (markets) and closed systems (commons) and view their allocation issues more in terms of game theory (figure 27.6).

Today's restructuring debates, whether of perestroika in the Soviet Union or economic reforms, deregulation, and so forth elsewhere, are all debates about two key issues: (1) what is valuable under new conditions? and (2) who, what, when, why, and how to regulate or deregulate? All economies are, in essence, sets of rules, derived from various cultural value systems, that determine in diverse ways what goals are important and what activities and jobs are valuable· in attaining these goals. The failure of economic models of development concerns their inability to embrace these diverse goals and values that differentiate cultures and attempting instead to impose formulas regarding "correct" policies, capital-labor ratios, and models of "efficiency" and "productivity" not only alien to many cultures but also ignoring the productive role of natural systems.[27]

The new debate about what constitutes sustainable development is about all these issues and going beyond neat formulas to decode the various "cultural DNA" of each specific society to find out what their people consider important and what menu of goods, services, and amenities they consider optimal. Breaking through economist rhetoric, it is now clear that the role of government is primary, whether intervening to foster market or command and control methods of governance, in both industrial and developing countries.[28]

Many see that it is less a matter of whether a country is centrally planned, mixed (as most are), or capitalistic, since the effects of the underlying industrial model are similar, but more a matter of whether societies are cybernetically designed to incorporate feedback at every level of decision making—from the family and community to the provincial and national levels, from those people affected by the decisions. Thus, the instinct of leaders in centrally planned societies (and oversized corporations) is to decentralize decision making and incorporate more of this feedback, using prices (hopefully corrected for social costs) and votes—that is, democracy. But prices and votes are not the only forms of feedback that complex societies need to correct their decision making. Other

Figure 27.6
Differing Models of Economists and Futurists/Systems Theorists Describing Rules of Interaction and Value Systems

ECONOMISTS

Markets

Private Sector
Individual Decisions
Competition
"Invisible Hand"
Antitrust Laws
Property Rights
(Government Protects and Enforces)

Commons

Property of All Humans
(Focus on Individual-Based Rules of Interaction)

Public Sector
(Often Assigns Monetary Values/Shadow Prices)
Public Choice Theory
Monopoly and Oligopoly Under Regulation
Consortia (Cooperation)
Market Intervention to Correct Market "Failures"
Communal or "Socialistic"
"Mixed" Economies

FUTURISTS/SYSTEMS THEORISTS

Open Systems

Divisible Resources
Individual Decisions
Win-Lose Rules
Adam Smith's Rules
Laws Enforce Win-Lose Property Rights
(Government Protects and Enforces)

Closed Systems

Indivisible Natural Resources, Amenities
(Valued By But Not Necessarily the Property
of Humans)
Arena of Public Decisions on Resource Allocation
and Rule-Making, Access to Tax Supported Goods
and Services
Win-Win Rules
Cooperative Agreements, Treaties, Etc.
To Prevent Lose-Lose Outcomes
(i.e., "Tragedies of the Commons")
Communal, Traditional Mutual Aid, Nonmoney,
Informal Sectors of Production and Exchange

vital feedbacks include genuinely free, even muckraking mass media, especially television, civic and other consumer and worker organizations, and free associations of all kinds, including business groups, as long as none can drown out the others or obtain unfair access to the political and economic processes—and all the newly perceived feedbacks from nature: acid rain, ozone depletion, and desertification. All of these new issues are much better suited to the expanded, interdisciplinary frameworks of systems theory, futures studies, and posteconomic policy tools such as technology assessment, environmental impact statements, social indicators, and the like than the cul-de-sac of economic theory. A macroeconomic management focus, in addition, can simply precipitate debates back into the old left or right axis of the cold war struggle between communist and capitalist ideologies.[29]

Today we can take off these old ideological spectacles of economism and also see that the history of the twentieth century has largely been about experiments at governing human societies at current, unprecedented population levels. As a biological species, we have no repertoire of experience or behavior beyond that learned in small communities and tribes in decentralized, rural, agricultural settings.[30] Most of the experiments of this century—at urbanization, nationhood, and agglomerated governance of larger, diverse regions and ethnic populations—have been less than satisfactory, for we are a young species. Efforts at synthesizing ideologies capable of organizing larger loyalties and productive efforts, whether around kings, generals, or religious leaders, or massive public undertakings, crusades, and even the ubiquitous fomenting of xenophobia, have all proved unstable. They have culminated in such ghastly organizing efforts as Hitler's Third Reich, two world wars, Stalin's gulags, and Mao's China. Now the game has changed irrevocably, and we humans must learn to overcome our disabling belief systems: all those -isms, from nationalism and tribalism to religious intolerances and communism, capitalism, and even industrialism. It remains to be seen whether environmentalism can avoid crystallization into yet another set of dogmas.

As we approach the twenty-first century, we are truly at a turning point. It will now avail us little to continue to argue about who is to blame for the past colossal mistakes. Neither is it helpful to perpetuate cold ware rivalries by rubbing salt in the wounds of the Soviets, the Eastern Europeans, or the Chinese about the demise of communism. It is time to give a decent burial to both Karl Marx and Adam Smith and reframe the old debates in much broader contexts and interdisciplinary terms. We can remember that most of humanity's failing organizational endeavors were undertaken at least in the name of progress and improvement of the human condition. Today we have all learned much from these experiments, however horrible, and leaders of both socialist and capitalist countries can learn something from each other. State-enforced cooperation requires leavening with incentives for individuals, and state-enforced competition and individual profit maximizing require ethical frameworks. Socialist leaders are exploring mixed, regulated market economies in the West and find little that conforms with neoclassical economics textbooks. Instead they see the similarities of predominantly government-regulated and created markets, which they seek to learn more about. For example, Deng Xiaoping's economic reform dictum is, "Government regulates markets and markets guide enterprises." The Chinese are falling behind in democratic reforms but are ahead of the Soviets in economic reforms.

Nowhere are the cries heralding the triumph of capitalism and the marketplace more hollow than in the new brand of economism that labels itself environmental, or resource, economics or, even more pretentious, ecological economics—desperately trying to catch up with events and new policy issues. One of the problems is the overcrowded state of the economics profession and the excessive numbers of new graduates rolling off academic production lines, leading to the ambulance-chasing effect we see in the legal field. Here again we see the same kind of bifurcation of economists' values between short- and long-term concerns: between economists who have staked out the market niche of helping to bale out the declining sectors of industrial societies (companies irretrievably committed to unsustainable or excessively resource- and energy-intensive processes, goods, and services: from nuclear energy and devastating weapons systems to non-recyclable packaging and private, fossil-fueled automobiles). There are also those economists who have thrown their lot in with the emerging sectors based on ecological principles of long-term sustainability (companies in renewable energy, conservation, recycling, remanufacturing, renewable-power mass transit, health maintenance, disease prevention, organic farming, etc.).

When in the service of these two divergent sectors and their goals and values, economics naturally looks very different. For the unsustainable sector, it tends to be the economics of rearguard actions: playing for time, lobbying against regulation, promoting market solutions, such as trading pollution licenses, and the like. For the emerging renewable sector (mostly start-ups and small companies) it tends to be fighting the old giants and their market power and prior dominance over the rule setting, quantifying the social and environmental costs of prior subsidies and incentives, and so forth. Thus at last is economics unmasked as not the value-free science it claims to be but merely a profession (with little quality control at that), with all the biases and social value commitments of any other profession. From this standpoint, economics too is an ideology—all the more suspect in its quantitative and technical pretensions. Economics has colonized our democratic processes by casting important clashes between old and new values as resolvable via cost-benefit ratios and risk analysis, with all the discredited underlying baggage of welfare economics, Pareto optimality still foisted on an unwary public. For example, the value of a salt marsh (one of the most productive systems on the planet) is compared with infilling for a housing development in price-determined terms, or using the "willingness to pay" principle, which asks voters with no financial stake in the housing development how much they would be willing to pay so as to keep it a salt marsh. These absurdities, which are common to most applications of this kind of economics, need no further comment.[31]

Values are the primary forces in all human societies (despite Marxian theory). Values drive all the different economic systems, which are simply programs of rules (in computer terminology), as well as their outputs (various configurations of technology furniture and diverse infrastructures, education systems, norms, etc.). Indicators such as the gross national product (GNP) perform the comparator function to see that the program is running properly according to the rules. When changes in external conditions occur, such as all societies are experiencing as today's globalization processes accelerate, citizens must find many new forums beyond merely voting occasionally in elections in order to clear the backlog of issues and values clarification that must be hammered out. This must be done in vernacular language, not confused by economic algorithms concealing obsolete values and assumptions. We see these new forums at corporate annual meetings, on television and radio talk shows, and in the massive increase in most industrial societies of citizen movements for consumer and environmental protection, corporate responsibility, human rights, animal rights, and so on, and all their myriad newsletter and press releases.[32]

It is no wonder the old two-party politics is failing, dominated as it is by the interest groups of the unsustainable sector and their prior market and political power. Until the new values and ethical concerns are given their due in political parties and the mass media, voters will continue to defect from the process. For similar reasons, macroeconomic management is failing, using models that are still too short term, static, and based on the assumptions of equilibrium, all at heroic levels of aggregation: levels of investment, interest rates, and unemployment that do not allow for the necessary detail and questions, such as the kind of investment and the criteria for measuring productivity. New consensuses cannot be located because all these macroeconomic indicators cannot deal with the new specific and structural issues in the real world (figures 27.7 and 27.8). Today we see many new initiatives to reformulate the GNP and augment these macroeconomic indicators with specific indicators of social performance: in health, education, and environmental quality in many countries.

The debate now shaping up between economics versus long-term environmental ethics has been brewing for over a decade. Economists whose intellectual investments and clients are tied to the declining sector have been lobbying environmentalists and insisting that it is we who need to learn economics rather than that they need to learn ecology and systems sciences. Economists still claim that economics provides the best overall theoretical framework for policy, while environmentalists insist that it is economics that must now find its place in broader, interdisciplinary models.[33] Obviously economists prefer market solutions and their own narrow models of efficiency and productivity, with which they are familiar, as well as the propensity to reduce everything possible to money coefficients or shadow prices. Ecologists and system theorists use many other coefficients (time, hectares of land, infant mortality, literacy levels, etc.), and this "politics of research methods and epistemologies" shows few signs of resolution.[34] The Bush administration has endorsed, predictably, such market solutions as effluent taxes, incentives (subsidies), and pollution licenses. All

Figure 27.7
The Economic View

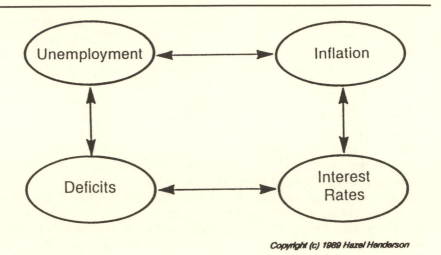

these should have a place in the mix of options. The most controversial proposal is that these licenses to pollute should be able to be traded between companies in newly expanded markets so that companies in compliance with air quality standards, for example, can sell their rights to spew out more pollution to companies that are still violators or companies that want to come into the area and site a new polluting facility.[35] This perversion of market theory was used in some cases during the Reagan administration, and I have made detailed arguments against it elsewhere.[36] Such policies grow, like noxious weeds, out of neoclassical market theory and economic textbooks that do not recognize the way markets are distorted by power, unequal access to information, and income opportunities.

This kind of misapplication of market theory to political, social and public health problems grew out of the famed Chicago School of Economics. Its leading proponent is Milton Friedman, coauthor of *Free to Choose*, which highlights the main concern of his theorizing: individual freedom in the market rather than the new concerns of the global commons.[37] These doctrines of the Chicago School have pervaded many of the nation's law schools and are taught as "Law and Economics." They assume that our democratic political system is simply analogous to yet another marketplace, where conflicts can be worked out between private parties and interest groups using such welfare economics principles as compensation for damage caused to others by market activities or their willingness to pay to avoid harm, thus avoiding the need for much regulation. Some of these ideas still work in small communities where the social fabric is intact and moral and ethical sanctions apply to control purely self-interested behavior.

Figure 27.8

A System View of the Global "Vicious Circle" Economy (Fast Feedback Loops)

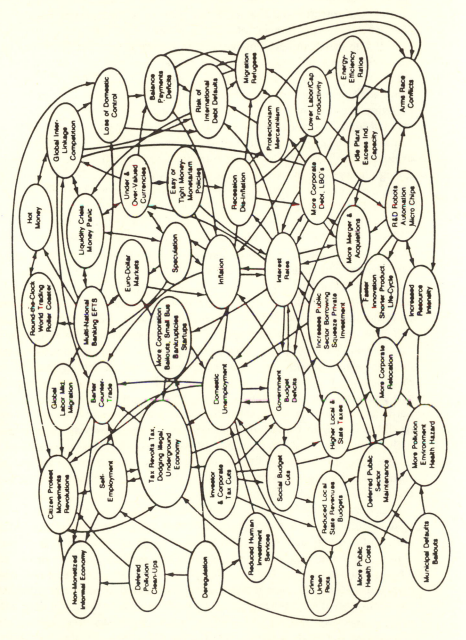

However, it is hopelessly outdated where common resources must be shared—air, water, or open space—in today's crowded, urbanized societies, where win-win rules are needed for equitable access. Even Judge Robert Bork in his unsuccessful confirmation hearings for a Supreme Court seat testified that he had abandoned his belief in much of this theorizing behind law and economics.

Although these misplaced market theories are perhaps most of all inappropriate for dealing with environmental and global commons, they are espoused by many in the Environmental Protection Administration, the Congress, and even some environmental groups with persuasive staff economists. The marketing-pollution-licenses proposals are often thrown in with the whole range of other less questionable uses of the tax code, subsidies, incentives, and other price signals, which can nudge change as well as or better than some regulations (such as higher gasoline taxes, which are essential, in my view). On the whole, I favor taxing and user-fee approaches over subsidies and incentives, which too often create a set of client companies or whole industries. These, in turn, soon have the additional market power to lobby for the perpetuation of such subsidies, creating tilted playing fields for newer market entrants. For example, *Project 88: Harnessing Market Forces to Protect Our Environment,* a study sponsored by Senators Tim Wirth and John Heinz, contains many useful policy proposals to create new markets and price signals.[38] At least, the truth that it is humans who create markets, and not God, or magic forces, is clearly stated, and the costs to taxpayers of these additional bribes is acknowledged, along with attempts at comparison with new revenues from effluent taxes and comparisons with regulation and costs of legal and enforcement delays and of the endless lawsuits involved. The assumption is that all of these intricacies and interacting variables can be modeled with economic tools and that environmentalists who participated were fully cognizant of the flaws in these models. However, economic theory is so perversely impenetrable that one has to be an expert in order to critique its deeply buried assumptions, and it is more likely that the noneconomists were overawed or did not wish to display their incomprehension. However, the report also includes recommendations that markets be created to trade pollution rights and licenses as well: for controlling air pollution, acid rain, greenhouse gases, and surface water and groundwater pollution. These need much more critical examination and rebuttal on many grounds.[39]

These marketable licenses to pollute imply that a right to pollute exists, in spite of protestations to the contrary, and since there is no constitutional right to pollute, the whole approach sends the wrong signal. The spectacle of private companies trading together the rights of third parties to breathe clean air is sinister. Human rights cannot be abridged so easily, particularly when neither the potential victims nor their representatives are seated at the negotiating table. Thus, creation of these types of pollution markets invades the social and political arena in new ways that must be widely debated and not discussed merely within economic concepts of efficiency. For example, the *Project 88* report was directed by economists with funds provided by foundations and a citizen-based group. The Environmental Policy Institute served only as "fiscal agent" for the project "as part of an effort to stimulate diverse points of view about environmental problems." Various environmental group representatives agreed to be listed as contributors, reviewers, or staff, with further caveats that the report did not necessarily reflect the views of their groups or the "fiscal agent's other funding sources." As an old science and public policy hand, *Project 88* looks to me like the brain child of a particular financial and economics constituency more committed to the rear-view mirror issues of baling out the declining, unsustainable sector than focusing on creating markets and price signals to fertilize the growth of the emerging, sustainable sectors of the future.

Several arguments are used in favor of marketing pollution licenses:

1. Regulation has not worked well, and pollution is a fact of industrial life.
2. Since pollution cannot be eliminated, why not just recognize this reality and tax or license it?
3. We need to use both the carrot of subsidies and the sticks of taxes and regulations.
4. Offering the right to trade their pollution permits enables companies that are cleaner to make more money by selling these permits to dirtier companies.
5. These policies will give us more efficiency and bang for the pollution control buck.

These arguments are less than persuasive for the following additional reasons beyond the constitutional one already cited. First, it is egregious to claim that regulation has not worked well; much progress has been made. Only during the Reagan years has it begun to fail badly since the policy of his administration was to deregulate the entire economy, and the EPA was singled out for systematic budget cuts and generally decimated. Second, one of the real blocks to better enforcement has been that the burden of proof in pollution and toxic hazards in the environment was placed on the general public and the EPA and other enforcement agencies rather than, as in the case of the Food and Drug Administration, where companies and all manufacturers have to take on the burden of proof that the substance be tested until it meets the GRAS (Generally Regarded As Safe) standard. This reversed burden of proof allowed endless, costly legal delays and required enforcement agencies to hire thousands of scientists and lawyers to testify through appeal processes that dragged out over years. This generally prevented the logical regulation of these hazards at the source. The new California Toxics Law, Proposition 65, implemented in 1988, puts the burden of proof back into the marketplace, thus saving taxpayers millions and speeding up the regulatory process, applying toxic status to more chemicals in the past twelve months than the EPA managed under the Toxic Substance Control Act in the past twelve years.[40]

The fight over marketing pollution licenses has only just begun. As Jon Mills, former Speaker of Florida's House of Representatives, says,

If these rights exist, what is to stop me and a group of my environmentalist friends from going into that same market and out-bidding all the polluting companies? We could take them off the market—but then, that's what we *pay our government enforcers* to do! Oh, you say that only *polluters* can enter these markets, *not* law-abiding citizens? What is fair about that?

I might add, what will stop us then from setting up markets to trade licenses to commit felonies? And will there ever be enough money in the public treasury to bribe everyone to abide by the laws?[41]

The good news about all this cultural confusion over our changing values and goals, ethics, and regulations is that these issues are reaching higher thresholds of public awareness and debate—in the Congress, on Wall Street, in the public sector, in the community, schools, and the family. The whole world has changed, and we are now debating how we need to change the game, the rules, and the scoring system. Arguments for using the magic of market forces to achieve social and regulatory goals have been a constant and sensible refrain in American politics. Our confusion was that we were blinded by economic dogma also to hold the contradictory belief that we did not actually create these markets but rather that they were derived from some original state of grace or "human nature." As I have noted elsewhere, invoking human nature to buttress one's political beliefs or policy is a very old strategy. Furthermore, while it is true that, as Adam Smith said, humans have a propensity to barter—indeed we have been doing it since we came out of the caves—the social innovation of creating a nationwide system of markets as a primary resource allocation mechanism is a fairly recent and brilliant human invention.[42] It was only some 300 years ago in Britain that a package of social legislation to create this national system of markets was introduced and passed by Parliament. It rolled back ancient cultural customs of feudal obligations and rights and the older resource-allocation methods still used by many societies (including ours and Britain's): reciprocity and redistribution.[43] In fact, one of the most critical errors of economic theory has been the omission of the informal, unpaid sectors from its models (parenting, do-it-yourself, mutual aid, volunteering, food raising, bartering)—what I refer to as the "love economy," which all societies bogging down in "economism" are now rediscovering (figure 27.9) as the unseen half.

We should create new markets to help eliminate pollution or keep it within nature's regenerating tolerances. But let us take credit for our intelligence rather than keep up the pretense that these are magic forces, that the propensity of humans to barter was invented by Adam Smith, or that capitalism is the only context in which they are or can be used. And let us remember that all human societies depend on sets of explicit and implicit values, ethics, and morals—the more of which can be agreed to and inculcated as part of our responsibilities that go along with our rights, the less police and external enforcement will be needed.[44] Indeed, we can use markets much more than we do now to shift our wasteful, unsustainable sector into the future and create whole new industries

Figure 27.9
From Economics to Systems View

Interactive Productive System of an Industrial Society
(Three-Layer Cake with Icing)

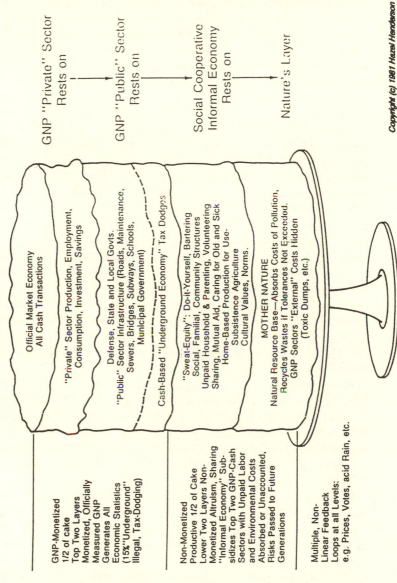

GNP "Private" Sector Rests on →

GNP "Public" Sector Rests on →

Social Cooperative Informal Economy Rests on →

Nature's Layer

Official Market Economy
All Cash Transactions

"Private" Sector Production, Employment, Consumption, Investment, Savings

"Public" Sector Infrastructure (Roads, Maintenance, Sewers, Bridges, Subways, Schools, Municipal Government)
Defense, State and Local Govts.

Cash-Based "Underground Economy" Tax Dodges

"Sweat-Equity": Do-It-Yourself, Bartering Social, Familial, Community Structures Unpaid Household & Parenting, Volunteering Sharing, Mutual Aid, Caring for Old and Sick Home-Based Production for Use-Subsistence Agriculture Cultural Values, Norms.

MOTHER NATURE
Natural Resource Base—Absorbs Costs of Pollution, Recycles Wastes if Tolerances Not Exceeded. GNP Sectors "External" Costs Hidden (Toxic Dumps, etc.)

GNP-Monetized
1/2 of cake
Top Two Layers
Monetized, Officially
Measured GNP
Generates All
Economic Statistics
(15%"Underground"
Illegal, Tax-Dodging)

Non-Monetized
Productive 1/2 of Cake
Lower Two Layers Non-
Monetized Altruism, Sharing
"Informal Economy" Sub-
sidizes Top Two GNP-Cash
Sectors with Unpaid Labor
and Environmental Costs
Absorbed or Unaccounted,
Risks Passed to Future
Generations

Multiple, Non-
Linear Feedback
Loops at all Levels:
e.g. Prices, Votes, acid Rain, etc.

based on cleaning up and recycling, as well as future sustainability and even environmental enhancement and restoration.

To move forward and achieve these goals, there already is a wide consensus among economists and environmentalists that we must, as soon as possible and by a range of appropriate means, move to full-cost pricing—that is, internalize as quickly as possible all the longer-term social and environmental costs of production back onto company balance sheets so that the products and services may be truly priced. Obviously there are many long-term costs that we cannot hope to account for fully, such a depletion of ozone and public health risks, which is why we can never rely on only prices. Other forms of feedback must be used where most apt for the problem at hand. These external costs can be internalized by regulations, mass media exposés, votes, public opinion, consumer action, boycotts of offending products, and "buycotts" of environmentally superior products,[45] larger bounties on recyclable cans and bottles, not to mention the sales efforts of pollution control companies, recycling and conservation companies, and the continued educational campaigns of environmental groups and their lobbying efforts. Better consumer information and product labeling are already creating their own marketing opportunities:[46] in pesticide-free organic foods, natural cosmetics, environmentally sound lines of paper products, household cleansers, and solar and energy-saving light bulbs and fixtures, as well as the upstream industries helping old companies change their processes, conserve their energy and recycle their by-products and former pollution and waste back into their production stream or find new uses for these unappreciated resources.

All of these new markets are either values driven or regulation driven. For example, at a recent meeting of the World Business Council, one of my fellow speakers, Dean L. Buntrock, president of Waste Management, Inc., a multi-million dollar corporation, began his talk by stating clearly that his company and its spectacular growth were "regulation driven." Moving further upstream to the securities markets, we see the outstanding success at promoting better environmental practices of the socially responsible investing movement, whose investors now account for $450 billion worth of assets screened for their longer-term social and environmental concerns. Here again changing values created this growing market niche, at first scoffed at by Wall Streeters. The movement's Valdez Principles and Sullivan Principles (covering investment in South Africa) are now regularly covered by the financial press for their effects in corporate boardrooms.[47] The energy conservation market is still holding its own, from its creation by the Organization of Petroleum Exporting Countries and energy-efficiency standards set in the 1970s and not completely rolled back in the Reagan era. This market is poised to resume growth in the United States as we rediscover our energy dependence on imports has increased and that our competitiveness internationally is still hampered by the fact that it takes the United States two and a half times as much energy to create an equivalent unit of GNP as it does Japan or Europe (figure 27.10). With new problems posed by global warming trends, the shift from fossil fuels to further conservation and alter-

Figure 27.10
Relative Decline of the United States

Some Overlooked Fundamentals:

* Investment Lag in "Human Capital" Resources: Education, Re-Training, Children

* Energy Sector Still Relatively Inefficient: Energy/GNP Ratio v. Japan, Germany, etc.

* Health Sector: Inefficient Use of Huge Investment (12% of GNP v. Performance of Other Countries, e.g., Denmark, Netherlands, Canada, Sweden)

* "Waste" Management: Costly Focus on "Disposal" Rather Than Recycling Back Into Production (Japan Recycles Over 50% of "Waste")

* Environmental Costs and Resource Depletion Rates Too High: Inefficient Subsidies Still Leading to Erroneous Pricing of Resources

* Aging, Decaying, Inefficient Infrastructure

* Inefficient Tax Code: Subsidizes Waste, Resource Depletion, Over Investment in Automation and Plant Relocation

* Consumer Oriented Culture: Low Savings Rate

* Short Term View Prevails In Business and Politics, As Well As Culture

* Productivity in the Services Sector Lags Behind Japan, Germany, Etc.: U.S. Trade in Services Fell Into Deficit in 2nd Quarter of 1989 for the First Time Due to More Earnings of Overseas Investors in the U.S. (Now An Indicator of U.S. Net Debtor Status in World Economy)

native, renewable energy is inevitable. In fact in my own environmental work, it is necessary to move even further upstream and survey all these social and values shifts as well as globalization and planetary ecosystem trends in order to see where new markets are emerging, as well as new commons, where new win-win rules still need to be negotiated and new treaties written (figure 27.11).

The new opportunities in both the new markets and the new commons include environmental restoration and enhancement, reforestation, new uses for renewable, less-toxic plant substitute—inputs into hundreds of manufacturing processes. As I predicted in my earlier books and papers,[48] the paradigm shift from focusing on mechanical, inorganic sciences and production methods of early industrialism, to the postindustrial focus on biological systems and information-rich methods, has now occurred. I described this paradigm shift as one in which a problem of production would no longer instantly invoke visions of machines, factories, or hardware but engender more careful thought and scanning of eco-systems for their inherent capabilities and their untapped potentials, which human knowledge can use and augment and shape to our needs more deftly. An example of this kind of rethinking of what development means on a living, crowded planet is the budding industry of desert greening, which promises to be a huge global market well into the twenty-first century. Many different methods are practiced today, and some areas, such as Florida, have all the native plant species and agricultural biotechnologists to create a new export industry, along with water-quality management technologies now being honed by environmental necessity. Venture capital companies are beginning to see the new opportunities, and several new firms are being launched.

New visions of world trade in the twenty-first century go far beyond the confines of economic theories of nations competing via comparative advantage or protectionism in a global marketplace. In the new era of global interdependence, countries will learn strategies beyond competing over today's narrow range of goods, such as automobiles and consumer electronics. They will practice the other two important trade strategies: cooperation, when commons require win-win rules, such as in space development, and, more important, creativity (rethinking the game itself). Today we are trying to impose industrial conformity on all trading partners by extending economic theories of protection to today's lengths of trying to homogenize everyone's social and cultural values, as is now occurring in the "structural impediments" debate with Japan. Instead nations can learn that each culture and its host ecosystem has produced truly unique gifts to offer in world trade, and the game will shift from "hardware" (shipping goods around) toward "software" (expertise, technique, social innovations). This cultural niche model is derived from ecological theory (where diversity is a basic principle) and mirrors the cooperation and symbiosis that is just as common in nature as competition. Competition, cooperation, and creativity are important strategies, appropriate in various circumstances, and no economic algorithm from either socialism or capitalism can be applied dogmatically.[49] Examples of such cultural niche export strategies include those in the Netherlands, where a

Figure 27.11
Exploring the Evolving Global Playing Field

New Markets, Industries

- Telecom Services
- Desert-greening
- Pollution control
- Renewable Energy
- Recycling-eco-resource Mgmt.
- "Caring" Sector (Day-care,
  Counceling, Re-hab, Nursing)
- Infra-structure (Extending
  Transport-Telecom etc.)

New Commons

- Space, Earth Systems Science
- Electromagnetic Spectrum
- Oceans-Water Resources
- Atmosphere-Ozone Layer
- Security-Peacekeeping
- Forests
- Health
- Global Economy

bedrock export with no competitors is the export of hardware and software of dyking out the sea, from the unique Dutch 2,000 years of expertise, which they routinely export to Bangladesh and the city of New Orleans. With global climate trends, this may also prove to be a growing market. Similarly, one of Britain's most successful exports since World War II has been eccentricity: the sheer creativity of its young rock musicians and punk fashion designers. In this way, we may be able to savor each other's cultural diversity and thrive on it, as we do on each other's food and art.

By far the largest global environmental ethics market is now emerging out of the winding down of cold war arms expenditures and the rechanneling of some of these trillion-dollar annual budgets into coping at last with the real Horsemen of the Apocalypse: hunger, disease, ignorance, and destruction of our planetary life-support system. Growing world trade in these basic goals of all humanity awaits only our fuller recognition that our tightly interwoven global economy is also a commons, requiring more win-win rules and agreements on debt, currency fluctuations, special drawing rights, and rethinking what a level playing field might look like once we take off our economic spectacles. Debt must be dealt with beyond the currently fashionable swaps for nature or equity (often based on murky ethical premises). The world's bankers and finance ministers need to face up to the fact that the de facto has occurred already, and most of the recent remedies merely acknowledge some of this reality. Writing off Third World countries' debt is a necessary but not sufficient starting point for further recycling of surplus currencies into more organized secondary markets for discounted country junk bonds, as I have termed them.[50]

As this Third World debt is put behind us, the global playing field can be buttressed by placing an ethical floor under it: composed of an extended lattice of agreements and protocols on toxic chemicals, worker and consumer protection, environmental standards, and eventually leveling some of the really serious differentials in wages (measured not in GNP terms but in purchasing power equivalents.[51] These differentials in exploiting human labor, just like excessive differentials in consumer and worker safety and environmental protection, are what drives the excessive, unhealthy migrations of populations across borders looking for work and companies looking for short-term market advantage. These massive migrations fuel the globalization processes and the twenty-four-hour-day financial casino, where money is divorced from real wealth and becomes mere blips of information on thousands of trading screens, where time windows of opportunity to exploit differentials in currencies and interest rates are collapsing to mere nanoseconds.

Much of this ethical lattice of treaties, agreements, and protocols to raise the ethical floor to level the global playing field is already in place via the United Nations special agencies and such treaties as that in Montreal in 1987 on chlorofluorocarbons and the Law of the Sea, which has been waiting for the United States to ratify it after a decade of delaying tactics. Only when this ethical lattice is in place can ethically aware, responsible companies live up to their moral codes without fear of unfair competition by others willing to cut corners and exploit people and the environment for short-term gain.

Most of the great ethical and moral leaders in the short history of our human family have preached similar ethical imperatives, usually encoded in the classic systems theory statement of the Golden Rule, and have reminded us that the god is within us as well as without. We have free will, reason, compassion, and the intelligence to read the feedback signals from every level of our societies and environment. No subject is more important to our survival than exploring our values, ethics, and potential for altruism, as well as broader self-interest. When our individual self-interests are seen in the larger context of the human family on earth, we see that they are all identical. It is in every one of our broadest self-interests to help create and undergird the ethical and environmental markets of the twenty-first century since they provide our best assurance of survival and truly human development.

NOTES

1. *Economist,* September 2, 1989, citing the growth of "green" policies from 1973, and E. F. Schumacher's *Small Is Beautiful* to Mrs. Thatcher's "conversion from Iron Lady to Green Goddess."

2. F. F. Fukuyama, "The End of History?" *National Interest* (Summer 1989).

3. William K. Stevens, "Evolving Theory Views Earth as a Living Organism," *New York Times,* August 29, 1989.

4. See, for example, Garrett Hardin, *The Limits of Altruism* (Bloomington: Indiana University Press, 1977).

5. Pitirim Sorokin, *The Ways and Powers of Love* (1954).

6. See, for example, Hazel Henderson, *Creating Alternative Futures: The End of Economics* (New York, G. P. Putnam's Sons, 1978).

7. See, for example, Mary Daly, *Pure Lust* (Boston: Beacon Press, 1984).

8. David Ehrenfeld, *The Arrogance of Humanism* (Oxford: Oxford University Press, 1978).

9. Fritjof Capra, *The Tao of Physics* (Berkeley: Shambala Press, 1983).

10. Erich Neumann, *The Great Mother,* trans. Ralph Manheim, Bollingen Series (Princeton: Princeton University Press, 1955); Marija Gumbutas, *The Goddess and Gods of Old Europe* (Berkeley: University of California Press, 1982); Joseph Campbell, *The Power of Myth* (Garden City, NY: Doubleday, 1988); Riane Eisler, *The Chalice and the Blade* (New York: Harper & Row, 1987).

11. The native American ethos of submitting all policies to the test of their effects on "the seventh generation" typifies this longer-range ethics. It is explored in Gary Paul Nabhan, *The Desert Smells Like Rain,* (Berkeley, Calif., North Point Press, 1982).

12. H. Henderson, *The Politics and Ethics of the Solar Age* (Berkeley: University of California, 1982).

13. See, for example, President Carlos Andres Perez of Venezuela, foreword to *Toward a New Way to Measure Development, The South Commission* (Caracas, Venezuela, 1989).

14. Charlene Spretnak and Fritjof Capra, *Green Politics* (New York: E. P. Dutton, 1984).

15. *Economist*, September 23, 1989, carried a special "Survey: The Third World," which outlines the classic economism view: that these countries should not give up hope and that the 1980s were "a temporary setback."

16. Ibid. The *Economist*'s editors in their September 23 survey do not include the ecological criteria in comparing Third World countries, which they espouse so vigorously in their Survey of the Environment in their September 2 issue.

17. "Environment Magazines Spring Up," *New York Times*, September 28, 1989.

18. H. Henderson, *The Politics of the Solar Age* (Garden City, NY: Doubleday, 1981).

19. "Costing the Earth," *Economist*, September 2, 1989.

20. "Growth Can Be Green," *Economist*, August 26, 1989, p. 12.

21. David Collard, *Altruism and Economy*, (Oxford: Oxford University Press, 1978), makes a heroic effort to tease out from economic theory the few papers and studies on the subject of longer-term ethics.

22. H. Henderson, "Post-Economic Policies for Post-Industrial Societies," *ReVision* (Winter-Spring 1984–1985).

23. *Business Week*, September 25, 1989, p. 166.

24. Herbert Simon, "Rationality as a Process and Product of Thought," *American Economic Review* (1978).

25. Henderson, *Politics of the Solar Age*, 1988 ed.

26. Perez, *Toward a New Way to Measure Development*, pp. 147–53.

27. Henderson, *Politics of the Solar Age*, pp. 245–406.

28. *Economist*, September 23, 1989, in its Third World Survey agreed that "in the 1950s and 1960s, economists set the third world on the wrong track" and that "government intervention (whether expert or inept) was the key variable."

29. Ibid. In its Third World Survey, for example, the *Economist* frames its entire fifty-eight-page discussion of these "development issues" *within* economic theory, as if these macro-*economic* management variables were *primary* (trade and export policies, currency differentials, fiscal and monetary approaches), rather than recasting these issues in line with their discovery that all these policies are simply policies of *government intervention*, which is primary. Social, cultural and environmental variables were largely ignored.

30. In "Do Good Ethics Ensure Good Profits?" *Business and Society Review*, 70 (Summer 1989), social scientist Amitai Etzioni and anthropologist Tiger point to these deeper cultural and anthropological factors and how our history of living in small groups allowed us to rely on "full disclosure" and social sanctions—mechanisms we need to reinvent to fit our crowded world.

31. Henderson, *Politics of the Solar Age*, pt 3 deals with these issues in detail.

32. H. Henderson, "Information and the New Movement for Citizen Participation," *Annals of the American Academy of Political and Social Science*, 412 (March 1974): 34–43. Philadelphia.

33. H. Henderson, "Ecologists versus Economists," *Harvard Business Review*, (July-August 1973).

34. H. Henderson, "Toward an Economics of Ecology," *Columbia Journal of World Business* 7, no. 3 (May-June 1972).

35. "Searching for Incentives to Entice Polluters," *New York Times*, October 8, 1989.

36. Henderson, *Politics of the Solar Age*, pp. 245–82.

37. Milton Friedman and Rose Friedman, *Free to Choose: A Personal Statement* (New York: Harcourt Brace Jovanovich, 1980).

38. *Project 88: Harnessing Market Forces to Protect Our Environment, Initiatives for the New President,* Public Policy Study sponsored by Sen. Tim Wirth, Colorado, and Sen. John Heinz, Pennsylvania, Washington, D. C., 1988.

39. "Searching for Incentives to Entice Polluter," *New York Times,* October 8, 1989, contains additional objections raised by David G. Hawkins, senior attorney of the National Resources Defense Council, to the Bush administration plan to apply such trading rights to automobile pollution, where reduction of pollution is not fungible, as it may be in the case of specific pollution or toxic substances.

40. Christine Russell, "California Gets Tough on Toxics," *Business and Society Review,* no. 70 (Summer 1989): 47–54.

41. Jon Mills, director of the Center for Government Responsibility, Holland Law Center, University of Florida, Gainesville, Florida, in a personal communication with the author, August 24, 1989, and taped for the PBS television special, "Profit the Earth," April 9, 1990.

42. Henderson, *Politics of the Solar Age,* pp. 155–241.

43. Karl Polanyi, *The Great Transformation* (Boston: Beacon Press, 1944).

44. See, for example, *Draft Declaration of Human Responsibilities for Peace and Sustainable Development,* presented to the United Nations General Assembly by the Government of Costa Rica and President Oscar Arias Sanchez, 1989 (fall session).

45. See, for example, Council on Economic Priorities, *Shopping for a Better World Guide,* (New York, 1988, 1989).

46. These new labeling systems include Germany's Blue Angel Seal and Canada's "Eco-Seal," both offered to companies that can comply with environmental standards regulated by government.

47. "Who Will Subscribe to the Valdez Principles?" *New York Times,* September 10, 1989.

48. Henderson, *Creating Alternative Futures,* chap. 1,

49. Hazel Henderson, "The Imperative Alternative," *Inquiry* (June 1986).

50. Henderson, *Toward a New Way to Measure Development,* pp. 147–53.

51. See, for example, "Feeling Poor in Japan," *Economist,* June 11, 1988, p. 33.

Index

About the Editors and Contributors

GREGORY H. ADAMIAN is president of Bentley College.

WALTER W. BENJAMIN is professor of religion and applied ethics, Hamline University.

KAREN BLUMENFELD is director of environmental policy and management studies at Alliance Technologies Corporation.

BRIAN EDWARD BROWN is professor of religious studies at Iona College and an attorney in New York.

ROBERT A. BUTLER is chief litigation counsel for Union Carbide Corporation.

VAN C. CAMPBELL is vice-chairman of Corning Incorporated.

D. KIRK DAVIDSON is visiting assistant professor at George Washington University.

WILLARD F. ENTEMAN is provost and vice-president of academic affairs at Rhode Island College.

BRUCE A. FINZEN is a partner of Robins, Kaplan, Miller and Ciresi and U.S. counsel for the government of India in the Bhopal gas leak disaster litigation.

ISABELLE FORTIER is a research assistant at the School of Business Administration, Laval University.

ROBERT FREDERICK is assistant professor of philosophy and assistant director of the Center for Business Ethics, Bentley College.

PETER A. FRENCH is the Lennox Distinguished Professor at Trinity University.

KENNETH E. GOODPASTER is the Barbara and David Koch Professor of Ethics at the College of St. Thomas.

HAZEL HENDERSON is an author, futurist, and consultant.

EDWIN C. HETTINGER is assistant professor of philosophy at the College of Charleston.

JOAN WHITMAN HOFF is associate professor of philosophy at Lock Haven University of Pennsylvania.

W. MICHAEL HOFFMAN is professor of philosophy and director of the Center for Business Ethics at Bentley College.

B. W. KARRH is vice-president of safety, health and environmental affairs at E. I. Du Pont de Nemours and Company.

JOAO S. NEVES is associate professor of management in the School of Business, Trenton State College.

LISA H. NEWTON is director of the Program in Applied Ethics at Fairfield University.

THIERRY C. PAUCHANT is assistant professor in strategic management at the School of Business Administration, Laval University.

EDWARD S. PETRY, JR., is assistant professor of philosophy and research associate of the Center for Business Ethics, Bentley College.

JAMES E. POST is professor of management and public policy at Boston University.

DAVID POWELL is a research associate at the Center for Corporate Social Performance and Ethics, Faculty of Management, University of Toronto.

GORDON P. RANDS is a doctoral candidate in the Department of Strategic Management and Organization, University of Minnesota.

GEORGE SAMMETT, JR., is vice-president for corporate ethics, Martin Marietta Corporation.

RAJIB N. SANYAL is assistant professor of management in the School of Business, Trenton State College.

JOHN A. SEEGER is professor of management at Bentley College.

RICHARD SEIBERT is vice-president of resource technology for the National Association of Manufacturers.

ARTHUR SHARPLIN is Distinguished Professor of Management and Marketing at McNeese State University.

PAUL STEIDLMEIER is assistant professor of strategic management at the School of Management, State University of New York at Binghamton.

ROBERTA B. WALBURN is a partner of Robins, Kaplan, Miller and Ciresi and U.S. counsel for the government of India in the Bhopal gas leak disaster litigation.

LAURA S. WESTRA is associate professor of philosophy at Auburn University.

RONALD S. WISHART is vice-president of public affairs at Union Carbide Corporation.